INDIANA
UNIVERSITY

Midwestern Pioneer

Volume I / The Early Years

INDIANA UNIVERSITY

Midwestern Pioneer

Volume I / The Early Years

THOMAS D. CLARK

INDIANA UNIVERSITY PRESS

Bloomington & London

For

Elizabeth Marye Stone

CONTENTS

List of Illustrations

following page 142

List of Illustrations

PREFACE

INDIANA UNIVERSITY is a pioneer institution of higher learning in the Ohio Valley. At the inception of the university the frontier of the Old Northwest was in the early stages of settlement. The newly chartered school shared in the major portion of two township grants of public lands which insured it a meager start toward legal organization in 1820. In time the Indiana Seminary was to experience periods of biting economic stringency arising from the vicissitudes of mismanagement of its public lands and monies, and a failure of the new state to make additional financial contributions to its operation.

There was in the Indiana Constitutional Convention of 1816 a handful of delegates who had a glimmer of the significance of higher learning in a raw rural frontier society. These delegates, however, did not comprehend the demands of such an institution. They hoped the seminary of their dreams would combine the teaching of the classics with the practical arts and sciences in such a way as to give enough training to Hoosier youth to fit them for positions of leadership in the state.

When the doors of Indiana Seminary were opened to classes in 1825 the central challenge became at once the broadening of its instructional base in such a way as to shatter the narrow parochialism of the classical academy curriculum which prevailed in America. There had to be developed a practical educational program and philosophy which unlettered people in the throes of pioneering in virgin country could understand and accept.

The earliest curriculum of Indiana Seminary and University was formulated within the context of two eras of American higher education, 1825–1902. The decades down to 1880 witnessed an eternal struggle to survive, in which little change or innovation could be made. The post-Civil War era took Indiana University headlong into the vortex of the American intellectual revolution which only the most open minds could fully comprehend. Actually the central historical significance of Indiana University down to 1885 was the desperate fight its supporters made for it in order to sustain it in a society which forced it to function under the surveillance of a wilful sectarian religious domination. Its second burden of history was financial in nature. The meager income from endowment and public land sales of two townships was scarcely enough to keep life in the college. On at least three occasions before 1885 the university was saved from economic collapse only by the most heroic dedication of a few citizens, trustees, and professors.

An era ended abruptly for the university in the fall of 1883. A largely innocuous social incident of that year, to be discussed later, turned the institution toward new philosophical and educational channels. Its purpose at this latter date was narrowed to excelling in the liberal arts and planning for future expansion of its offerings. To succeed in accomplishing this required bold if not brash modern administrative leadership. It was fortuitous that the trustees elected Professor David Starr Jordan to the presidency. A young, eager, and even bumptious scientist, Jordan was well schooled in new university management. He sensed the strong surge and purpose of the university in a rapidly emerging modern American civilization. Bubbling over with energy and egotism, Jordan preached Darwinism to fundamentalist Hoosier audiences, and sold them on the wonders of the biological and physical sciences. He introduced the elective system, revised the entire curriculum, and hacked away the last vestiges of the limiting academy tradition. Too, he broke the stultifying precedent of having a ministerial presidency with its eternal sectarian entanglements.

This book in no way intends to belittle the enormous efforts of Andrew Wylie and Cyrus Nutt. These men were truly dedicated to their tasks, and like their successor, Jordan, they steered a direct course to accomplish a degree of excellence within the context of the curriculum and state of learning in their times. The personal impact of Andrew Wylie will persist in Indiana University so long as the riddle of his personality remains unsolved. He and Cyrus Nutt set dependable and positive courses.

Indiana University is one of a relatively small number of American state universities whose histories span two full eras of

American higher education. Its history reflects graphically the forces at work in each of these ages. It would be easy indeed to dismiss the record of the institution as that of a backwoods school tucked away among the hills of southern Indiana and away from main thoroughfares of travel where it was permitted to doze away almost a century in intellectual self-satisfaction and public neglect. This, however, was historically not so. Its faculty, from the beginning, reflected rather broad, cosmopolitan educational backgrounds. Many of the professors were trained in European universities, and most of them seemed alert to the challenges of international educational theories and progress. For instance, Baynard Rush Hall demonstrated bright talents as the author of *The New Purchase*. John Hopkins Harney became the successful editor of a seminal newspaper. Andrew Wylie brought from Pennsylvania some learning and a high sense of education and scholarly purpose.

The fact that Indiana professors were offered good positions by other universities throughout the latter three-quarters of the nineteenth century reflected something of their qualifications. With the appointment of David Starr Jordan to the presidency in 1884 a current of genuine educational excitement began to run through the university. The intellectual and innovative virility of the universities of Michigan, Cornell, Wisconsin, Johns Hopkins, and Harvard helped to bring about an Indiana renaissance. It is one of the truly remarkable facts in American higher education that Jordan, John Merle Coulter, and Joseph Swain were able not only to get Hoosiers to accept innovations, but to embrace them with enduring affection. In a state where citizen and legislator alike were ready to swing the scimitar of blind religious partisanship with such deadly effect, almost no one crusaded against the teaching of the modern sciences, or the holding of liberal scientific views, or taking modern approaches to the solution of man's problems.

Jordan viewed the challenge of the American university as limitless. He said, "In like spirit the Morrill Act was framed, bringing together all rays of various genius, the engineer, and the psychologist, the student of literature and the student of exact science, 'Greek-minded' men and tillers of the soil, each to do his own work in the spirit of equality before the law." This became a central philosophy of Indiana University.

No doubt there was reflected in the philosophy of all the Indiana presidents a sense of the deep physical earthiness of economic development of the state. Implanted in Indiana was the conviction that men discovered truth by original investigation. No matter how stringent the financial conditions of the past, there were men like Richard Owen, Daniel Kirkwood, David Starr Jordan, John C. Branner, H. C. G. von Jaggermann, John Merle Coulter, and Carl H. Eigenmann who built national and international reputations.

This volume represents the first half of a hundred fifty years of searching by the university for dependable directions and stable public support. The struggles of Indiana University in this period were perhaps no more strenuous than were those of most other state universities. Indiana survived, sometimes only by the grace of God, and in doing so won a major victory.

There are three older histories which were written by authors who felt intimately the heartthrob of the university they served and loved as long-time professors. Theophilus Adam Wylie, Samuel Bannister Harding, and James A. Woodburn presented much of the history through which they lived. The challenge I have faced has been to produce a fresh interpretive account that does not repeat what these earlier historians have said. To do this has necessitated a patient and thorough reexamination of the various collections of documentary materials in university and state archives. Fortunately the original records of the university are intact except for the important *Trustee Minute Book* for 1860–1883. I have had to fill in this vital gap from many sources such as faculty minutes, official state reports, personal memoirs, published speeches, personal correspondence, and contemporary newspaper accounts.

My book no doubt suffers from lack of access to this basic record of the Civil War and Reconstruction years, but the nature of the loss is in degree only, not a total lack of information. A serious gap appears in Indiana University's record in another area, as it no doubt does in that of other state universities. There are no extensive collections of professorial papers. Even David Starr Jordan's correspondence in Stanford University Archives is disappointing because of its lack of information about Indiana. Thus I have been largely denied the privilege of peeping behind the scenes through the observant eyes of professors who saw the institution develop even during its most informal moments.

Writing the history of a state university which has enjoyed such a long existence is somewhat akin to publishing a rural weekly newspaper. Names parade before the author in endless procession. Everybody who has served as a staff member or who has sat in university classrooms has in some way left a personal imprint on the institution. Yet to note all of these would turn the narrative into a historical catalogue which would reflect little or none of the educational activities of the institution. It must be assumed at the outset that a university is a human place where scholarly reputations and traditions are made or tarnished by human beings, but scores of them must remain nameless in the process.

I have spent all of my mature life in a university community as a student, professor, and trustee. I know full well that the formal and official record is often impressive in its failure to reveal the full story. The inside human aspect of a university often perishes with the death of men or with their softening and fading memories. Indiana I am sure is no exception. There survives in various sources enough color to give the history a rich and human tone, a fact which lifts it out of the slough of dull administrative officialdom.

This is not an authorized history. I came to Bloomington almost completely uninformed about the university's background and was given free access to the most confidential archival collections. President Elvis J. Stahr, Jr., gave me written assurance at the outset that I would be allowed to see all the university records without "let or hindrance." At no time have I had occasion to take this letter from my files. No one has in any way attempted to influence me by presenting an "official view" of the institution. Its administrative officials have followed the precept that Indiana University exists to search for the truth, however much that truth might pain someone. There exists in the university a marked reverence for the past which at times lends in the minds of many people a shade of the romantic to its history.

I have not intended to create an encyclopedic sourcebook. It has frequently been difficult for me to discard accounts of incidents of some significance to conserve precious space. Nevertheless I have undertaken to present as much of the story as possible and to hold to the ancient adage that "one does not have to eat all of an egg to savor its quality." Not wanting to overwhelm the reader I have not included footnotes, but I have made an effort to document much of my material internally in the text. The notes from which this book was written are deposited in the University Archives in both topical and chronological arrangement for ready reference. A bibliographical note concludes this volume and a much more extensive one will conclude Volume II. In organization I have been able to follow with some faithfulness a chronological order.

I have tried at all times to remember that a public state university is a sensitive human institution where the line between statehouse and campus is often thinly drawn. Presidents and trustees have gone from Bloomington to Indianapolis seeking desperately needed funds, and to sell the proposition that the public university is one of a democratic society's most effective barriers against the tyranny of ignorance. Often they have found themselves in sharp competition with other equally meritorious state services. Because of this fact there has always existed a public sensitivity which has forced individuals to choose between the sanctity of the campus and the charity of the state institutions, or between the collective intellectuality of the university and the narrower personal views and prejudices of the individual citizens. This has ever been the marshland of the state university, and Indiana, like its neighbors, has striven heroically to keep its feet free of the bogs.

In the preparation of a book of this sort the author becomes only one of many who contribute. Mrs. Mary B. Craig of the University Archives and her staff, Miss Dolores M. Lahrman, Mrs. Joyce de Roos, and Mrs. Aliyya Emeruwa, have gone beyond the call of duty in the search for records and other materials. Mrs. Craig has been most constructive in reading some of the finished manuscript. I am deeply indebted to George Challou, Leo LaSota, John Werner, Robert Stinson, Eric Gilbertson, James H. Jones, and David Warriner who have been diligent and alert in research and final checking of the manuscript. In time they have produced literally thousands of notes. Mrs. Barbara Buckley Lambert has been tireless and efficient in research, filing, typing, and checking. Thomas Buckley has read the galley proofs with great care.

Mrs. Dorothy Collins and Professor Donald F. Carmony have been most generous in both reading and facilitating the preparation of this study. Mrs. Ann Moore and Professor Leo Solt of the

Department of History have been expert in making administrative arrangement for this project. My son Thomas Bennett Clark has read most of the manuscript, as have my wife Elizabeth Turner Clark and my daughter Elizabeth Stone.

When all of this is said, I have no further right to infringe on the generosity of these kind people. The book is my own personal responsibility, and I alone am accountable for its contents and interpretations.

May 1, 1970   THOMAS D. CLARK

INDIANA
UNIVERSITY
Midwestern Pioneer

Volume I / The Early Years

[I]

The Foundations of a Public University

Iᴛs ɢʀᴏᴡᴛʜ from tiny, fumbling, and narrowly conceived beginnings in the early nineteenth century to the large, modern "multiversity" of today, Indiana University may stand as a prototype of the American state university.

Like many other midwestern institutions of higher learning, the university originated as a land grant college. In the Ordinance of 1787 establishing the Northwest Territory, from which five states would be created, Congress spoke to its future settlers: "Religion, morality and knowledge being necessary to good government and the happiness of mankind, Schools and the means of education shall forever be encouraged." Although Indiana at the time of its admission as a state was still a wild, thinly settled frontier region with few of the amenities of civilization, the author of its first constitution in 1816 provided for a state university, and in 1820 the legislature formally authorized the establishment of the new institution.

The members of the Constitutional Convention seem to have had three main purposes in mind. The first object was to develop an elite group of educated men who could serve as leaders of the new commonwealth. They also looked to the new seminary to carry out the mission of spreading the Protestant religion in the raw western country. Finally there was a desire, though it was vaguely defined and poorly projected, to train men in technical and scientific fields to cope with the physical and economic problems of the growing state. Yet few of the founders had any clear concept of what a university was or should be, and the conflict between advocates of the traditional classical learning and those of the practical arts such as law, medicine, agronomy, and geology bedeviled the university for many years.

In fact, the legislators who enacted the law of January 20, 1820, bringing the Indiana Seminary into existence were far from being convinced that higher education was a responsibility of the state. Nor did they have any plan for educating the masses of people beyond the most elementary levels of rural schools with short sessions. No one knew at what level higher education began, nor was there any clearly defined concept of what public higher education was supposed to accomplish.

The use of public land and state privileges for the promotion of colleges and seminaries did not begin in the nineteenth century. Older schools such as Harvard, Yale, Bowdoin, Dartmouth, William and Mary, and Princeton had received public aid in the form of varying amounts of crown land grants. These schools, with the possible exception of William and Mary, were not public institutions. In 1780 the state of Virginia applied the William and Mary principle of public support to Transylvania Seminary in the western country. By 1805 four of the states had either created or provided for state universities. These were Georgia, North Carolina, South Carolina, and Ohio. Two or three of these state institutions grew out of small struggling public or religious academies or had begun at the academy level. In 1809 Ohio chartered Miami University, and two years earlier the federal government had made a gift of a township of public lands to the support of a university at Vincennes. These were some of the public precedents existing when the delegates gathered at Corydon in 1816 to draw a blueprint for the future state of Indiana.

Because of such historical precedents the grant of two townships of federal lands to the new state of Indiana with which to maintain a seminary of higher learning had the weight of public policy behind it. In negotiating the Bill of Sale to the Ohio Company Associates on July 23, 1787, Congress had inserted the provision that "not more than two complete townships . . . be given perpetually for the purposes of an University . . . to be applied to the intended object by the legislature of the state." Donald G. Tewksbury says in *The Founding of American Colleges and Universities Before the Civil War*, "This latter provision established a precedent of far-reaching significance for the development of higher education in the new nation. All twenty-one new states admitted to the Union before the Civil War, with the exception of Vermont, Kentucky, Maine, and Texas, were made recipients of land grants by Congress, following the precedent established in 1787 in the grant of land to the Ohio Company." In Indiana this grant became confused because of factional politics. The question has often arisen, in both state history and the courts, as to whether or not Congress actually gave the second township of land to Indiana. It can be answered categorically that it did under the terms of the Ohio Associates grant. For some reason the United States Supreme Court overlooked this fact in 1852. The only significant question is when precisely the transfer of the Gibson Township was made to the state. In the Supreme Court decision this was a fact of some importance.

In making generous grants of public lands to the incoming states, members of Congress demonstrated no great zeal for higher education or for raising the level of American culture or advancing the sciences. They thought in more immediately practical and expedient terms. By granting blocks of land in strategic locations they sought to create a demand for lands which in turn would speed up the sale of the public domain and reduce the national debt. The adoption of the Ohio principle was followed by no pronouncement of educational philosophy and policy, nor were the states bound by the central government to establish any particular grade of institution, so long as it bore the title "seminary," "college," or "university."

In the years of ferment immediately following the War of 1812, when the stream of westward moving population emptied itself into the Indiana Territory, few of the pioneer settlers realized the urgent need to make educational beginnings. Most of them merely wanted to claim fresh lands and to build new homes. This new Indiana society was not concerned with cultural institutions, nor was it eager to assume even the slightest burden of obligation to support a college. In 1816 most of the people in Indiana had arrived in the Northwest within the past decade, possibly a majority of them since 1814. Among this mass of restless pioneers there were very few individuals with educational qualifications enough to teach even the most elementary grammar school, and none perhaps who had taught in a college classroom.

The eloquent arguments uttered in and out of the Constitutional Convention in 1816, and subsequently in the General Assembly in 1820, must be considered as pure forensics. The reasons given for the creation of a seminary or college had little to do with the frontier conditions of Indiana at that time. Yet, however idealistic the arguments of this period, there was some conception of the importance and power of higher education in a virile and growing society. One cannot be certain how much or how little the small coterie of crusaders for the establishment of a seminary knew about educational experience in Britain or along the Atlantic Coast of the United States. Nor can we say whether the backers of the Indiana Seminary had any clear notion of what kind of institution they wanted. Did they have in mind a state seminary which would depart from the old, narrow pattern of church-controlled colleges to make higher education a central secular force in American life? Did some of the early supporters of the seminary share with Thomas Jefferson the concept that a state school should grant the utmost freedom of choice of courses and disciplines? Did these leaders hope to satisfy the demand for both practical and classical learning? Only one thing was clear: the school would be public in nature, and it would be the apex of the public school system. There appears never to have been a thought that at some future date the school might be surrendered to a parochial administration.

Basic educational philosophies in Indiana originated from many sources. Emigrants from all the older states, from Pennsylvania southward to Georgia, came to the northern shoulder of the Ohio Valley in the rapidly expanding nationalistic decades. Those who were literate knew something of the University of Pennsylvania, the College of New Jersey, or William and Mary. A few of them may even have been conscious of Jefferson's plans for the democratically motivated University of Virginia. Most of them, however, had gained an inkling of higher education nearer home. Some had either attended Transylvania University in Lexington, Kentucky, or knew of it from reading western newspapers or from ministerial sources.

Although no one can say with any certainty from which intellectual soil the taproots of an educational institution spring, in the case of Indiana University it seems significant to take a look at what was happening in the oldest and nearest collegiate institution in the western country. Transylvania University was chartered as a public seminary with the thought that it would serve all the people in the practical fields of engineering, medicine, and law, and that it would also provide the classical curriculum then prevalent in American colleges. The need for roads, canals, and town planning demanded that the college graduate have a knowledge of mathematics and surveying; frightening recurrences of deadly epidemics demanded trained doctors, medical research, and discoveries to combat smallpox, malaria, and systematic disorders. The complexities of the new land systems of the West created an urgent need for lawyers, whether people liked them or not. Even the early American diplomatic snarls arising in the West, and the increasing legal demands of the new states, made training in the law imperative if western political society were to thrive. These were some of the demands that burdened Transylvania and were to burden the newly created Indiana Seminary.

The intellectual origins of Indiana University had their sources far away from Corydon or Bloomington. Its history reflected most of the crosscurrents and contradictions that gave American higher education generally such a slow and uncertain start. No one in Indiana was sure what the central objective of higher education ought to be. Were the central European and British systems the answers to the needs of a new country? What were people being educated to accomplish? How was a so-called practical education to be provided by a school which had to draw so heavily on the ministry for instructors? These were the central issues in Indiana University down to the election of David Starr Jordan to the presidency in 1884.

There existed in Indiana in 1828, when the seminary became the college, neither the talent nor the courage to overcome the influence of classicism. There was an ever present consciousness of the tremendous demands made by the surrounding physical world, but these forces were seldom allowed to penetrate curriculum or

classroom. Lack of educated individuals in Indiana society necessarily cast the university under the control of clergymen.

Laboring under tight ministerial administrative control, Indiana University was unable before 1884 to shake off the grip of
traditional practices more appropriate to a college than to a
university. In this it resembled other public universities in the new
states. Frederick Rudolph said in his book on *The American College and University*, "The threat to the old order was recognized
and squarely met, and the reformers were so successfully routed
that for almost fifty years the American college was necessarily
put beyond the sympathy and understanding of the American people. Stagnation rather than dynamism became the order of the
day. Self-satisfaction overtook the American College." It is doubtful that self-satisfaction ever overtook Indiana University in the
half century mentioned by Rudolph, but during most of its pre-
Jordan years its program of instruction bore little relation to the
needs of the people of Indiana.

Between 1825 and 1890 Indiana University was unable to
assume full and effective status as head of the Indiana school
system, although it was legally a part of that system. For at least
two decades little of its instruction was much beyond the college
preparatory level; for many years student enrollment was mainly
in preparatory classes. Not until the post-Civil War era of the
commissioned high schools was the university able to pull away
from the stultifying burden of training students in the most
elementary subjects. This alone was enough to keep the institution
from developing into one of scientific and intellectual significance.

For the first three-quarters of a century of its existence, Indiana
University had to import most of its senior teaching staff from
universities located in other states and from foreign universities.
Thus the philosophies of the people of the state and those of the
professors were often in conflict. Years later David Starr Jordan,
as President of Stanford University, was quoted by Lewis E.
Akeley in *This Is What We Had in Mind*: "He said when he
first went to Indiana University he found a faculty from Yale
and Harvard and Princeton who did not do things that Hoosiers
could understand. As a consequence, he had not made much progress until he began sending his Hoosier graduates to the Atlantic
side of the Appalachian mountains to get their Ph.D. degrees.

They then returned to him with their doctorates and with their Hoosier character unimpaired." Like many of Jordan's statements this one was considerably overdrawn. Nevertheless many of the professors who came from the outside brought with them the English classical academy concept of higher education. When the native Hoosier asked the university to consider his practical problems the professors found it difficult to give him help. The Hoosier wanted railroads, canals, roads, banks, doctors, schools, and agricultural advances. The classicists such as Baynard Rush Hall and Andrew Wylie contended that a man should be drilled in the ancient philosophies and languages, and thus prepare himself for later specialized training in the practical fields. The academists, however, were never able to specify where and how in Indiana this kind of post-academic training could be acquired. Added to the confusion was the persistent contention by the state's ministry and church members that the university existed largely for the purpose of training Protestant ministers. The conduct of the university reflected a strong belief on the part of presidents and professors that personal morals and religious commitments were indeed basic considerations of higher education.

Of even more importance, Indiana legislators reflected three basic frontier anxieties. First, there was decided opposition to levying taxes of any kind for the support of a college. The taxpayer, in their minds, should not be expected to finance the training of teachers, lawyers, and doctors, who in turn would bleed the public by charging fees for their services. Second, whether of Jeffersonian, Jacksonian, or Whiggish loyalties, Indiana politics was a coarsely woven fabric of backwoods egalitarianism, the product of social and geographical conditions rather than of philosophical and political concerns. This kind of Hoosier mind considered only the immediate present and its primitive demands. It did not look very far ahead, nor could it comprehend how a progressive school system might benefit the growing commonwealth. Finally, too many voters and their representatives were unable to distinguish between the implications of public education and those of schools supported by religious denominations. Hence they viewed the state university as a costly and corrupting interloper and competitor for the public's support.

In its first half-century of existence Indiana University represented an interesting experiment in American higher education. It was created and operated as a state institution, falling under rigid and sometimes jealous state controls, but it was denied direct public support. Its enemies seldom if ever were intellectually honest enough to acknowledge this fact. Legislators were quick to criticize but adamantly opposed to giving direct financial aid. There is perhaps no more eloquent example than that of Indiana University of the fallacy of the American belief that a grant of public land would endow an institution in healthy and growing condition. The Indiana experience, of course, was only one of many such cases, but it is doubtful that any of the others endured so many crises and reverses. Even the grants of two townships of land were to be called into jeopardy by political finesse and selfish maneuvering, and the life of the university hung by the slender thread of a single senatorial vote in 1854. Having survived the reverses created by the issues which arose over its lands and accumulated endowment, Indiana University was denied the bigger plum of sharing in the land distribution authorized by the Morrill Act of 1862. Thus the university was steered into the backwater of liberal arts classicism without the support necessary to begin realizing its original objectives.

For a century and a half the university has labored to define clearly its mission as expressed in the dynamic blueprints of the constitutional and legislative mandates. Only Miami in the old Northwest has endured so long and undergone so many of the woes of a public university in an America that took fully a century to discover a university's true mission. Indiana has had to do this in the face of political reactions which at times have severely limited its objectives. When the decision was made to create a new institution—Purdue University—with Morrill land support, Indiana University was forced to redefine its central mission within the context of the humanities, the social sciences, and the new physical sciences. These were the challenges which the institution accepted in the 1880's when it broke with the past and hired a scientist president. Changing times and a major shift in the social needs of the people of Indiana gave the university not only a new mission, but likewise a fresh dynamism in a society that came to depend more on current sciences than on the lore of ancient civilizations.

Indiana University did not exist during its maturing years in vacuous isolation in out-of-the-way Bloomington. Every current that passed through American education influenced it. It is impossible to consider its history apart from that of the whole American college and university system. The details were different—the experiences were common ones. The dynamic forces that steered the struggling state universities toward the realization of their central mission and helped them to survive were native and indigenous.

[I I]

University of the West

A S THE ROISTERING EIGHTEENTH CENTURY tumbled headlong
into the nineteenth, human society on both banks of the
great Ohio artery was in a state of ferment. Well named,
Indiana Territory was the home of more Indians than white men.
When the territory was created in 1800 only a few holes had been
bored in the great forests along the Ohio River. Later settlers
had begun to move onto the Whitewater River of the Northwest
Territory and after 1805 they were nesting among the coves of
the Ohio, at Madison below the mouth of the Kentucky River, at
Clarksville opposite the Falls of the Ohio, and on down the river.
Puddling in land-claiming fingers along the lower valley, they
made their way over the trails to the ancient French outpost of
Vincennes and elsewhere along the Wabash.

Indiana Territory was not only one of the most heavily forested
areas in the republic, but almost all of it was still claimed by the
Indians—Miami, Wea, Piankashaw, Potawatomi, Shawnee, and
others—who lived there. Governor William Henry Harrison,
conscientiously attempting to satisfy the settlers' craving for land,
was busily engaged in reducing these Indian claims by a series
of treaties. The "New Purchase" treaty that opened the central

portion of Indiana to settlement was not negotiated until 1818, two years after statehood. Not until the 1830's would the Indian claims in northern Indiana be gradually extinguished.

Before coming to Vincennes as governor of Indiana Territory at the age of twenty-seven, William Henry Harrison was the delegate from the Northwest Territory to Congress. As the representative of the western settlers, he sponsored the Land Law of 1800, which divided the public lands half in sections and half in 320-acre lots to be offered for sale at $2.00 an acre, and permitted installment payments over a period of five years. For the first time the interests and desires of the western settlers prevailed over Congress' desire for revenue.

Driven by an insatiable land hunger, immigrants crowded into Indiana Territory. Despite the growing resentment of the Indians, which culminated in the Battle of Tippecanoe in 1811 and despite the outbreak of the War of 1812, the tide of settlement abated little during the war years. The Land Law of 1800 had set this human riptide running, and every wave of newcomers hurled men against nature's stubborn maze of forests, faint trails, and eternal mud or dust. The American frontier had early cast its first settlers into a common and deeply etched mold of backwoodsman; he was the hunter, a squatter on the public domain just outside the law's reach. He was followed by a transition class, half hunter and half farmer, who would either move on or join the permanent settlers. This last group conformed to no type but endeavored to reproduce the communities from which they came. Families who came from Virginia, Pennsylvania, the Carolinas, Kentucky, and Tennessee, as either immigrants or squatters, brought with them little more of the niceties of life than a crude sense of modesty expressed in their coarse garments; in Indiana they were given the name "Hoosier." The leveling effect of nature led to informal cooperation and neighborliness as well as to an unrestrained individualism. The educational needs of the new country were as down to earth and practical as the use of frow and broadax, and as urgent as the building of a cabin and gnawing away enough trees for a clearing in which to plant corn.

There was a pulsating religious fervor among these pioneers of the earlier Jeffersonian era in the West. Religion had its meaning largely in terms of individual salvation. Scriptural interpretation and pulpit discourse were devoid of deep theological insights or social gospel. Each individual had a conscience, and a hope of ultimate salvation. In 1800 and 1801 the great revivals at Mud River and Cane Ridge in Kentucky had lit the blaze of religious fervor, and emigrants crossing the Ohio River widened its perimeter. By the time settlers were crowding into the new territory, the frontier had become religiously conservative, if not literally fundamentalist, and personal morals became basic matters of public concern. However rough and unpolished society was, it was not rowdy and profligate in the terms of Natchez-under-the-Hill or New Orleans. Rowdiness on the rivers battened on the flow of naive persons from farms and settlements extending from Pittsburgh to Cairo, but this wickedness floated on by without really touching Indiana much beyond the first tier of Ohio River bluffs.

Methodists and their circuit riders, hardshell Baptist fundamentalists, Presbyterians of three or four narrow disciplines, the newly formed Campbellites and Stoneites, fresh from the outpourings of Mud River and Cane Ridge, Quakers from North Carolina, and Catholics from Maryland, Bardstown in Kentucky, and abroad all flocked to Indiana Territory. Wherever clearings, ferry landings, and crossroads coagulated knots of settlers into villages, churches rivaled courthouses as places of central importance. The seasons, the productivity of the land, and the individual lives of men were all set by the everwatchful eye of a personal God.

The bumptious, eternally optimistic breed of Jeffersonian Republicans, having seen their guiding genius safely sworn into office as President in 1801, were frantically founding new states, writing and rewriting constitutions and building new towns. They were flexing their economic muscle to pressure the United States government into maneuvers with wily Old World diplomatic chess players for free and unrestricted use of the central river system. These were years when the people felt the throb of power and were inspired to visions of future national grandeur. A vast unbroken wooded littoral was not a stubborn barrier, but a natural domain out of which would pop cabins, clearings, towns, and roads. Here honest citizens would implant domestic and cultural institutions, and would bring up from their ranks honest, industrious, God-fearing leaders to take the measure of the times and the country. From the Monongahela to the Wabash men tolerated the present and anticipated the future. Jeffersonian Republicanism on the frontier was one part politics and nine parts braggadocio, hope, and enthusiastic faith in a homespun egalitarianism and progress.

Among the settlers who came to Indiana Territory were some who brought in their cultural baggage a sense of the necessity of education in the scheme of settlement. The Land Ordinance of 1785 had reserved section 16 in each township for the maintenance of public schools. Federal land grants seemed a painless way of financing schools, seminaries, and colleges. But devising a scheme of financing was far easier than defining the objectives for which such schools would strive. The frontier mind found itself hopelessly in conflict. Should youth be taught the mathematics of western surveyors, or the theoretical principles of the ancients? Would they study the law necessary to equip them to serve backwoodsmen who were yanked before illiterate magistrates and circuit judges, or that of classical Greece, Rome, and England? Would they learn more about the soils of the plains of Attica and the ancient valleys of Rome than of the burgeoning loam of the Whitewater, White, and Wabash rivers? Would they study to become teachers, ministers, and "statesmen," or to become men with more practical tools in a land that demanded the utmost in democratic simplicity and earthy practicality?

In 1802 petitions from Indiana Territory prayed of Congress a grant of land to establish schools and seminaries in the "Illinois settlement of Vincennes, and that of Clark's grant, near the Rapids of the Ohio." Congress responded on March 26, 1804, by providing, among other things, that the Secretary of the Treasury should select a second township for the support of a seminary in the territory.

Deeply involved in the beginnings of higher education in Indiana Territory were several exciting personalities who stood with one foot in the path of the raw frontier and the other on the high road of civilized history. An overshadowing political, diplomatic, and social figure was William Henry Harrison, Virginian, territorial governor and politician, Indian warrior and treatymaker, and landed gentleman. Harrison was of the Jeffersonian tradition, but how much he was a part of his early background and how much he was influenced by family connections or by what was happening in Ohio and other states can only be inferred. Certainly he had had wide influence in developing the Northwest Territory. Many men in that territory had dreamed of establishing a university from 1792 until the incorporation of Ohio University in 1804. Harrison knew intimately, of course, the land grant provisions for the maintenance of education in the land ordinance of 1785.

Few if any men brought to Indiana Territory as much training and experience as did the Swiss immigrant, John Badollet. Born in Geneva in 1758, he studied at the Academy and became the close friend of two of his classmates, Albert Gallatin and Henri Serré. The friends dreamed of establishing a utopian society in the great American wilderness, but they lacked funds to pay the passage of all three. Gallatin and Serré sailed first, arriving in 1780, and Badollet went to France to prepare himself to be a Lutheran minister. He followed his friends five years later, and became a western Pennsylvania farmer. In 1792 the governor of that state appointed him to study means of improving navigation on the Youghiogheny and Monongahela rivers, and later he was chosen to locate an east-west passage over the steep Laurel Hill barrier in the Allegheny Mountains. Gallatin, who now was Secretary of the Treasury, no doubt influenced Thomas Jefferson to appoint his friend in 1803 to locate roads in Indiana Territory, and the next year to be registrar of lands at the newly created land office in the territorial capital. At Vincennes Badollet led a crusade to establish a public library, and became a trustee of the seminary.

The attorney general of Indiana Territory named by President Jefferson in 1808 was Benjamin Parke, a New Jerseyite, who came to Vincennes by way of Kentucky. In Lexington Parke studied law with James Brown and Henry Clay and became their apostle across the Ohio River. He was a protégé of Dr. Samuel Brown, who had introduced smallpox vaccination to the frontier and created the Transylvania Medical School. Brown was a pioneer educational statesman in the Ohio Valley. He viewed the mission of higher education through the wide-angle lens of trained doctors coming from first-rate medical schools, and of lawyers who were taught the theory of law along with the practical techniques of jury trial and courtroom maneuvers in dealing with illiterate jurors and magistrates. Parke was to be an influential figure in the beginnings of higher education in Indiana Territory.

Jonathan Jennings was born in New Jersey but grew up in Pennsylvania. His father was a Presbyterian minister, and both his parents had degrees in medicine. Their son, who studied law at Washington, Pennsylvania, was twenty-two years old when he arrived at Jeffersonville aboard a flatboat in 1806. For a few months he stayed in Charlestown before moving on to Vincennes, where he was admitted to the bar in 1807. Two years later Jennings returned to Charlestown to begin a successful campaign for election as territorial delegate to Congress. He would play a decisive role in shaping territorial and state educational policies.

When the territorial legislature chartered Vincennes University on November 29, 1806, the legislators set a high purpose for the institution. It was to be the guardian of the independence, happiness, and energy of the citizens of the republic, "under the influence of the destinies of Heaven." It was to polish bright the lamps of science, literature, and the liberal arts. As a wide force in the maturing of Indiana civilization "the University would improve the intellectual qualities of the people as the ablest advocate of genuine liberty, the best supporter of rational religion, and the source of the only solid and imperishable glory, which nations can acquire."

As with most American frontier institutions, the Board of Trustees was made up of nearly every person of prominence in the territory, including William Henry Harrison, president, Henry Vandenburgh, Waller Taylor, John Badollet, Peter Jones, tavern-keeper, Francis Vigo, trader, and George Leech and Luke Decker, farmers. Jonathan Jennings' name was soon added.

The charter authorized the university to receive the seminary township as provided by Congress in 1804, but little income could be obtained from this "capital" source for several years. John Gibson and Jonathan Jennings spoke for the Board of Trustees in a petition to Congress in 1807, which gave reasons for supporting pioneer higher education and for receiving funds more quickly. They did not want citizens of Indiana Territory to be "subject to the in-roads of ignorance, superstition, and faction, which are inevitable consequences of the want of the benign influence of

[1 7]

education and the liberal sciences." The petitioners told Congress that an enlightened and virtuous people is the only depository of public liberty. They wished "to carry the said institution [Vincennes University] into immediate effect on a liberal plan, so as to be reached by all classes of citizens, without encroaching upon the capital of said institution." In a flight of frontier oratory, they continued:

> Your petitioners seeing that our excellent government (which was purchased at the expense of the lives of thousands of brave men) is liable to be assaulted by the various arts of cunning and intrigue, of designing, ambitious and desperate individuals, and also subject to the attacks of silly and often deadly arts of foreign politics, your petitioners, therefore, being convinced that the only safeguard and secure shield, against the dark cunning of individuals and of foreign governments, is the blaze of science which will reach the mind of the plowboy, as well as the most wealthy citizen; and wishing to secure to the citizen domestick happiness, and stamp the principles of our government upon the plastick minds; but not having the means to apply the remedy with a strong and steady hand, we therefore pray that you may pass a law, laying a small tax on salt made at public works in this territory, and also by a tax on Indian traders.

These were the reasons for establishing a seminary, and the proposed means by which it could be established and maintained until the township land could be sold at satisfactory prices. The document reflected the Jeffersonian philosophy of egalitarianism on the one hand, and on the other the near impossibility of securing much local support from the small and scattered population in the territory. The small tax on salt at public works, of course, was to be levied "in this territory," as would be the tax on Indian traders. Payments for public lands in a territory were federal revenue until the territory achieved statehood; it was then granted control over public lands within its boundaries. The petitioners were therefore asking for a return of part of the federal taxes collected in the territory.

Later the Board of Trustees of Vincennes University came down from the Olympus of oratory to the mudstained realities of the Wabash. They now had to find teachers and students qualified to undertake the teaching of the arts, sciences, and languages, including the mother tongue. They now had to polish bright the lamps of science, the arts and literature in terms of their times and their community. Here was a situation that demanded the intellectual sparkle of Badollet and the practical capabilities of Francis Vigo and Luke Decker. Beyond the first state aspirations, the university would extend the benefits of Anglo-American civilization to its Indian neighbors. The natural children would be admitted free of cost, but apparently no ambitious native forsook the lore of the woods for that of Homer and Virgil. An equally liberal gesture was made to women, but they were to be trained in a separate institution.

The history of Vincennes University in the territorial period can be summarized in the few words so often used in describing most pioneer American educational efforts. There were no funds, few teachers, no buildings, and few students. Early board meetings reflected ignorance of how to operate even the simplest kind of school. Public apathy in Indiana Territory toward Vincennes University was as thick as the mire in the Wabash River bottom. The trustees looked to the future, when sufficient population would have moved into the territory to enable it to sell the 23,040 acres of Gibson County lands to good advantage. In the meantime, however, there was urgent need of funds. Resorting to that device that Americans have ever conceived to be both a profitable and a painless means of raising money, the trustees organized a lottery. The Vincennes lottery, however, was a miserable failure. Money had to be refunded on the meager number of tickets sold, and the scheme written off as a needless and disastrous added expense.

At the meeting of the trustees on August 29, 1807 Jonathan Jennings who had just arrived in Vincennes to begin the practice of law, was elected a member over two opponents. Jennings had been appointed clerk of the board ten days earlier to replace George W. Johnston. In the meantime William Henry Harrison had resigned from the board on August 12, but was reelected on September 17. Friction developed over several issues, all of them ultimately involving Governor Harrison and Jonathan Jennings. When Harrison was again made president of the board, he appointed a committee to investigate Jennings' activities as clerk. Jennings had certified the publication of a pamphlet written by "Sand and Rosin"

(General Washington Johnston and Luke Decker), in which they defended the election of Davis Floyd as clerk of the territorial legislature. By the time the special committee reported, Jennings had moved to Clark County. The future relations between Harrison and Jennings were strained even to the point of open hostility.

The history of education in the decade from 1807 to 1816 can be summarized as one of frustration and failure. Promoters of education had a gleam in their eyes but little or no experience in establishing schools. Internal political pulling and hauling, personal struggles for power, the long-drawn-out War of 1812, and the agitation to create an independent state distracted attention from the high purpose of bottoming the new commonwealth with an educated citizenry. The feud between Harrison and his opponents at times became dramatic, and although he gained the stature of a major frontier military hero at Tippecanoe and the Thames, he was unable to restore himself to his former position of power at home. There was as much or more hunger for power on the part of Harrison's opponents, the traditional stance of the outs, as there was conflict over basic social and political principles.

On December 11, 1815, the Indiana Territorial Legislature passed a petition formally requesting statehood. This instrument asked that a township, in addition to the one in Gibson County, be reserved for the establishment of a seminary. As in the earlier petition that had procured the Gibson County township for Vincennes University, the legislators bolstered their plea with the emotionally charged phrases of "useful knowledge," and "best guarantee to our civil institutions." By this time, however, Hoosiers knew more about the realities of acquiring funds. They said, "as Congress must know something of raising money in new counties for the use of universities, we think we do ourselves but justice in asking a reserve of one entire township to be located at some suitable place on the United States Lands in this territory."

The enabling act of April 19, 1816, made favorable response to the territorial petition. In section 6 of the act, provisions were made for reservation of an additional township, thus making two in all. This township was to be "reserved for the use of a seminary of learning, and vested in the legislature of said state, to be appropriated solely to the use of such seminary by the said legislature." Congress had now established clearly the policy of land grants for the purpose of subsidizing academies and colleges. Whether or not this was the second land grant is inconsequential.

In Indiana an entire township was to be reserved in addition to the one already donated to Vincennes University. On June 19, 1816, a week after this issue had been introduced in the state Constitutional Convention at Corydon, a committee composed of Jonathan Lindley, Benjamin Parke, and James Noble was appointed to select a township to be designated by President James Madison. This they did in the area soon to become Monroe County, and they named the township for Oliver Hazard Perry, hero of the battle of Put-in-Bay.

Discussion of education as a state responsibility was begun at 8:00 A.M. on June 12, 1816, by the committee and was continued intermittently until June 27. The committee on education was composed of James Scott, chairman, later to become a member of the first Supreme Court of Indiana, William Polke, John Boone, Dan Lynn, and John Badollet. Most active in the convention discussion of this question were John DePauw, John Badollet, James Scott, Benjamin Parke, and James Noble.

Someone at Corydon had access to the New Hampshire Constitution of February, 1792. The special committee copied almost verbatim the first half of the educational clause entitled, "Encouragement of Literature, & c." Four interesting amendments and additions were made to this document. First, the Indiana clause was made to read, "for the use of schools and seminaries." There then was added a considerable body of original materials relating to funds arising from sale of federal land grants, and restricting the sale of seminary lands until after the year 1820. Again the Hoosiers returned to the spirit, if not the precise wording, of the New Hampshire article by instructing the legislature from time to time to "pass such laws as shall be calculated to encourage intellectual, scientifical [sic] and agricultural improvement, by allowing rewards and immunities for the promotion and improvements of the arts, sciences, commerce, manfacturers, and natural history of the country."

Yankee constitutionalists justified their concern with education and the arts and sciences in a thoroughgoing proclamation of the Puritan-Protestant ethic. To them it was mandatory "to countenance and include the principles of humanity and general benevolence, public and private charity, industry and economy, honesty and punctuality, sincerity, sobriety, and social affections and generous sentiments among people." Hoosiers apparently were unimpressed with this Yankee lecture and agreed only to "countenance and encourage the principles of humanity, industry, and morality." There was no dawdling at Corydon with "sobriety and social affections."

The constitutional delegates refused to bind the General Assembly to a rigid principle of public support of education. Provisions were made to contribute fees from persons exempt from militia duty, "except in times of war," and fines assessed for any breach of the penal laws were to be distributed among the counties to maintain seminaries.

After stating so firmly reasons why New Hampshire should maintain a system of seminaries and public schools, constitutional delegates of that state, with Yankee terseness, said no more. Hoosier delegates, however, feeling the deep impulses of frontier egalitarianism and penury, provided that "it shall be the duty of the General Assembly *as soon as circumstances will permit, to provide by law, for a general system of education, ascending in a regular gradation from township schools to a state university, wherein tuition shall be gratis, and equally open to all.*" To date no other state had made such a sweeping constitutional commitment to education. Ohio's convention had opened that state's schoolhouse doors on a basis of equality, but it remained silent on the subject of remitting tuition. Tennessee and Kentucky ignored public responsibility for education. In fact, it is impossible to state with any certainty who promulgated the generous Indiana tuition-exemption clause. Delegates at the Corydon assembly were largely from Virginia (12), Pennsylvania (7), Kentucky (6), Maryland (5), and New Jersey (2). The other eleven were from various states, Ireland, and Europe. Clearly the makers of the constitution overestimated income from sale of lands in the two isolated townships, they lacked a sense of what costs would be involved in opening and operating a university, and certainly they had a narrow concept of the future growth of such an institution, limitations that would haunt Indiana University during its entire history.

Fortunately the educational committee of the Constitutional Convention was composed of men of unusual experience and background for the early West. These men were not merely buckskin pioneers who had bright hopes for their region. They hoped to improve the lot of the common man, but they were not the hard-knuckled frontiersmen who trailed cheap lands across the Ohio or who hardened their hands at the handles of a plow. All of them had a background of cultural influences before they came West. The five men on the educational committee embodied most of the spark of dynamic cultural interests in Indiana in 1816.

It is impossible to separate the move to organize a system of public schools from the intense power struggle that went on in the territory from 1807 to 1816. Jonathan Jennings, the newcomer, and James Noble, leader of the Harrison faction, Thomas Posey, Waller Taylor, and William Hendricks were leaders of the other factions (although Hendricks was not a member of the convention, he made his presence felt in Corydon.) In the convention, it was said there was a general agreement among partisans of Jennings, Noble and Hendricks to make them Governor, United States Senator, and Congressman, in that order. This was the way it turned out, whether or not there was an actual trading agreement among the factions.

The first two years of statehood were devoted to organization of the state government. On December 7, 1819, Governor Jonathan Jennings told the General Assembly that the time had arrived to consider the establishment of schools. He said he believed it would be useful to locate the seminary near one of the townships set aside for its support, because this would at once enhance the value of the lands, and he thought Perry Township in Monroe County was the more desirable. As reasons for his choice he gave fertility of soils, a healthy climate, its central location, and distance from the Ohio River. After 1820, said the governor, the legislature could authorize the sale of these lands.

The governor was too much a politician to let legislators off with a simple statement of administrative opinion. With a good Jacksonian oratorical flourish he said, "The future reputation and prosperity of the state, must greatly depend upon the means of education generally being diffused, and attended with the least possible expense." "Ignorance," he continued, "has generally been the offspring of Despotism, and ruinous to the rights and liberties of mankind." He asked the legislature to proceed with legislation looking to the establishment of schools, and during January, 1820, this was a central issue before the Assembly.

In the second reading of the seminary bill on January 15, 1820, William Drew moved to amend the proposed legislation by striking from it the provision that 2,000 acres of the township lands in Monroe County be forever reserved as a glebe for use of the seminary and its professors. This was done, and then Senator Drew sought to delay further consideration of the bill until the next session of the Assembly, which would meet in December. The bill had its third reading on the seventeenth, and a vote resulted in a tie of five to five. The President of the Senate, Ratliff Boon, voted affirmatively. Drew next attempted to cause defeat of the bill in the House, but that body refused to accept any of the Senate amendments except the one pertaining to the perpetual glebe. Drew then failed in a final attempt to persuade the Senate to stick firmly by its amendments.

William Drew represented a considerable bloc of Indiana public opinion. He was a large landholder and lawyer, strong-willed and of impressive personality. His reputation as attorney for either side of an issue was high. He was deeply involved in the bitter personal political feuding of the early statehood period, and was Senator from Franklin and Fayette counties from 1819 to 1820. His actions in the Senate reflected a conservative and frugal attitude toward the state as well as a sharp political factionalism in the Assembly.

On January 19, 1820, the bill entitled "An Act to Establish a State Seminary and for other Purposes . . ." was sent to the governor for his signature. Jennings signed the bill on January 20, and Indiana was embarked in the field of higher education.

[I I I]

Laying the Bottom Rail

E NACTMENT OF THE LAW creating Indiana Seminary in January, 1820, was little more than legislative formality. Of greater significance was the fact that active and decisive steps were taken to organize an entire state system of public schools. A legislative planning committee consisting of John Badollet, David Hart, William W. Martin, James Welsh, Daniel J. Caswell, Thomas C. Searle, and John Todd was created on January 9, 1821, to carry out the law's mandate. This body was instructed to prepare a report to be ready for presentation for the next session of the Assembly. It was to do more; actually it was to produce an outline of a plan of procedure. It reiterated the democratic proposal that a school system "ascending the regular gradation from Township Schools to a state seminary, wherein tuition shall be gratis and equally open to all" be established. The committee was strongly admonished to see that no distinctions were made between the rich and the poor.

Only three of the panel of seven members actually served. Daniel J. Caswell was made chairman. Others, because of death, illnesses, or indifference, never attended a committee meeting. Within a remarkably brief time the three produced one of the truly fascinating documents in American social and cultural history. They observed that the cession of lands by the central government was generous, even though Indiana was deprived of taxes for a time by withdrawal of two townships from immediate sale. In the long run, however, they recognized that both state and nation would profit. Proper disposal of the land would produce money enough to establish "a permanent fund—sufficient in amount not only to disseminate the general and more necessary branches of education in the several townships, but also to furnish such endowments to a university as with some assistance will enable this state to occupy in a literary point of view a highly respectable standing," but this in time only. "High attainments in literature," they informed governor and legislators, "are not the results of a moment." They cautioned careful disposition of funds because a mistake in that matter would be fatal to the whole undertaking.

The committee estimated that within the current boundaries of Indiana there were 22,312,960 acres of salable public land which promised a possible income of $1.25 to $5.00 per acre, one thirty-sixth of which would be set aside to support schools. Because of this heavy stake in the public domain, the committee prepared an elaborate procedure for sale of school lands. If the college townships were sold advantageously, then Indiana College should be established as the beginning of a university. They pleaded,

> Make it respectable, or indeed useful, it is respectfully suggested, that it will be necessary to place a president at the head of it, whose duty it shall be, besides exercising a general superintendency, to participate personally in giving instruction to the highest or first class in College Logic, Metaphysics, Moral Philosophy and Criticism. A professor of mathematics and natural philosophy, a professor of geography, ancient and modern, and astronomy, a professor of Latin, Greek and the Hebrew languages [should be appointed].

They looked ahead to the teaching of law, theology, and medicine, and the establishment of a university. For the latter subject they even outlined a curriculum.

The committee gave voice to an expansive dream. The lands immediately available were expected to bring a total income of $260,772, from which $60,000 could be spent annually, and $40,000 more could be used in erecting buildings, and the purchase of a library and philosophical and chemical apparatus, although this reflected a bit of erroneous addition. The annual interest of 6 percent on $200,000 would solve all faculty problems, and the seminary would be on its way into the future as a full-blown college.

While governor and legislators wrestled with the problems of establishing state government and public schools during 1819 and 1820, Jesse Brandon, editor of the *Corydon Journal*, became cynical. So far, he said, the legislators had never demonstrated capacity or patriotism enough to carry into execution any plan for educating the masses of the people, and "for bringing instruction home to every man's door." He hoped some scheme could be devised to educate every youth in Indiana. The Assembly had the necessary constitutional and statutory provisions as well as the experiences of other states before it, and if it now went astray the people would be convinced its members were devoid of intellectual acumen. He warned, "Let them take care how they squander away the resources of the state upon universities or colleges, to which the masses of the people can have no access, and from which little else than pedantry and aristocracy issue forth. Projects of this kind have already received too much countenance from the legislature." Jesse Brandon thought it was just about as absurd, "in the present state of improvement, to erect such establishments, as it would be to provide a *great cannon* to defend the state, instead of arming every citizen with rifle or a musket. Let education be generally diffused and colleges will grow up of themselves."

Despite the carping of editors and the indifference of the people, Indiana Seminary had become a legal fact. Now it had to be located on the ground and plans made for its operation. Where the school should be built involved consideration of numerous facts. Indiana in the first quarter of the nineteenth century had a genuine health problem. The lowlands of its heavily forested river bottoms were thought to generate the ague in about the same ratio as cool nights in early autumn bathed the region in wet, impenetrable fog. This vaporish miasma was chill- and ague-ridden. Exposure to its toxicity was an almost certain guarantee of sickness, thus consideration had to be given to health. Closely coupled with miasmic threats was availability of drinking water from natural sources. The seminary would have to be located close to an everlasting spring of proper size to supply so large a quantity of water.

Creation of Indiana Seminary at Bloomington in 1820 was not unlike a mass conversion in a backwoods revival meeting. One of the first responsibilities of the new school would be to look after the morals of the youth with even more diligence than parents had exercised. Morality came first and learning second; morality involved stern discipline administered well away from the morally distracting fleshpots of borderland society. Society along the immediate Ohio River frontier left much to be desired. Untinged with the rowdiness of the river trade, the freewheeling gamble with destruction which came from periodic floods, and the constant flowing back and forth of foreign social elements from the Gulf of Mexico to the Great Lakes, Bloomington was difficult to reach. An advertisement appeared in the Bloomington *Post*, June 8, 1836, explaining that stagecoaches operated from steamboat landings at Madison, Louisville, Jeffersonville, and from Leavenworth and Indianapolis. Once a student reached the town there were rewards; one of them was the fact that board could be had for $1.50 a week. The town, said the Board of Trustees, was fifty miles south of Indianapolis, eminently healthy, pleasant, flourishing, and far enough from the river to be cheap. More important, "The state of society [in Bloomington was] sufficiently removed from the rudeness of vulgar manners on the one hand; and silly affectations shewing over emptiness on the other," narrow sectarian bigotry excluded.

Finally there were the matters of the division and sale of school township land by locating the school in close proximity to it. Geographic centrality also played a part. In 1820 both the backwoods county of Monroe and its tiny county seat, Bloomington, were hardly inviting places for the location of a rising midwest seat of learning. Immediately following the War of 1812, the area which became Bloomington was still in the woods and still on the border of Indian territory. It was not until two years after the framers of the constitution in 1816 devised the educational article in the constitution that John Ketcham located his mill in the vicinity. In that year, January 14, 1818, the legislature created Monroe County, named in honor of the President of the United States, and appointed commissioners to locate and name a town where a courthouse could be situated.

Bloomington in 1820 was scarcely more than a dot on the vast map of forestlands of south central Indiana, and "Monroe Post

Office" was little more than an air pocket in a postmaster's hat. Lots had been auctioned on June 22 and 23, 1818, and the town was on its way.

In this period settlers were rushing across the Ohio to satisfy their yearning for more and better lands. Among these earliest settlers of Monroe County was one Dr. David H. Maxwell. As a pioneer of Monroe County he exhibited more than ordinary intelligence about the local situation. From his Kentucky background he had already developed a good amount of political acumen, and he saw the location of Indiana Seminary on Perry Township lands as a tremendous advantage to those owning property in this area. One can only conjecture how much influence he exerted on legislators and the governor in this matter. Indiana was no different from the states that fed settlers into the region. Laws and public policy decisions were one part conscientious efforts at statesmanship and two parts pressure and personal nudgings by shrewd and self-interested lobbyists in legislative gathering places. David Maxwell, Kentuckian, knew the art of nudging full well from experience in Frankfort.

This was the situation when the Board of Trustees, created by the legislative act of 1820, set about locating the seminary. The first board was composed of Charles Dewey, Jonathan Lindley, David H. Maxwell, John M. Jenkins, Jonathan Nichols, and William Lowe. It was vested with the power of a corporation and was instructed to hold its meetings in Bloomington with a view to selecting a site from adjoining Perry Township. Only four of the six members of the Board of Trustees met on June 5, 1820, to locate the seminary. Because Jonathan Lindley and Charles Dewey were ill (with the ague no doubt), they adjourned until July, when the seminary was located near a large spring along the northern border of the township, approximately a quarter of a mile south of the newly established courthouse.

The chartering act instructed the board to construct two buildings, a seminary hall and a professor's house. There seems to be no conclusive contemporary record as to when the buildings were actually started. The board reported, however, they were still under construction in 1824. In 1921, John W. Cravens, writing from notes gathered from secondary sources, said work was begun on April 17, 1822. The class hall or seminary building was a two-story oblong brick structure with evenly spaced windows and the projecting mid-roof bell tower so characteristic of contemporary academic and public buildings. Originally it was intended to be a replica of Nassau Hall at Princeton. The professor's house was a similar but smaller structure enlarged somewhat by addition of a lean-to type of shed. Fortunately for the record, Thomas Carter Perring drew a ground floor plan to scale of the academic building; this plan is still in existence. The professor's house was constructed at a cost of $891 and the class building for $2,400.

There are no doubts as to the precise date when Indiana Seminary was chartered by legislative act, and apparently the date on which the Monroe County site was chosen and buildings were begun is reliable enough, but the precise date on which classes actually began is not certain. So many published sources have said with such positiveness that it was May 1, 1824, that this has been accepted as an established fact. This matter, however, presents an intriguing problem in evaluating historical evidence. The Board of Trustees was largely responsible for the confusion. Professor James A. Woodburn was sufficiently dubious of the date that he wrote a fascinating little essay in historical criticism, raising questions about precise semantics of earlier reports. He, however, along with John W. Cravens, was willing to accept the May date. Woodburn examined Banta's history and David Maxwell's report to the legislature in 1828, along with Baynard Rush Hall's *The New Purchase*. Hall wrote in a delightful style and produced a highly useful and fascinating book, but because of his slightly veiled anonymity he was master of vagueness. More precise was John Hopkins Harney's statement to Andrew Wylie on July 4, 1828. He told Wylie, "This institution formerly called the State Seminary was commenced at this place little more than three years ago under favorable circumstances." Harney seems to have been exact in most of his statements, and if the period had been a little more than four years he would have said so. Banta, it must be remembered, wrote largely from memory, and Maxwell prepared his four-year report in 1828, in which he measured the timespan of the seminary in terms of a single class.

Apparently the only contemporary records to survive are two newspaper stories which appeared in the *Indiana Gazette* in January and April, 1825, and Harney's letter. On January 8 the paper announced, "The Trustees of this institution are authorized to inform the public that the Seminary buildings are now in a state of preparation, and will be ready for the reception of students by the 1st Monday of April next; at which time the 1st session will commence under the superintendence of the Rev'd Baynard R. Hall, whom the trustees have engaged as teacher." Three months later the editor reported in an editorial that, "on Monday last [April 3] the State Seminary at this place went into operation agreeable to previous respectability of our state, we congratulate our fellow citizens." Professor Woodburn apparently never saw the *Gazette* announcements firsthand, though he seems to have known about them. Despite Woodburn's uncertainty the present author is convinced that Monday, April 3, 1825, is the correct date.

The question arises, however, as to when an institution of this nature has its actual beginnings. Does it begin with the chartering by the legislature, location of the site, construction of the first buildings, selection of the first professors, or the actual opening of classes? If it were not for sentimental and antiquarian emotions of people these things would have severely limited meaning.

Of appreciable significance was the appointment of the first teachers. Baynard Rush Hall (1793–1863), a native of Philadelphia who lived in Gosport late in 1823, was appointed the first professor. Hall was a Presbyterian minister, trained in Union College and Princeton Theological Seminary. He came west in 1821 or early 1822 in search of a livelihood. For a year or two he entered the backwoods life with zest. By the time he became professor in the newly formed seminary he had toned down much of his eastern manner and had come to understand the Hoosier backwoodsman on his own terms. Hall was a warmhearted person who quickly developed affection for his neighbors, but at the same time he perceived the limitations of their intellect.

Hall never overrated his own capacity to teach a broad spectrum of courses. He was a product of two "gerund grinding" colleges of the East, and in Indiana he never pretended to be able to teach anything but Latin and Greek; this was the extent of his teaching in the seminary. All the eloquent speeches about practical things to serve the New West were forgotten, and students at the seminary spent long hours grinding away at learning by rote two ancient languages. When Hall arrived in Bloomington he found himself the center of a small storm. The argument was over what kind of education young men of Indiana should receive. The People wanted them to have "a practical education," and Hall argued this was class discrimination. Everybody should have, he said, the foundation preparation for "the best *intellectual* education, for both rich and poor." To Hall this meant four years of Latin, Greek, and mathematics. Years later he wrote in his book, *The New Purchase*,

> And many were the friends he [Hall] would have bought; ay, he could have made some money too, had he spoken in favour of Patent Picture Books that represented truth and falsehood too, enigmatically; and had he abused classical learning! Had he delivered Taylorian twattle! or sent two boxes of dried bugs! or a chest of flints! with a pair of globes, a double wooden cone, and other toys to common schools! And had he not advocated heathen establishments, where poor darling children read about Jupiter, and Venus, and other he and she divinities, instead of those noble, man-confiding, common schools, which in some places so abhor *all gods*, as to acknowledge *none* either by public prayer, or the reading of Divine Revelation!

In reporting on the affairs of the seminary to the legislature in 1828, Dr. David H. Maxwell said, "During the first three years one teacher only was employed by the trustees, and the Greek and Latin languages alone were taught during that time." To use Hall's more colorful phraseology, this occurred in a place and time where "we now obtained as much knowledge by the time we could carry a rifle, or tree a raccoon, as our grandmothers had acquired in a long life! And all this was real American, United States' learning! —useful, practical stuff!—such as would enable a fellow to get his own bread and butter; or in New Purchase terms, his hog and hominy!"

No one in Indiana knew in 1820 exactly how to administer a college. Thus through ignorance and inexperience a most complicated system of administration was established. Hall said, "By a recent charter of our college, it was appointed that the Faculty should oversee the Students; the Trustees, oversee the Faculty; the Board of Visitors, the Trustees; and the Legislature the Visitors;— the people in general engaging to oversee the legislature, and the people of Woodville [Bloomington], the entire whole! The cause of education was, then, well overseen!"

All of this watchful oversight involved approximately twelve students and a professor who was paid $250 annually for his services and who was allowed to accept $150 worth of trade articles a year for preaching in a Presbyterian church. Not until 1827 was the faculty expanded to two members. In that year John Hopkins Harney, a native of Paris, Kentucky, and a graduate of Miami University, was employed to teach mathematics. In that year Hall said he had only three pupils "professedly studying even Latin! and that only to understand *law-terms*! the rest are literally in the R. R. R. and Jogerfree! Indeed, in a population of some twelve thousand *bodies*, we can count but twelve *souls* as classical scholars in any of the schools, public or private." Thus the need for practical subjects arose.

Other changes were necessary. Somewhere and by some means both board and faculty had to find a way of giving vitality to the seminary. Early supporters of the seminary—constitutional delegates and subsequent legislators—clearly intended that the institution soon become a college or university. As Hall indicated no one had an administrative plan for the school. Supervisory responsibility was left to the Board of Trustees, and they thought only in terms of opening a school with a very small faculty, then awaiting future developments.

Unlike Thomas Jefferson, who at that moment was deeply engrossed in planning the University of Virginia, the Board of Trustees of Indiana Seminary lacked sufficient wisdom and experience to think of their school in rarified philosophical and intellectual terms. No provisions were made for a president or principal of a one-teacher school which could raise an annual salary of only $250. In the intervening years, 1820 to 1828, many problems emerged, and in January, 1828, in an effort to solve them, the legislature created Indiana College. By doing so that body began to think of an enlarged curriculum and an expanded teaching body. The legislature was still looking to the future, this time to the moment when a genuine college course could be instituted. In fact the first three or four years of the seminary's existence were years of anticipating its transformation into a college.

This age was one in which Hoosiers generally were seeking

ways to mature their culture at the grass roots. A young Virginian, Enoch Tackett, who had followed the land rush out to Decatur County, wrote John Latham of Loudoun County, Virginia, on June 9, 1828, that he was pleased to hear that Latham was moving to the West. With more than a bubble of optimism he said,

> The people of this state profess a great anxiety to have the science of literature more among them than it is. Schools are much wanting in this state and the inhabitants are less divided about schools than they are with you. I think the Indianans are more on an equality than any class of people with whom I have become acquainted for it is nothing uncommon with them if their neighbor is a little behindhanded, to unite their forces and get his toils beforehanded—Teachers here are very scarce and particularly good ones—my school is very large and have applicants almost every day. This is a great country for teachers but not as good as it will be in a few years, money will be more plenty though I think we share pretty well with our neighbours.

Faculty and Board of Trustees of Indiana Seminary and legislators gave indications that they hoped it was a great country for teachers, and that money would be "more plenty." They had joined forces to help a new state that was educationally "behindhanded" become "beforehanded."

By the time Indiana College was formed, the local community and Indiana as a whole had split into numerous religious factions and there was intense sensitivity on this subject. David H. Maxwell wrote Andrew Wylie on June 5, 1828, "It is . . . evident, that our society is yearly becoming more refined. Our citizens generally are moral, and a large proportion of them are professing christians of the Presbyterian, Cumberland presbyterian, Methodist, Baptist, Covenantors, and New light or christian Orders." Central Indiana was a region of fervent camp meetings, and religious zeal was comparable to the intense nationalism and land fever of the post-War of 1812 period. The hardships of the panic of 1819 had kindled the flame even higher until religious fundamentalism became a tightly interwoven strand of Hoosier domestic culture and Jacksonian politics, and no one could differentiate between the two. The stern Protestant ethic was the code by which inrushing settlers ordered their lives and institutions. Indiana Seminary could claim neither size nor complexity enough to represent both religious and political factions in equitable balance and the people themselves were too illiberal to recognize that it was immaterial what religious or political views men held, so long as they were competent to perform acceptable instructional functions. The office of teacher in the public view was like that of constable or sheriff; it was one to be rotated. This Harney knew full well.

The early Indiana student himself appeared in Bloomington with almost no perspective beyond the township horizon. He came seeking training of a form and purpose he knew not, but training which would not shake his childlike faith, revise his political loyalties, or loosen the right hand of parental control. He was bound in the web of tight-minded denominationalism, the temperance reformist crusade, and the great concept of "practicality." Most of all he was practically devoid of former education. He and his parents expected the seminary to be but a social and spiritual lean-to to the backwoods home itself, and the professors to assume roles of *in loco parentis*.

Denominational rows were further stirred by the fact that instructors supplemented their starvation incomes by serving as pastors of local churches. The public objected to paying additional salaries to augment even the modest salaries of professors who were also sectarian ministers.

By 1828 a crisis of life and death proportions faced Indiana Seminary. Its curriculum, if such it could be called, was strictly limited to two areas of learning. Its faculty was also limited, and was perhaps incapable of meeting the immediate needs of the people who lived in the vast green world about them. On top of this the state faced problems of political maturation. There was in 1820 a population of 147,000; in 1825, 185,000; and in 1830, 343,000. This inrush of people left nothing untouched, and no place or institution remained the same from year to year. No matter what personal issues arose in connection with the seminary, the impact of expansion and extension of political boundaries and organization, rising demands for internal improvements, need for better banking facilities, improved conditions of public health, better markets, and better communication were issues that kept local society in constant turmoil. Every season of settler emigration brought revolutionary demands and changes to Indiana, and at the same time a growing consciousness of Hoosier nationalism. These conditions demanded greater efforts from the seminary and a broader sense of public service from the state lest it lose its youth to expanding western neighbors.

The seminary could not escape its dilemma. Hall and Harney considered themselves inadequately trained and too inexperienced with educational management to offer work beyond the sophomore year, and now the school had at hand students it had trained but could not offer work for the last two years. Closely associated with this crisis was the generalized nature of the legislation which had created the seminary, but which failed to define in practical terms the means by which ultimate objectives could be attained. The eloquent section of the constitution providing for the foundation of a school, and the legislation chartering it, were the handiwork of men who cast their visions and dreams in terms of Oxford, Harvard, Yale, William and Mary, and, maybe, of the Jeffersonian university, without actually knowing firsthand what the problems of a functioning college in Indiana would be. Curiously one of the basic problems was the fact that both legislator and trustee created a headless and leaderless institution in which no planning took place. It is doubtful that they copied Jefferson in this respect.

Indiana Seminary had reached the full extent of its usefulness before it had graduated a class. The most important changes made in 1828 in the new charter were the creation of the college, with the office of president, and a proposed broadening of the curriculum to encompass four years' work.

Now the enormous task of finding a capable president confronted the board. As Hall said, "And now was to be found the *rara avis*—the white crow—a good President." Experience revealed that he should be a man who had already been president of a college. He and Harney went to work trying to locate such a person. Hall said Harney suggested Andrew Wylie, a recent president of Washington College in Pennsylvania. There are questions of whether it was Harney or William Hendricks who had been a student of the Pennsylvanian. At any rate Wylie's name was fixed upon by board and faculty. This young pedagogue was born in 1789 on a western Pennsylvania farm and had spent his early youth there as a laborer. He was tutored by his mother, and at fifteen years of age entered Jefferson College at Canonsburg, from which he graduated with honors. The second year after his graduation Wylie was made President of Jefferson College, and five years later transferred to the same position in nearby Washington College. A bitter dispute of an intradenominational nature had grown up between the two Presbyterian groups, and between the communities of Canonsburg and Washington. Wylie was caught in the cross fire, but not without firing a few shots himself. He was at loggerheads with the Presbyterian elders over fundamental theological viewpoints. Eventually he was forced to resign as President of Washington College, but he retained the pastorate of his church. Wylie's education was limited to the four years he spent at Jefferson College and his administrative experience in the presidency of the two struggling Presbyterian schools. He was a man of positive views who took the business of being a scholar, in form at least, with the utmost seriousness. He was approximately six feet tall, weighed over two hundred pounds, had a Scotsman's blond hair, and walked with the gait of a man who carried more than his coat on his shoulders. His facial expression indicated that he had a touch of haughtiness and detachment. In temperament he was stern, and some who knew him said he was devious.

Apparently the Board of Trustees of Indiana College had no more than a handful of sketchy recommendations for Wylie, and only the candidate's name, when they elected him president of the college on October 5, 1828. Wylie himself knew neither of Indiana College nor the board's decision until he received David H. Maxwell's letter telling him of his election. There followed letters from Hall and Harney, and no doubt one from Hendricks. Dr. Maxwell said he knew acceptance of the board's offer would involve genuine sacrifice. The salary was low, and he was being called "to enter upon a field of arduous labor." Too, he gave Wylie some idea of what "arduous labor" meant; the College had an endowment fund of $40,000 which was loaned out by authority of the legislature at 6 percent per annum. Thus the new president could count on approximately $2,000 a year of public money.

Dr. Maxwell undertook to portray to the Easterner the frontier country in the best light possible. He said he had resided in the state sixteen years as a physician, "and I unhesitatingly declare that Bloomington is as healthful a situation as any in our state, or in any of the other Western states." He then recited his experiences as a practicing physician to sustain his somewhat rosy picture. The seminary, he said, was a thriving institution with twenty-five students. It had a commodious three-story classroom building. A new edifice 81 by 35 feet was under construction; this building would contain the chapel.

The same month Hall and Harney wrote Wylie that they had proposed his name, and told him that if he chose to come to Indiana he would have an opportunity to advance religion and liberal education. "Hitherto," Hall said, "the smiles of Providence have been upon our Institution: & the very hand of God has visibly directed all events; & hence we cannot but hope that the same Being intends this as the scene of your future labours."

What Maxwell, Hall, and Harney did not know was that Wylie was being greatly discouraged by his wife, who never fully adjusted to the idea of moving to Indiana. Nevertheless Maxwell suggested that he come out to Bloomington to view the college and its community. He invited Wylie to come on October 29, when a large number of state officials, members of the Board of Visitors, would be present.

Following the October date Hall wrote Wylie that if he accepted the presidency of Indiana College he should plan to be present at the next board meeting, even though he would have to make a special trip west and then return for his family. This was to be a key meeting in which a curriculum would be planned, bylaws drafted, buildings planned, a library started, and many other vital matters discussed. He admonished the reluctant candidate that, "In all these things something must be done: —& it is highly important that it be done properly. Without you, even with the best intentions on the part of the Board, I am very confident *all* will be done more or less improperly." Too, Wylie was needed as a third instructor. He would be offered a salary of approximately $1,150, and if conditions improved this amount would be increased in the future. Hall also implied that he and Harney were only temporarily members of the staff; however, he and Harney would agree to stay all their lives.

Before Wylie reached Bloomington on his first visit a fresh row developed in the community over Harney's job. Wylie raised a question about this and asked David H. Maxwell for information. On December 18, 1828, Maxwell replied that Wylie's "unaccountable feelings and prejudices," which were aroused when he was in Bloomington, were groundless. If he indulged in these he would be confined to just one spot on earth. The facts in the Harney case, said Maxwell, were that he had been elected an instructor and Reverend James Ferris, a Covenantor, felt he was better qualified and more deserving for the position. Ferris had set his heart on the job and when Harney was elected he had stirred up the Jacksonian partisans of the community in his behalf. As Maxwell told Wylie, "Some of the party had by *downright lying* and other infamous means prejudiced the minds of several of the trustees who had no knowledge of the real state of affairs; and hence the vote that was given. The plans and arrangements of the parties were unknown to most of the Board until after the election was over." In time Harney was to become unhappily involved in a bitter dispute with Wylie which caused him to leave Bloomington. Ironically he became editor of one of the strongest Jacksonian papers in the Ohio Valley, the *Louisville Democrat*.

There were still more questions. Andrew Wylie must have driven the patient Maxwell to distraction. In answer to his query about the board Maxwell said, "A majority of them are men of intelligence, but not having had the experience in the management of a literary institution are measurably unacquainted with their duties as trustees." On the whole they were men, he believed, whose intentions were good; they were subject to error, but willing to right mistakes. He thought at the previous meeting the members had erred in electing Hall and Harney for a specific length of time; in his mind, tenure should be left to the will of the board. At the next meeting they would correct this error. "It is not my opinion," he said, "that any of the members of the board are bigoted, farther than an honest preference of their own religious views, may be so considered."

Dr. Maxwell said there was a Baptist minister on the board, and in Monroe and adjoining counties there were represented several other denominations. The "purchased" lands were held largely by yeoman owners, and there were large tracts held by land companies. Current emigration continued in an unabated flow, and in a short time settlement would extend from the Ohio to Lake Michigan. He described Bloomington society as civil and polite, "neither charge-able with '*rudeness*' nor entitled to the appellation '*refined*.' " In general he believed most of the people were moral, practicing Christians.

Dr. Maxwell's honesty and candor still did not persuade the reluctant Wylie that he should move west. He turned to his former pupil William Holmes McGuffey to help him make a decision. He told McGuffey the more he thought about moving to Bloomington, "the more I feel inclined to take the matter under serious consideration." But he knew if he did move he would face difficulties. He would break many ties, and at his advanced age (39) he was too old to make new acquaintances and to push forward a new educational enterprise. Bloomington's ruddy frontier society offered real problems, and, further, it was close to Oxford, Ohio, and would have to compete for its students with Miami University. The climate and general conditions of the section offered a serious threat to health. His reservations, which he mentioned to McGuffey, no doubt were stimulated by the opposition of his family. In Washington he preached regularly to a large and congenial congregation, a privilege he might not enjoy in Bloomington for many years to come. "Ah!" he asked McGuffey, "How shall I fill up the Faculty? What kind of fellow is Harney? Would *you* go with me?"

Perhaps Hall's urging that, "should you come hither, Sir, your influence may be exerted upon a very broad scale towards the noblest & most beneficial ends; the advancement of religion and of liberal education" influenced Wylie.

Thus far Indiana College prospered because "the smiles of Providence have been upon our Institution," said Hall, "& the very hand of God has visibly directed all events, & hence we cannot but hope that the same Being intends this as the scene of your future labours." Appealing further to Wylie's vanity, Hall said the public waited impatiently for his decision, "& great & universal will be the disappointment should you by a sense of duty be impelled to a declination of what may be termed, not merely the call of the Trustees, but of the whole state."

Bloomington, said Hall, was a new town in a new country. It had a different appearance from most towns in that it was improving rapidly. He cited evidence that it was as healthy as Dr. Maxwell claimed it was. In his three years in the place he said he had preached the funeral sermon of only one adult from his congregation and he had died from pulmonary troubles. Hall's own daughter had died of a peculiar eruption, and he could recall only six or seven deaths in the town.

Hall thought more virulent than the ague was the poison of the college's enemies, and the Harney case had brought these into the open. If Wylie accepted they would die and remain dead, otherwise they would destroy the institution. Too, the board, with the best intentions, would make fatal blunders from which they could not recover. What Indiana needed at the moment was the stern guiding hand of a man who knew from experience what a college was and how it should proceed with its educational program.

After long and painful delay on his part, Andrew Wylie accepted the presidency of Indiana College and arrived in Bloomington in time for the fall term of 1829. On October 29, he delivered his inaugural address, in which he set out his educational philosophy. There would be no radical change in the classical curriculum. He would exercise a strong parental hand, and he assured his audience that

> Purity of morals shall be made a primary object. Whenever any student shall shew symptoms of sloth, or of any other vice, commencing upon him, he shall be addressed on the subject; and, if admonition prove ineffectual, he shall be sent away. No indolent or dissipated youth need ask for admission, even for a day, within these walls. Let none think hard of this. Colleges were intended, not to reform the vicious, but to instruct those who wished to learn. They are schools not penitentiaries.

There was no doubt in Wylie's mind about the kind of studies Indiana College would offer, "and, in the first place," he said, "it is intended that classical learning shall hold its place—a grade of equal importance with any other kind of learning—in the course of literature to be pursued." Immediately he instituted a program of Latin, Greek, and English for freshmen; Greek, algebra, and Cambridge mathematics for sophomores; mathematics, astronomy, and mathematical and physical geography for juniors; and evidence of Christianity in connection with natural religion, political economy, Greek, Latin, and English classics, and moral and mental philosophy for seniors. With slight exceptions this was the core curriculum of Indiana College, later Indiana University, for the next quarter century.

There was some innovation in this program, especially in the fields of philosophy, political economy, and perhaps astronomy. None of the "practical" subjects were included. It was necessary for men of the West to understand languages, lawyers, doctors, farmers, legislators; everybody had to understand languages and history, otherwise "they would villify their benefactors and caress their enemies. . . . They would oppose their own best interest. They will forge chains for themselves."

Though no direct proof can be established that Andrew Wylie brought with him to Bloomington a copy of the famous *Yale Report of 1828*, there is sufficient internal evidence to assume that he did. His "Lecture on College Government" of October, 1838, contains in strong essence if not in specific wording the philosophy of the *Report*. It seems likely that the conclusions of the eastern committee went far toward shaping the course of higher education in Indiana until 1885. The *Yale Report* covers what at that date was considered the whole range of purposes of higher education, and it states that the function of the college was fundamentally to "discipline" and "furnish" the mind of the student and to supply him "Parental superintendence" during his stay in academia. The Yale professors took cognizance of American needs for special academies to teach the masses the functional arts of society, but the college must drill the select few in the higher arts in sophisticated courses in languages, history, mathematics, and philosophy. On these points Wylie based his presidency at Indiana University in the institution's important formative years.

Classes opened in December, 1829, with Wylie, Hall, and Harney as faculty members. The coming of Wylie wrought several changes. Junior and senior classes were added, a curious kind of elective was instituted which allowed advanced students to elect Hebrew instead of French. The program was made even more liberal than this; if any student wished to acquaint himself with any one of the specified branches he could elect to do so. The new president ignored the often stated principle of "tuition gratis" and persuaded the board to assess a tuition fee of ten dollars per annum for the first year, and fifteen dollars for the remaining three years. As a matter of fact, this provision of free tuition had never been honored. Even Hall had charged $2.50 per session. Thus Indiana

College was launched with forty enrolled students, and this number remained constant for the next three years.

Andrew Wylie never could have been classed an expert public relations man. Unlike Hall he did not bring in his intellectual baggage from Pennsylvania a will to become a confirmed Hoosier. He was a serious man engaged in the serious business of scholarship. In his relations with the everyday world he treated people with the studied detachment that he thought became the preoccupied scholar. Along the streets of the village he let people see the intellectual man shambling along in deep study, and when he had to expose himself to the public he did so formally. This was the manner in which he revealed himself to students and colleagues. A decade later, in a long address to the annual meeting of the Western Literary Institute and College of Professional Teachers, he told the audience,

> That mode of government which I intend imperfectly to sketch in the sequel of this discourse, may be denominated the "paternal," as being analogous to that which every wise and affectionate father exercises over his children, and which is the nearest image of that moral and providential government, which the great God, our Heavenly Father, exercises over us his intelligent offsprings. It seeks to establish its authority over the governed, not by a system of minute and paltry rules, which require the exercise of an espionage, as vexatious to the governors as it can be to the governed, but by addressing itself to the rational and moral faculties of the latter, and to their sense of honor, their interests, and their social affections and sympathies.

Nowhere did anyone state the principle of *in loco parentis* in clearer language. Wylie, however, had to admit that his system had not worked out as he had hoped, and there still had to be some of the old kind of direct supervision.

This was Wylie's Achilles' heel. He was able to win the affection and cooperation of some students but he incurred the deep enmity of others. It was a student incident which brought him face to face with his colleagues in a row that almost threatened the college itself. Beginning with Hall's first class, emphasis had been placed upon student orations. In one of the oratorical exercises of the college Wylie was accused of a breach of promise. In the spring of 1832 the faculty chose two student orators, and since the temperance movement was strong the student temperance society asked that it be allowed to supply a third speaker. Samuel Givens was chosen to speak. He asked President Wylie if he might come either first or last in the order and Wylie agreed.

The college orations on this occasion were held in the Presbyterian Church, which was then undergoing internal repairs. When the students and President Wylie appeared at the church, the procession was led by a band consisting of a bass viol, a fiddle, a clarinet, a triangle, and drum. A crusty old carpenter was still at work and when he saw the fiddle coming down an aisle he stubbornly refused to stop his work on the grounds that it had no business in the church. He kept on planing boards, throwing shavings over everybody and creating a great noise, and not until the audience agreed to pay him his full day's wages would he agree to withdraw and leave the temple to the devils.

In the midst of the hassle with the carpenter it was discovered that President Wylie had violated his promise to Givens and placed him in the middle of the program. This infuriated the youth and he refused to respond when his name was called. Wylie passed on to the next speaker but on Saturday morning in chapel he called Givens before the faculty and students to give his excuse for not responding. Givens explained he did not want his speech mixed up with the others. Wylie said in the commotion at the church he had forgotten his promise but asked the angry young Kentuckian whether, if the same situation developed again, he would make the same response; he replied that he would. Wylie denounced him as "a very mean man." Faculty and students entered a dispute which resulted in Wylie lecturing Hall and Harney before the students, and they—Harney and Hall—in turn accusing Wylie of duplicity and spying. There followed a hot exchange of letters between the professors and the president.

The Wylie-Givens dispute was complicated by a second semicomic incident. Harney had a habit of taking out a pocket knife and strapping it on his boot. Wylie saw this and dramatically accused the professor of threatening to attack him with a deadly weapon. Hall rose to the defense of his colleague and from that time on "the fat was in the fire," to use a good New Purchase term. Later Wylie and Harney met on a narrow log over a mud hole and confronted each other like two bulls; in this episode Wylie, a large man, butted Harney into the mire. In a resulting trial in the Presbyterian General Assembly, Wylie was victorious. By this time students had aligned themselves with one faction or the other, and the affair bordered on being childish and disgraceful. When Wylie returned from the Presbyterian General Assembly following his victory, seniors of the college lighted his way with $14 worth of candles.

Hall was to have an enduring say. In *The New Purchase* he detailed the quarrel with genuine discredit to Wylie. There was more to the quarrel, however, than the above stated facts. Fundamentally the three men would have found themselves at odds had there been no oratorical exercise or strapping of a pocket knife. Already they disagreed over methods of teaching. Wylie preferred a departure from the rote-textbook method where professors drilled students in memory exercises, whereas Hall and Harney were traditionalists. In the end Hall and Harney were discharged, which necessitated the hiring of new faculty members.

Hardly had the dust settled over the faculty "war" before students and faculty of Indiana College were confronted by a far more serious threat of destruction. In the summer of 1833 the Ohio Valley was swept by a scourge of Asiatic cholera which had been brought up the Mississippi and Ohio rivers by steamboats. This epidemic had broken out along the river at Louisville and Maysville in Kentucky, and had been carried inland, where it virtually depopulated the town of Lexington. On Saturday, August 9, some of the people of Bloomington were on their way to a morning church meeting. They passed the residence of George Johnson, where his Negro servant Auneka was gathering wood to start dinner. By 2 o'clock that afternoon Auneka's body was being hastily buried in an attempt to halt the spread of cholera. A student named Huntington from Indianapolis was taken ill and died quickly and was buried by faculty and students the next morning. A frantic exodus from Bloomington began, many people going on foot to get as far away as possible. President Wylie cautioned students to depart calmly and not overexert themselves on their way to their homes. Indiana College did not resume classes until the first of September. By then the cholera had run its course, and the professors thought it safe for students to return.

[4 5]

At the end of the college year in 1838 the *Louisville Literary Register* took a close editorial look at President Wylie, measuring his abilities in popular theological terms. The Kentuckian said that he

should be remembered not so much for his talent as reputation. He had written a great deal and changed his residence enough [that] his works and combative propensities in the field of theology and literature have sounded his name far and wide. He cannot lay claim to any great talent, or particular acuteness; and as to aiming the fire of genius, we doubt that he ever saw those mighty truths that like mystic stars, burn far up in the heavens of mind, even . . . through a telescope fashioned for his wants by another hand. But he often presents long established facts in a vigorous manner, and, by his occasional command of the rich and masculine Saxon, has at times interested large audiences. If we were asked what divine he most resembles, we could not say Channing, because the Unitarian of Boston is original; we could not say Bascom, because the Professor of Augusta is an orator; we could not say Dewey, because he is fervent; we could not say Moffitt, because the great revivalist, when he forgets his dandyism, has all the merits of the first three mentioned persons combined. No, the Doctor is rather of the good old round head school, and we all know the characteristics of that order.

Wylie's schedule for himself was austere. As outlined in 1830 by a student at the college, it was: up at 4:00 A.M., pray at 6:00, breakfast at 7:30, and recite at 9:00, recite again at 3:00, supper at 5:00, go to rooms at 7:00, and retire at 10:00, this six days a week. President Wylie acknowledged that he must be somewhat enigmatic to the Hoosiers. His public image, he knew, was a mixed one. People who liked him supported him fervently, while his enemies were equally vigorous in their opposition. The line between town and gown was at times impenetrable, and one had to learn to tolerate the other. The scholar's world was not that of the courthouse square, and his language was not that of the hitching rack and the county judge's office. Addressing the citizens of Monroe County on July 4, 1840, Wylie said,

A student, fellow citizens, is no idler. He works hard; he works every day: rain or shine his hay must be made. At night, too, he works while others sleep; works while others play, works on and on. There is no credit, often, for what he does, because his labors do not harden his hands, nor bring sweat from his pores. But his brain works—and there is the very place where that is elaborated which sets everything else to work in this working world— the brain! The workshop of the mind—where it manufactures thoughts, devices, cunning inventions—combines the elements of things, in ideas, into contrivances which, when brought out of the idea into act, fill the world with the products of all the arts of life! But while we, Fellow Citizens, are thus employed, it is our misfortune to be lost from your sight and from your sympathies. And it may be that we are even, on account of these our habits of seclusion and confinement, accused to you—accused of pride and selfishness; as if our imprisonment were our choice, and not imposed upon us by the duty which we owe to the public; or as if we cherished none of the feelings of humanity nor entertained a wish to be on terms of friendship and good neighborhood with those around us.

The people of Indiana were conscious of the existence of both Andrew Wylie and Indiana College. Wylie had come to stay. In 1835 he entered into an elaborate contract with two Bloomington builders to erect for him at what is now the corner of Lincoln and Second Street a fine brick mansion. This house was no doubt an effort to placate his wife Margaret, who had never become fully reconciled to the West. Based on a solid limestone foundation, it had a large basement, two main stories, and a fairly large attic. In short, it was a bit of affluent Pennsylvania transplanted into the midst of the Hoosiers, and the house was well adapted to a most gracious way of life. No doubt it was one of the better homes in the New Purchase area. This was an anchor, or perhaps more accurately an island, to which the Wylie family could retreat.

Despite his stiff, even sanctimonious manner, Andrew Wylie had a wry sense of humor. In May, 1837, he went East to become embroiled with the Presbyterians in a theological dispute in the national assembly. On his way he visited relatives in western Pennsylvania. To Margaret he wrote that he had just seen his nephew, Craig Wylie's, new wife.

I can't give you an idea of Craig's "better half." She surpasses in ugliness & repulsiveness anything in the shape of humanity that anybody ever married before, or I hope ever will, till the last of the long line of Eve's daughters has found a husband. In one sense *she* is without joking the *last*. The marriage however will undoubtedly work for Craig's good: which I prove thus: he must have married her for pure love, love founded on excellence and character (that be deep out of sight) to all but love & that are likely therefore to be lasting & they will be happy.

At least in the trying faculty sessions with errant students Father Andrew could always let his thoughts wander away to this misbegotten daughter of Eve who had crept into his family, and maybe student "crimes" seemed less horrendous. For president, college, and community the die was cast. Upholding a façade of learning, if not liberality of curriculum, Andrew Wylie strode down the streets of Bloomington between his fine brick mansion and the "cotton factory," as Mrs. Theophilus Wylie called the school building, on the edge of Perry Township.

Indiana College in its first decade had grown up on the knobless plains of classicism, elementary mathematics, and a surface consideration of the Constitution of the United States and political economy. The roof of the Wylie mansion had a flat deck and there one could scan the heavens with a hand telescope to learn some elementary astronomy. The College was an established institution in 1838; it had survived almost every woe that could face a frontier college. Now, as a boy orator said in 1837, was the time to take the third step and convert Indiana College into Indiana University.

[IV]

Andrew Wylie's Era

T HE SCHOOLBOY ORATOR OF 1837 was prescient when he beckoned lustily to the future in his speech, suggesting that soon Indiana College would become Indiana University, and that its fount of knowledge would be greatly enriched by this act. In the minds of the people, legislators, Board of Trustees, and Board of Visitors, the mere matter of changing academic titles would work wonders. All that was necessary was a legislative sleight of hand to produce the miracle. On February 15, 1838, the college, by legislative fiat, became the university.

One searches the record in vain for some expression of an enlarged educational philosophy, significant curriculum change, or faculty expansion. In 1836 there were four full-time professors, Andrew Wylie, Beaumont Parks, Ebenezer Newton Elliott, and James F. Dodds, and there were two tutors. Between 1837 and 1839 there were changes. Parks and Elliott went away to colleges in Illinois and Mississippi, and Theophilus Wylie, cousin of the president, and Augustus W. Ruter replaced them. Otherwise the status quo was maintained.

Meeting in extended session beginning September 24, 1838, the Board of Trustees revealed the full extent of their thoughts on raising Indiana College to university status. First responsibility was that of devising a curriculum. Along with an outline of general courses the board established a chair of law and elected Miles C. Eggleston, scion of a prominent old Virginia family and professor of law in Hanover College, to fill it. No one admitted having consulted Judge Eggleston, and consequently none knew whether he would accept the position. A special committee was instructed to look elsewhere for a professor if Eggleston refused the offer, which he did. Thus Indiana University just barely entered the door to achieving university status by a flick of the governor's pen and a fruitless search for a law professor.

Mere legislative action had no effect whatsoever on the flow of college life in Bloomington. The college bell continued to ring out the periods of study with no greater urgency than before. Life in the Boarding House was as hectic as ever, professors droned on through rote recitations, and students found the stagecoach tavern benches of classroom and chapel no more inviting or comfortable. For Andrew Wylie the lingering problems of college administration outweighed those now arising in the new university. His stern personal manner of discipline and code of student behavior begot troubles faster than he could solve them. Students were restive and rebellious under the wearing pressures of austere academic life. This being true, president and faculty sat frequently in star-chamber sessions, wringing from miscreant youths confessions of wrongdoing. They forced from the repentant ones apologies as fervent as the neighboring outpourings in revival brush arbors, or they stirred Jacksonian independence and anger from boys who stamped out of college in furious huffs.

The faculty court was still tingling from the reverberations of the Thomas-Bryant affair. This incident was provoked by that ancient source of collegiate irritation, the stealing of janitorial firewood. Even President Wylie had noticed that Bryant's winter supply of wood was vanishing at a phenomenal rate. Late one evening the enraged janitor came to the college and called loudly for a boy to come down. Charles Thomas responded and became engaged in a heated conversation with the master of the woodpile. Bryant was devoid of tact and subtlety. He boasted loudly that he could out-chop anybody in Indiana. Thomas said he could out-chop him, and implied that such a contest would not fully test his talent

[5 0]

with an ax. The janitor took a new tack, saying that students were lazy no-good boys who sat in their rooms all day reading books. Young Thomas bruised Bryant's ego further by saying he was too stupid to sit in a room and read a book, in fact he said Bryant did not know "A" from "B," whereupon the janitor dropped his ax and picked up a stick with which to hit the boy. Before Thomas could draw his knife he was knocked to the ground unconscious and bleeding. Bryant believed that he killed Thomas and rushed off to Dr. Wylie's house to confess his crime.

This incident threw the college into an uproar. Students milled about threatening to lynch the janitor and quickly the faculty became deeply involved in the row. Eleven days of testimony before the faculty revealed that Bryant was expert at hitting college boys over the head. He had committed similar indiscretions against students at Centre College in Danville, Kentucky, and hence had left that post. Thomas was cleared of his part in the argument on the grounds he had a right to defend himself. But the tedious faculty courtroom proceedings added more fuel to a feud already smoldering between President Wylie and the stiff-necked Connecticut Yankee, Beaumont Parks.

Hardly had the Thomas-Bryant incident been settled before Wylie and his court of continuous session were neck-deep in another case of student misbehavior. On a hot August day in 1839, two boys decided a good way to break the Bloomington doldrums would be to treat their friends to a jolly round of wine bibbing. They bought two bottles of brandy and smuggled them into the Boarding House, where approximately a quarter of the student body joined the escapade. Perhaps they could have committed no greater breach in this bluestocking age and place. The president and faculty were certain that youth had to be impressed with this fact, and they took positive actions to teach their lesson. One after another each tippler entered the faculty sanctum to confess that he had drunk the brandy, and that in all his innocence it had made him sick. (So sick did they claim to have been that it appeared Indiana University might be having a fresh outbreak of the Asiatic cholera.) Judge and jury expelled two boys, censured five others who promised never to drink again, and "frightened the others into everlasting sobriety."

University life in Bloomington never ran smoothly according

to the carefully kept records of the faculty. Erring students were forever falling into the clutches of Judge Wylie's court on charges of fighting, swearing, drinking, or irritating townsmen. Almost every meeting of chapel was a session of censuring wayward lads. While bored schoolboys fought and argued with the janitor and sent carping petitions to the Board of Trustees, the faculty itself was fraught with its own petty troubles. The feud between Wylie and Beaumont Parks renewed itself at almost every faculty assembly. It is now hard to discover the source of this dissension.

Parks seemed to think he would be a more competent president than Wylie. He was born in Norwich, Connecticut, in 1775, and had graduated from Dartmouth College with a Master's degree in 1802. Leaving Hanover (or Dartmouth) for the West, he went in search of a school to teach. After 1821 he opened and taught in Madison, Indiana, the first Latin school held north of the Ohio. In 1832 Andrew Wylie brought him to Bloomington as successor to his old adversary, John Hopkins Harney. For the next seven years this wilful pair quarreled almost continuously. Parks was picayune about the precise wording of faculty minutes, about the arbitrary rulings of the president, and about instructional methods. In the case of a fight between two students, William McCall and John R. Cravens, Parks took the part of Cravens against Wylie's sons, who were involved, and Wylie showed partiality to McCall. This incident caused a near revolt among the students, and Parks heated the cauldron of discontent more by raising accusing questions about what happened in an unrecorded faculty meeting. His colleagues proved him a liar and he stomped out of the room in a fit of anger. Later that year, 1839, he withdrew from the faculty, by invitation of the board, and went to Illinois, where he taught in a classical school for the next twenty years, but he did not depart until the Board of Trustees agreed to pay the rest of his salary for that year.

Wylie left much to be desired in his relations with his faculty. He and Ebenezer Newton Elliott, professor of mathematics, and physics, could not work together harmoniously. Elliott had come to Indiana with that colony of stern Reformed Presbyterians who emigrated from Chester, South Carolina. Among these was the Woodburn family, which was to be so intimately associated with Indiana University over the years. In 1836 Professor Elliott accepted the presidency of Mississippi College, and from 1861 to 1865 he served as a surgeon in the Confederate Army.

Between presiding over his court and rendering stern censures in chapel, Andrew Wylie turned his attention to the more basic needs of the university. It was his ambition to make good the boast that it would become "the leading institution of higher learning beyond the Ohio." He faced enormous handicaps, in which he could not always apply his ideas or correct the university's shortcomings.

In creating the university the legislature had increased the size of the Board of Trustees to a number almost rivaling that of the student body. New and returning members were John Law, Robert Dale Owen, Samuel K. Hoshour, James Blair, Joshua O. Howe, Chester G. Ballard, William Turner, and Leroy Mayfield. Among these newcomers were men who were determined from the outset to be troublemakers. On September 23, board members arrived in Bloomington to begin an extended session in which they were to discuss every aspect of the new institutional status. They reelected Andrew Wylie president, by a vote of 9 to 2, Joshua Howe and William Turner casting the negative votes. Owen, Law, and Thompson were then appointed a special committee to work with the president in the selection of a faculty.

Five standing committees of the board were created: Ways and Means, Library, Examining, Buildings and Grounds, and Claims. Among the various powers the legislature granted the trustees were electing "a president of said university and such professors, tutors, instructors and other officers of the same, as they may judge necessary for the interest thereof, and shall determine the duties, salaries, emoluments, responsibilities, and tenures of their several offices and designate the course of instruction in said university." In its initial meeting the board proceeded to draft the curriculum, examine students, hire faculty members, supervise library purchases, and even usurp the function of a buildings and grounds manager and the janitor. In every way the board took itself seriously, except when facing the political realities of a wholly chaotic condition of public finances in Indiana. This was a period when Indiana suffered from a serious economic depression which affected every aspect of life in the state. No part of the state's development was harder pressed than the recently expanded system of internal improvements.

Wylie, however, also had positive ideas about the university's reorganization. He wished to drop the academy even over the opposition of board members. Later when he changed his mind and asked that it be retained his opponents on the board accused him of duplicity. He reiterated his faith in the more liberal methods of teaching, although this also opposed the will of some board members.

Reflecting the lowly estate in which Indiana University was beginning operation, Andrew Wylie informed the trustees in a lengthy communication that much better provisions had to be made for the teaching of natural philosophy and chemistry. Storage cases had to be constructed to house instruments and chemicals. The college building was unsafe for use of inflammable materials; water was not available to conduct experiments or to quench accidental fires. Heating stoves were no good as sources of heat; besides they would be lethal in conducting proper laboratory procedures. Water had to be carried some distance from an open and polluted spring. He said the time had come to construct a separate science building. The penurious board, however, felt this request an unnecessary extravagance. They believed the financial condition of the university was so precarious that it would have to wear its new prestigious title in fancy rather than fact.

Members of the board had other, and they believed weightier, matters to consider. It was now time to dignify the institution by having an official heraldic seal cast and a diploma plate made so that recipients would be properly impressed with their accomplishments. A steward had to be employed to oversee the boarding hall, and a university band organized. Before this the college's musical equipment had consisted of a steel triangle, a viola, a fiddle, and a clarinet. These were the instruments which had angered the Roundhead Presbyterian carpenter. An appropriation of $150 was made: $30 to pay for the services of Director William McCrea, $20 for the band, and $100 to purchase instruments. Inference was made that if there were too few student musicians then townsmen might be enlisted in the band. Other problems in considerable numbers awaited solution with some degree of haste. One was moving of the disreputable old college privy onto a more solid university vault.

At the time of the transition from college to university status, life in Indiana and Bloomington was just emerging from the first phase of backwoods settlement. The intense depression following 1837 took a heavy financial toll. Thus this period of the university's history must be considered against a backdrop of economic stringency, a primitive way of life, and a diligent search for new institutional directions. Mrs. Theophilus Wylie left a colorful gauge of contemporary conditions. Responding to a student reporter in 1905, she gave a vivid picture of life at the moment when the university was being organized.

> When I came here in 1838, things were in a rather primitive state. There were no railroads then in this part of the country and the National road was just being built. We came from Pittsburgh to New Albany by boat and the rest of the way to Bloomington in a stagecoach drawn by four horses. The roads were very bad; the stumps of recently cut trees sticking up in the middle of the road-way and grazing the coach at every turn.

As the stagecoach entered Bloomington the coachman blew a long and loud blast on his horn, causing the horses to jump, and they turned the stage over. Mrs. Wylie had to scramble out head-over-heels through the window of the vehicle, and walk the rest of the way.

> . . . It was a pretty wild place when I first came. The farmers made almost everything at home. The houses were lighted by tallow "dips" and the farmer's wives went to church in their sun bonnets and wove their own linsey-woolsey. My own dresses came from Philadelphia, but they were nearly worn out before I could wear them. When women heard that a new dress had come from the East they would send miles and miles for the pattern and there was nothing to do but pack up the pretty silk dresses in a saddle-bag and let them go. I did not always like to see my nice silk dresses carried around the country in that way, but my husband comforted me by telling me that we had come west to educate the people and that this was part of my education.

Nevertheless the people were friendly, hospitable, full of questions.

A year after the arrival of the Theophilus Wylies in Bloomington, Indiana College ceased to exist and the university began operation. The institution lacked so many necessary things that no one really knew which problem to consider first. Obviously money was needed and it had to be available soon. The university had on hand $4,835.82 in cash, but it was well nigh impossible to determine how much money had accumulated in the endowment fund from land sales. The state treasurer was an incompetent elected official who kept his formal records on bits and scraps of paper which were unintelligible to everybody, including the treasurer. As best as anyone could determine, there should have been at the very least $70,000 in the accumulated fund. The Board of Trustees resolved that under no circumstances would they touch this backlog until it amounted to $100,000. This meant the university was placed on an impoverished budget during the important formative years. Furthermore the endowment rested in the hands of a blatantly political fiscal officer. It appeared that endowment money was loaned to favorites whose security amounted to little more than the fact that some of them had noisily supported Martin Van Buren and the Democrats. The trustees were practically powerless to rectify this state of affairs. State officials and legislators were glad enough to serve on the Board of Trustees and the Board of Visitors, and to exercise tight if not spiteful control over the university, but few if any of them intended to help stabilize its finances by making appropriations directly from the public till.

Van Buren's panic of 1837 not only slowed down the sale of land from the university townships, but it jeopardized collections for land already sold, and it reduced the prices of fresh sales to the lowest acceptable level. It is possible that some of the lands of the two townships sold for less than a tenth of their actual value. Under these circumstances to speak of either free tuition or an expanded educational program was to speak of eventually closing the university itself.

As the new board of the university struggled to adjust conditions to the changed status of the school, it was confronted with the grim fact that money on hand was insufficient to meet the university's debts. It owed $7,732.56, and there was only $6,697.25 in sight if all funds became available; and even this amount was visible only through a thickening fog of financial uncertainty. It was proposed that the state treasurer be requested to supply $5,000 from accumulated interest, and that $1,798.25 be raised by foreclosing two first mortgages on lands held by the Borland estate and by Wright and King. If these efforts succeeded there would still remain a shortage of $425.00. In addition to this it was proposed that a loan of $5,000 be negotiated with the Bank of Bedford, a move which was to provoke running arguments and to cause much personal embarrassment to President Wylie and the Board of Trustees. The trustees made it clear that they in no way would be personally responsible for the guaranty of the deficit. A novel proposal was made, that the legislature be requested to permit the university to share in the state's saline fund for ten years. This was a special leasehold fund which was derived from the sale or lease of choice mineral sites such as salt licks. In return for this privilege it would establish a normal school and admit young Hoosier men free of tuition and grant them free use of the library. This branch of didactics, as it was called, would be placed in the charge of a "professor" who not only would teach pedagogy but would travel over Indiana visiting all school districts every two years. On his visitations he would give advice on educational matters to public school teachers and patrons.

Andrew Wylie was certain that a university could not stand still in its natal tracks. It had to develop all of its parts in keeping with similar institutions across the country. One of the first needs was a good library. The college had received a generous gift of books from the library of William Maclure which had been purchased in Europe and included classic works in French, Greek, and Latin. They were presented to Indiana College in 1836 by Board President Jonathan Nichols. This laid the foundation, but the collection needed expanding. When confronted with this proposition the board felt that some rare books in the library should be sold and cheaper ones bought in their places. Wylie asked the trustees to follow Harvard's example and appropriate $5,000 annually to expand the university's library holdings. Bloomington, however, was not Cambridge, and Indiana University in the backwoods was not the old and settled Harvard University of the West. The board exercised little discrimination; its members tended to translate everything into terms of the will of a majority of the people. This meant the reduction of University functions to an equation with fundamentalist religion and the earthy terms of frontier politics. Thus the institution was forced to pitch its intellectual hay into low racks to please shortnecked citizens.

This Andrew Wylie learned when he purchased a copy of the classical *Thesaurus* for $300. Board members questioned whether the school could afford such an extravagance. They suggested that the book be sold and the university buy cheaper ones that would be just as startling to incoming students. They thought it best to buy books in American history and literature. Except for this rash purchase the committee reported the library collection in good order; all books were shelved and accounted for. The committee felt, however, that some of the "rare and curious books," which had come from various sources and had cost little, could be sold for profit.

Looking to the future the trustees compiled an extensive list of books that they thought should be purchased, provided they could be had cheaply. On this list was John Smith's *Generall Historie of Virginia*, the journal of Stephen H. Long, Captains Lewis and Clark's journal, Thomas Jefferson's *Notes on the State of Virginia*, Constantin Volney's *View of the Soil and Climate of the United States*, David Ricardo's *On the Principles of Political Economy and Taxation*, the *Tatler* and *Spectator*, Edmund Spenser's *Faerie Queene*, and the *Arabian Nights*. Few people in Indiana in 1839 could have compiled so excellent a list of books. It was evident that Robert Dale Owen sought to perpetuate at Indiana University some of the intellectual tools which he had collected at New Harmony in the form of books and scientific laboratory equipment.

In 1843 the university published an impressive catalogue of its library holdings. This booklet was modeled after Park's *Pantology* of the University of Pennsylvania. Under twenty headings the library's books were categorized and listed as the board had earlier requested. It is not clear whether board members or faculty members did this cataloguing. An extensive number of books were included under psychology, such titles as Sir Walter Scott's *Letters on Demonology and Witchcraft*, the Metaphysical Works of Immanuel Kant (eight volumes), and J. G. Spurzheim's two-volume *Phrenology, or the Doctrine of Mental Phenomena*. Judging from the published catalog it is questionable whether a single student during the first three decades of Indiana University's history could have found enough material in the library to study United States history.

There is some considerable evidence to indicate that the library existed as much for ornamentation as for use. It was open only on Saturdays, it contained no tables or chairs, and books could be used only under the most protective rules. The attitude toward books and users was ever that of vigilant watch-care, and the happiest possible condition was to have every book in its place and duly accounted for when the trustees' library committee came to make its annual inspection. This, however, could never be. A member of the board borrowed Volume I of James Shirley's six-volume set of *Dramatic Works and Poems* and lost it. It mattered not that the delinquent borrower was a board member, a lost book was an irreparable loss, and the university could not afford to ignore this breach of trust. To allow a board member to violate the rules was to set a dangerous precedent. President Wylie requested the trustees to force the borrower to pay for the entire set. In 1842 Shirley's inimitable poetry was still listed with Volume I missing.

The Board of Trustees thought they had more important matters to settle than to hunt for a missing volume of Shirley's deadly work. Agitation to remove the university to the capital city of Indianapolis had already begun, and at least two members of the board, Joshua O. Howe and William Turner, favored the suggestion. As their reason they gave the fact that the institution had declined in Bloomington, where "broils" and dissensions were unceasing. Religious bigots and brawling Jacksonians kept a fight going. If not held in check these forces would eventually destroy the university.

Advocates of a move to Indianapolis gave various other reasons why they thought the university should be located in that city. The legislature in 1840 even went so far as to request the Board of Trustees to sanction the move. A majority of the board, however, opposed removal and placed the legislative request on the table. They refused to act, first, they said, because it would cost $20,000 to make the move, and the university was already in debt. Students of moderate means, the sons of farmers and artisans, could not attend college if the fees were higher. The university had to be located where agricultural products could be purchased cheaply and boarding prices could be kept at a minimum. In Indianapolis boarding would be 50 percent higher, and there would be greater inclination to indulge in extravagances. Bloomington was a healthy spot, and many people had bought property in the town with the belief that the University would always be located there. Indianapolis was a wicked place and offered too many temptations. Finally the university would only mark time while awaiting removal. The board thus disposed of a troublesome issue for about the third but by no means the last time.

To distinguish between professorial appointments made within the university and those made at courthouses or in boards of deacons was nearly impossible. Though making what appeared to be careful and considered decisions, board members were not always dedicated to the cause of higher education at the cost of partisan politics. Trustees were no different from other members of Indiana society, and this was an extremely partisan age. Because of this they nearly defeated the central purposes of higher education at times. Holding to a passionate dedication to maintain equality of the individual, they often acted without using sound judgment in deciding on some of the internal policies of the university.

Somehow the trustees and university patrons seemed to hope that young men would attend classes for four years and come away socially and intellectually the same backwoodsmen they were at the beginning of their college careers. Paradoxically they hoped the catalyst of the classroom would achieve results without altering the graduates' manners or personalities. The conflict remained between the purposes of the university as an effective operation, local egos that had to be served, and flourishing intolerance of intellectuality. What Indiana University needed was a president who could understand and tolerate Hoosier foibles and failures and lead the people to actively support the university in its growing years.

Unhappily Andrew Wylie, with all his show of erudition, was not such a man. He could neither understand the backwoodsmen's differing views or their limited mental processes nor could he communicate his own ideas to them in easy informal terms. An example of this was his promise to speak about the university at a public gathering in Washington, Indiana. A son became ill and he had to send two students as substitutes. Later his friend, Judge David McDonald wrote that everybody in town had anticipated his coming, "Methodists, Catholics, Presbyterians—everybody intended to hear you." The women had cooked mince pies, made jellies and sweetmeats, "even the chickens seemed to anticipate the moment when they should, *sans ceremonie*, be beheaded to please the appetite and inhabit the abdominal regions of a great man." Judge McDonald said the Presbyterians would never forgive Wylie for sending them two Campbellite preachers. "That was the 'unkindest cut of all,' your unpardonable sin, 'worse than witchcraft.' " He said his friends had to face all of this in the "face and teeth of the scriptures which saith that 'Campbellism and every other ism not 200 years old are dramatic heresies!—that the Presbyterians, the round heads, the fifth monarchy men, and those other sects that rose up about the time of the Rump Parliament, are the only true saints, and that confession o'faith is the only point where human bliss stands still."

The lawyer told Wylie that he should get out in the state more. He thought Wylie owed this much to Indiana. Following such a course, McDonald said, he could make liberal assurances to the friends of the university, and he could dispel foolish prejudices that were borne against the school. McDonald wanted the school to remain in Bloomington, and well beyond the legislators' reach, but he was afraid of what committees might try to do. In closing his letter he observed that Wylie's widely publicized Fourth of July speech was fresh and original, but he must be told that the Van Burenites regarded it as a "leetle of whiggery."

It had been evident since the opening of the seminary itself that the university's well-being depended upon a reduction of ridiculous prejudices and spites arising from a sharply divided political community. At no time was this dark cloud shifted from overhead, nor did a ray of hope shine through it. At nearly every meeting of the Board of Trustees it was clear that state officials were serving a spoils system with university money by the nature of the loans which were made. The university's income was shrinking and legislators were highly indifferent. The Board of Trustees and faculty in the 1840's had to design and operate an academic program, not because of its intrinsic merit but because it was feasible within severely limiting circumstances of the times.

Reflecting this fact was the first university course of study after 1838. Wylie was assigned instructional responsibilities in the moral sciences, mental philosophy, rhetoric and rhetorical composition and reading, logic, evidences of Christianity, and the Constitution of the United States. There was to be a professor of mixed mathematics, and to this position the board appointed Jacob Ammen, a Virginian born in Botetourt County, and a graduate of the West Point Military Academy. He had been an assistant instructor of military tactics at West Point; at the time of his appointment to the faculty of Indiana University he was professor of mathematics in Bacon College at Harrodsburg, Kentucky. For some reason Ammen failed to arrive in Bloomington on time and had to wait a year to begin his duties. In fact the board debated whether or not to allow him to begin at all. The course in pure mathematics had no designated professor. Greek and Latin were taught by Professor John Irwin Morrison, a Pennsylvanian, a graduate of Miami University, and a member of the Indiana legislature who had written the legislation creating the office of State Superintendent of Public Instruction. Theophilus Wylie, a Pennsylvanian and cousin of Andrew Wylie, joined the faculty in 1837 as professor of natural philosophy and chemistry. This was the faculty, and it is clear that the board was motivated in its plans by efficacy, not ideals.

While the Board of Trustees struggled with almost insuperable problems, Andrew Wylie had problems of his own. He wrote friends complaining about the bigotry and petty political squabbles in Indiana, and about the dissension within the Board of Trustees. He was scarred by his conflicts with Ebenezer Newton Elliott and Beaumont Parks. His wife was still not fully reconciled to living in Bloomington despite her fine new house. If the financial condition of the university worsened it would have to close because of bankruptcy. He could see little prospect for improvement within the immediate future. On top of these troubles, students were restive. On one occasion they carried their grievances to the Board of Trustees, bitterly criticizing president and faculty.

It was at this unhappy juncture that Congressman Henry A. Wise of Virginia wrote his old teacher that only recently he had shown Wylie's published address on the classics to Daniel Webster and that famous orator "was highly delighted with your classic speech, and I think I would prefer his judgment over a performance of the kind to [that of] any man, 'on the continent.' " Wise was curious to know why Wylie remained in Indiana.

> Why, in the name of all that is refined, do you stay buried in the mud of Indiana? What a wider and fairer field is here in the east country. Moral economy is like physical, depend upon it. Put the grub hoe in the grubby ground, the keenedged instrument in the garden for the flowers & the seed. You are no woodcutter—are wanting nicer work—I always thought so when you went West.

West is great—a great country in limestone, land, hogs, horses, & Hoosiers—but believe me East is the field of feeling and thought. You are in advance of the civilization there—that is what is the matter, and *here* is the place—I mean in some of our Eastern cities where you would be most useful for here the people [would] be most adapted to your line of improvements. Can't you come to Boston, N. Y., Phila., Baltimore or Richmond? They are rough Yankees in the non slaveholding West. So what Lindsey [Philip Lindsley] has thrown away even upon Nashville. I congratulate you upon your personal triumphs and your foes, but they will not leave you alone. Worth must abide the shots of malice. I was not surprised to hear that you or any other pious man had been disgusted with the bigot broils of the Presbyterian Church.

Henry A. Wise was an astute man. The Philistines were not to leave Wylie alone. Buffeted by heartless forces which he neither understood nor could always identify, Wylie found his job as President of Indiana University growing daily more burdensome. Undoubtedly he must have reflected many times on the wisdom of his decision to come to Indiana. Perhaps he recalled Henry Wise's advice one morning in July, 1840, when his wife received a note from Orville, Orful, or (alias) Jacob Nider. In this blunt communication Jacob gave no evidence of having been nearer a school than his chicken coop. He wrote, "Mis Wiley owes me fur these here things that she took from our cupe. Wun chicken and wun rooster 25, wun pese of butter 10, too lofes bred." She owed $.45 in all. "These witnesses," said Jacob, "said you tuk these here things when you was at the picknick now if you honest you will pay this you can send it to me Jacob Nider." The Justice of the Peace's record in the ensuing slander case did nothing to lift Wylie's spirits in trying to educate the masses. The Justice wrote, "Mr. Orful Debry (or Orville) (alias) Jacob Nider is hereby summon to appear before court tomorrow July 17 to answer a charge of *slander* against the plaintiff [with satisfactory evidence] to prove him guilty of slandering—the honest & humble defendant [stated,] I am very sorry someone stole your chickens of plaintiff. I was not the guilty perpetrator & didn't even know you had chickens & or furthermore that you kept your bread & butter in the cupe."

Outside the university Wylie faced other shattering conflicts.

Before coming to Bloomington he had become embroiled in a dispute with the Presbyterian elders over the narrow, strictly Calvinistic course they pursued. His dissatisfaction continued and during a trip to Philadelphia in 1839 he became involved in renewed doctrinal infighting. Finally in 1841 he withdrew from the denomination and had himself ordained a deacon in the Episcopal church. Next year at Vincennes he accepted the vows of a rector. From that date until his death he was an active minister, but he hardly curried local favor by going over to a faith that he had once criticized severely.

Andrew Wylie found himself in a permanent quandary after 1840. He no doubt was tempted to heed Henry A. Wise's invitation to return to the East, and certainly Mrs. Wylie would have welcomed an opportunity to leave Bloomington. The Board of Curators of the newly founded University of Missouri asked him to come to Columbia, Missouri, for an interview in the early spring for possible appointment to the presidency of that institution. He had been recommended by Governor James S. Rollins, a former student and a friend. In a letter to his son Craig, President Wylie revealed a genuine interest in the Missouri post, but he had grave doubts that it would be a pleasant place. He inquired of Governor Rollins if there were trouble and strife in Missouri. He unburdened himself as to his problems in Indiana and told Rollins if there were similar frictions to those plaguing him in Bloomington he would not want the post. He was convinced he did not want another appointment in a university under state jurisdiction.

It is now clear that Wylie had ample reason to be cautious. The Missouri board was divided in its sentiment. Some of its members were opposed to hiring an eastern man, and could not be persuaded that Washington, Pennsylvania, was not "East." Thomas M. Allen, a Boone County farmer and Disciples of Christ minister, wrote Wylie that some of the board

> did not much like an *Eastern* man, he might be an abolitionist. The next thing we heard was that Doctor Wylie was very unpopular, the Institution was dwindling in Indiana. . . . I have written Governor David Wallace and the Hon. Wm. Hendricks for information; but in order to prevent your injury "with them," or the people of Indiana, I let them know you were not an appli-

cant, nor never had been for a seat in our Institution, but your name had been presented, in connection with other gentlemen, by your friends here.

Harassment and troubles dogged Wylie's footsteps. He had to sit by during the summer of 1838 and witness a tedious and bitter argument between William C. Foster, a retiring member of the Board of Trustees, and Cornelius Pering, principal of the Female Seminary. Foster was a contentious man, and he and Wylie had clashed frequently. Foster, in his correspondence published in the Bloomington *Post*, charged the president with having overstepped the bounds of his authority. He said Wylie had gone to Philadelphia and purchased $1,500 worth of books when the board had authorized only the purchase of maps of the United States and Indiana for $6.00. Moreover, said Foster, he had laid plans to corrupt Indiana youth. Among his purchases were worthless and obscene books which should be denied places on the shelves of all college libraries. Offending further, Wylie had bought an expensive edition of Milton's works when a much cheaper one would have been just as satisfactory. To pay for his indiscretion the board should withhold $200 of his salary.

To establish his authority, Foster said he was a scholar of English literature, having read several hundred books in the field. In reply C. Pering said that Foster was a silly, vainglorious ass, comparable to a Billingsgate fisherwoman. He was as capable of judging a list of classic books "as a barnyard cock was the interior of a Jewelry store." Instead of being pinched by the limitation of $1,500 President Wylie should have been allowed to spend $5,000. If Foster was worried about the $300 classical *Thesaurus* then he could take comfort in the fact that several colleges in Ohio would be glad to pay $500. Calvin E. Stowe of Lane Seminary in Cincinnati not only had paid $250 for a *Thesaurus* in Paris, he had bought in addition $5,000 worth of other books.

Foster levelled other accusations at Wylie, saying he had discriminated against Beaumont Parks, James F. Dodds, and Augustus W. Ruter by refusing them votes in the faculty meetings. He implied that Wylie could hear only Presbyterians. Taunting Wylie further, he wrote, "you have been complimented, and highly eulogized for presenting 4 or 500 dollars worth of books to the College, and for procuring a seal & plate for diplomas: and the impression is sought to be made that you *done* this of your own free will, and the books were donated by you. Not so fast Doctor, you were authorized by the Board to do this."

Wylie, said Foster, sat smugly behind the curtain supplying Pering with information while drawing a $1,400 a year salary. "You . . . perhaps fancied that your dignity would be compromised by coming in collision with me. But Sir you must recollect as a trustee of the College of Indiana, I am officially to say the least your equal: and I trust my private character, will at any time bear an advantageous comparison with yours." Looking back on this ridiculous dispute we may see something strangely reminiscent of Bottom in Foster's tirades which he, the great scholar of English literature, should readily have recognized.

Whether or not Wylie was popular in Indiana depended largely on who answered the questions. It is easier to describe issues that arose throughout the decade 1839 to 1851 than to analyze Wylie's relationship with faculty and townspeople. In the spring of 1839 Orson Barbour, a student, was accused by other students, including Wylie's son Craig, of having insulted one of the literary societies in an oration. Young Wylie and another boy undertook to beat Barbour, and in the following commotion the people of Bloomington took sides. Craig Wylie was arrested after the fight, which provoked further emotions. As a result several students left the university, thus reducing the school's enrollment to thirty-eight. This was what the Missourians referred to when they said Indiana University was dwindling.

About the time of the Barbour affair Dr. William Foster brought further charges of assuming too much authority against President Wylie. These included having appointed James Darwin Maxwell, a professor in the preparatory department, without board confirmation, failing to read the university's bylaws to the students in chapel, duplicity and ungentlemanly conduct, and misrepresentation and falsehood. Foster had failed in earlier efforts to remove Wylie, and he now hoped with the backing of the bigoted Joshua Howe and Chester G. Ballard of the Board of Trustees to succeed. A second bitter public controversy followed with lengthy coverage in the Bloomington *Post*. The Board of Trustees sought information through a kangaroo court in which a score of witnesses were grilled by Dr. David H. Maxwell for the defense and W.C. Foster for the plaintiff. On April 2, 1839, after an exhaustive hearing, the board issued a strong resolution vindicating President Wylie. Chester Ballard resigned in a huff on April 4, 1839, and was succeeded by the ever faithful Dr. David H. Maxwell. The board made a second resolution, of greater importance. It removed James F. Dodds, Beaumont Parks, and Augustus Ruter from the faculty, thus practically depleting the teaching ranks. This action was not taken, however, before several students had submitted a petition declaring their dissatisfaction with Dr. Wylie.

There was not enough money to do anything more than pay the meagerest sort of salary. Wylie was paid $1,300, the professors received $1,000 each, and the tutor $600. Even this low budget produced a deficit of $440 still owed in faculty salaries. By extremely close management there were funds to pay the janitor $100 per annum provided he rang the bell with clock-like regularity, made fires, swept the rooms, kept the grounds in order, made building and equipment repairs, and did everything else required of him. In order to lighten the janitorial load the campus was to be placed in charge of a professor of engineering at $50 per year if such a person could be found. It was thought that a local farmer could be induced to cut the grass on the grounds for the privilege of salvaging the hay.

In the opening of the decade of 1840, two new divisions of the university were proposed. The first was a department of civil engineering. Agitation for this department began in the summer of 1836. Dr. David H. Maxwell made an eloquent plea in the public press for the teaching of engineering. In an article that appeared in the Richmond *Palladium*, June 4, 1836, he contended as a member of the Internal Improvements Board, that the time had come for universities to concern themselves with the practical things in their states. Internal improvements were being undertaken all across the nation, and Indiana had grave need for specialists trained as engineers. He said a class would be organized in June in Indiana University, and students could enroll in engineering or related subjects upon the payment of a $20 per term tuition fee plus $10 more to finance field work. Dr. Maxwell based his announcement on the assumption that Professor Ebenezer N. Elliott would teach the various mathematical and engineering courses. This course failed to mature because Professor Elliott resigned from the faculty and it was impossible to find another professor who could teach such a wide spectrum of technical subjects. Nevertheless, some desire to establish an engineering school prevailed in the university until after the founding of the land grant college of Purdue.

The second new division was the military science department. A room was equipped for the purpose of storing arms in the main building. Professor Ammen, a graduate of the West Point Military Academy, was placed in charge of drill instruction. The board stated that military exercises would be purely optional, but once a student enrolled for drill he would be required to attend all exercises. This interest in military instruction was stimulated partly by a lingering horde of difficulties with Indians along the upper Mississippi, and partly by the increasing tension between the United States and Mexico over the Texas annexation dispute. There is no doubt that Professor Ammen himself had promoted the idea of drill. One thing is certain, the performance of the Hoosiers with General Zachary Taylor's army in the subsequent Mexican War failed to reflect even a vestige of formal military training or proper credit upon the state.

Indiana University struggled from year to year with meager financial support, a severely curtailed faculty, and almost no scientific equipment. For instance, in October, 1840, the board consented to President Wylie buying a mercurial pneumatical trough on his trip to Philadelphia, provided he could find a cheap one, and if he could persuade a Pennsylvania merchant to grant him credit. Again in 1848 he was permitted to purchase $200 worth of scientific apparatus. Otherwise the university operated with such materials and equipment as the faculty, students, and janitor could devise.

While trustees and faculty concerned themselves with the multitudinous problems of converting a backwoods college into a university and fought off avowed enemies and meddlers, the central question of diversifying the institution's program persisted. Ostensibly, the title was changed to include a department of law. When Miles C. Eggleston rejected the invitation to be professor of law in 1839, the special committee of the board was largely frustrated in its search for another competent candidate. At the July meeting, 1841, it put forward the name of Tilghman A. Howard, but he was slow making a decision and after unseemly delay refused the offer.

Nevertheless the trustees went ahead and selected four texts for law courses. These were the inevitable Blackstone, Chitty, and both Stevens and Gould on pleading.

A year later, at the June meeting of the board, the committee was still without a candidate, and the board turned to Judge David McDonald of the Tenth Circuit Court of Indiana to accept a part-time professorship. Judge McDonald had an interesting background. He was born in Kentucky at McBride's Run within the shadow of the mecca of the Disciples of Christ at Cane Ridge. His youth was conditioned by the precepts of this faith. His elementary schooling was limited in Kentucky, and even more so in Indiana. He wished to become a Disciples minister, but was diverted by a growing interest in the law. On January 1, 1829, he entered the office of E.H. McJunkin in Washington, Indiana, and on February 1, 1830, was admitted to the bar of Knox County. Between that date and 1841 he served as a county attorney, a member of the legislature, and as circuit judge. When he accepted the professorship of law in Indiana University it was as a practical procedural lawyer rather than legal theoretician and scholar.

In a burst of generosity the Board of Trustees suggested a salary of a thousand dollars a year, but this sum was reduced to one hundred dollars a month per term. The board suggested divided terms of three months each, but Judge McDonald reduced this to a single one of four months to mesh with his duties as circuit judge. Even at this it was necessary to reduce the Tenth Circuit by legislative act, by dropping Morgan County. Judge McDonald as professor of law was given use of specially fitted rooms in the academic building and was permitted to conduct his classes apart from the rest of the university program. He even could award diplomas written in English to graduates upon the payment of a five dollar severance fee.

This was a brave beginning toward establishing a true university. Within four years, however, the financial condition of the institution became so precarious that the school could no longer pay a law professor's salary or maintain its department of science. In September, 1846, Judge McDonald was informed of this fact; however, he was told he could continue to hold classes and collect the $20 term fee for his own use. Also he could have use of the classrooms, a supply of firewood, and enjoy all other privileges already granted his department. He accepted this revision of plans, and employed Judge William T. Otto of the Second Circuit Court to assist him. In 1852 Judge McDonald moved away to practice law in Indianapolis and left the university with a weakened law department with Judge Otto as the entire staff. Years later, in a journal prepared for his children, McDonald said, "My connection with the Indiana University was highly advantageous to me, as it brought me into intimacy with that great and good man President Wylie. During that time I picked up a good deal of learning, and amongst the rest I studied Latin."

The period of the middle forties, when the nation experienced considerable turmoil over expansionist issues, was in many respects the most promising the university had enjoyed to date. In the year 1846–47, for instance, the income of the institution had risen to $6,300 and the faculty budget was $4,700. In this year the board felt free to spend $23.00 in renovating the old building and adding the thousand dollar surplus to the endowment fund. This was the first time that the school had operated with an excess of funds. The student body in 1844–45 exceeded a hundred members, although during most of the next twenty years it dropped below this figure. The ratio of students to faculty remained somewhere near sixteen to one, but preparatory school students still accounted for approximately half of the total university enrollment.

The faculty had expanded to six members by 1847. Andrew Wylie carried the heaviest curriculum burden, teaching moral and mental philosophy and belle lettres. Daniel Read taught natural philosophy which included chemistry, biology, and physics. Alfred Ryors, later to be president, taught mathematics and engineering, Judge David McDonald offered classes in law four months of the year, and Matthew M. Campbell was principal of the preparatory school. Narrow as it was, this curriculum marked an advance in the school's constant struggle to broaden its academic offerings.

Hoosiers, like everybody else in the Ohio Valley and the Northwest, felt the impact of the roaring forties. This was reflected in Andrew Wylie's commencement address in September, 1847. Lecturing the departing seniors, and the public audience even more, he stressed the power of religion and the eternal watchfulness of a personal God. He took occasion to condemn the British for their sanctimonious attitude toward American slavery when they had planted the institution on these shores. He viewed the split among the Protestant institutions in America over slavery as threatening the central virtues of faith, charity, and all other good works. Men, no matter what the issues or form of government, ruled themselves under the watch-care and the sufferance of God. He said, "government is to be regarded with a reverence, I will say with religious reverence as being 'ordained of God,' to interpret and execute, to a certain extent the eternal law of righteousness. The subject has the right to interpret it." He admonished them to respect and serve the worldly powers but never to transgress the supreme law. He came close to stating the prevailing Calhoun philosophy of the "higher law" which some Southerners put forth so ardently: the citizen who loved his country would strive to see that it was always in the right, and he must realize that when the country opposed right it was on the brink of ruin.

At the moment President Wylie spoke, Americans were being called upon to give searching attention to such issues as the international boundary disputes, the annexation of Texas and slavery expansion, the war with Mexico, and the eternally nagging Indian policy. Wylie hoped the United States had God on its side. He believed the country was fundamentally right in its conflict with Mexico, but at the same time the individual citizen had both the right and obligation to raise questions, make moral judgments, and do his own thinking on these issues. These were unusually liberal sentiments to be spoken by a Whig in such parlous times, when Americans were emotionally explosive toward the world about them.

Wylie's squabbles with students continued. A pair of students complained to the public through the columns of the Bedford *Sun* about Wylie. The two, William E. Williams and H. H. Trimble, were involved in an incident which had occurred in a meeting of the Philomathean Society. They had invited a guest to attend the meeting of the society in violation of the organization's rules. The record is unclear as to what, if anything, happened. The results were that Williams was denied an honorable discharge from the university, and that Wylie insulted Trimble by apologizing to a group of students for having invited him to a social function. Williams charged Wylie with refusing to call him a gentleman, being passionate and intemperate in his remarks to him, and implying that he and

Trimble were dogs and murderers. The charge Wylie resented most, however, was that he had been less than a paternal friend and impartial judge to Williams and Trimble.

The Board of Trustees conducted an extensive hearing into the Williams-Trimble affair. David McDonald sat as judge, and the investigation was conducted under court rules. All charges except one, that the president had apologized for inviting Trimble to a social function, were dismissed. Once more the university and Wylie were demeaned over student discipline.

Students reflected the public nature of the times. While the nation was being highly sensitized in the political and public areas, students were expressing sharp attitudes toward the university and its parental watchfulness. On February 26, 1848, J. McG. C. Holden wrote the editor of the Bloomington *Tribune* a letter explaining why he refused to accept a diploma in law from the university. Holden was enrolled in Judge McDonald's classes, and technically was not a student in the university. He claimed he had finished his work and had been proffered a diploma but had refused to accept it because, "I could not consistent with my opinion of the *man*—receive a diploma with the name of the president of the institution upon its face." He refused to state reasons for his attitude, though he said they were many. Some day, in his opinion, Hoosiers would learn how much they had been humbugged by Wylie. Holden told his readers that although he left the university without a diploma in his pocket, he brought away a clear conscience.

In refuting Holden's wild claims, Judge McDonald informed the public that no diploma had or would be offered the lad. He was a very poor student, and was an unfit candidate for the bar. It was they, the lawyers, who had refused to graduate the youth, they said. Holden had claimed to the law professors, so he said, that he did "*not want the old Dock's name to his diploma.*" The law professors replied that these remarks were "impertinent, malignant and stupid in *him.*" He had been dropped from law classes because of failure to study and for "*loose* morality." The argument went on for a couple of months in a half dozen lengthy and vitriolic articles. There was little substance to Holden's charges, but his attack, to which Wylie never responded, damaged the president's public image in his closing years in the university.

The final year of Wylie's administration saw registered in the university 163 students, 58 of whom were in the preparatory school, and 28 in Judge McDonald's law classes. This meant there were 77 students enrolled in university classes. The faculty in 1850 consisted of T.A. Wylie, David McDonald, Daniel Read, William T. Otto, and Charles Marshall. The latter was an addition to the faculty as successor to Alfred Ryors as professor of mathematics. He was a recent graduate of the University of Virginia and had been highly recommended to Andrew Wylie by William Holmes McGuffey to be professor of pure mathematics and engineering. Apparently faculty members were hired at this time with a slender amount of personal information about them. Marshall was a lad of nineteen years, and when he arrived in Bloomington his youthful, almost childlike, appearance created a sensation. The president tactlessly expressed his consternation, and this angered the proud young man. Further, the board was most reluctant to confirm his appointment, despite the fact he was a mathematical genius.

The Bloomington *Indiana Tribune and Monroe County Farmer* commented on December 1, 1849,

> Mr. Marshall is, as we learn, a grandson of Chief Justice John Marshall, and is quite a young man. However we understand that Mr. M. says that he will not always remain young, and that any objection to him that may exist on account of his age will be growing less every day! He is a very pleasant and dignified looking young man, and we doubt not will prove himself equal to the important duties of his chair.

A feeling of insecurity in Bloomington caused Charles Marshall to resign at the end of the year. He went to Baltimore, where he read law, and in time became a leading attorney. Although Marshall's youthfulness may have startled the elders in Bloomington his teaching performance was good; he won the affection and confidence of his students. One student was Walter Q. Gresham, who served Benjamin Harrison as Postmaster General, and then left the Republican party to become Grover Cleveland's Secretary of State in the first Cleveland administration.

On Tuesday, November 11, 1851, an era ended abruptly. Andrew Wylie, indulging in one of his two hobbies of horseback riding and chopping, cut his foot about November 1, while cutting wood about a mile from his residence. The wound bled profusely and he was seriously weakened before he could be taken home. A couple of days later he apparently thought he had gained enough strength to resume meeting his classes and to deliver a long and enervating address to the Monroe County Agricultural Society. In this speech Wylie came closer than ever before to understanding the life and ordeal of the common man in Indiana. Having grown up on a farm he had some firsthand appreciation of the farm way of life, yet as a scholar he had long ago detached himself from the soil. This address was delivered with Wylie seated before his audience. Like all of his speeches, this one was long and involved, parental in tone, and idealistic in concept. This address exhausted him, and on Sunday, November 9, he contracted pneumonia. By 3:00 P.M. of the eleventh he was dead.

For over two decades Andrew Wylie had been the predominant personal force in the formation of Indiana College and University. Following with Calvinistic fidelity his precept of personifying the university, he had served the institution as spokesman, scholar, and father-master. Wylie was Indiana University's first publishing scholar. Stooped over his desk evenings at home at Second and Lincoln streets, he prepared long and involved commencement and public addresses, which were later published. He demonstrated both thoughtfulness and erudition.

In August before his death in November, he told the graduating class,

> The laws of man's nature forbid that he should prolong his existence, and, indeed, that he should exist at all, in the state of a separate, independent, individual. Unless he enters into the bonds of domestic society he must, by the common law of mortality, depart from his place, leaving no one to fill the vacancy. And this shows that the family is not a piece of human policy, but an ordinance of nature, and of Him who is the Author of nature. Though man may modify, he cannot destroy it, without, at the same time, destroying himself. If he pulls down the pillars of this temple, he is crushed and buried under its ruins.

Andrew Wylie's death left a vacuum for Indiana University; no one could fill his place. He left the historian a difficult task of appraising his worth and meaning to higher education in the Middle

West. It is difficult to say that the university expanded or thrived under his management. There were forty students enrolled when he arrived in Bloomington, and there were 74 in the university proper when he died, more than two decades later. The budget in 1829 was approximately $5,000, and in April, 1852, the board reported an endowment of $72,400, and an income of $6,770. Expenditures were $5,420, almost precisely the same as they had been in 1829. The president's salary was $1,200, and professors received $1,000 each.

So far as a quantitative statement can be meaningful in appraising the intellectual contribution of the university to its constituency, there were enrolled in the Wylie years 1,532 students. This compared with 2,145 at Harvard over the same period. Comparative enrollment, as given by the Census Bureau, for several universities for 1850 were: Dartmouth 221, Harvard 358, Yale 453, Columbia 135, Princeton 251, Georgia 144, Miami of Ohio 66, Michigan 64, Virginia 222, and *Indiana* 97. The states listed had total college enrollments as follows: Massachusetts 719, Connecticut 647, New York 752, New Jersey 332, Virginia 756, Georgia 395, New Hampshire 221, and *Indiana* 337. Indiana University graduated an average of six students a year between 1830 and 1851, or 140 in all.

There were four professors in the beginning of Wylie's administration and five at the end. In the intervening years there were remarkably few innovations in either educational philosophy or curriculum planning. Wylie and the Board of Trustees had held religiously to the old and poorly adapted English Academy concept of a classical university. The most original phases of teaching were Wylie's own penetrative instruction in modern political theory and constitutional development and the organization of a law department; otherwise the curriculum centered about the classics. Educationally it may not have been entirely unfortunate that the president bore a lion's share of the teaching responsibility, but administratively it was all but self-defeating. He left too little time for planning, public relations, or viewing the broader educational scene in maturing America.

Andrew Wylie by nature was incapable of meeting and understanding Indiana's common people. When they did meet, both he and they were uncomfortable. There is no doubt that he was af-

flicted with a strong intellectual snobbery that kept him from un-
bending. Later Wylie's son Andrew alluded to this. When a visitor
came to Bloomington whom his father considered his intellectual
equal his whole manner changed. He would become talkative and
was most hospitable in every way. He would take his guest on long
walks or horseback rides, and sit until far into the night conversing.
On the other hand if a less intellectual visitor arrived, no matter
who he was, Wylie's manner became cold and reserved, "not so
from study or design, but as the manifestation of an inward feeling
too strong to be kept under, and of which he was perhaps himself
unconscious at the time. This perfect honesty of his character always made him disagreeable to knaves and double-dealers every-
where, and they never failed to hate and to persecute him." To his
own children President Wylie was an enigma. When Andrew was
asked to write a biography of his father he pleaded incompetence.
"My father," he said, "was a man of great reserve and abstraction
even in his own family. His whole time was filled with either reading, study, or writing, or manual exercise connected with something
which he regarded as useful." It is interesting that among his
father's most cherished friends there was not one who lived in Indiana.

Andrew Wylie's educational views and Indiana University's
limited program were synonymous. The school was thoroughly
parental in its approaches, regarding the correct moral behavior of
its students as more important than maintaining an aggressive
educational program. Faculty minutes reveal a staff constantly engaged in petty matters of student discipline. The professors were
jealous of their dignity and prerogatives, and stood militantly at
the bridge to see that neither was slighted. Almost no hint appears
that professors were primarily concerned with intellectual responsibilities or even recognized them. President and faculty accepted—
apparently without revision—the Board of Trustees' dictates on
curriculum. The course of study hardly changed over three decades;
the trustees surprisingly revealed remarkably little consciousness
of the need for an adaptable education.

Wylie and his administration refused to acknowledge that
America itself had undergone fundamental changes in almost
every aspect of its life. They never really understood the emerging
challenge of a public university. Wylie kept most of his aspirations

thoroughly to himself and left the university to flounder in a troubled sea in the decade of the 1850's. His administration did not approach carrying out the objectives of the constitutional charter of higher education. By 1851 they had hardly made a dent on the glittering exhortation: "for a General Assembly shall, from time to time, pass such laws as shall be calculated to encourage intellectual, scientifical, and agricultural improvement of arts, sciences, commerce, manufactures, and natural history; and to countenance and encourage the principles of humanity, industry, and morality." Indiana University was to await the passage of at least three more decades before these objectives became central to the institution's purposes.

Andrew Wylie wrote his own best self-summation in his remark to the Reverend Dr. Elihu W. Baldwin, President of Wabash College. "If there were a stump in the road," he said, "you would walk quietly around it, but I would blunder against it, battering and bruising my shins."

[V]

A Season of Frustration

THE AMERICAN POLITICAL CAULDRON boiled hot in the 1850's. The nation had come through the Mexican War with success, and the Treaty of Guadeloupe-Hidalgo had vastly expanded the continental boundaries of the United States. The Whigs had elected their last president, Zachary Taylor, and then found themselves with Millard Fillmore as chief executive. The political Goliaths who had dominated the national scene for the past three decades were now at the end of their careers. Political realignments were taking place as new faces appeared on the scene, but more important were the biting national issues which led to the threatening political explosion of 1850. The great Compromise of that year pulled the American people back temporarily from the brink of disaster, but by no means healed political wounds or formed a basis for lasting peace. Gold rushers had populated California within the past two years, and in an even more important way opened roads across the continent to what became two far western states, California and Nevada. At the time of Andrew Wylie's death, Mrs. Harriet Beecher Stowe was publishing segments of *Uncle Tom's Cabin* in the *National Era*, and soon her book would appear and raise an emotional storm.

Amid the clatter of national change, railroad builders covered drafting boards with plans while orators and promoters organized new companies and pushed major rail expansion. The South and the Great Lakes states campaigned vigorously for the eastern termini of transcontinental lines. In Indiana the transportation barrier was rapidly being penetrated by the building of highways and railroads. A new age had dawned in the state with almost the suddenness of a spring cyclone. The state's population had increased to 988,416 in 1850, and its traditional insularity was yearly being shattered by new economic and social contacts with a much larger world. Farmlands reached full production, new industries began operation, and a fresh inflow of Europeans and Easterners emigrated westward. Northern Indiana now became more influential in making state policy decisions.

On the educational scene, Indiana University found seven denominational competitors in Wabash, St. Mary's, DePauw, Hanover, Notre Dame, Franklin, and Concordia Colleges. Beyond this the common school system made headway toward maturity and acceptance. The challenges of the university were now much greater. The university, however, faltered during this wave of progress because of a lack of funds and aggressive leadership. The Constitution of 1851 ignored the university in the public school clause, and the legislature offered no material support. On June 17, 1852, the legislature enacted a lengthy statute setting forth in great detail the functions and modus operandi of the institution. This act clearly demonstrated a desire to exercise strict legislative control without appropriating funds to support the school. Even more fundamental was the university officials' need to vigorously cultivate the Indiana public good will. The institution was not well known, it had scores of enemies, and old fights within the faculty and board sapped much of the school's vitality. Though Andrew Wylie had left behind a legacy of personal scholarship and devotion to the cause of education, he had also left a grim liability of considerable public hostility. All of this had to be mollified, and at the same time the university had to be thrust forward.

In Indianapolis the legislators sensed not only changes of the new age as reflected in the revised constitution; they were also aware of educational forces at work throughout the state. In a series of legislative acts and political maneuvers between 1851 and

1855, the executive leadership of the university changed hands. It is difficult to fathom local reasons for changes from the available records. It is clear, however, that at least three special interests were busily engaged in seeking advantages. There was a virulent religious rivalry among the Protestants; each denomination sought to assert its influence in Bloomington. Though functioning well outside the pale of bare-knuckled partisan politics, spites and rivalries were funneled into the institution through board members, who operated in a larger field than education. The shifting sands of political loyalties and alignments contributed further to dissatisfactions.

The Indiana Constitution of 1851 all but ignored the University. It repeated an abbreviated form of the original education clause: "Knowledge and learning, generally diffused throughout a community, being essential to the preservation of a free government; it shall be the duty of the General Assembly to encourage, by all suitable means, moral, intellectual, scientific, and agricultural improvements and to provide, by law, for a general and uniform system of common schools, wherein tuition shall be without charge, and equally open to all."

Beginning with legislation dated June 17, 1852, and concluding with an act dated March 3, 1855, the Indiana legislature made considerable statutory headway in restructuring Indiana University. At present it is all but impossible to discover from surviving records what precisely provoked legislators into this extended period of concern with the university. It is clear, however, that public irritations caused by Andrew Wylie, continuous petty bickerings in Bloomington, and the incapability of the university to achieve the expansive objectives prescribed for it in the charter had important bearings on the course of events. There is every reason to believe that partisan politics played an important part in this interim period while the university sought new administrative leadership. The Whig party had reached, if not passed, the nadir of its power; this fact is reflected in subsequent proposals to broaden the practical aspects of the university's program in terms of the main interests of the people of the period.

Before the reorganization act of March 8, 1852, had been signed by the governor, a joint meeting of Senate and House was called on March 6 to assemble "instanter" for the purpose of electing a new Board of Trustees for Indiana University. Eleven men were elected to the board, but by April 10, 1852, this number had been reduced to eight. John I. Morrison of Washington County was the only member left from the preceding board. The new trustees assembled in Bloomington on April 10, 1852, and began an extensive reconsideration of the university. The school had a "reliable income" of $6,770, and expenditures amounted to $5,420. The president was to be paid $1,200, three professors $1,000 each, the janitor $80, and $600 was appropriated to the preparatory school.

In the spring of 1852 the faculty submitted to the Board of Trustees a report that inner stirrings among Indiana youth indicated that the university should have broader objectives. They expressed willingness to work with zeal and enterprise to make needed changes. This report caused the board to consider an enlarged spectrum of university offerings. Motivated by the faculty, the fervor of its new membership, and the fermentation of the age, the board set out to bring Indiana University more nearly into harmony with the fresh challenges. Many past suggestions had been made concerning the offering of courses in agriculture. The week before Andrew Wylie died he had addressed the farmers of Monroe County on the importance of farming and agriculture. A vast majority of the people of Indiana in this age were farmers or had farm-centered economic interests. The time had come, thought the board, when it should take notice of the needs of rural people for the kind of education best suited to Hoosiers' everyday life. It recommended that there be included in proper season a course in agricultural chemistry, and that the university assume the lead in keeping up with advanced agricultural literature and improvements.

On November 6, 1851, the Indianapolis *Indiana State Sentinel* rejoiced that Governor Joseph A. Wright had contributed $1,000, perhaps from private funds, toward the establishment of an agricultural professorship in Greencastle College, provided $9,000 more could be raised. The editor said he hoped "the scheme as originally proposed by Gov. Wright and others, may yet be carried out, and that similar professorships will be established in all the colleges of the State. Such a department would be peculiarly appropriate in the State University." The *Vincennes Gazette* agreed.

If there is any one branch of learning which deserves more attention than another it is the science of Agriculture, and yet we find
it almost in the rear of all others—There are many young men
who resolve upon some one of the so-called "learned professions."
. . . A man cannot be expected to succeed well in any avocation
unless he understands it, in truth, he should know all about it,
and how can farmers expect to make fortunes, unless they know
what substances enter into the composition of the plants they
would produce, which of these substances are wanting in their
lands, and what manures will supply them. We hope to see something else other than talk upon this subject.

It was a tragedy that the university, for lack of financial support,
was unable to pioneer in the field of agriculture.

Public pressure and the new board were pursuing a trend which
was established later by passage of the federal Morrill Land Grant
Act. Taking note of the changes that were occurring in other applied
fields in the state, the trustees recommended that a course in practical and theoretical engineering be organized. The proponents
of this expansion said, "The numerous public works now in process
of construction renders civil engineering, a most important branch,
together with practical illustrations in the field, would meet one of
the present demands of public education in Indiana, and add a new
class of students to the University."

The time had come to break the hold of the classical reading
curriculum leading to the bachelor of arts degree. Practical considerations outweighed the traditionalist conventions; the board
voted to add the bachelor of science degree to the university's
offerings. Courses, it said, should be instituted to prepare students
in chemistry, mathematics, and natural philosophy. Expressed in
this action was a consciousness of the past and the difficulties associated with preventing a snobbish barrier growing up between
the classics and the sciences. The two degrees should have equal
weight, and science courses should have the same place in the university's offerings as the traditional ones.

Indiana University was again designated as the head of the
state's educational system. The legislative act of June 17, 1852,
reiterated the statement of the act of 1828, that the school "is hereby recognized as the University of the State." To insure that it hold
this place provisions were made that the trustees admit two students

from each county free of tuition or other official fees. This was in fact a legislative restatement of the provisions of the court decision rendered in 1845 in the case of *McDonald v. Hagins*, in which university officials were instructed to admit two students free of charge, including to the law courses of Judge David McDonald. The act of June 17, 1852, was fundamentally a rechartering of the university. It went into extensive detail in prescribing modes of university operation, including instructions to the board to advertise the institution's commencement program in the Louisville *Journal*, the New Orleans *Picayune*, the Indiana *Journal*, and the *Indiana State Sentinel*.

In an effort to destroy the public sense of university aloofness during the Wylie years, legislators provided that a member of the faculty should be chosen annually as a public lecturer to visit at least fifteen counties of the state to explain the university, its principles, organizations, and educational facilities. This lecturer was admonished not to disparage the claims of learning in other institutions of the state, and no two of the lectures should be delivered in the same county.

Further provisions were made to publicize Indiana University. The Board of Trustees was instructed to organize a normal department in which both men and women were to be admitted to the university free of cost, provided they sought to qualify themselves as teachers in the Indiana public schools. The board had anticipated this provision by authorizing the organization of a normal school at its meeting on April 15, 1852. The trustees said, "There is no measure in regard to the State University more urgently required, by public opinion than this, through this department the common school system of the state will be brought into connexion and sympathy with the University."

Perhaps legislators went further than they realized in the normal school clause. In order to bring women students into the normal school of the university it would be necessary to construct a separate building for living quarters and classrooms. Neither parents nor legislators were yet ready to face the fact that eventually the sexes must confront each other in the daily routine of life. The public believed the college years were the socially explosive ones of youth. The Board of Trustees actually got underway an investigation to see about accommodations for women students, but they led with their weakest card by appealing to citizens of Bloomington to help finance such a program.

A department of engineering was established, and the board hired Robert Milligan as professor of mathematics, natural philosophy, and civil engineering. Milligan was an Irishman from County Tyrone who had graduated from Washington College in Pennsylvania and came to Bloomington by way of Flat Rock, Kentucky. He remained a member of the faculty at Indiana University for two years and then resigned to teach at the Disciples of Christ Bethany College of Virginia; he later accepted the presidency of Bacon College in Harrodsburg, Kentucky. Milligan was another member of the Christian Church who came directly to Indiana from the benign Disciples' environment of Cane Ridge in Bourbon County, Kentucky.

The bells tolling Wylie's funeral had hardly ceased ringing before the Board of Trustees began the search for a new president. Again that body thought it wise to seek an outsider who would bring to Bloomington new educational views, no handicapping political entanglements, and hopefully, no religious bigotry. The throbbing pains of old infighting and personal animosities were still present. Eulogies of Wylie's service were interspersed with reminiscences of his problems, and the board hoped to take a new departure, but nevertheless they sought a sound, safe, congenial, commonplace scholar of deep religious convictions.

John Hiram Lathrop of the newly organized University of Wisconsin promised to be in harmony with the mores of the Middle West and its deep-dyed rural nature. Lathrop was an upstate New Yorker, trained at Hamilton College and Yale University. In addition to his liberal arts courses at Yale he had taken law and continued work in this field after his graduation. However, he returned to the classroom as a professor of mathematics, and natural philosophy. He taught in several schools including Hamilton College. In 1840 the Board of Curators of the University of Missouri, after having considered Andrew Wylie, called Lathrop to the presidency of that embryo institution. In Columbia he enjoyed unusual success in organizing the university and in keeping divergent groups quiet long enough to open classes. By 1849 opposing cliques had destroyed Lathrop's effectiveness and he moved on to be chancellor of the newly chartered University of Wisconsin. No doubt this appointment was influenced by Eleazor Root of Waukesha, who had graduated from Williams. Lathrop was glad to escape the "broils" of Columbia and accept a $2,000 salary in Madison. His inaugural address indicated how thoroughly imbued were frontier Americans with the idea of progress.

Lathrop reiterated the philosophy that had led to the founding of Indiana University. "If we feel," he said, "we could discharge our obligations to the species, and become, in our turn, its benefactors, we shall tell to our sons more than our fathers told to us." He saw in the university and education a heavy obligation. "The UNIVERSITY of modern times, acting in unison with the other public schools of the civil state, is the appointed instrumentality by which this instruction is to be rendered. The university is the depository and the almoner of the intellectual treasures of the age." This was the man the Indiana University Board of Trustees sought to carry on the building of their university. Lathrop, however, was unavailable.

The Board of Trustees next elected Henry Barnard, Superintendent of the Connecticut schools and principal of the state normal school. He later became editor of the *American Journal of Education*. Earlier Barnard had attracted national attention by his work as secretary of the Connecticut Board of Educational Commissioners and in the organization of the schools of Rhode Island. As the Indiana board had done in the past, it neglected to discuss the Indiana presidency with Barnard before his election, and consequently no one knew whether this ambitious Yankee could be enticed into coming to Bloomington. Nevertheless the Board indicated its deep interest in the training of teachers by electing Barnard. That year his name was carried in the catalogue as president-elect. One can only wonder what chapter in American educational history might have been written had this pioneer accepted the Indiana presidency. Provisions were made that, if Barnard refused the board's offer, a special committee be instructed to employ the Reverend Alfred Ryors. He was subsequently elected by a vote of 6 to 2, and was notified of his employment.

Like Wylie, Ryors was a Pennsylvanian of Scotch Presbyterian faith, and an 1834 graduate of Jefferson College. Immediately after college he accepted a position as principal of the academic division of Lafayette College at Easton, Pennsylvania, but within a year he moved to Ohio University in Athens as professor of mathematics. In the spring of 1843 he accepted a similar appointment in Indiana University, where he remained five years before returning to Ohio University as president and successor to William Holmes McGuffey. During his stay in Bloomington he was ordained a minister by the Salem Presbytery.

Ryors' return to Bloomington in 1852 was fraught with sore disappointment. He was a marked man from the beginning. The university was disorganized, personal animosities developed quickly, and funds were lacking to support a good program. After he had been in Bloomington six months he resigned, but he consented to remain a short time longer before moving on as minister to a church in Madison, Indiana, and later as professor of mathematics in Centre College in Danville, Kentucky.

Ryors had no real personal impact on Indiana University. Financial conditions of the institution were so critical during his brief administration that he had no opportunity to accomplish anything of lasting value. Internally the entire university academic organization needed drastic revision. New faculty members had to be employed, but there was no money with which to pay them; new courses had to be instituted, but there were too few professors. Despite its hard plight this was in many respects one of Indiana University's heroic moments. A small corps of faculty members kept classes going, but they accomplished little more than maintaining the course of the university's continuity.

At its meeting on April 28, 1854, the Board of Trustees saddled the university with a cross that was to bear heavily upon the institution far into the future. There are still irritations caused by this act. So desperate were the trustees to raise money that they devised the ingenious scheme of giving a free and "perpetual" scholarship with every one hundred dollars subscribed. These scholarship certificates could be used in both the university and the preparatory school. The board undertook to cloak this offer in a legal agreement specifying that only "One scholar at a time may be kept forever, free from tuition fees in any of the classes of the academical or Literary Departments of the University in such studies as are or may be necessary to graduation." Perpetual scholarships could not be assigned or transferred, they could not be used to serve two students at once; the donor during his lifetime could assign them

[8 6]

to a son or grandson, and upon death the privilege of use descended through male heirs or to other designated male persons. In case of a holder dying intestate the certificate descended to legal legatees. The purchaser could send to Indiana University any boy he chose, except one guilty of an immoral act or who was known to be disobedient. Subscribers who paid fifty dollars to the building fund would be entitled to a half scholarship good for four years.

Three years later William K. Edwards reported that he had signed eighty-eight certificates, raising an undetermined amount. This was a small sum indeed to compensate for the great amount of ill will and bickering generated in the future over use of the scholarship. It became necessary in 1890 for the board to revoke this agreement. This scheme in no way solved Indiana University's financial problem, in fact it scarcely made a dent on it.

Theophilus A. Wylie said in his history of Indiana University that everything went on prosperously until April 11, 1854. This was hardly the case. Wylie had not seen the closely guarded minutes of the Board of Trustees. Student enrollment was off, the faculty was undermanned, and enough serious financial woes had accumulated to threaten the closing of the university. At Ryors' resignation the board made William M. Daily president. Daily's qualifications were limited. He had attended elementary schools in Ohio, graduated from Indiana University, and had served as a Methodist minister on several charges. He was a noisy camp-meeting type of orator who could rustle the leaves on a brush arbor, or raise the shingles on a church. Energetic, opportunistic, and ambitious, he ever had his eyes on the main course.

It seems clear that Daily's selection as president of the university was influenced by Governor Joseph A. Wright, who thought an ardent Methodist, loyal Democrat, and university graduate could save the institution from financial ruin. Immediately before his selection Daily was a member of the board, but when news came that Ryors was on the verge of resigning he removed himself from that body, and then informed the board that Governor Wright wished to meet with it at a convenient time. The result was that on August 3, 1853, Daily was elected to the presidency. Problems met him at the university gate. Ryors remained only briefly as professor of mathematics, and Judge David McDonald went away to Indianapolis to practice law. It was now necessary to give serious attention to reestablishing a teaching faculty. Daily became professor of mental and moral philosophy and belles lettres. Elisha Ballantine, a New Yorker and Presbyterian minister, joined the faculty in 1854 as professor of mathematics, civil engineering, and modern languages. Daniel Read taught ancient languages, James Hughes was made professor of law, and James A. Woodburn served as academy principal and part-time language professor. Except for civil engineering and law, the curriculum was actually no stronger than it had been in 1828.

In 1853 only the most astute management could have produced progress in the university. The resignations of Alfred Ryors, Daniel Read, and Robert Milligan had virtually brought the older part of the instructional program to a halt in 1856.

Daily tried manfully as administrator, teacher, and public relations man to serve Indiana University in his first year as president. It was said he had learned his Latin under "Old Dock Wylie," reading the text as he rode a Methodist circuit. He pleased the students because he used a politician's approach to problems, and in class adapted the dramatic eloquence of the circuit rider to establish his points. D. D. Banta says he was dramatic in manner of speaking, often startling backwoods congregations with his overworked phrase "uncapping hell!" or puzzling them with his sermon on "Zapnath-pa-a-Neak!"

In his inaugural address, August 2, 1853, Daily delivered a fundamentalist sermon. He attacked Darwinism with the same vigor with which he had upbraided the devil. In this address he said, "The theory of a gradual rise of man, from the stupidity of barbarism into civilization and refinement, is almost as absurd as the old Egyptian notion that men originally grew like mushrooms from the mud of the Nile, or the much more modern infidel notion, that they were monkeys, and have gradually ascended to the grade of men, which means that we are a race of monkeys, slightly modified." He told his audience that Indiana University would look to the Bible "as the great textbook of human duty; and endeavor to form a high character of moral excellence, by an appeal to the sense of religious obligation, and principles drawn from this book alone." He seems not to have been concerned in this moment of fresh beginnings that the university's constituency was crying out for men of scientific training who could help keep Indiana abreast of national progress. Daily's inaugural was in fact a pronouncement that the stated purposes of the university would not be realized under his leadership. The school's program would proceed on the old basis of work-a-day teaching largely by rote and drill.

Neither William Daily nor the Board of Trustees seemed willing to carry out immediately the elaborate program which had been suggested by faculty, legislature, and trustees in 1852. Fifty-eight students were enrolled in the university, and there were four full-time professors. The curriculum, through changes of personnel and accident, had been allowed to get out of date. There were, it is true, courses in law, natural philosophy, and civil engineering. Elisha Ballantine offered a valid course in mathematics, but the classical language program had deteriorated, especially after the departure of Daniel Read.

Daily, as it turned out, enjoyed a remarkably short space of time in which to joust with Charles Darwin over the origins of man before a more immediate calamity occurred. At 2:00 o'clock on the morning of April 9, 1854, a brakeman on a passing freight train spotted fire and smoke emerging around the cupola of the old university building and aroused the people of the town. Before help could arrive, however, the building was engulfed in flames, beyond salvation. Wild rumors spread as to the fire's origins. Some said that a band of robbers and thieves had set the building on fire in order to draw attention away from the stores around courthouse square; this rumor circulated even though no one had heard of such brigands being in the community. A more plausible guess was that students had been making and smoking cigars at the base of the stairs and had thrown lighted butts into the janitor's trash pile. Whatever the cause, the building and its contents were a total loss. In 1856 Daniel Read gave members of the Philomathean Society a graphic description of this tragic moment.

> When that old college building, uncomely in aspect though it may have been, but around which clustered so many sacred associations; when your Society halls, adorned with so much good taste from the little savings of your pocket money; when your Society libraries, collected book-by-book, with so much pains; when the college library—that monument of the judicious learning of Dr. Wylie; when these all were lying in ashes—not a book

saved—the very bell which called you together a molten mass; blackened and tumbling walls the only memorial; when the same dastard villainy which had before deposited the anonymous or fictitious letter, had at last applied the midnight torch, and fraud and incendiarism were in secret places chuckling over their work; when dismay sat upon the countenances of all good citizens; in that dark hour, some of you of this Senior class, and some of the two preceding ones, met, a little band, in that dilapidated room of the old college building and resolved to stand by the University.

This was indeed a dark moment. No one knew whether the university could survive this blow. The main building was gone, and with it the school's records, library, and most of its equipment. As though a ghostly hand had set the fire, this monument to the labors of Andrew Wylie was obliterated. No accumulated cash resources existed to restore the uninsured building. At this juncture the board had only two avenues open: to sell the university's remaining lands, or to secure permission from the legislature to issue bonds secured by these lands. A third but highly unpromising solution was the solicitation of funds from the public.

In the spring of 1857, the Board of Trustees made a candid report to the Indiana General Assembly. The university was caught in financial panic. The Board of Trustees in 1853 had made a contract for a new building and this agreement was binding; the institution had to go through with it or suffer serious damages. The building, however, had been planned to supplement, not replace, the one which burned. It was partly constructed and when finished would cost approximately $22,135. The people of Bloomington and Monroe County had been generous in their support, but they could not be expected to finance the university. The only funds the Board of Trustees had at hand were those which had accumulated in the endowment. The legislature was asked to allow more of the lands to be placed on the market so some purchase money could be made immediately available. This, however, was a moment of national economic crisis brought on by the panic of 1857. Money was scarce, unemployment was high, and large numbers of individual Hoosiers were hard pressed to earn a living. Under these conditions the university had low priority among public concerns.

To sell university lands in this period was to sacrifice them to depression and the trustees had hoped to hold the lands as security in the negotiating of loans. In their opinion the time was past due when the legislators should assume some fiscal responsibility for the institution which they had so glibly proclaimed head of the state's school system in 1852. One of Indiana's urgent needs, said the trustees, was school teachers. Fees from tuition yielded only $676, a sum not equal to the salary of a single professor. "A great mass" of students, they said, were enrolled in the university under the free county scholarship plan and paid nothing. If teachers were to be trained there had to be serious public consideration of cost. Indiana should stop importing its teachers from other states and educate its own sons to assume this responsibility. It was suggested that special public funds be made available from which students could pay their way through the university, if they agreed to teach a certain number of years in the Indiana public schools. The state normal school at New York, the trustees said, operated under such an arrangement. In the opinion of the board, the university had justified the faith of its creators. Many of its graduates now served in offices of high public trust. More young men of promise would be graduated in the future. The reason the university had not sent a greater number of graduates from its halls was severe limitations of resources in every department of its operation. Legislators were told, "It is unfortunate that one of man's frailties is impatience. No great design is suddenly accomplished, and it would be as wise to find fault with the sun because he does not suddenly dart to the meridian, as to complain that the University has not already accomplished, with very limited means, all the great results which the friends of education expect from it." The need was far greater than a mere handful of private individuals in Monroe County could solve by popular subscription. The legislature continued to turn a deaf ear to the frantic pleas for help.

This was a period of pervasive unrest and there was almost a constant background clamor of dissatisfaction with the operation of Indiana University. Much of the criticism originated in the petty sectarianism of the local church bodies, a good part was of political origin, and the rest grew out of the poverty-stricken conditions of the university itself. The institution was unable to fulfill its stated mission, and, as the board warned, it could not be expected to achieve instantaneous results. Unhappily the great mass of Indiana's population was wholly indifferent if not hostile to the university.

William Daily was a most unfortunate choice for president during this critical era. He was a self-professed opportunist, apparently he had serious defects of character, and certainly he was involved in religious squabbling within and without his church. An even more damaging charge of lack of courage and determination may be made against him. In two private and confidential letters to General Joseph Lane, Daily revealed his anxieties. In the first letter, written in November, 1854, soon after he became president, he told Joseph Lane that the Supreme Court in the Vincennes land case had robbed Indiana "of nearly all our endowment fund." The institution could not continue to pay salaries unless the legislature acted quickly. He wanted Lane to talk to General Caleb Cushing and see if there were not a federal appointment which he could give a steadfast Democrat, but "Let it be something worthy of my position, so that I would not have to compromise my own self-respect, or that of my family."

Three and a half months later Daily again wrote Joseph Lane confidentially seeking his aid with legislators in his bid for a seat in the United States Senate. He told Lane he could tell legislators how they could find a good and true Democrat. "I would write with more freedom only for one circumstance, this is confidence. My name has been used, and is still used. I wish you were here— You might do us some good. You might do me some good."

If Joseph Lane interceded for his friend it was in vain. Back in Bloomington, Daily was soon to face an even greater test. On July 12, 1858, a rival minister, Dr. Alexander M. Murphy, brought numerous charges to the Board of Trustees against the president. None of these complaints perhaps contained genuine substance concerning the bigger university program. They did, however, reflect the volatility of public temper and the vulnerability of William Daily. Behind these charges were frictions between the university's president and the Methodists. Even though largely unexpressed in the public press, the issues asserted themselves in the nature of religious controversy, and more particularly in the perils of a fundamentalist minister who headed a state university. Dr. Murphy presented eleven detailed charges, some of them a bit sensational. The board cleared visitors from its room and proceeded to sit as a judicial hearing body.

President Daily was charged by his attackers with not having followed the proper formula in the commencement exercises of 1854, and by failing to do so he had brought "reproach and disgrace" upon Murphy. He had failed to obey the instructions of the board to deliver an original lecture each Sunday in chapel. From time to time he had read portions of books, other ministers' sermons, and had shamelessly pirated Gilfillan's *Books of the Bible* as though he had written it himself. In this instance one of Daily's famous camp meeting sermons returned to haunt him. He was charged with having preached a baccalaureate sermon on *Zap-nath-pa-a-Neak* (in Hebrew *Zaphenat-paneach* is Pharaoh's name for Joseph). In this bit of plagiarism he was charged with compounding literary grand larceny with error by assuming *Zap-nath-pa-a-Neak* was a leader or prime minister. The sermon, when published, was said to disgrace the university.

Once he began enumerating grievances, Dr. Murphy's pen outran his reason. Daily was accused of being an incompetent teacher who only pretended to instruct his classes. He disregarded truth and was quick to conceal it to obscure misdeeds when doing so served his personal interest. In the field of business, the president was accused of not paying his debts to Bloomington merchants, and he had not, even though he had been urged to do so, paid the $250 he had pledged to the university building fund. More offensive, said the self-righteous Murphy, Daily was given to tipping the sacramental wine jug, and at some unspecified time had graduated a senior who was beastly drunk. In the classroom the president allowed students to be insolent and coarse and in return for this leniency students were said to have treated him with incivility. In this way Daily had ruined the characters of young men. By personal example, Murphy said, the president had slipped the latches of Gomorrah in his attempts to seduce Adeline Ruthie, a maid at the Wylie home, but Ruthie proved uncooperative. In this connection the board voted unanimously to accept Ruthie's story. In 1857 Daily was said to have transferred his affections to Dicey Rudiwill at Wylie House with a comparable lack of success. Finally Murphy declared that Indiana University was presided over by a lecherous and lewd man who had repeatedly attempted to seduce other women in Bloomington.

The Board of Trustees officially received Mr. Murphy's charges on July 14, 1858, when he and Lawyer Sheeks were on hand to confront Daily and his lawyers, Buskirk and Dunning. Murphy declined to submit the names of witnesses and when pressed to do so expressed the desire to withdraw the charges. It is evident from the record that Murphy had not anticipated the stern reality of a confrontation with his victim and the Board of Trustees. The trustees, however, were unwilling to dismiss the case and voted unanimously to appoint an investigating committee consisting of Samuel Campbell Willson, William C. Tarkington, and James Ray Bryant to evaluate the accusations. After spending several days reading a large volume of documentary materials submitted by both sides, and even in comparing Daily's baccalaureate sermon with *Zapnath-pa-a-Neak*, the committee prepared its report.

On August 10, 1858, the trustees again came to grips with the Murphy issue. They felt Daily had plagiarized the *Zap* sermon, and voted 6 to 0 against him. Ultimately he was cleared even of this charge. They sustained Murphy's charge that Daily was a poor disciplinarian and seemed to have agreed he was a lecherous man. Other charges were dismissed. This hearing lasted three months and ten days, cost $240 in board expenses, and resulted in almost complete confusion. The trustees voted to keep the records confidential, not to be examined by anybody without the board's approval. Daily was left, partially sustained but convicted on two moral charges, which destroyed his further usefulness to the university. His troubles were to multiply; the Methodist conference censured him for a second time in what Daily called an "ecclesiastical persecution." Nevertheless he was cast out of the conference.

William Daily resigned the presidency of the university on January 26, 1859. In his letter of withdrawal he branded all charges against him as "*basely and maliciously false* and wholly the result of a foul conspiracy, as I shall clearly show in due time. Over this prosecution a popular clamor is raised, which may in the estimation of the Board, be prejudicial to the interests of the University." Daily was correct, the furore had hurt the university. Though it is difficult to determine positively, the records seem to indicate that classes continued without interruption but the school's program idled in a state of ineffectiveness. Again it was necessary for the board to search for a new president, this time with less to recommend the university to a prospective candidate than ever before.

Daily's departure, officially at least, caused no sadness among the faculty. At the very moment he was composing his resignation letter, that body was wrestling with the momentous problem of whether to allow J. J. Johnson to forgo the study of Latin. Two days after the board accepted the resignation of Daily his former colleagues sat in the president's room comparing roll books. The professors adopted no resolutions of appreciation on his departure nor took further notice than to say he was not present at the next faculty meeting. On February 4, Theophilus Wylie was appointed president pro tem and school was kept as usual.

The trustees met in Indianapolis on May 5 and 6, 1859, to consider election of a new president but there was lack of a quorum. On July 11 and 12 called meetings in Bloomington had to be canceled for lack of a quorum. Late on the 12th six members had assembled, and for two days the matter of finding a successor to William Daily was discussed. In the final vote four of six members present favored John H. Lathrop, and one voted for Daniel Read. So anxious were the trustees to have an answer from Lathrop that they sent a special messenger to Madison, Wisconsin, to inform him of his selection and of their eagerness for his early decision.

While board members awaited the answer they once again considered a problem which had often concerned them in the past. No progress had been made on the legislative mandate to add courses in agriculture to the curriculum. John S. Tarkington was appointed to correspond with Colonel James R. Bryant, John O. Wattles, and such other persons as he chose about the possibilities of their donating lands on which to conduct agricultural experiments. Unhappily the minutes of the board for the next decade were destroyed by the university fire in 1883, but one can reasonably surmise that nothing came of this correspondence. The legislative record indicated there was no financial support with which to carry out its instructions.

The *Weekly Vincennes Sun* announced on September 3, 1859,

that Professor Lathrop had accepted the presidency of the university. Faculty minutes noted that Dr. Lathrop had arrived and that a meeting was called in the president's room, in which Theophilus Wylie formally resigned the chair and Lathrop was installed. Following this little ceremony the faculty conferred on the problems confronting the university. If Lathrop brought with him from Madison plans for changing procedures in Indiana University he never revealed them. He fitted into the regular routine outlined by the faculty, and for the year of his administration the institution operated in the same way as it had in the days of Andrew Wylie. On March 23, 1860, Lathrop lectured on "The Moral Law." The Bloomington *Republican* commented that the sermon was tolerably long, well prepared, and full of provocation for thoughtful persons, but they had to be thoughtful. With a little more energy in his manner the "Doctor, we think, would make a very popular lecturer. Every word and sentence seemed to have its proper adaptation and force." This journalistic grammarian gave no indication that Lathrop's speech came nearer than the banks of the Tiber to touching problems relating to Indiana. Later the same paper noted that Dr. Lathrop had been invited to deliver the annual address before the literary societies at Wisconsin, but the press of duties in the university forced him to decline.

The last bit of feverish gossip about William Daily and his ill-fated administration was simmering down as the university again got underway with a new president. John H. Lathrop promised a quiet, comfortable routine of university management that would make no radical departures from past procedures. Then came news that the troubled Board of Curators of the University of Missouri had elected him professor of English at a substantial increase over his Bloomington salary. The curators recalled his effectiveness as the guiding force in that university's foundation. Now on the eve of the Civil War, Missouri was being completely reorganized with a new board, a new faculty, and possibly a new mandate. Lathrop, mothlike, chose to return to the flame. In a short time after his return he was again made president, to undergo all the woes of a border state in civil war.

As President of Indiana University Lathrop was able to allay much of the old bickering which had so unsettled the academic community for the past three decades. He walked the streets of the town greeting people with backwoods joviality and equality. Hardly a sidewalk punster, he was nevertheless human. It was more difficult for the sectarian feudists and snipers to unsheath their poison arrows against such a pleasant sincere man. This man of peace was educationally unaggressive, and the record of his single-year administration reveals no innovations, no forays into fields, and no curriculum expansion.

That Lathrop established good rapport with his colleagues is documented by the fact that he was as adept as they in comparing roll books, publicly dressing down obstreperous student offenders who dawdled about the Bloomington fleshpots, and maintaining the decorum of boring chapel periods. When Lathrop's decision to return to Missouri was publicized the Indiana faculty was quick to express its sense of loss. They were once again to be without a presiding officer and realized they were losing one "whose scholarly attainment would adorn any institution with which he might be connected." Reciprocating the same kind sentiments, the departing president said, "I deem the happiest year of my professional life" the year spent at Indiana University.

While the Indiana trustees still hunted for a successor, President Lathrop and his family prepared to move to Columbia. Late in September they departed Bloomington to begin a hectic career in the storm of the Civil War. Sandwiched between news columns telling of the crumbling nation, the Bloomington *Republican* found space to extend the Lathrop family its warmest good wishes. The editor assured the ex-president that his year in Bloomington had established him as a scholarly gentleman. The *Republican* admonished Missourians to receive the Lathrops with cordiality and respect.

In 1928 the Board of Trustees and faculty of Indiana University still remembered with a glow of cordiality that Lathrop had spent a happy year with them. On his one hundred third birthday they congratulated him in a lengthy message.

By 1861 the university had established a definite sense of direction, had driven some of the offensive bigots away, sensed a need for a broader educational base, and had persuaded a reluctant legislature to consider some of its needs. Since 1855 it had occupied the new building, a fairly commodious example of "board of trustees" gothic. To build it the institution had obligated itself to the amount of $15,000. Architecturally the new building was a blurred transitional structure combining the romantic concepts of an age wedded to the Waverley Novels and those of the first phases of the chromo society and taste. Except for loss of records, library books, and literary society collections, the fire of 1854 was not wholly a disaster. With its big square base, narrow windows, peaked gables, dented cornices, and slightly Islamic cupola, in a vague way the building symbolized a fresh moment in American cultural history.

Before the newly appointed Cyrus Nutt had settled into the president's room, the American people found themselves hoisted on the forked spear of debate and ultimate dissolution of the republic. The university historically had been a political and social middle ground where Northerners met Southerners, and both had played roles in its development. A colony of South Carolinians had been active in the formation of the institution. Graduating class rolls each year contained the names of boys who had crossed the Ohio to enroll as students. Now this sentimental tie was to be severed. Ironically the university approached these uncertain days first in search of a president, and then with a new administrator just come to office. There were 102 students registered in 1860–61, but the university was now forced to become a provincial island while the red winds of war blew about it. Now it could only operate largely as a holding institution, and await the return of more stable times when once again there would be pressure to train teachers, engineers, scientific farmers, lawyers, and preachers. For the time being the tasks were to keep a faculty, enforce discipline, and preserve order in the chapel.

[V I]

Redefining the
University's Objectives

J OHN H. LATHROP'S SERVICES to Indiana University were
severely limited. This was true partly because of his fatherly
indulgent personality but largely because of the unsettled
conditions of the times. The university's financial plight, the
gathering storm of civil war, and local religious and political
dissensions were not conducive to creative educational planning
or curriculum expansion. Lathrop demonstrated no inclination
toward aggressive leadership which would have provoked an
intellectual revolution under the most favorable conditions. Actually he did little more than restore harmony to the tiny faculty,
smooth Methodist feathers ruffled by William Daily, placate
meddlesome townsmen, and let the passage of time take care of
problems as they arose.

Nevertheless Lathrop's departure created a considerable vacuum of despair for generating any progress in the immediate future.
The university was not only burdened with debt, but also impending financial recession, public indifference, reckless management of
its endowment, and by exceedingly unsettling morale problems
growing out of the loss of the Vincennes land suit. These things

either eroded public concern or by their very complexity stunned board and university community alike into a state of intellectual coma. More fundamental was the inability of the Board of Trustees and the president of the university to begin realizing the institution's broader educational objectives. There was no lack of constitutional and legislative mandates, but these official sanctions were little more than mocking platitudes in the face of a paucity of leadership and economic resources.

Nowhere was the idea of using public lands as a painless source of revenue given a more realistic trial than in Indiana. Not even Michigan had all the experiences of its older Northwest neighbor. Here not only federal but state lands were made available. By 1860, however, it had to be said in all honesty that the scheme had failed because it could not provide more income than was necessary to keep university doors open.

Lewis Bollman, an Indiana graduate, compared the handling of the university's lands with the management of those granted the University of Michigan. In Michigan the governor, after rigorous prodding by the university's board, vetoed an irresponsible act that would have allowed lands to be sold 'for the bare official minimum of $1.25 an acre. He observed that in contrast Indiana lands were placed on the market at minimum prices, with first-class lands selling for as little as $3.50 an acre. "Thus prematurely," Bollman said, "the lands were forced upon the market, and sacrificed. And this was the fate of the sixteenth sections, for common school purposes. Neither should have been sold for twenty-five years. The attempt to establish the College was as premature as the sale of the lands. It should have followed, not preceded, the successful establishment of the common schools, for it is the outgrowth of these."

The Indiana alumnus denounced the legislators of Michigan as demagogues who wished to toady to squatters who were as devoid of educational desires as wolverines. Control of Indiana school lands rested with the same kinds of legislators, a procession of inefficient and patronage-minded state treasurers, venal local land agents, and politically inspired governors. The Board of Trustees of Indiana University had only a minimal amount of power in administration of the institution's lands. The result was not only failure all around to produce a dependable operating income for the university, but creation of such a state of confused management that no one could tell precisely at any given moment what funds would become available to the school from year to year. Proponents of the subsequent Morrill Act could have learned much about the weaknesses of this type of institutional support if they had investigated the Indiana experience.

Official records of this period yield a fixed notion that the university functioned in a *classics* vacuum where trustees, presidents, and professors appeared to be oblivious to the fermentation which spurred the great national crusade to establish universal public education. Indiana's four minister-presidents seemed to have been myopic sectarian gropers determined to assure a narrowly prescribed academic orthodoxy, to maintain strict parental oversight of students, and to assure at all times respect for professorial dignity.

Long after the surge of the westward movement had passed well beyond Indiana there remained a near backwoods religious fanaticism which expressed itself in an acrid blend of raw rural adaptation of the puritanical ethic and an indigenous camp meeting spirit of fervent revivalism. Hoosiers had difficulty coming to grips with the earthy practicalities of a maturing state and national culture. This was a time Americans gained tremendous momentum in expanding land, economic, and political frontiers. Inventors and scientific pioneers were rapidly destroying the old folk mores of the past. Yet Indiana University and its community seem to have been only mildly concerned about the growing threats to the unity of the republic. This was true despite newspaper columns and editorials pertaining to the great debate. Even the most modest prophet saw that a moment of future reckoning was inevitable.

In Bloomington, professors and students left little or no evidence that they were concerned with or even knew the momentous Illinois debates were taking place. Not even the shattering Dred Scott decision of the Supreme Court in 1857 was noted in the university record. It now became tragically clear that the timid flame of interest which Andrew Wylie had fanned into vigor in his courses on the Constitution of the United States had flickered out. The trustees were more interested in being caretakers of the university's program of well-conducted senior examinations, com-

mencement speeches, and chapel decorum than with pending dis-
union and civil war. In 1861 the university's age-old worry of
insufficient funds was so active that the ominous turning back
of the *Star of the West* in the Charleston Harbor early in 1861
went unnoticed in their future projections.

Nevertheless, Indiana University graduates somehow grew up
with the age. Some of them became governors, congressmen, state
and territorial legislators and judges, and teachers. Among them
were also preachers, lawyers, and one became a major mining
engineer in the Far West. Congressman Robert Roberts Hitt of
the class of 1855 entered the diplomatic field and served for a time
as secretary of the United States Legation in Paris. Later he was
made assistant Secretary of State. In 1858 he shed a certain
amount of notoriety if not glory upon his alma mater when he
transcribed full stenographic notes of the Lincoln-Douglas debates,
thereby creating an invaluable set of documents for historians to
pore over in the future.

In the opening semester of 1860 there were four full-time professors in the university, plus the adjunct professor of languages,
who was also principal of the preparatory school. The law professor
functioned separately and was paid on a contingent basis. Theophilus Wylie occupied the all-embracing chair of natural sciences
and was president pro tem. Elisha Ballantine taught languages,
the newly appointed Henry B. Hibben was professor of English
literature, Daniel Kirkwood taught mathematics, and James Woodburn was principal of the preparatory school and adjunct professor
of languages. James R. M. Bryant taught law as a sideline to his
Bloomington practice; he was not strictly considered a member of
the faculty. Thus the teaching program was reduced to the barest
essentials in courses. In 1865 Amzi Atwater said of the school, "I
use the term University, for that was its official designation, but
there was little about the institution to differentiate it from the better
western colleges except for its small law class of seven Seniors and
eight Juniors. . . ." This condition reflected the stultifying plans
made by the trustees and the almost total neglect of the university
by state officials. Any meaningful talk of conducting courses in the
new fields of agriculture, engineering, or professional education was
for now purely academic. The university was entering a decade in
which it would be merely a holding operation.

To replace John H. Lathrop the Board of Trustees once again turned to the Methodist clergy. In July, 1860, Cyrus Nutt was chosen president at a salary of $1,300. This choice not only continued the ministerial succession, it further fixed the idea that the public educative process was first of all a religious obligation. Without a doubt, appointment of Cyrus Nutt pleased the Methodists and Democrats, though it is hard to determine reactions of the moment. Unfortunately the Board Minutes from 1860 to 1883 were lost in the fire of 1883. Because of this loss it is necessary to turn to other, often less dependable, sources of secondary information. These seldom reflect the true nature of problems considered by the board, the precise financial condition of the university, or the voting records of individual trustees.

Cyrus Nutt was a man of impeccable Methodist background. A native of Ohio, a graduate of Allegheny College, a minister and presiding elder, a professor, and a college president, he fulfilled most qualifications for an American university president in the 1850's. Of equal significance, he was well known in Bloomington, where he had served the Methodist church. He had taught Greek and Latin in the preparatory department of Allegheny College, in the Fort Wayne Female College, and as president of Whitewater College of Brooksville, Indiana. At the time of his election at Indiana he was president and professor of Latin and Greek in Asbury University (DePauw).

When the Bloomington *Republican* announced the board's choice of a new president on July 27, 1860, the editor commented, "We consider the Board as being fortunate in securing the services of a man so well qualified for the position, as we believe Dr. Nutt to be." President Nutt bore in his broad countenance the mark of frontier Methodism and its arduous circuits, the camp meeting, and the rawness of the western country. Combining the hardiness of Francis Asbury and the gentleness of the Prophet Elijah, he came to Bloomington in August to plan for the opening of the university. These plans, however, promised no future revolution and no belaboring the past. He assumed the head chair after the faculty meeting had been opened with fervent prayer, and proceeded to the business of assigning courses and hours for the academic day. He gave a heavy overtone of religious procedure for the rest of his administration. His faculty meetings resembled more the gathering of a quarterly conference than an academic assembly in a public state university.

The temper of the times no doubt had enormous bearing on the operation of the university. Disruptive forces had worked overtime in the past decade and now inevitably made themselves felt in the university. Actually the university had not grown since 1850, its student body hovered between 80 and 100, only twice exceeding the hundred mark. The Bloomington community was distinctly borderland, geographically and sentimentally, and the rise of church schools offered serious competition. Too, this area of southern Indiana was in fact a microcosm of the lower Middle West and the borderland South.

With the rising pressures of the presidential campaign of 1860, the local debate of issues and emotions often rose in an angry crescendo over loyalties and sectional views. There occurred many instances of political realignment which bore upon the university. Dispossessed Whigs searched for a new party, and many disgruntled Democrats crossed the party line to support the new Republicanism. In this community there were people of deep southern origin, many of them coming from as far away as Piedmont, South Carolina. Expatriate Kentuckians and Tennesseeans had maintained loyalties to their states, and even to Virginia and North Carolina. The increasing influx of Easterners who were constitutionally opposed to everything Jefferson Davis and John Breckinridge symbolized proved a counterbalance. Thus the local emotional loyalties had to be sorted out in the great sectional and slavery debates.

University professors and Monroe Countians alike sought a course of action that would be sane, peaceful, and effective. On February 2, 1860, a mass meeting was held in the court square over which Judge George A. Buskirk presided, and former Governor Paris C. Dunning was speaker. Dunning advised the community to take a nonpartisan, nonsectional course to preserving the Union. In response the gathering reached the consensus of adopting a borderland stance by which the valley states on both sides of the Ohio would seek a compromise of differences then being expressed by both Southern and Northern militants. Specifically the local citizenry favored the Crittenden Compromise as a means of preventing dismemberment of the Union and needless battlefield bloodshed. An

ardent unionist in this meeting accused the Bloomington postmaster, a Breckinridge partisan, of canvassing the town seeking signa-
tures to the Crittenden Compromise, an act which was said to have
resulted in the calling of the meeting. Resolutions outlining a course
of action were adopted at the meeting, but not until feelings were
bruised. The majority favored extension of the Missouri Compromise line, a reinstatement of the terms of the Compromise of 1850,
toleration of slavery where it already existed, and enforcement of
the Fugitive Slave Law. Opponents of this proposal said, "By
adopting the Crittenden plan we would destroy our present form of
Government; become protectors of slavery, and offer as much to
traitors in arms, by way of appeasement, as the South asked for ten
years ago."

In the mass meeting Dr. W. C. Foster, Andrew Wylie's old
nemesis, was appointed a committee of one to draft resolutions. He
reported his summation of what he believed to be the tenor of the
crowd in strong Jacksonian rhetoric.

> That "while the lamp holds out to burn, the vilest sinner may
> return." That in view of its Bible doctrine, we hold that all con-
> ciliatory measures should be adopted to prevent a collision be-
> tween the south and the north, and when all the arguments are
> exhausted, and a conciliation rejected, then we advise coercive
> measures to be pursued to prevent the desecration and dissolution
> of the Union. The Union must be preserved at all costs.

The Bloomington assembly was too pacific, however, to accept
Dr. Foster's strong expression of coercion. Then Dr. J. G. Mc-
Pheeters, a former president of the university Board of Trustees,
calmed tempers by offering a more mollifying resolution reiterating
the importance of border state neutrality and constructive national
compromise. The people, he said, should stand steadfast for the
Union but not at the price of coercion.

Under pressures of the moment it was not possible for Hoosiers
to retain moderate and compromising attitudes. Already the southern states were seceding and the Union was being torn asunder. On
April 12, 1861, defiant guns on the Charleston Battery removed the
last vestige of hope for compromise. People in Bloomington reacted
to the news from Fort Sumter somewhat according to the places of
their origin. Some pro-Southerners cheered the beginning of the

war as an act of liberation from some vague form of oppression. Around the courthouse square local Confederate supporters incensed loyal Unionists with their intemperate remarks. Constantly supporters of Jefferson Davis and the South involved their neighbors in hot-headed arguments. Fist fights occurred, and one man was clubbed to the ground because of his treasonous words. An overwrought Mexican War veteran killed a secessionist after the two had exchanged profane sallies.

The Indianapolis *Daily Journal* reported on August 7, 1861, "Several disturbances of the peace have recently occurred in Monroe County, occasioned by the violent language of some sympathizers with secession and the rebel government of Jeff. Davis." Earlier, in May, the Bloomington *Republican* said the A. Seward and Sons foundry would contribute a hundred pounds of brass and cast a cannon for the Unionists if someone would contribute the rest of the necessary metal. The editor thought the proposition reasonable and it could be met if the people would bring in old brass and copper ware, andiron knobs, boilers, and the like. Students of the university displayed an interest in military drill, "affording them wholesome exercise and imparting competent knowledge." Thus in a small way the war had begun before the doors of the university.

Yet most of this excitement over the war was among townspeople. The faculty minutes from 1860 to 1865 reveal very little concern that the Civil War was in progress. Not even John Hunt Morgan's scare raid north of the Ohio in July, 1863, disturbed the monastic complacency of the professors, or stirred students to unusual action. Staff and students alike kept to their daily routine of reciting, misbehaving, cutting classes, and being censured by the faculty court. Courthouse square brawling was left to the unwashed masses. For the larger community of university graduates, however, the war became as real as the gore of Shiloh, Gettysburg, and Chancellorsville.

Sixty-six graduates and professors can definitely be identified as having seen active service in one or the other of the armies. No doubt there were many more. Of these there were eight Confederate officers, including Major Charles Marshall of Baltimore, who was aide-de-camp to General Robert E. Lee. Among the Unionists there were three generals, seven colonels, seven lieutenant-colonels, three majors, ten captains, six lieutenants, and nine privates. The rest were chaplains, surgeons, paymasters, sailors, and drummer boys.

There was not a single important battle of the war in which an Indiana University graduate did not fight. Theodore Read, son of Professor Daniel Read, was among the first 75,000 volunteers who responded to Abraham Lincoln's call for troops. He rose to the rank of general, and fought at Fredericksburg, Manassas, Yorktown, Harrison's Landing, and Antietam. W. C. L. Taylor fought as an amphibious soldier aboard the *Monitor* when it confronted the *Merrimac* in Hampton Roads on March 9, 1862, and lived to fight at Second Bull Run, Chancellorsville, Spottsylvania, and Petersburg. John W. Foster was first major, then colonel of the Thirty-sixth and Sixty-fifth Indiana Volunteers. He was present at the surrender of Fort Donelson, at Shiloh, Perryville, and was the first Northern soldier to enter the beleaguered city of Knoxville.

At least a half dozen Indiana graduates marched with Generals William T. Sherman and George H. Thomas from Chattanooga to Atlanta, and some went on to Savannah and Columbia. There were enough Indiana graduates with Sherman and Thomas at Resaca to have convened a respectable alumni meeting. In the western Confederacy, Indiana alumni helped to make military history. They fought at Island No. 10, Vicksburg, Jackson, Nashville, Franklin, Stone River, and Chattanooga. Both the armies of the Tennessee and the Cumberland contained graduates of the university.

In 1858 Lucien Greathouse, a fifteen year old native of Illinois, entered Indiana University as a junior, and in 1860 he graduated with A.B. and A.M. degrees, and then began to study law. Before he could enter that profession, however, he responded to Abraham Lincoln's first call for volunteers. Greathouse entered the army as a private, but was quickly made a captain. By 1864 he had risen to the rank of brigadier general, and was the youngest man to date to hold that rank. He was killed in the storming of Atlanta on July 22, 1864. At the end of the war General William T. Sherman was asked to select the soldier whom he considered the outstanding hero of the war, and he chose Lucien Greathouse. In announcing his choice Sherman said, "Where all have been brave it seems invidious to mention one name, but we must speak of Colonel [sic] Greathouse. He is the bravest of the brave."

The war drew away from the classrooms two or three active

staff members. One of these was Henry Bascom Hibben, who had followed Cyrus Nutt to Bloomington from Asbury University. Hibben was the first professor of English literature, even though some courses in this field had been offered before. He joined one of the Indiana volunteer units at the outset of the war as chaplain and was also present at Donelson and Shiloh.

A lack of students, but more crucial, a lack of funds, caused the trustees in 1861 to discontinue the literature professorship Hibben had held. Ten years later they were attempting to reinstate the course but with little success. Hibben was not available because President Lincoln had appointed him to a permanent naval chaplaincy. The board's search for another literature professor became a matter of concern. The editor of the Bloomington *Progress* said on August 23, 1871, that when a professor was found he hoped he would "know all about the English language, it is earnestly hoped that the trustees will select a man who can spell correctly words of one syllable. If any one of three gentlemen who were so agitated last Wednesday, see fit to continue this into a 'fling,' as they termed the notice in which titles nor toadyism was indulged in, we can assure them that it is a direct charge. Office hours 7 to 6." The incident which had provoked this editorial belligerency was a report published by three concerned citizens of Monroe County who took it upon themselves to report on the quality of teaching in the schools. They reported to a teacher of English, "you spelt fust rate, and you've sifered purty good, but you hain't sot still durin' the performance."

In the same year that the teaching of English literature was dispensed with for lack of a professor, the legislature provided by statute that a state geologist was to be chosen, and that while he held office he would be regarded as a member of the university faculty. The law instructed this new professor to collect duplicate samples of minerals and other scientific specimens. One set was to be placed in the Owen Cabinet in the university. This was one of the most significant archaeological and geological collections to be found on the North American continent. Its contents were assembled by David Dale, Robert Dale, Richard Dale Owen, Alexander Maclure, and the erudite William Maclure of New Harmony fame. The cabinet contained specimens of soils, minerals, rocks, and fossils of a great variety. David Dale Owen purchased from a Dr. Krantz of Germany the skeleton of an *Icthyosaurus* from the Lias at Boll, Wurtemberg. Owen himself had exhumed a gigantic atheroid (*Megalxonyx*) near Henderson, Kentucky, and it was in the cabinet. There were rare specimens of almost every fossilized form to be found in the Ohio and Mississippi valleys which had been collected by the Maclures, Girard Troost, and the Owens. Sometime in 1859 or 1860 this huge collection was transferred to Indiana University, where it filled a three-story and basement wing of the new building. On May 11, 1861, the legislature instructed the Board of Trustees of the university to appropriate $1,000 from the Vincennes land sales fund to be spent in enlarging the cabinet and the university library. Legislators did not, however, indicate the price or terms of the purchase of the cabinet. Apparently not all this collection was bought at once, and certainly it was not all delivered at one time. On March 7, 1870, the Bloomington *Progress* announced that the geological collection recently purchased by the university in New Harmony was being delivered. This addition consisted of approximately thirty tons of rocks.

David Dale Owen was the first geologist of Indiana. Since the arrival of the famous New Harmony scientists he had been busily engaged with Alexander Maclure in surveying and collecting geological specimens. In 1837 he began his services to the state and immediately thereafter reported on the availability of coal and the presence of a good quality building stone. Between 1838 and 1859 David Dale Owen was employed in far-reaching geological projects, most of them supported by the newly formed United States Geological Survey. In the latter year, 1859, he was again appointed geologist for Indiana, but with the understanding that his brother Richard would actually become the field geologist. Richard resigned his professorship in the University of Nashville and came to Bloomington to take up his duties with the Indiana Survey. Before he could make a start on his duties, however, the outbreak of the Civil War disrupted his plans, and in 1861 Governor Oliver P. Morton appointed the young scientist a lieutenant-colonel of the Fifteenth Indiana Volunteers. He was promoted to the rank of Colonel of the Sixtieth Indiana. He was present at Fort Donelson, the fall of Vicksburg, Rich Mountain, and was in the Red River campaign. During the winter of 1861–62 he commanded the prison camp in Indianapolis, which had charge of 4,000 Fort Donelson captives.

On December 18, 1863, he returned to his position of professor of the natural sciences in the university.

The university itself did little more than keep its doors open with a slender schedule of classes during the Civil War years. Enrollment fell to an average of 78 students per year. This did not mean, however, that its problems lessened or disappeared. The war interfered in many ways with the institution, most important of all it prevented both growth and future planning for the years when the conflict would end. One of the important issues the faculty considered in this era was the question of whether to give instruction in military science. This body agreed to so long as students could elect it on a purely voluntary basis. Two years after the end of the war the faculty again considered the question and decidedly favored continuing military training. On June 19, 1867, President Nutt was informed that the United States Army would supply an officer-instructor at War Department expense.

In the opening session of the university in 1868–69, Major General Eli Long was on hand to reinstate military drill where Jacob Ammen had left off. The university was asked to pay $25 a month of General Long's salary and the army would assume other costs. Long's appointment became active on October 15, 1868. By this time the faculty had changed its mind and required all freshmen to take military science, for which the army would supply uniforms and arms. This burst of enthusiasm for the military in 1868 stemmed from three sources. The Grand Review in Washington at the end of the war had stimulated enormous public enthusiasm for the army, victory in the Civil War was a great achievement for a civilian military corps, and the provision in the Morrill Act of 1862 for military training caused the university to become seriously interested in the science.

By 1871 the university company was well organized with four staff officers, and there was such a wave of local enthusiasm that professors Hermann B. Boisen and Tilghman Mallow joined the ranks as high privates. It was even said that Dr. Nutt proposed to take the course. Colonel James Thompson, the new commandant, rode the wave of excitement and suggested that every student and professor should participate in the drills. Perhaps the praying colonel felt that his cow pasture soldiers would be ready for a second phase of the Civil War. The Indiana *Student* predicted that Kirkwood and

Wylie would also soon shoulder guns and march off to an imaginary Antietam. This all took place safely after Appomattox, and three times a week in the spring of 1869 the "boys in blue" answered the colonel's call to arms and turned the campus into a parade ground getting ready for the commencement dress parade.

The editor of the *Student* listened to the click of the heels and rifle butts and observed, "How brave these soldiers are, it is only necessary to state that they have begun a war of extermination against snakes, and at least three of the images of man's arch-enemy have been destroyed."

Not all Indiana students were fired with the martial zeal that sent Professors Boisen and Mallow charging the snakes on the outskirts of the college grounds. "Imbellis," or W. Cooper, wrote in the student paper, "In some things there is sense, and in some other things there is not." To him the military presence on the campus was "neither sensible, profitable, or pleasant." He saw no reason for compelling a hundred sophomores and freshmen to leave their studies to march with "stately tread" up and down the campus pursuing some invisible foe. He wrote with a touch of anger that, "It is unpleasant to be marched up and down the campus like a race horse. It is unpleasant to get out of bed the next morning sore as to every muscle and fibre." The answer was for students to petition against this practice.

"Imbellis" reflected a changing mood. The South was sorely defeated and was suffering under the light provisions of the Reconstruction military commands. By 1874 military ardor at Indiana University had cooled. The university no longer hoped to secure location of the agriculture and mechanical college in Bloomington, and now the faculty favored dropping military science. Professors wished students to expend their energies in the study of engineering and other subjects.

While Colonel Thompson's callow army paraded up and down the campus, Cyrus Nutt and the trustees wrestled with a much greater challenge. In January, 1864, the president and Richard Owen were appointed a committee to work with the legislature and Governor Oliver P. Morton to bring about the creation of an agricultural and mechanical college under the terms of the Morrill Act. This act had been before Congress for at least five years, but it was not until July 2, 1862, and in the absence of Southerners, that it was finally passed. Once before, in 1858, the bill had passed Congress, but was vetoed by President James Buchanan. Passage of the Morrill Land Grant Act climaxed a long public discussion on the subject of American agricultural and technological education. New York State had experimented with such training, but it failed for various reasons. Now the federal government opened the way for a grand national experiment to be financed by sale of public land scrip. Indiana University unhappily was in no position in 1862 to take immediate advantage of the terms of the land grant act. Under its terms the state was entitled to 390,000 acres of land scrip which had to be sold. Tragically there were insufficient public lands left within the state to permit direct control by the university, and the state's rights philosophy, that no state could hold lands in another commonwealth, prevailed. Besides this Governor Oliver P. Morton and the legislators had their attention focused solely on conduct of the war.

William A. Gabe, editor of the Bedford *Independent*, said on April 15, 1865,

> Bloomington is "pitching in" for the state agricultural college, in which farming is to be taught by actual experiment, rather than mere theory. From our knowledge of the soil around the vicinity of "Young Athens," we would suppose that all experimental teaching would fail. Still we hope our neighbors will succeed, and if Bedford is successful in getting a female college, we will furnish their farmer boys with wives.

To Cyrus Nutt and the Board of Trustees the issue of establishing the agricultural college in conjunction with Indiana University had far more significant implications than supplying girls of a visionary Methodist female college with husbands. No state by 1865 had managed to get the windfall of federal land subsidy so thoroughly ensnarled as had Indiana. It appears on the face of the record that very few people in responsible positions had even read the terms of the Morrill Act. Once again they muddled along allowing township level politics and denominational rivalries, if not strife, to completely obscure the main objectives of the land grant legislation.

On March 4, 1865, Cyrus Nutt reviewed in a clear and concise statement the terms and intent of the Morrill Act. By that time, however, at least three highly impractical and nullifying schemes had been proposed to the legislature. One of these sought to place endowed chairs of agriculture in Indiana University and four of the denominational colleges, including Wabash, Hanover, DePauw, and Northwestern Christian College. In addition a central laboratory and agricultural college would be established in Indianapolis. These departments and the central college would be financed by use of dividends from sale of land scrip after 20 percent had been reserved for constructing buildings and equipping farms and laboratories. There was a proposal that a soldier's home be built with the money, and a third scheme proposed that the federal money be turned over to the public school system. A fourth proposal said an independent college should be established in one of the counties and this college made a coordinated school of Indiana University.

Unfortunately the Dunning Bill in the Indiana Senate was passed too late in December, 1865, to receive consideration in the House before legislative adjournment. Between 1865 and 1869 four local petitions were prepared and submitted to the legislature seeking the location of the agricultural and mechanical college in as many places. One was the offer from the university and the citizens of Monroe County as partially outlined by Dr. Nutt in 1865. He raised at the time at least a half dozen fundamental questions, most of them based upon realistic figures, about the income that would be derived from the sale of 390,000 acres of land scrip at the low figure of $.50 per acre. He made the proposal to locate two professors in ten denominational and sectarian colleges appear not only ridiculous, but financially impossible. At 5 percent interest on the estimated capital fund the land grant act would supply only $335 per professor.

President Nutt proposed that the legislators pursue a practical course of first making an inventory of public institutional resources already in hand. In Bloomington the trustees had removed the tuition fees in 1860, thus students in agriculture would be spared the cost. "The doors of our University," he said, "are freely open for all! It is no small honor that our own has been the first to establish a college free for all." Michigan claimed this honor, but it still charged $10 for the first session, and $5 for each succeeding one. At Indiana all students could attend without charge all lectures on the campus. There already existed an organized faculty teaching courses so necessary to the education of farmers and engineers. There was already a military department and Colonel Richard Owen was an able officer and teacher. The existence of the magnificent Owen Cabinet, which was still being expanded, was an indispensable asset. Chemistry and geology laboratories were in existence as well as a preliminary soil survey made by David Dale Owen of every county in Indiana. A good library was available. In short, said the president, "The whole property of the University becomes subsidiary to the State Agricultural College. . . . It [the university] is the child of the commonwealth, and should be an object of interest to every resident of the State."

In addition to the things listed above, Dr. Nutt said the endowment of the university approximated $112,000. Buildings were estimated to be worth $50,000, and unsold lands were believed to be worth $500,000. Thus the addition of $300,000 of Morrill land scrip would produce an appreciable sum in both endowment and income.

The people of Monroe County offered to purchase an experimental farm worth as much or more than that tendered by any other locality. All of this, said the president, would approximate $400,000. Colonel Owen's scientific knowledge and his European educational background were assets of incalculable value. There was also available the necessary administrative organization to permit immediate functioning of the new college.

President Nutt perhaps did his cause some injury when he argued so stoutly against locating the agricultural school in Indianapolis on the grounds that the city in time would become a great commercial metropolis, and its environs would not be conducive to agricultural experimentation or the proper environmental or moral training of farmers. Bloomington might be small and isolated, he said, but so were Oxford and Cambridge, New Haven, Cambridge (Massachusetts), and Charlottesville. The agricultural colleges of Europe were located in small towns. He argued against the placing of agricultural chairs in church-related schools on the grounds of the narrow sectarian objectives of the institutions. Finally, contrary to much popular belief, Indiana University was not a sectional institution serving only the southern part of the state. In Nutt's mind whatever decision the legislature made it must remember an agriculture college could not stand alone, its students had to have access to the various facilities of a liberal arts college.

Dr. Nutt was perceptive and aggressive in his attempt to secure the location of the agricultural and mechanical college in Bloomington. There were, however, all sort of special interests and petty forces working against the university. Political manipulators sought to locate the central function of the new college in Marion County, and though powerful enough to hold a balance of power, they were not influential enough to actually secure the college. One source of Indianapolis irritation was the annual legal battle over the lots around what was known as University Square in the city. This plot of land had a long and troubled history. Apparently it was originally given to the university in one of the several land grants. In time squatters settled on the west side of it and had to be moved after considerable difficulty. In 1850 the legislature authorized its sale to Asbury University but nothing came of this. In 1856 Colonel J. R. M. Bryant, trustee, and Robert A. Chandler, citizen of Morgan County, brought suit over the lots on the east side of the square with the belief if they won this would win a quitclaim title to the whole square for the university. In 1858 Judge Bryant asked further for power of attorney to take possession of the square. Because of this extensive litigation feelings in Indianapolis were bruised, and political toes were trampled.

A matter of unfortunate timing no doubt was a basic reason for failure of Indiana University to procure the addition of the agricultural and mechanical college to its organization. The Dunning Bill was passed too late for further action in 1865, the Lot or Square 25 issue was sensitive, and postwar politics were too unsettled for prompt or fully intelligent decision making in such a matter. Within the four years between 1865 and 1869 at least four counties sought the location of the land grant college. Each of these places offered various inducements in the form of local support. The debate went on until March 2, 1869, when John Purdue, the wealthy Pennsylvania-born Lafayette merchant, offered to add $100,000 endowment to the Battleground Institute's bid, provided the college was located near Lafayette, and that the school bear his surname. At a special session on April 8, 1869, the legislature accepted the Tippecanoe County-Purdue offer and located the new school in West Lafayette. This ended one phase of Indiana University history. Failure to secure the land grant college made an enormous difference in the university's future objectives.

The legislative act of April 8, 1869, which established Purdue University as the land grant college of Indiana, unintentionally revised the constitutional mandate on higher education of 1816. The intent of that document was to establish a seminary of higher learning, and to insure that the state would, "from time to time, pass such laws as shall be calculated to encourage intellectual, scientifical, and agricultural improvement." The act also invalidated the Assembly's own mandate of 1852 in which the Board of Trustees was instructed to organize in the university a department of agricultural instruction. Under the Act of 1869 the university had to reconsider its future objectives within the narrower contexts of the liberal arts and professions.

This was a decisive moment in the history of Indiana University. Up to this date trustees and faculty conceived of the university's mission as a universal one. Now its program was largely restricted to the liberal arts. Thus it was to become increasingly difficult to convince legislators and the people that the university served the state in a practical way. Internally the university administration was forced to seek support to permit the organization of professional courses which would serve nonagricultural and nonengineering constituents.

While legislators debated and haggled over the issue of establishing a land grant college they revised another policy. In 1867, for the first time, the legislature assumed a slight responsibility for the direct financial support of the university. An appropriation of $8,000 annually was voted the institution. Two years later Judge George A. Buskirk told Monroe County Republicans that the state university "is now in a more critical condition than it ever has been." He said when Judge James Hughes represented the county in the Assembly the school had received its first appropriation. At the last session Judge Buskirk said he had procured an additional appropriation of $7,000. This fiscal legislation was nonrecurring and could be allowed to lapse at the end of the year without creating adverse public reaction. Buskirk had introduced a bill at the last session to make future appropriations mandatory, but the Democrats had destroyed a quorum in order to prevent the ratification of the Fifteenth Amendment to the federal Constitution.

Someone, maybe Judge Buskirk, was successful in representing the university's needs to the legislature for 1872. In that year the Assembly appropriated $30,000 for a new building and gave a hint that a session the next year would appropriate an additional sum, which it did. In a February issue, 1873, the Indiana *Student* was jubilant over the fact that salaries of the president and professors could now be increased, and at the same time an additional sum of $20,000 was made available to complete the new building. A comical typographical error in the report of the salary scales of the university staff made it appear that President Nutt would receive $25,000. This was enough to completely unsettle the man.

The Bloomington *Progress* attributed the legislature's generosity to the work of Senator Friedley. With jubilance and a sigh of relief Cyrus Nutt told students,

> The legislature has adjourned; the University is safe; none of the departments of the University will be cut away; write this to your friends. . . . We have passed through a trying ordeal; the eyes of a State were directed toward us—granger eyes, as it were ready to ferret out & punish any irregularities found in the management of our monies. But thanks to our efficient managers, our faculty & Board of Trustees, we have shown the State that we are doing good work, that the money, so munificently donated by the State, has been placed where it would "do the most good."

The university was unfolding in many areas, especially in student activities. Just returned from the war, veteran students brought to the university knowledge of the new game of baseball. M. A. McDonald, called the "father of baseball at Indiana," said, "When I arrived at the University in 1866 everything pertaining to baseball was crude. There were no regulation bats, no gloves, no masks & no pods or shields of any kind used." Home base was a piece of flat iron thrown on the ground, and the bases were bags stuffed with straw. The batter took his stance over or near the plate in any position he chose and without admonition from the referee. Bats of varying sizes and shapes were supplied by the individual players. The first diamond was laid off southeast of the old college building in the flat ground of the "draw." In 1867 interest in the game had increased and a team was organized under rules and players were assigned specific positions. A lad named McIntyre was the barehanded catcher, and Homer Bothwell was the "clean clothes" dandy. This was the beginning of organized athletics at Indiana University.

These were milestone years. The students, on February 22, 1867, celebrated George Washington's birthday by issuing the first number of *The Student*. This name emerged from what the editor said had been a national search for a title. In a bit of college boy buffoonery it was said that eight "great literary lights," among them Andrew Johnson, came to Bloomington and struggled mightily to come up with a proper title. The editor declared that Washington Irving suggested "Prairie Flower," James Gordon Bennett, "The Elevator," George D. Prentice "proposed to call it 'The Indiana Drawer,' *draw* being a very popular word with certain classes, and the name would thereby be constituted an element to its success." Henry J. Raymond thought "The University Lightning Rod" exceedingly appropriate, "as it would undoubtedly be the means of silently conducting all the superfluous gas generated in the fruitful craniums of certain 'smart students,' either to immortal glories in the skies, or perhaps, to its more appropriate place, the dominions of Pluto under the earth." "His majesty Andrew, earnestly insisted on the singular appellation of 'My Policy Gazette,' strenuously adhering to the principle that all 'Big things' are controlled by policy." Greeley was disturbed by a noisy temperance meeting taking place in the room overhead and could think of no appropriate name. Finally "Henry J. Raymond, by a heroic stretch of imagination and herculean wielding of brain power, was delivered of the word *Student*."

The Washington's birthday edition expressed pride in the faculty, which then numbered eight members, including George A. Bicknell, professor of law. The editor in good country weekly style said he would hold to high purpose and bright hope. He promised Indiana University students that the paper would be neutral "in politics, but not on vice and corruption; independent in religion, content to advocate morality, without being orthodox or sectarian." The junior and senior promoters hoped to make the journal reflect student thought and opinion and describe conditions of academic life. *The Student* was controlled by the junior and senior classes. In this bold fashion the fledgling newspaper set out to inform the American collegiate world.

Almost immediately the editor's pride was blunted by a smug Easterner who edited the *Magenta*. He requested in 1873–74 that the Hoosiers discontinue exchanging their paper with him. The Indiana editor fired back with information that wrappers had not been removed from the snobbish little Eastern rag, and the virginal copies could be returned at once. "We western people," he said, "don't like boat racing, gaming, etc." The ink was hardly dry on the youthful editor's salutation before he involved himself in a ticklish racial incident. It was apparent at once that the days of national Reconstruction had brought many changes to both Indiana and the university. Students and institution alike found themselves caught up in the currents of social readjustment. On May 3, 1867, just two months to the day after the Radicals in Congress had pushed through the Military Reconstruction Law creating five military districts in the South, *The Student*'s editor observed acidly that white women were working in the cotton fields in Georgia, Tennessee, and Virginia while black women refused to do so.

In the next issue of the paper the editor said he had been psychologically wounded and humiliated on Sixth Street, where he had met a young Negro and had greeted him with, "How are you Sambo?" The Negro held his head high,

eyes front, he passed us by with a dignified air that would well become any lord or baron. Consequently, we are disgusted with ourselves, & find that every editor is not always free from disrespect & insult. We raged, we tore, we stamped, we swore, we rent our clothes & fought the air & were about to lower his dignity by tossing a brick bat after him, but recollecting a certain provision in the civil rights bill, & a vision of gloomy dungeons & military bastiles presenting itself to our mind we concluded to cage our wrath & submit to the insult like a true martyr. It once was that the white man refused to speak to the Negro; but now, the American citizen of African descent (alias said Negro) refuses to speak to the white man. . . . We are in favor of the "nigger" in his right place, but we want it distinctly understood that we are radically, uncompromisingly, unchangeably, everlastingly, combinedly & editorially opposed to American citizens of African descent, & we hereby forewarn all persons claiming such title, not to come within a radius of one square mile of our sanctum, for fear of incurring the awful peril of our eternal wrath.

Much of this, of course, was adolescent bombast, but it did get published without a challenge. If the "concerned" Radicals of the period existed on the Indiana campus as they did in the Indiana congressional delegation in Washington they did not come forward to express themselves.

Strangely there is no mention in the faculty minutes of the national Reconstruction issues. Certainly the impact of the national struggles during these years was felt in Bloomington. On December 5, 1872, *The Student* reported that it had irrefutable proof that the Ku Klux Klan had a toehold in the university. "Would it not be well," said the reporter, "to send for a division of Grant's Ku Klux squelchers?" The year before, the faculty had received a petition signed by forty-seven students, a fourth of the university's enrollment, requesting that colored people be excluded from the university chapel on Sunday afternoons. The faculty made no comment on the content of the petition, but referred the petitioners to the Board of Trustees, who controlled such matters.

However much many Hoosiers may have reacted like Southerners to the excesses of Reconstruction, the old southern ties were temporarily broken. No longer did Southerners come north to Bloomington to seek an education, partly because of financial straits, but largely because of the sectional enmities growing out of radical Reconstruction.

[VII]

The End of Sectarianism

THE POST-CIVIL WAR YEARS were for Indiana University the dawning of a new era. The institution began to feel the national cultural impulse which stirred what J. C. Furnas has called the "Chromo American Civilization." This was a time in American history when professional crusaders worked the byroads in behalf of moralistic causes. Religious fervor was stirred annually by technicians who manipulated evangelistic outpourings. Public speakers used the newly connected rail lines to peddle "culture" from the platforms of universities, church auditoriums, and county courthouses. There must have been at least one speaker abroad in America who was willing to discuss, for a fee, any subject man could suggest. Many in this army of transient educators came through Bloomington. There were the temperance crusaders, who at least once a month tanned demon rum's tough old hide in the university chapel. Women's rights advocates followed in quick succession on each other's heels. Multitudes of self-proclaimed authorities debated the evergreen subject of conflict between science and religion. Man, the universe, nature, psychology, and the human mind were subjects of prime interest. "Professor" R. E. McDuff, phrenologist, preached a simple gospel of understanding by feeling the lumps on human heads. He spent several days in Bloomington explaining the local citizens to themselves. Between formal lectures in the university chapel he rubbed the heads of Indiana students in search of their capabilities and weaknesses.

The Lecture Association of the university was active in its search for speaker talent. The Reverend James W. Malone of Illinois, a Negro, spoke of the Fifteenth Amendment. Will M. Carlton, described as "this celebrated American Poet" and author of "Over the Hill to the Poor House," "The Burning of Chicago," and "Betsey and I are Out," spent two days in the university cashing in on his horrendous description of the great Chicago conflagration. His vivid portrayal of this catastrophe was hardly more vicariously satisfying than was Anna Livingston's description of her Uncle David's adventures in equatorial Africa. Mrs. Josephine R. Nichols explained "Boys" in eloquent fashion to a chapel full of the animals. Dr. N. A. Payne, an itinerant naturalist and human character expert, attracted most of the university's students to his courthouse lectures on the natural sciences and human character. His afternoon levees in Parlor Number One of the Bloomington Hotel competed with Dr. Richard Owen's sounder discussions of scientific topics.

The prince of all lecturers who found their way to Bloomington was the Reverend Theodore Tilton, the New York abolitionist and clergyman friend of Henry Ward Beecher. The editor of the Bloomington paper said Tilton "thoroughly aroused our quiet little town on the important subject of Marriage and Divorce, or Home Sweet Home." He topped off this bit of domestic felicity with "The Right Use of the Mind." Other lecturers came and spoke their pieces and went away quickly to be forgotten, but not so with Dr. Tilton. In 1872 the Reverend John L. Gay (or Gray) was a member of the university faculty, a North Carolinian, professor of English and an Episcopal clergyman. For some reason he was fired by the Board of Trustees in 1873 and for a time he was forgotten. On March 17, 1875, Henry J. Raymond's *New York Times* ran a full page covering his testimony in the notorious Beecher-Tilton adultery trial. Gay's testimony was highly sensational, and related graphically to Tilton's lecture in the Indiana University chapel in 1872. Professor Gay intimated in answer to the lawyers that Tilton had told his Indiana audience to follow nature in the formation of marriages, thus implying a brand of free love if not sexual promiscuousness. He was reported as saying that Tilton would not allow either the church or state to regulate or interfere with marital relations. If he had his way he would crush both state and church, and illustrated his point by crumpling two bits of crisp paper. Gay said Tilton told the Hoosiers that if any two among them had expressed enduring love for each other they were as married as if they had the sanction of the law and the benediction of a priest. He also said if they came together in this manner they could dissolve the union in the same fashion, and it would become the duty of the state to care for their children.

Gay's implication that Theodore Tilton had lectured in Bloomington under the sponsorship of the university faculty infuriated those gentlemen. In a fit of temper they recorded in their minutes that they had had nothing to do with bringing the New York clergyman to the university, and they took this occasion to denounce their former colleague. In fact they called him a liar in a nice professorial way. This spark of fury enlivened an otherwise dull set of minutes, and the Beecher trial gave the university a bit of left-handed national publicity.

The stream of culture flowed a bit unevenly in Bloomington during the decades of 1870 to 1890, whether it was fed by mountebank scientists, exploitative nieces of famous men, the wronged Dr. Tilton, the great female army of temperance and woman's rights apostles, or local faculty members and student talent. A. M. Cumings of Nashville, for instance, captivated "the wit, beauty, fashion & wealth of the town assembled in the college chapel" early in the evening of George Washington's hundred and thirty-fifth birthday. With all of this, however, the editor of *The Student* in 1871 expressed dissatisfaction with the fact that the university was "behind the age, & even behind its hopeless rivals in the West, in its lecturing department." It failed, he said, to attract such famous talent as Mark Twain, George Washington Cable, Henry Ward Beecher, Anna Dickinson, and Olive Logan. He might well have added the popular lecturing prostitutes Victoria Claflin-Woodhull and Tennessee Claflin, who pleased American audiences of the day. Some students felt there was perhaps too much lecturing. One suggested that a bundle of straws be placed on the platform at many of the popular lectures so they could be distributed among the audience and people could tickle one another to stay awake and hear the lecture.

In these years the nation was stumbling through the enormously upsetting period of Reconstruction, and above the smoke and din of political and economic chaos had begun the sober business of drawing the American people back together in a celebration of the first century of freedom. Freedom of another sort occupied the thoughts of the Board of Trustees in Bloomington. Once again this body considered the long standing issue of admitting women to the university. Isaac Jenkinson, Fort Wayne newspaperman and lawyer, suggested at the board meeting in 1866 that the quickest way to meet the feminine drive to achieve equality was to admit girls to university classes. The following year at its June meeting the board voted to "admit such ladies as might apply for instruction in one of the four college classes." This was a momentous occasion which made both heavy and irksome emotional demands of students and professors. In the following October the faculty relaxed tradition and announced that subject to board approval ladies would be admitted even to the "masculine" courses. Looking back on this moment some years later Sarah Parke Morrison told her friend Frances Higgins that her father, John I. Morrison, of Washington County, and President of the Board of Trustees, had urged her to seek admission to the university. She told Miss Higgins, "I possibly had a dim perception that I ought to go first but nothing more, if that, for the idea of women entering men's Colleges had not then dawned upon the average feminine mind much less upon the male intellect." She compared the first round in the fight to assert feminine equality to a groundhog's appearance on a sunny day.

Sarah Morrison did not enter upon her pioneering venture unprepared. She had graduated in 1857 from Mount Holyoke College, and since then had had several educational experiences. Her two years at Indiana University, however, tested her stamina to remain unruffled amidst arrogant stares and intolerant slights and remarks. She said she had to undergo the additional test of correcting deficiencies in her preparation.

Following Sarah Morrison's first year of success twelve more girls were admitted in 1868. Four of these registered for scientific courses, three chose mathematics, and the others studied the classics. By this time the presence of girls on the campus and in the classrooms had almost become an accepted fact; not fully, however, until additional radical changes were made. To head off a confrontation on the social front, Professor Amzi Atwater was given the task of organizing a "feminine" literary society. The next year the faculty approved the new organization.

The traditional social order took considerable readjusting before women could be made to feel welcome in the university. For instance, in planning for the commencement of 1869 professors were perhaps more worried about Miss Morrison's graduation than they had been by her admission to classes. They were afraid she would be subjected to the curious and hostile stares of the audience. Even worse, she would have to walk across the stage to receive her diploma and her ankles might be exposed to immodest views.

As grave as a little ankle exposure may have been in this age, it was of secondary importance as compared with the fuller meaning of the event. Indiana University's monastic period had ended. Professors and male students surrendered reluctantly, but they surrendered, even if they were sometimes ungracious in their acceptance of the new students. There were still questions: should professors treat women students with Victorian deference, should they insist they take special and easy courses, or should sex be ignored altogether? Later Miss Morrison revealed her answers to these muddling questions.

> The ghost would not down—no woman, after men had declared the doors open, [would falter]: I studied the Catalogue—So much Greek, and I had forgotten even the alphabet! It would later take two years hard study—I did not know how hard—to make that up—For they did not have [easy?] courses of electives then but the old-fashioned grade-grind of Ancient Languages, a sound course of it. And if one could slip along, it must not be the elective woman, who must show for the credit of her sex that her brain was fully as capable as that of the male. That woman must come up to the mark. Must be careful to establish no precedent injurious to her interests.

The male students contested the ground all the way. When the question of whether Miss Morrison could take part in the debates and orations was raised, they were horrified. These were manly arts reserved for the male. Sarah Morrison had other ideas. She remembered Lucy Stone and Susan B. Anthony and asserted her rights. She had set out to destroy the myth of the "female college" in Indiana, and she was equal to the task.

Women in the university presented some new problems to the Board of Trustees. They had to make some extra physical arrangements for them—a ladies' retiring room in the new building, and revised student rules to prevent loitering and loud talking near it— and they had to define the educational and professional objectives of female graduates in Indiana society. The principal career for university trained women was teaching. With their prospective entry into this field Indiana University would at last begin to come to grips with a long standing problem. For almost a half century much had been said about training teachers and strengthening the mode of public school instruction, but very little had been accomplished.

Since 1832 the Board of Trustees had dabbled with the idea that the university should concern itself more with the plight of Indiana public schools. It was said after 1856 that a majority of the students held county scholarships, which in a vague way implied a commitment for them to return to their home counties to teach for a few years. In 1871 the faculty agreed with the board's philosophy and proposed the discontinuance of the university's preparatory department. The faculty said that prospective university candidates could best be prepared for admission by the local high schools. By this time the larger Indiana towns had organized high schools, and the movement was spreading across the state.

One of the best high schools was located in Bloomington. The Board of Trustees, believing that Bloomington's high school could perform the function of the old preparatory department, made arrangements for it to accept inadequately prepared university applicants. In June, 1871, the board "Resolved that we think it advantageous to discipline and to the character of our institution that immature minds should not be admitted [to the university], yet we desire provision be made for the preparatory studies necessary to admission, as many cannot obtain them in their own counties, the same to be open on equal terms to both sexes."

In January, 1874, the State Board of Education considered the matter of college preparatory education and it listed the high schools that gave proper preparatory training for admission to the university. Students would be admitted without examination if the superintendents of the approved high schools would certify their training. Recognized in the first list were the high schools in Logansport, Princeton, Franklin, Plymouth, Aurora, Muncie, Vincennes, Rushville, Greensburg, South Bend, New Albany, Shelbyville, Terre Haute, Goshen, Mt. Vernon, Evansville, Elkhart, and Kokomo. Strangely, Indianapolis was not included in this list. This was the beginning of accreditation in the state even though Asbury University had issued a previous set of qualifications which the university faculty refused to accept.

About this time the faculty sought to expand the university's own educational program. In June, 1874, it proposed an ambitious program of postgraduate work in the fields of English, philology, public speaking, analysis and criticism of English, Anglo-Saxon, German, ancient languages, engineering, physical sciences (analytical chemistry, geology, comparative anatomy, mathematics, and astronomy), the metaphysical and empirical sciences, political economy, history of civilization, and the philosophy of history. This was indeed an ambitious undertaking for a faculty of approximately ten professors. It was especially impressive when one remembers that the undergraduate program desperately needed expanding and restructuring. The library was poor; Amzi Atwater called it "diminutive." The books were confined to one room and Professor Theophilus A. Wylie served as part-time librarian.

In the decade and a half that Cyrus Nutt was president of the university, the institution underwent fundamental changes. Andrew Wylie had experienced no greater challenges than did his successor. Nutt, like Wylie, was unable in the end to fend off the animals of partisan and sectarian dissent. His last year in office was sorely troubled by an undercurrent of carping and malicious criticism. Destruction of the Minutes of the Board, a volume of the Indiana *Student*, and the local newspaper seriously handicaps a search for facts concerning the closing months of the Nutt administration. For some unexplained reason the old president found himself at loggerheads with students. They claimed he had been in the presidency too long, and that he had "lost his dignity and respect" in dealing with them. There appeared on the streets of Bloomington an underground newspaper or "bogus" entitled

The Dagger. The contents of this sheet are not precisely known except that it was an attack upon President Nutt.

Nutt lived in a period of Indiana history in which political and religious infighting was no respecter of person or institution. Results of these squabbles were disaster for the victim, only the specific details were different. The Daviess *County Democrat* and the *Indiana State Sentinel* gave the best insight into Nutt's dismissal. The editors wrote,

> At a full meeting of the Trustees of the State University at Bloomington, Dr. Nutt was dismissed as President of the University by a unanimous vote. There were no resolutions passed, and the chair of the President was declared vacant with a degree of abruptness that makes the word "dismissed" very appropriate. Dr. Nutt was not informed of the action until after the graduating exercises, and although he appeared considerably surprized at first, he soon regained his self-composure, and remarked that he would quietly abide by the decision of the Board. The salary of the office was raised from $2500 to $3600.

The faculty and townspeople were well aware that all was not well at the end of College Avenue. On July 24, 1875, Theophilus Wylie, at that time in Fort Wayne, noted in his diary, "Board met Monday & Dont know what they have done. They have removed Dr. Nutt & I suppose by outside pressure & prospects rather gloomy for next year." The university was not in session at this time and the faculty minutes are silent on the change of administration. Available records suggest that both political and religious forces were at work. If the latter, they were surely not of Methodist origin because within ten days after his removal the ex-president was unanimously elected minister of the Bloomington church to complete the unexpired term of Reverend M. Haight, who had accepted the editorship of *The Western Christian Advocate.*

Immediately after the board had removed Cyrus Nutt, W. K. Edwards of Terre Haute, a member of the Board of Trustees, wrote Theophilus Wylie, "Dr. Nutt does himself a gross wrong, to charge that it was an offence to his church, in declaring his chair vacant." This seems to indicate that internal troubles in board and student body were the reasons for his dismissal. The board's action caused

Cyrus Nutt biting grief from which he never recovered. His pastorate in Bloomington was short. Almost immediately after his appointment he contracted what Dr. J. J. Durand called "bilious intermittent fever." On August 23, 1875, Dr. Wylie recorded in his diary, "Dr. N. died this A.M. 4:15, in great agony." At the funeral in Greencastle the next day, Wylie made a brief graveside statement in which he referred to the troubles Nutt had experienced in the university, apparently absolving the president of any mismanagement. There is no doubt that the board had fired him; the reason however, remains vague.

Measured by many criteria Cyrus Nutt was perhaps the best of the "preacher presidents." The resolutions adopted by the faculty following his death indicate that he not only enjoyed the loyalty of his colleagues but their warm affections. He served the university during one of the most frustrating periods in American history. He no doubt lacked imagination and vision when compared with James B. Angell and Andrew White of the period, or with David Starr Jordan. He did not extract from the age all that it might have yielded the university, but he faced enormously difficult problems with Indiana people, the churches, and the legislature. Possibly the Board of Trustees itself deserves inclusion in this list. Nutt himself proved able to accept change with grace, and he indicated in his speeches and actions that he understood the role of university education in a maturing Hoosier society. Cyrus Nutt brought Indiana University, a scarred and uncertain institution, to the divide of the ridge between the ages of preacher presidents and gerund-grinding classicism to the watershed of Darwinism and the new social gospel in the gilded age of American society.

By 1875 the Indiana Board of Trustees had become experienced if not skillful in searching for a president. In their hunt for a successor to Cyrus Nutt the board favored William Torry Harris of St. Louis, Professor Jonathan Tenney of Williams College, and Professor Edwin D. Sanborn of Dartmouth, but they did not reach a decision before adjournment. Five times in the part twenty years they had gone looking for candidates. Following the discharge of Cyrus Nutt there was urgency for several reasons to find his successor. W. K. Edwards suggested to Theophilus A. Wylie on August 18, "Delay in selecting a successor is not desirable, but it is best to take time, and make certain of securing the right man.

Progress up to this time has been very slow, and there is no prospect of knowing how soon, the trustees may succeed."

The principal reason for the urgency was to prevent special sectarian and political interests from gaining the upper hand. There is evidence that this was a real threat. In the absence of adequate contemporary materials it is difficult to be specific as to who the "wilful powers" were. Trustee Edwards' statement "right man" has to be interpreted in the light of a prospective president's religious, political, and educational background, in that order. It is clear the board's definition of "rightness" was more nearly that of the Noah Porter type than of a James B. Angell or Andrew White. Indiana trustees still thought in the strict moral and religious terms of the first half of the nineteenth century when they came to view a presidential candidate. They had not yet learned the lesson that college administration had become a distinct academic profession, not a subsidiary to the interests of a church body.

In its search for the "right man" the name of Lemuel Moss, a Baptist minister and university president, came into prominence. The forty-six year old University of Chicago president was born in 1829 in Bullittsville (now Shepherdsville), Kentucky. He graduated from the University of Rochester and the Rochester Theological Seminary; afterwards he served as printer, professor, and editor before he was elected to the presidency of the Baptist University of Chicago in 1874. The Board of Trustees of Indiana University were able to entice him to Bloomington largely because Chicago was a starveling denominational institution in a booming, bruising commercial city. Though the record is vague it is known that Moss came to Indiana at a higher salary than Cyrus Nutt had received, and that his appointment was made early enough in September for him to be present at the opening of the school. Faculty minutes show that Theophilus Wylie, Daniel Kirkwood, and Richard Owen comprised a welcoming committee which greeted Moss at the Monon station and then escorted him to the Orchard House. That evening the entire faculty called on the new president to discuss university affairs, and the following morning he attended chapel, where he heard welcoming resolutions read by Daniel Kirkwood, Amzi Atwater, and Thomas C. Van Nuys. They hailed Moss' election "as a cheering indication of continuing prosperity of the University."

Moss was a large man with wavy hair, a slanting Roman face, sensuous lips, and slightly heavy eyes. His manner was that of a stern no-frivolity preacher disciplinarian. He entered upon his duties with a sternness that recalled Andrew Wylie. Since 1872 the student enrollment had declined from 190 to 132. Perhaps Nutt had influenced this decline, at any rate Moss' first concern was with increasing enrollment and broadening the curriculum. It was now clear that Indiana University could only hope to thrive in this age of an expanding America by relating itself intimately with the state and the times. Before this the old curriculum had proved acceptable if unprogressive largely because it resembled that of sleepy old-line and outdated colleges all across the country.

The advent of the land grant colleges, emphasis on the sciences, professional demands, and the burgeoning of national literature and history, plus the rise of the neighboring universities of Michigan, Wisconsin, Cornell, and Ohio State, all created a broader intellectual swirl that would eventually envelop Indiana. These were visible facts to which President Moss and his faculty, tucked away in Bloomington, had to give more than casual consideration. In this connection Moss proved a better administrator than a mere faculty chairman. He demonstrated some genuine capacity for broader and bolder administration.

Moss had hardly settled himself in his new presidential chair before Alex M. Gow of the Indiana Committee for the Celebrating of the Centennial of National Independence asked him to raise funds to send a student representation to Philadelphia. This request was followed by an even more urgent one from John Eaton, United States Commissioner of Education, requesting Indiana to rent a student headquarters. This sudden burst of national attention startled president and faculty. They were not accustomed to sending students away from Bloomington to represent the university, certainly not as far as Philadelphia, where expenses and moral discipline would be burdensome. They were equally startled at the request to send a faculty delegation. Later the professors decided to present themselves in spirit at least by sending their autographs.

Bloomington was so far from Philadelphia, and Indiana University had so many problems of greater local importance, that Moss said he wished to wait and see what other universities did. On December 14, 1875, David Hough, acting chairman of the

Centennial Commission, asked the university at least to prepare pertinent exhibits which would include faculty autographs, photographs, catalogues, and materials from the famous Owen Cabinet. The university responded favorably, and a generous collection of items was placed on exhibit, attracting much attention. When the centennial ended and the exhibits were returned to the state, the university materials fell into the hands of James Henry Smart, Superintendent of Public Instruction, who claimed them. It took everything short of the state militia to make him give them back to the school.

Hardly had the battling with Superintendent Smart ended before the faculty was confronted with a problem of prime importance. Since 1842 the university had maintained law classes on a contingent basis, but in the third quarter of the nineteenth century this no longer seemed possible or desirable. Either the legislature had to give material support or law classes would have to be discontinued. This was the end of the trail so far as the faculty and trustees were concerned. The university faculty itself was seriously weakened by the resignation of Colonel Thompson because of ill health and the absence of Thomas Van Nuys, who was studying in Europe. The professorial ranks were now reduced to four members, Moss, Wylie, Ballantine, and Atwater. If the university was to continue its academic program, additions had to be made at once to the teaching staff.

The change of presidents and the financial difficulties of the university in no way slackened public service calls made upon the institution. The Reverend W. P. McNary sought use of the chapel to lecture on "Free Masonry the Most Gigantic Humbug in the World." He was refused on grounds the faculty did not wish masonry—pro or con—discussed in the chapel. Nevertheless, public pressures were great for use of the auditorium. The Presbyterian Missionary Circle could not well be turned away, and certainly there was more social and political liability in turning Elizabeth Cady Stanton away than in permitting her to take arrogant mankind over the jumps of discrimination. Dr. J. G. McPheeters interceded in behalf of Professor R. A. Proctor, asking that he be allowed to speak in the chapel on astronomy. The star lecturer, however, was President James B. Angell who spent ten days lecturing in the university. His sponsors collected $62.75 in admissions, paid his expenses of $22.27, and sent him back to Ann Arbor with $40.48 jingling in his pocket.

The procession of lecturers continued endlessly. Moss and his faculty spent almost as much time discussing their appearances as they did the misdeeds of students. Students, however, made themselves heard on many subjects. Forty of them signed a petition asking the faculty to allow organization of a mixed literary society. This was too bold a step for the moment. It was trying enough to have women in the university, but allowing men and women to share membership in a common society was the late nineteenth century equivalent of open housing.

The university's poverty generated shabbiness. The two new buildings presented imposing external appearances if one did not examine the unsightly weeds, bushes, and debris surrounding them. A suggestion to the faculty that trees be planted about the stark buildings was tabled while that body approved giving special attention to cleaning the grounds, especially at the rear of the buildings. The faculty provided some notion of the surroundings of the buildings when it complained in May, 1877, that the railsplitters working at the rear of the classrooms were making entirely too much noise. It was suggested that workmen be brought in late in the afternoon so they would not disrupt classes with their chopping and mauling.

Lemuel Moss was a self-important, bustling man who regarded his position with pope-like seriousness. Because of this he never endeared himself to the university community. He gave a perfect demonstration of his pomposity in the fall of 1877. An Italian organ grinder strolled by the university leading a performing bear. Dr. Richard Owen saw him and dismissed his class in geology and sent Lew Munson out with some change to invite the man and bear to entertain the boys. By this time Professor William Ballantine was persuaded to dismiss his Greek class to enjoy the show. The Indiana *Student* said, "The man struck up his timeless wail & the bear began his laborious gyrations, when suddenly Dr. Moss flounced out of the west back door of the Preparatory building, hurried up to the group & in language more forcible than decorous ordered the bear and man off the premises." The organ grinder offered to refund Dr. Owen his money, but the latter refused. Said the *Student*,

The two minstrels wended their way out of the campus, the students scared, yet angry, sneaked off to their recitations, Professor Ballantine & the Greek class suddenly became absorbed in Herodotus. Dr. Moss having broken up the picnic went back to his "Vatican" & left Dr. Owen, provoked, embarrassed, & grieved standing on the steps contemplating the unfortunate end of the amusement he had planned for the students.

Students, however, have long memories, and there came a day in Moss' administration when all four classes extracted their pound of flesh with vengeance. Moss no doubt was at the moment contemplating the university's fortunes in the next decade while revealing himself as a pompous, thoughtless, and arrogant man.

The university strove throughout the decade of the 1880's to strengthen its program and to fix its location permanently in Bloomington. Actually supporters of the university were forced to attack on three fronts. The two buildings were woefully inadequate for university functions. By 1880 plans were underway for the projection of additional buildings. One of them was to serve the needs of chemistry and physics with special laboratories, classrooms, workshops, and storerooms. Already the Owen Cabinet and the geological collection made necessary the construction of new quarters with laboratories and lecture rooms. The growth in interest in the arts and literature had gone far beyond the capacity of the old buildings, so had the need for larger assemblies in the chapel. The library had once again begun to grow, and there was need for a separate and fireproof library building. Other academic fields were being expanded and were demanding more space.

A new age was dawning in the area of university functions and needs all across the country. The Board of Trustees learned this as early as 1878 when Indiana students requested that any plan for future buildings should include a gymnasium. This caught the governing fathers by surprise. They had no idea of what the students were requesting, and they spent some time trying to find out. Some unimaginative soul wrote across the student petition, "Saw your own wood!" A student complained that sitting in the university buildings on a cold night was akin to a retreat to the Arctic region. New and better heating facilities had to be provided if students were to remain healthy. Some progress was made in this area early in 1883. Two steam boilers were installed, failed to function properly, and had to be reset. Gas fixtures were installed in the old buildings to provide lights, and serious attention was given the constantly nagging problem of water supply. The latter problem was one which caused greater irritation than mere human welfare and comfort in Bloomington. Repeatedly it was used as an argument for removing the university to Indianapolis. Now that the trustees were back before the legislature asking for greatly increased building funds the dogs of removal were once again aroused. All sorts of reasons were advanced as to why the state should invest no more money in Monroe County. The editor of the Bedford *Star* said that Mr. Vanzant, the Bloomington undertaker, had buried 1,129 persons in nine years. This was evidence enough that the university was located in a "dreadful place."

Tugging and hauling over the Bloomington location aroused people all across the state, and their sentiments were reflected in legislative actions. The editor of the Greencastle *Banner* felt, however, that the university should remain in Bloomington. He again gave moral reasons. Students were removed from the greater temptations of the metropolis, even if they did create some of their own in the Monroe Valhalla. In the *Banner*'s opinion Indiana then had just the right geographical distribution of its colleges, and to move the university would destroy that balance. In the fall of 1833, 166 students had enrolled, and this, said the Bloomington *Saturday Courier*, is "some kind of action that will stop all the talk about the removal of the State University. The preachers," said this editor, "can all testify that there is not a better location for the State University than Bloomington." One minister said to the *Courier*, "You have a beautiful, enterprising little city, I never saw a place of its size with better streets nor better behaved people. I have been here six days and have not seen a drunken or disorderly person." This was accepted by the newspaper as proof positive that the university should remain in its present location.

For the Board of Trustees and faculty there was a more fundamental matter at stake. The legislature had to be persuaded to appropriate money for the badly needed buildings and to stabilize the university's future income. Early in February, 1883, the educational committee of the legislature visited Bloomington to inspect the university. Local interest was high and when the train arrived at about eleven o'clock there was a tremendous crowd gathered about the depot. The *Saturday Courier* said,

> In fact the greeting was a little too boisterous as the way the crowd pounced down upon the train when it came to a stand still it reminded one of a mob of lynchers after their prey. The guests were escorted around the South end of the depot, and the crowd rushed pell mell around the North end so they could get a good view of the visitors as they come [sic] around to the Orchard House at the rear of the depot. The visitors looked with astonishment at the crowd, and the crowd stared at the visitors as if they were a band of wild Commanche Indians.

At the university chapel the legislators heard speeches emphasizing the need for strengthening the university at once and extending its usefulness. The editor of the *Courier* was anxious that nothing unpleasant happen, but at the National House, where a fine dinner had been prepared, the natives rushed in and preempted tables so some of the legislators had to wait for the second table. Despite this unpleasantness the lawmakers seemed to depart with a favorable impression. On March 17, Representative John Graham came home from Indianapolis with the feeling that the legislature would support the school. Later that year it was reported that W. W. Durand was being pressured to run for the office of representative from Monroe; if he consented then the university's interest would be well served.

Indiana University's future was at stake in this strategic moment. Universities all across the United States were expanding and adjusting curricula and faculties and venturing away from the old classics confinement. There now was some slight awareness in Bloomington that faculty and board had to rethink the educational objectives of the university and to make plans to reach a larger student constituency.

President Moss felt this so definitely in November, 1881, that he tried to redefine for the Board of Trustees the university's objectives.

> It is an institution for the largest liberal culture, & the instruments which centuries of proof & experience have demonstrated as most efficient for this culture as to be cherished & rendered as effective

as possible. Language, literature, history, philosophy, mathematics (pure and applied), & the great principles of the sciences of nature, are to be wisely wanting that the strong & broad men & the best facilities are most eminently qualified to meet the emergencies & use the opportunities of life. If ever the world called for men of wide outlook & deep insight & comprehensive views of society & its destiny, it calls for them today. No institution in the commonwealth has such a responsibility as our own to this most urgent demand.

This was hardly a classic statement, but it did indicate the president's willingness to meet the university's challenge.

At the same meeting the president pointed out to the board that the legislature had been guilty of an immoral act. He had been employed at a salary of $3,600, but "Two years later the legislature, arbitrarily, unlawfully, & without inquiry ordered my salary to be reduced to $2,500, & the Trustees thought it necessary or prudent to obey the order." Moss told the board that Indiana University faced a crisis, and that it would be cowardly and sinful for him to desert it. It was for the time his duty to take this insult from the legislature and from members of the board but he was unhappy.

In 1883 catastrophe struck Indiana University. The new building, constructed in 1873, was set on fire by lightning at 10:30 P.M., Thursday, July 12. Fortunately a heavy rain had fallen and the roofs of neighboring buildings were wet. The courthouse bell was rung and volunteer firemen rushed to the campus, dragging behind them the new steam pumper, but this machine quickly exhausted the water supply of the university cistern, and the engine had to be moved farther away to the creek on Walnut Street. The building burned quickly. Lightning had followed an underground telegraph wire into the structure and set the internal framing on fire so that the blaze was out of hand before the fire was discovered.

Unsuccessful efforts were made to remove most of the contents from the burning building. It contained the 85,000 specimens of the geological and archaeological treasures of the Owen Cabinet, the 14,000 volume library, David Starr Jordan's ichthyological collection, and the law library. The dollar loss was estimated by the Board of Trustees to be approximately $111,000. The three-story building itself had cost $33,000 when it was constructed in

1872. The state had paid $30,000 for the Owen Cabinet, and additional money had been spent on its arrangement, cataloguing, and exhibit. The library was valued at approximately $40,000. No attempt was made to evaluate the Jordan collection. The university carried $27,454.50 in insurance, which the several companies paid immediately.

For a month after the fire Indiana newspapers carried garbled stories of the tragedy. Some stories gave the impression that the entire university was destroyed, and this caused advocates of removal to bark even louder. Now was the time, they said, to leave Bloomington for the bright lights of the capital city. On the Sunday morning following the fire the Reverend J. E. Brant anticipated this campaign and preached to his congregation on the significance of the university remaining in Bloomington and Monroe County. He pleaded with his flock to exert itself in supporting the school. Away in Buffalo, New York, at the time of the fire, President Moss sent instructions that a handbill be prepared announcing that the regular session of the school would open in September and classes would be held as though nothing had happened.

Letters and contributions flowed in from over the country. One of the first was from President James B. Angell of Michigan. All the Indiana college presidents sent their regrets. James S. Rollins, the oldest alumnus, sent his sympathy from Missouri, and Sarah Parke Morrison sent $5.00 from Knightstown. The Board of Trustees lost no time in acting. On July 24 it resolved to rebuild and on August 27 it recognized the fire as an act of God, and regarded it also as a summons to advance the university toward the position of effectiveness and influence it ought to occupy. The institution, they declared, would remain in Bloomington; however, it seemed desirable to relocate it. The old campus contained eleven acres, at least half of which lay along the creek and were unfit for use. It was an established fact, said the board, that the population of the state was expanding, and Hoosiers were increasing their industrial activities.

The editor of the *Saturday Courier* asked, "Why wouldn't this be a good time to make a bold strike—secure new and sufficient ground, and on it place the new buildings? With the amount of funds now at the command of the trustees, and with the aid they certainly could obtain from the vicinity, would furnish ground and building facilities fully equal to those now afford [sic] by the present locality." He suggested that the old university buildings be turned over to the preparatory school, and Dunn's Woods east of town be purchased. Laberfew and Prospect hills would also be desirable sites.

Bloomington's plight in the summer of 1883, said the Bloomington *Saturday Courier*, was comparable to that of Leyden in the great siege of 1574. At the end of the struggle William of Orange had offered the people, as a reward for their courage, either exemption from taxation or the location of a great university. They chose the university, and Bloomington should do the same. The people should obligate themselves to raise money, and to provide a more favorable location. By the middle of August a petition was being circulated asking the county commissioners to appropriate $50,000 to be secured by a bond issue. It was said that an owner paying taxes on $5,000 worth of property would be indebted only $4.00 a year, plus interest on $4.00 or $4.10 in ten yearly installments. Assessed valuation of Monroe property was about $6,000,000. This proposal met some opposition. In November a "Tax Payer" wrote the *Saturday Courier* that the people of Monroe County are in a "good state of very considerable excitement." He thought benefits from the university to the county were very remote. For the people to permit themselves to be taxed would only invite other lawless acts by the commissioners. He contended the county officials could only raise money for county purposes. There were other attacks, but the commissioners' decision stood and President Moss was notified of this fact on September 8.

Immediately thereafter, the search for a new site of forty or fifty acres began. A critic said of this that it was a selfish move on the part of the faculty, which sought good pasturage for their cows. The faculty, however, ran true to professorial form and resolved at its meeting on September 15, 1883, that it would be to the university's best interest to rebuild on the old campus. As could be expected, none of the proposed sites was perfectly satisfactory. Dunn's Woods was too expensive at $400 an acre, the cheaper thirty-acre Milligan tract was too far from town, and other places were equally undesirable.

At its meeting in September the board settled on the size of the new buildings, made plans to hire an architect, and chose Dunn's

Woods, but hoped the land could be bought for less than $300 an acre, and without the reservation of lots nearest the town. The Dunns expressed themselves as not being anxious to sell because they wanted to keep their fine meadow, and they hoped to make good profits from the sale of town lots. At a meeting in Indianapolis on October 5, the trustees voted by a majority of one to buy the Dunn tract at $300 an acre, allowing Benjamin Dunn to reserve a 375 foot strip across the west end of the tract. Immediate plans were made to erect two main buildings. One of them, two stories high, would be adapted to the use of chemistry, physics, and the other sciences; the other would be a fireproof building to accommodate the library and the liberal arts. It was thought that a solid fireproof brick structure could be erected at a cost of $40,000, or built of wood for $25,000, and the second building would cost $37,000. The science professors were asked to view the plans and make suggestions. On his way home from Europe, David Starr Jordan stopped in Indianapolis and discussed plans for the science structure with G. W. Bunting, the architect, and Trustee James L. Mitchell. He differed sharply with the board and architect over the dimensions of the rooms, and at last persuaded them to agree to increase the size of the science building from 3,000 to 4,000 square feet. That same day the board approved the final plans, and in March the contract was awarded N. Y. Nichol and Son for $59,982, from which G. W. Bunting would receive $899.43. At its June, 1884, meeting the board asked for bids on additional buildings.

On June 10, 1884, the cornerstone of the larger of the new buildings was put in place and the board announced it would be called Wylie Hall in honor of Andrew Wylie, the first president, and Theophilus A. Wylie, long-time professor. The second building would be named in honor of the Owen brothers, Robert, David, and Richard. The street running west of the campus would be called Nutt Avenue, another street would be named for David H. Maxwell, and Dunn's Woods would henceforth be called University Park. The contractor worked rapidly, and in November, 1884, the Indiana *Student* announced that the new buildings were almost completed. The paper, however, criticized the appearance of Owen Hall and quoted from Casper Kremer's edition of Horace to describe it: "Suppose a painter wished to couple a horse's neck with a man's head, and to lay feathers of every hue on limbs gathered here and there, so that a woman, lovely above, foully ended in an ugly fish below; would you restrain your laughter, my friends, if admitted to a private view?"

Late in 1885 the university moved from the old campus to the new and on January 9, 1886, the Bloomington *Saturday Courier* announced, with a note of triumph,

> The State University is rapidly recovering from loss occasioned by the fire two years ago. The chemical laboratories are models, and occupy almost all the first floor in the main building. All of the books in the library are new and well selected, $8,000 having been expended on books this year. The University is making the departments of Chemistry, Zoology, Geology, and History specialities. The Senior class numbers twenty, nearly all scientific students: the Freshman eighty-four. The probable successful candidate for the State Oratorical Contest is a member of the junior class.

Despite his pomposity, financial handicaps, and other worries Lemuel Moss brought a certain sparkle to Indiana University which other presidents often lacked. In 1881, for instance, he convinced the Board of Trustees that they should purchase for the president's office a typewriter—just three years after Christopher L. Sholes had perfected the machine. He asked for a mechanical typewriter, "To relieve me from some of the drudgery & discomfort of constant use of the pen. I can readily explain to you the typewriter, & its methods of work if you are not familiar with it. The instrument I want will cost $100, & I believe I shall count it another favor if you will buy it for me." Evidently the president had no secretarial aid and expected to operate the machine himself.

President Moss was never without ideas. He flooded the board with direct requests; he discussed with them problems that arose and suggested solutions. One of these was a request for official sanction of the anniversary dates of the university. He asked what would be a proper and official founding date to place on the new seal which he was having cast. The board gave four dates which the university had celebrated as anniversaries, and then declared the old date of 1830, which appeared on the earlier seal, was improper; it should be 1820.

President Moss occasionally encountered problems in relationships with his students. Discipline was very much on his mind. He became involved in a public controversy in the spring of 1883 with William R. Asher of Martinsville. Since September of the preceding year this case had hung fire, and young Asher had been suspended from the university in December, 1882. The central issue was whether Asher should represent the university in the State Oratorical Contest. A committee composed of David Starr Jordan, Orrin Banner Clark, Thomas C. Van Nuys, and Charles H. Gilbert was appointed to investigate the case. They substantiated claims that the defendant had plagiarized speeches, cut classes, done poor class work, and violated promises, and they asked that his name be dropped from university rolls. President Moss talked with the boy to try to persuade him to withdraw gracefully. But Asher refused and maintained that he had every intention and legal right to speak in the annual state contest. There followed several petitions from citizens which claimed the president of the university had not told the boy why he was being discharged. This was indeed a delicate issue which had to be handled with tact and finesse, both of which Moss possessed, when he wished.

Where his predecessors had on the whole been modest if not poor public relations men, Moss had a keen appreciation of public notoriety and approval. He was a good lecturer and was in popular demand, lecturing at times in places as far away as Toronto, Lake Chautauqua, and the eastern cities. He even took a leave of absence one semester to fill speaking engagements. Before Indiana audiences his favorite topics were "Student Discipline" and "How to Get On."

On November 8, 1884, Judge D. D. Banta, long-time member of the Board of Trustees, appeared before that body and announced that Lemuel Moss had suddenly resigned the presidency of the university, and that Miss Katherine Graydon, professor of Greek, had also resigned her position. Banta either presented to the board at that time, or students themselves presented, six affidavits sworn to by a party of students known as the "Moss Killers." These lads, in collusion with Uncle Tommy Spicer, the janitor, had bored holes through the ceiling of Miss Graydon's office and classroom and kept vigil on the roof to see what happened below in the chamber. On one occasion, they saw President Moss unlock the door and

ANDREW WYLIE, *President, 1829–51.*

THIS PICTURE SECTION *selected from the archives gives some of the flavor of early Indiana University. Included are names, sights, scenes, groups, and the ten presidents that helped shape the university during its first century.*

ALFRED RYORS, *President, 1852–53.*

WILLIAM MITCHELL DAILY, *President, 1853–59.*

JOHN H. LATHROP, *President, 1859–60.*

CYRUS NUTT, *President, 1860–75.*

University buildings in 1876, the Board Walk, and stepping blocks laid across the muddy street. The Science Building, to the right, was destroyed by fire in 1883.

LEMUEL MOSS, *President, 1875–84.*

DAVID STARR JORDAN, *President, 1885–91, Professor of Anatomy, Botany, and Zoology, 1875–91.*

JOHN MERLE COULTER, *President, Professor of Botany, 1891–93.*

JOSEPH SWAIN, *President, 1893–1902, Professor of Mathematics, 1883–1902.*

Indiana University campus in Dunn's Woods, 1898.

William Lowe Bryan, President,
1902–37, Instructor, then
Professor, 1884–1902.

Carl H. Eigenmann as a senior,
1886. Professor of Zoology,
1886–1927, Dean, 1908–27.

"Political Meeting on the Square," painting by Theophilus
A. Wylie, ca. 1839. The original now hangs in Chancellor
Herman B Wells' office.

Elisha Ballantine, teacher,
Acting President, and Vice
President, 1854–86.

David H. Maxwell, Board of
Trustees, 1820–37, 1839–52,
President, 1820–37, 1841–52.

The carpenter shop, at one time the men's gymnasium.

Baynard Rush Hall, first professor
and teacher of Ancient Languages
in Indiana Seminary, 1824–31.

Theophilus Adam Wylie,
Professor, 1837–52, 1854–86,
historian of the university.

South side of the Old Chapel in 1876. Shown here are the
stage, the stage tavern benches, and the old "stop" organ.

Charles Marshall, Professor of Mathematics and Civil Engineering, 1849–50.

Daniel Kirkwood, Professor of Mathematics and Astronomy, 1856–86.

Gustav Karsten (fifth from the right) and his hiking club, 1889. Seated fourth from the right is Theodore Dreiser.

Amzi Atwater, Principal of the
Preparatory School, 1865–68,
Professor of Latin, 1870–93.

James Albert Woodburn, Pro-
fessor, 1890–1924, historian of
the university.

Indiana University baseball team, 1893. Professor Charles
Sembower, is third from the left in the top row.

Thomas C. Van Nuys, Professor and Head of the Department of Chemistry, 1874–95.

Horace Addison Hoffman, Professor, 1885–1920, Dean, 1894–1920, Vice President, 1919–20.

Indiana University football team, 1893.

John W. Foster, A.B., 1855, Secretary of State, ambassador, and jurist.

John Hopkins Harney, Professor of Mathematics and Natural Science, 1827–32.

Mitchell Hall, at one time called Maxwell Hall. This was for years the center of the cultural arts at the university.

*Richard Owen, Professor of
Natural Philosophy and
Chemistry, 1863–79.*

*"Uncle Tommy" Spicer, univer-
sity janitor and friend of
students.*

*The Owen Cabinet display as it appeared in 1876. Seven
years later this priceless collection was destroyed by fire.*

Judge David McDonald, first professor of law.

Henry Sanders Bates, the "Philosophical Shoemaker," Registrar, 1893–95.

A law class in the old science Building, 1876.

Isaac Jenkinson, Trustee, 1866–70, 1875–1906, Board of Trustees President, 1889–1906.

Sophie May Sheeks, Registrar, 1888–93, Assistant Librarian, 1893–96.

Indiana University co-eds, 1868. Sarah Parke Morrison is in the front row, fourth from the left.

THE STUDENT

"LUX ET VERITAS."

Vol. XXI.   INDIANA UNIVERSITY, MARCH 5, 1895.   No. 22

THE STUDENT is published every Tuesday of the college year by the Publishing Association of Indiana University. Subscription price, $1.50 per annum, or $1.25 if paid before January 1st; 50 cents per term; 10 cents per copy. Address all communications to THE STUDENT, Bloomington, Indiana.

WERTER D. DODD, '96.   -   -   Editor-in-Chief.
ERNEST O. HOLLAND, '95.   -   Revising Editor.

Associate Editors.

EDWIN C. CRAMPTON, '97.   FLORA LOVE, '95.
THOMAS LARGE, '96.   EDNA HENRY, '97.
ROBERT C. BROOKS, '94.   C. A. ZARING, '95.

ASSISTANT EDITORS.

EDITH B. WRIGHT, '96.   BENJAMIN F. LONG, '97.

CLAUDE G. MALOTT, '95.   -   Business Manager

Entered in the Postoffice at Bloomington, Indiana, as second-class matter.

A FEW weeks ago there was no little talk about some athletic benefits which were being devised. For a time we were led to believe that the debt was to be paid and the Association was to begin the season with a surplus on hand. Now it seems that all interest has relaxed and the season is to begin with the characteristic loose management. We must say, however, to those who have this matter in charge that we expect them to make some effort to discharge this debt, and if they do not do so, we shall consider that they have not done their duty.

ON FRIDAY night, March the 8th, the State Oratorical contest will be held in Indianapolis. Seven colleges and universities, Hanover, Earlham, Butler, Franklin, Wabash, DePauw and Indiana will be represented. Almost as much of the interest of an institution in oratory is manifested by the representation of students at the contest as by the strength of the orator. If the yell is given with a vim it is understood that oratory is flourishing; if faintly, it is understood that oratory is on the wane. It is at these contests that many students obtain their conceptions of college oratory and receive inspiration to enter succeeding contests; and we advise all students who intend to compete for future honors in this direction to hear these seven orations on Friday night. Since the recent debate was supported in such a half-hearted manner by the students and faculty we should be very conservative in making an estimate of the number certain to attend this contest; we hope that it will be at least twice as large as that in attendance at the debate.

AS THE base ball season draws near, we reflect that in our competition with other colleges in other things we have not made a record this year of which we can boast with any degree of pride. In base ball is our only hope of victory. Here we have a record to sustain as well as new conquests to make. It would be less humiliating to us to be last in foot ball than second in base ball. We hope nothing will stand in the way of selecting the best players possible for the nine so that we may have the best team yet sent out. To you, ye invincible nine, we entrust the reputation of the University. May you prove worthy of the trust.

THE GENERAL crusade that is being carried on by the college papers against cribbing is indicative of two things, a low standard of student morality and a growing desire to raise that standard. There is scarcely a student who would not resent th

The Student, March 5, 1895. Four years later it became a daily paper.

conceal a gift in a book case. Miss Graydon came in and went straight to the hidden packet and unwrapped it, then President Móss reappeared and there followed a slightly affectionate scene that involved more than a mere professional greeting. For three or four days before Moss' resignation Indiana newspapers carried stories implying more intimate relations than student affidavits claimed was the case. The editor of the Bloomington *Saturday Courier* said on November 7, 1884,

> The daily newspapers of the last three days have been teeming with sensational articles touching the Moss-Graydon scandal, and it is understood the matter is being investigated by the Trustees of the University now in session here. For these reasons we feel loth to devote a great deal of space to the unhappy and shocking affair. Putting pressure upon all sorts of rumors we have been able to boil them down to the following effect: Many months of private scandal and suspicions on the part of certain members of the faculty and the students of the University eventuated on the 28th proximo, in the formation of an organization to develop the facts as to what occurred between Dr. Moss and the woman in question at their clandestine meetings at the latter's room on the third floor of the University building. The room was the Greek Room, and, as assistant Greek professor, was occupied by Miss G. and here she was ostensibly earning the $1600 per annum paid her by the taxpayers of Indiana. On the night of the day mentioned six students selected on account of their trustworthiness, and representing each of the collegiate classes assisted by the Janitor (Mr. Thomas Spicer) worked their way through the roof above the Greek-Graydon recitation room, and . . . [perforated] the ceiling of the room so as to show its floors at every point.

Every day for a week the "Moss Killers" saw, according to the editor, "Dr. Moss and Miss Graydon, the beautiful Greek professor, kissing, hugging, etc."

There was more to the newspaper story, and it repeated the contents of the affidavits which students had delivered under such a heavy seal of secrecy to the board. Either they or board members divulged the contents.

This incident had sharp public repercussions. Miss Graydon was a member of two prominent Indianapolis families and they became militantly defensive. Katherine Graydon's indiscretion was indeed mild enough, but rumors, gossip, and imaginings, stimulated by innuendo of the press, made it seem much greater. The Indianapolis Presbyterian church congregation of which Miss Graydon was a member became involved in the public furore. The Reverend W. H. Carrier was forced to resign his pastorate because of the split which occurred in his congregation. Mr. Carrier wished to remove the young woman's name from the membership roll, very much to the displeasure of the Merrill and Ketcham families.

Miss Graydon went on, after this incident, to have a long and respected career as professor at Butler University. Moss, however, apparently had no defenders. He hastened away from Bloomington, leaving his family to dispose of his library and home. Behind him he left a mighty roar in the press. The editor of the Lafayette *Leader* perhaps spoke for his professional fraternity when he wrote, "Dr. Moss of Bloomington University, must be prepared to run for office, if the recent publications about him are true. When old men set such an example, what can be expected of the boys?" In Chicago Lemuel Moss became an agent for a manufacturing firm which produced patented water heaters to be attached to cooking stoves. Later he went back to editing a religious magazine, and for a time preached in Philadelphia. He died in 1904 in New York City.

For Indiana University this became a sharp breaking point with the past. The line of six "preacher presidents" was at last broken, and the Board of Trustees now felt safe in turning to the scholarly academic field to find a fit president. Because of the wide publicity of Moss' resignation their task was made somewhat difficult.

In its attempt to conclude the Moss-Graydon incident the Indiana *Student* raised more suspicion than it allayed. The editor, William J. (Lowe) Bryan, said the paper would not record the details because the public press had done that. However, he said that there was error in all the reports except that published in the Chicago *Tribune*. The university paper said it was satisfied to stand on the record of the Board of Trustees, and to forget the details it actually knew about the incident.

Actually the Moss-Graydon scandal was far less significant than the newspapers made it out to be. Years later President William Lowe Bryan, Miss Graydon's successor in Greek, perhaps best summed up the situation when he said she sat on President

Moss' knee, and "on the brink of disaster." Yet this may well be considered one of the most timely if socially unfortunate, incidents in Indiana University's history. Nothing short of a major social shock could have caused the trustees and legislators to break so sharply with the past. Of significance was the fact that the time had arrived all across the country when major revisions in university academic programs were mandatory. In this intellectual age the new physical sciences, social studies, and demands of the learned professions rapidly pushed the old moralism and static classicism into eclipse. If Indiana University was to justify further public support and patronage it too had to become a functional part of this age of advanced learning. It needed new educational leadership that clearly saw what the challenges of the university were, leadership with the knowledge and academic seasoning to bring out the university's potential.

Indiana University's failure to recognize earlier its intellectual challenges was exemplified by Lemuel Moss' ambivalent statement to the legislature in 1878:

> Centuries of experiment and use have pretty well settled throughout Christendom, and for all time, the chief materials and methods of higher education. There may be great improvements in details and better facilities for the work, as these are constantly changing and growing, but there can never be much change in the prominent and characteristic features of the scheme. Our intellectual and spiritual powers are to be developed and grained by the acquisition of truth, for which undoubtedly the human soul was made.

[VIII]

Father Andrew's Children

THUS FAR in the history of Indiana University emphasis has been placed upon the organization, administration, and financial vicissitudes of the institution. The student has peeped around the corners, but he has not appeared in center stage. Student life in the university reflected the ups and downs of the institution. Involved in the changes in conditions of student-university relationships were matters of discipline, physical accommodations, intellectual objectives, and the eternal pressures demanding the broadening of curriculum. Changing conditions of Hoosier society were reflected in the personalities and natures of the boys who enrolled before 1867. The quality of the educational program, the richness of its traditions, and the university's sense of accomplishment lay with its students and alumni.

In 1885 the nature of Indiana society was no less Victorian than it had been in 1840, but a new economic and social age in the nation intruded upon the agrarian commonwealth. Old family and community ties were loosened, and, even more important, early economic lines were either being opened or redirected. Civil War and Reconstruction, and the various humanitarian crusades which followed, exerted decisive influence upon the outlook, demands, and personal standards of behavior of Hoosier students. They became adapted to the new age and changing mores much more rapidly than did their parents, trustees, and faculty. Perhaps this was always true in Bloomington.

When Indiana University opened its doors in 1825 the state was still buried in the backwoods. Bloomington was on the outer fringe of the spread of population, and the act of pioneering was in full swing. There were many courthouse towns, a scattering of villages, and no cities or large concentrations of population in the state. The people were oriented to a way of life on the land; the rhythm of human affairs was coordinated with that of the seasons, crops, and life cycles of domesticated farm animals. The five leading employment opportunities open to Hoosier youth in the decades from 1825 to 1850 were farming, the ministry, crafts and trades, law, and school teaching. Engineering, business management, manufacturing, banking, and the scientific fields awaited another era to achieve ranks of major importance.

The first ten students who struggled along backwoods trails to reach Bloomington and the tiny seminary on the edge of Perry Township were frontiersmen. Their domestic backgrounds were those of at least three generations of log cabin-corn patch Western settlers. Their homes were largely of the primitive coon skin, tallow dipped, corn land abodes of pioneers. Not far southeast of Bloomington in the university's formative years, the Lincoln family struggled to place a crude roof over its head and to open enough ground to plant corn. They were thus engaged when constitutional delegates sweated over the draft of a new state constitution at Corydon, and when the committee located the seminary in Bloomington.

The earliest students to present themselves in Bloomington were Lincolnesque in background and experience. They made their laborious ways to the town hoping to study the "three R's," although only three of them had been exposed to more than the most elementary schooling. A dispute developed at the outset between students and Baynard Rush Hall over what they were to be taught. They had not even heard the word "relevance," but they sought to start at the foot of the ladder of practical learning by enrolling in the most elementary beginning studies.

Baynard Rush Hall conducted a drowsy village school in which he drilled farmer boy-frontiersmen in Greek and Latin grammar, even though they had little or no inkling of English forms. They spoke with the nasal drawl of the Valley frontier, pronounced words in the flat manner of at least three generations of American backwoodsmen, and formed their phrases in the picturesque colloquialisms of people who regarded speech as a rough tool of direct and brusque communication. Nothing, however, could have been further from Professor Hall's mind than "encouraging the trades and commerce, the arts and sciences, and agriculture." To him Latin and Greek were the intellectual pediments of a sound education. Prospective students had been forewarned in newspapers that they would need the texts, Ross's *Latin Grammar*, latest edition, *Colloquies of Corderius, Selectae e Veteri, Selectae e Profanis, Caesar, Virgil*, and Mair's *Introduction*, Volpy's *Grammar*, latest edition, a *Testament*, and *Graeca Minora*.

The Hoosier pioneers who first presented themselves in Bloomington to seek a seminary education were clad in rough homespun and butternut dyed trousers, wore crude floppy hats, were shod in ill-fitting cowskin shoes, carried man-sized pocket knives, and were total strangers to neck ties and nightshirts. They had never known anything but hearty frontier table fare, and were able to accept the primitive accommodations of the town without complaint, in fact they would have been uncomfortable with any other kind. In his report of Board of Trustees proceedings on June 20, 1854, John I. Morrison wrote, "The larger portion of students in our university are aspiring young men from the middle and even the very humble walks of life; many of them having, by their own efforts, procured the means of an education, and not a few of them for the sake of learning, denying themselves, what most would consider the necessaries of life."

Most of the earliest students lived with Bloomington families, becoming temporary members of their adopted households. Those who found lodging in the limited facilities of the seminary accepted the *pater familias* of the president and his Eastern wife. For many years students gathered their own firewood, molded candles, did their laundry, made their beds, and sometimes grew their vegetables. For about a half century cost of board ranged from $1.50 to $3.00 a week. On one occasion Andrew Wylie announced in the catalogue that an industrious boy could make do on even less money.

In the classrooms Hall, and then Harney, treated their charges like children. They set a stern pattern of decorum which was not changed appreciably until the administration of David Starr Jordan. As much emphasis was placed upon discipline as upon learning, and both required constant humdrum drill. Backwoods lads arrived in Bloomington with one set of social mores, and the seminary professors had another. Throughout the university's early history the faculty dealt with such disciplinary lapses as drinking, uttering profane oaths, drawing pocket knives in anger, fighting, threats of duels, insubordination, pranks, and general rowdiness.

Everybody from Baynard Rush Hall in the beginning to William Lowe Bryan in the twentieth century considered one of the major institutional functions to be that of turning a raw natural and nearly illiterate human resource into learned gentlemen who were as conversant with Claudius, Virgil, Cicero, and Cincinnatus as with Jonathan Jennings, William Henry Harrison, George Rogers Clark, and Anthony Wayne. It was expected from the outset that the institution's students would quickly take positions of leadership, and they could not be permitted to betray this trust in their formative years. Out of the first ten, three became lawyers, two doctors, three became ministers, and one each was tanner and merchant.

Employment of John Hopkins Harney in 1827 gave breadth to the curriculum. Mathematics had about as much practical meaning in the New West as any subject which could have been taught. This academic expansion, however, hardly had a chance to prove itself before the arrival of Andrew Wylie in 1829, and, no doubt, with the Yale University blueprint for American classical education.

One of Wylie's most pronounced intellectual fixations was his belief that college discipline should be that of a strict Presbyterian home. Repeatedly in the catalogues, and in his annual reports to the Indiana Legislature, he insisted, "The society of a college ought to be a family, in which the Faculty is the parent, and the pupils the children—of different tempers and attainments, and therefore to be treated differently, but all under the same kind and paternal government. And those who cannot be governed in this way, it would be wrong to educate, if it were possible." Earlier the president had written in a most positive vein, "I would not be understood as supposing that a case can ever arise in the government of a college, wherein it would be proper for the teacher to *consult* his pupils, or seek their advice as to his measures: for this would be the utter subversion of his authority."

A decade later Andrew Wylie had come to appreciate more fully the streak of independence in Hoosier youth. "It may, however, be remarked," he wrote, "that the students [of Indiana] are in a generation of more mature years, than those of colleges in the older states. It is not infrequently that ministers of the gospel are found in the classes of the University." This latter fact was to cause grief because many narrow sectarians conceived the primary objective of the university to be the training of ministers, and often for their own particular sect.

For a century Indiana was to be an institution most sensitive to the place of religion in American life. The first six presidents were ministers, and so were a majority of the professors. Throughout most of the nineteenth century students were hourly made conscious of the subject. Some classes even were begun with prayers.

But the moral atmosphere of Bloomington was not entirely wholesome and pious. There existed in the town several saloons or "doggeries," as they were called in the new West, and occasionally students yielded to temptation and visited these places. From time to time a prostitute would appear on the scene. As small and gossipy as the town was, wayward lads who accepted such hospitality were almost certain to be found out and placed in jeopardy. W. Barkman, for instance, was brought before his mentors and charged with having visited a disreputable house to witness some unusual dancing. A Julia Hughes had invited him to come back and suggested he bring along his friends. On a second visit there were three boys in the party. The faculty dismissed one of them and suspended the other two, and Barkman was sentenced *in absentia* because he had fled to Gosport to avoid testifying against the gracious Julia.

In the same faculty session W. Norton was charged with attending an Irish wedding where liquor flowed as freely as the waters of Shannon. He admitted he was present at the wedding and had imbibed the joyful emotional spirit of the occasion, but he neither drank nor was disorderly. He was accompanied by Mrs. Snodgrass and Miss Buskirk. What disturbed the faculty, however, was the fact that the celebration had been held in W. Mone-han's saloon.

Perhaps student indiscretions of this sort, said the faculty, grew out of the fact that parents were too generous in the amounts of money they gave their children. Not all the exploitation of students, Andrew Wylie told legislators, was by saloon keepers and lewd women. There were sharks among Bloomington businessmen who preyed upon students. They took advantage of the "indiscretions of the generous, the confiding, the inexperienced." This in the president's mind was one of the reasons why the student body dwindled in the early 1840's. Repeatedly the president published the suggestion that parents be frugal with the money they gave their sons. If they felt compelled to send along money then it should be deposited with some responsible person in the town who would dole it out as it was needed to pay college bills.

So long as students could be kept on the campus they could be reasonably well controlled. Under his watchful eye, Wylie told legislators, the students could not waste their time on *tricks*. In this the president was perhaps not fully informed. He must have contemplated this when devilish boys stole the laboratory skeleton from the university closet and drove it seated in a sleigh through the town in a snow storm. This incident greatly incensed townsmen. If the youths were not defying the clutches of death in their macabre sleigh ride, they aggravated local citizens by milking their range cows, they whooped and hollered in the streets, and even got into knife-drawing altercations in the churches.

Drinking liquor was anathema in the university, and remained so for generations to come, but there was less objection to the use of tobacco. Students chewed tobacco and smoked cigars and pipes. These were almost universal habits among American backwoodsmen. As late as 1867 the first editor of the Indiana *Student* complained about the "companions of the tobacco *worm*" who spat in the wood boxes in the classrooms. He said every time the professors turned their heads boys spat into what they thought were obscure nooks. "We have heard it said, that the monkey and goat chew tobacco, but it would detract from their decency and cleanliness, as animals, to compare them with these fellows, who, as they enter the recitation rooms, can be seen to shoot for the wood-box or some corner of the room. Afraid to spit their tobacco saliva where the professor will see it. . . ." He even accused the "worms" of expectorating in the chapel. The editor, signing himself "Reformer," said he thought persons visiting the university would conclude "there are no rules prohibiting the use of tobacco, or if there are, they are not enforced. There are rules for this purpose, but it is not possible that the faculty can keep a strict watch for tobacco chewers all the time." He flung a final self-righteous stone at the tobacco addicts, "keep up the practice of chewing, & by-the-by, every young lady in Bloomington will fall in love with their *juicy lips & sweet perfumed breaths!*"

During the first century of the university the Board of Trustees and faculty exhibited a nagging concern over attracting students to the institution. Their records have a thread of fear running through them on this subject. The university's isolation and the extremely primitive conditions of roads and travel facilities were serious drawbacks. Bloomington was not only land- and forest-locked, it was not located on a main inland trail or road, nor did it have immediate prospects of ever being so located. Nearly every early traveler to Indiana mentioned being in New Albany, Jeffersonville, Washington, Vincennes, Madison, and Gosport, but not one of the better known visitors seems to have reached Bloomington. A trail, and later a road, led southward to Paoli and eastward to New Albany and the Falls of the Ohio, another came by way of Salem, Uniontown, Columbus, Nashville, and Bloomington.

Students during the earliest years came on foot or on horseback. D. D. Banta described Austin Shipp's journey on foot from Johnson County by way of Columbus. He carried a bundle mounted on a stick and foraged for his food and lodging along the way. One account describes two students coming from the Ohio River country on a single horse by following frontier practice of "ride and tie." One boy rode for awhile, then hitched the horse and walked on, while the other caught up and rode until he passed the walker and hitched the horse. William McKee Dunn described his journey to college riding behind his father on a single horse. It took them two days to make the trip from Crawfordsville through almost unbroken wilderness between that town and Greencastle. There may have been a few stages in operation in the earlier years, but this service was severely limited and erratic. After 1854 rail connections were opened. Until the outbreak of the Civil War, Indiana University students brought almost no luggage to Bloomington. The earliest ones brought no trunks, suitcases, or other types of baggage. The clothes on a boy's back with a change of shirts and socks tied in a bundle just about comprised his wardrobe. Students no doubt bought in the town such other bare necessities as they needed to make themselves presentable. Certainly not until the late forties was the Indiana college man conscious that he was more than a frontiersman seeking an education on the plainest possible personal terms. Clothing was a necessity of comfort and modesty, not an adornment. Its very plainness was a badge of Jeffersonian-Jacksonian-frontier democracy. Townsmen and professors were dressed little if any differently. Andrew Wylie appears to have been the best dressed man of his day in Bloomington, maybe in Indiana.

Once stagecoaches began operating from the Falls of the Ohio, the university had greater appeal for out-of-state students. A stagecoach line was begun in 1835 that operated on a regular schedule between Louisville and Bloomington. Early advertisements of the institution gave specific directions on how to reach Bloomington, but even the most satisfactory route required two to four days of travel from the river and steamboat connections under favorable conditions. Students underwent the hardships of travel to come from other states to Indiana. Virginia, Kentucky, Tennessee, Ohio, Mississippi, South Carolina, Pennsylvania, and Illinois were represented in the early student bodies. When Andrew Wylie came from Pennsylvania he had brought along several Pennsylvanians who elicited a bit of animosity from the Hoosiers. They branded "Wylie's men" foreigners and implied they were undesirables. Nevertheless university newspaper advertisements continually sought enrollment from other states. The president announced in the catalogue of 1845 that the railroad had been completed between Madison and Columbus. Students could come by steamboat to Madison, by train to Columbus, and by stage from Columbus to Bloomington once a week.

In his annual legislative report in 1848, David H. Maxwell made a brief analysis of the number of Hoosiers attending college. He found that one hundred of them went to other states, while twenty to thirty outsiders came to Indiana University. In every graduating class until 1860 there were several representatives from the southern states. It was believed necessary to attract these "foreigners" in order to keep enrollment up. On occasions the Board of Trustees instructed the president to advertise the university in the Louisville and other Ohio and Mississippi valley newspapers in a search for more students.

In the early advertisements university officials undertook to capitalize on the healthful location of Bloomington. It was, they said, well back from the river and poisonous swamp miasma or recurring fever epidemics. Students would find a rapidly growing town. Some years it doubled in size; for instance, in 1844 it had a population of 1,300 persons. It was populated by virtuous democratic people who looked cheerfully to the future. There were no appreciable vices in the community and few saloons.

The promoters of a stage line in the *Indiana Journal* of May 15, 1835, advertised the university in glowing terms. "No institution in the United States," they said, "can be better situated than this. It is on a high, healthy and rich tableland, with a President and Faculty eminently qualified. At this college tuition can be procured at $15.00 per annum—board at $1.25 per week & all expenses, except clothing do not exceed $75.00 a year."

They further emphasized that Indiana University enjoyed the bucolic pleasures of isolation, and said "here, in this delightful and retired situation, the student must enjoy the full fruition of thought & reflection. The Society of the town; the cheapness of the board & tuition & the rising celebrity of the college, all unite in making Bloomington not only a pleasant retreat, but especially interesting to the enquirer after moral and scientific education." Maybe Bloomington and Indiana University were all the things Wylie claimed for them, but the town still was hard to reach, and remained the butt of many student jokes. This continued to be true even after the coming of the New Albany and Salem Railroad in 1854. Since 1835 David H. Maxwell had promoted the railroad idea, and the arrival of the first passenger train was the realization of his dreams.

In 1828 David H. Maxwell had taken pains to assure Andrew Wylie that the town was located on a healthy site. What he did not say, however, was that at long periods during summer and fall the land became semi-arid and its stone underlay prevented the digging of satisfactory wells or the finding of water. The university from the date of its opening lacked a dependable water supply and had no immediate means to remedy this situation. So long as the student body was small and the flow of the nearby spring was fairly adequate, there was water. Trees, however, were removed from the campus and the balance of nature was seriously upset with the result that the vein faltered and the water became polluted. This proved to be one of the university's sorest physical problems for more than a century of its history.

The great majority of early students came from middle and lower middle class homes. This by no means implied they were strangers to the bath. Early they requested that the university provide them either with crude tubs or a shower for their weekly use. The bathing problem was not solved until well into this century. The editor of the Indiana *Student* in January, 1868, observed,

Now as it is impossible for each student to have a private bathing room, it is to the public bathing house that we call attention of the board of officers connected with the University & the medical men of the town who have the care of students & welfare of the community at heart. We do not ask for a magnificent structure such as those spoken of in ancient history, but one of convenience only. Let it be established in a place where there is plenty of fresh water. There is a very large cistern of water connected with the University, & no use is made of it, except a small portion for experimental purposes. There is also a room joining the laboratory room that might be used for the bath room. . . .

A problem related to that of the water supply was the eternal one of providing decent and bearable sanitary facilities. From 1825 until the first decade of the twentieth century the university's personnel depended upon enlarged versions of a crude backwoods privy. Board minutes reveal that the trustees often had to deal with this issue. In 1838 a committee was instructed to remove the facility to a new location, plant trees and shrubs about it, and gravel its walkway. There can be little doubt that failure to deal with this problem properly imperiled the institution with a deadly threat of ill health.

All the boasting about Bloomington's healthfulness could not erase the fact that there were recurrent outbreaks of typhoid, smallpox, and other epidemic diseases prior to 1910. In fact in 1910 a major fright was caused by an outbreak of typhoid fever.

As described elsewhere the great cholera epidemics of 1833, 1849, and 1851 reached Bloomington. The one in 1833 struck with deathlike suddenness, but there was forewarning of a possible outbreak of the disease in 1849. On January 13 of that year the editor of the *Indiana Tribune and Monroe Farmer* said that cholera was sweeping the towns of the lower Mississippi Valley. Bloomington should prepare itself for another outbreak. He advocated cleaning the streets, alleys, and cellars, and removing every other infectious nuisance. After this had been done the community should await the appearance of the scourge with composure. The anxieties of these moments were reflected in faculty and board minutes. With regularity, the secretary of the faculty recorded the absences of professors who were at home either because of personal illness or illness in their families.

The *Tribune and Farmer* editor was not content to sound an editorial warning, he sought additional alleviating measures that would spare the town a cholera epidemic. He read in the London *Lancet* an article which advocated removal of every cesspool, pig sty, slaughterhouse, and "domestic nuisance." The British editor suggested other preventives including the removal of all partitions from houses, and a process of cleaning and fumigating that practically destroyed the rest of the buildings. The Hoosier editor declared, these are "so excellent, and address themselves so directly to the common sense of every man, that I think they cannot fail to produce a beneficial result." There are, however, no published descriptions of gutted houses in subsequent issues of the paper.

Although Bloomington citizens were hospitable in accepting students into their homes as boarders, public boarding presented some fundamental problems to faculty and students alike. The faculty could not exercise as full and strict disciplinary control over the boys as it wished. On the other hand boarding house families undertook to exercise too much discipline at times. A special Board of Trustees report in 1830 described this aspect of university life. Lodging, said the trustees, was the most expensive item involved in attending the university. By instituting a boarding program for the school this expense could be reduced to between fifty and sixty-two and a half cents per week. The trend in many

American colleges was away from dependence on private lodging to the establishment of boarding clubs under university jurisdiction. Before Indiana University students could enjoy such an advantage, however, the institution would have to erect a boarding-house on the campus. This idea no doubt was promoted enthusiastically by Andrew Wylie because this was the only way by which he could apply fully his philosophy of parental discipline.

After almost a decade of discussing the housing problem, the Board of Trustees finally authorized the construction of a university boarding house. Board of Trustees minutes seem to indicate that on September 27, 1838, the structure was ready for occupation and had cost $3,147. University officials would oversee the operation of the house, but students were to bear the expenses. William Russell was employed as proctor and caretaker. He was to keep the building in repair, maintain order in the rooms, see that meals were prepared, and in his spare time work on the university grounds. In turn students kept their rooms cleaned, worked in the boarding house vegetable garden, supplied their firewood and candles, and did kitchen chores. This accounted in large part for the extremely low prices of board. The university boarding was from $.50 to $1.00 cheaper than in the town.

A decade after the boardinghouse was opened Andrew Wylie reported to the legislature that the entire building and three additional rooms were used by the boarding club. He said that the $1.50 a week cost was half of the amount paid for board in the town, and maybe the fare was better. Something of this question was revealed years later when a student wrote, "Hash—This excellent article of diet is extensively used at some of the boarding houses of this place. It is a good thing for three or four hundred meals, but as a constant diet it isn't so good."

John H. Ketcham estimated as late as the 1850's that university students were paying only one to two and a half dollars for board per week, and a minimum amount in addition for laundry. These were the figures which both Wylie and Daily reported in the catalogue from 1829 to 1859. The boarding house had helped to keep prices in town at a modest level. This institution does not present a very pretentious appearance in the surviving pictures of it, but in 1838 it was considered a "rather large building" with dining rooms, a kitchen and bedrooms on the first floor, and cubicles or bedrooms on the upper floor. Ketcham said the rooms were cheaply furnished by students and they presented an austere and frugal appearance. So long as it set a good table the house enjoyed a good patronage. In spite of the quality of the fare and the cheapness of the price, however, the boys complained.

Maybe the boarding house rules were far too strict for some of the free ranging lads who gathered in from the Indiana countryside. They were bound not to swear, drink, gamble, or to engage in any sort of misconduct. They were to remember at all times that they were "Father" Andrew's children, and as such they were supposed to think intellectually on all subjects, even while hoeing the cabbages in the garden.

Whatever else the student did he was to remember that one of the major objectives of the university was to cultivate the moral and religious man. Every school day opened with chapel exercises at 8:00 or 8:30 in the morning. In chapel the president read a passage of scripture and offered up a prayer. There was singing accompanied by some kind of musical instrument, possibly an old fashioned melodeon. Once the songs and scriptures were concluded the president turned to the everyday affairs of the university. He made announcements, delivered homilies on the mission of man in the universe, and censured recalcitrant students who had run afoul of faculty rules or city ordinances. Some of these sessions were little more than oral castigations of students. The most vivid memories many Indiana University graduates took away from Bloomington was of the boring chapel exercises. The chapel itself was an unadorned room located in the main building. In the forepart was a small stage large enough to seat the faculty and a lecturer, and the rest of the room was crowded with stage tavern or hitchcock benches with rigid upright backs and hard board seats. Each unit seated six boys, and sometimes it took some scrounging to accomplish this with larger lads. There was not really a comfortable seat in the whole main body of the chapel. In 1836 when the new chapel was ready for use it was located on the first floor on the west side of the new academic building. Later it was moved to the third floor, and after 1856 it was on the second floor of the building constructed after the fire. This latter room was practically as described above except that it was well lighted by several windows, and adorned by elegant gaslight chandeliers.

The Board of Trustees felt that six days' chapel exercises were not enough to serve the spiritual needs of the students. On Sunday afternoons the president again read the scriptures and preached a lengthy sermon. The latter was often the subject of an editorial or news story in the next issue of the Bloomington paper. Often Wylie irritated his fellow preachers because he took the occasion in the Sunday services to comment on their sermons, and sometimes to refute their statements. Andrew Wylie and his five preacher successors took the Sunday afternoon assemblies most seriously. Students, however, could pass up the service if they had attended a church of their parents' choice that morning.

For many students the tremendous emphasis on religious exercises proved uninspiring, and frequently they revealed this fact by committing indignities in the sanctum. Attendance was mandatory and was checked by professors calling the roll. The rule was that students should be inside the room by the last tap of the bell, at which time the janitor was instructed to lock the door to keep out the laggards. The janitor, however, often favored the boys, and tolled the bell slowly to allow the hindmost to get in their seats on time. Occasionally a lad arrived after the doors were locked, and he either had to sneak in through a window or go away in trouble. Sometimes a lad answered the roll from the outside.

In 1871 W. F. McDonald was charged in a faculty meeting with having disturbed worship by clambering over the windowsill. He explained that he was anxious to hear the lecture and he had committed this unseemly act on an impulse. Because he had not premeditated his misbehavior the faculty gave him a sentence of three months on probation. The Jenckses were not to be outdone by a McDonald, and Joseph Jencks reached the star-chamber for causing disorder in the chapel when he answered roll call by reciting a Latin sentence. This case was difficult for faculty members to handle because of the emphasis the university put on the classics. Nevertheless they rapped the boy's knuckles in a public censure.

The faculty prosecuted many cases of improper chapel behavior. W. Palmer was charged with appearing in chapel under the influence of liquor, lying down on the bench during the songs, and sitting during prayers. He was further accused of having his knife open, and laughing while Dr. Nutt prayed. Nearby W. Shannon had stuck a pin in a lad during prayers, and he also had his knife open. W. D. W. Browning on another occasion was brought before the faculty for misbehaving in chapel. He had also committed a gross indiscretion in the classroom. When called on to go to the blackboard to inscribe a part of the Latin assignment he drew a comical picture and placed Professor Atwater's name under it, and then shouted a lusty Anglo-Saxon epithet at the professor when he was reprimanded.

During a cold spell in March, 1863, W. L. Prather and an unnamed band of confederates removed the pipes from the chapel stove, then put in a charge of wood. Acrid smoke filled the room and broke up chapel all right, but Prather must have questioned his act as a means of gaining respite from President Nutt's long prayers and the daily tongue-lashing of fellow students. He found himself before the angry faculty being quizzed about his misdeeds. He was foggy about his role in the stove pipe incident. He seemed to be able to recall in a vague way that he had said something about putting wood in the pipeless stove. He admitted lunging against the chapel door with his shoulder and then rapping noisily, but he said it took this to attract President Nutt's attention. He had no knowledge of sassing the president when he did come to the door. Prather blandly assured the faculty he believed his actions were correct, and in all honesty he could not promise to do better in the future. He was unsure about what self-incriminatory commitments he might have to make. Prather tried the patience of the faculty so much, and was so honest in his blunt answers, that his case was dismissed. The faculty no doubt realized that the decorous scholars who arrived on time at the chapel wrote letters, read textbooks, slept, and sang in painful discord. Amid the scrounging and twisting on the hard seats, the boys' tempers flared and occasionally the offended ones drew their pocket knives and swore.

One of the most vexatious of all chapel antics was that committed in March, 1873, by W. E. Maxwell, who became bored by the lengthy oratory during the law commencement, so broke the tedium by sowing handfuls of beans and birdshot over the audience. He offended further by bringing a dog to chapel, and he would not remove it when commanded to do so. The faculty revised his deportment record and barred him from public performances. To faculty and parents this dastardly act was almost akin to stabling a range cow in the chapel.

The faculty was faced with two disciplinary problems it did not know quite how to solve. At the Sunday chapel services town and country boys came in and created a din. University students added to this vexation by loud and unnecessarily long clapping after even the dullest speaker had finished.

The chapel bell was a local clarion. It heralded the rising hour of the day, meals, chapel, and opening of classes. For many students it was a heartless tyrant that reminded them of their moral and intellectual omissions. It drove them relentlessly through the university's weekly and annual calendar. This trusted sentinel had to be given the utmost protection lest it disappear. Its rope was in constant peril. The janitor reported on February 25, 1859, that he could not perform his official function because someone had slipped through the Philomathean Literary Society Hall and had cut the golden cord. Neither janitor nor faculty were able to spot the culprit, but they found themselves in a dispute with the wronged Philomatheans, whose righteous indignation had to be assuaged. They were especially angry because the faculty ordered their door to be bolted. This caused strained relations between the two groups for several weeks.

Just before the Christmas holidays in 1867 the editor of the Indiana *Student* commented on the chapel bell's weird tone. He discovered the clapper had been stolen and the janitor was beating the bell with a hammer. "This is an outrage," said the editor, "that has not been committed for some time, and we hope we shall not hear of it again. We cannot believe that any of the students who are attending college at present, would be guilty of such a *low* deed. The person who did this surely has sunk to the nadir of meanness, & there is nothing too low which he could not pander." Editorial scolding and faculty grilling accomplished nothing. The clapper was still missing and no one had clue enough even to fix a suspicion on the lowdown thief. The faculty arraigned a number of prime suspects but their inquisition produced neither evidence nor bell clapper. Perhaps the thief remained in seclusion pondering his next foul deed.

In 1871 Colonel James Thompson, a military-religious fanatic, felt the routine of the campus should be militarized and he worked out a scheme of bell ringing similar to barracks bugle calls. The first bells, or matins, were to be rung at five minutes to eight and at

8:25 A.M. Throughout the rest of the day the janitor was required to be as precise as his tricky old watch would allow. But neither the faculty nor the officious Colonel Thompson could outwit ingenious Hoosier youth. They were always ready with a new trick to disrupt chapel exercises. These ranged from hiding a rooster in the president's pulpit to pinching, scrounging, and giggling, and outright rebellion.

Use of the chapel was a constant problem for board and faculty. Local denominational groups wished to use it for purposes of their own. On July 20, 1841, the Board relaxed its rules and provided that the chapel would be opened on Sundays, "to the reception of ministers of every denomination of Christians & their congregations on the Sabbath for the purpose of worshipping God." Until that time Andrew Wylie had decided who could use the auditorium and for what purposes, but he was criticized by the local ministers, who feared that the university would become little more than a Presbyterian seminary. When ministers were not tugging at the president, the temperance crusaders pursued him. They sought use of the chapel and student body to convey their militant messages. From 1835 to approximately 1890, Demon Rum was pounded to a pulp almost monthly in the university's chapel. The crusaders appeared to believe that the school was a training ground for "faces on the barroom floor." They had no opportunity to read the faculty minutes to learn otherwise.

Ministers sometimes took the occasion to criticize the university for not training more preachers. In August, 1849, Andrew Wylie gathered that the Reverend Levi Hughes had expressed such a notion from his pulpit. He took occasion in chapel to refute him. He quoted Hughes as saying there were forty students in law while there were only two interested in the ministry, and they were Presbyterians. In a long newspaper reply Hughes denied that he was author of the statement about the forty candidates in law and only two for the ministry. Neverthless he expressed the attitude of many ministers in Indiana.

As student enrollment increased and some changes occurred in the university, maintaining a rigorous program of compulsory religious activities became more difficult. In 1886 the Board of Trustees sensed these changes in attitudes and reluctantly began to moderate their stand on chapel attendance. They made the

Sunday services optional, however, the board minutes are confusing as to regular morning chapel exercises. It appears that there was at least a single semester in which notices and announcements were posted on bulletin boards and chapel attendance was optional with the students. Attendance under this system, David Starr Jordan told the board in 1888, was actually better, but in November, 1890 the board proceeded to enact a new compulsory attendance rule. By 1891, however, John M. Coulter reported that out of 355 students 189 remained away from chapel for one reason or another. By that time the whole tenor of American student life had undergone fundamental changes, and so had the religious attitudes of large numbers of Americans.

The main objective the student had in coming to Indiana University was to receive adequate training in the institution's classrooms. Some mention has already been made of the general university curriculum and special courses. From the students' perspective the catalogue outline of material to be covered in four years seemed most formidable. In 1841 Andrew Wylie said in his special report to the state legislators that the college was no more than a grammar school when he came in 1829. He could well have added that it was little more in that trying year, 1840, when all sorts of difficulties confronted it. The old *Yale Report* formula had been followed religiously. Some one, maybe Andrew Wylie, noted in contemporary handwriting in a copy of the 1838–39 catalogue when there were only three professors, "a college must be made up of three persons at least." Out of the eighty-nine students the catalogue claimed were enrolled, twenty-seven were students in the preparatory school, and six were "irregulars." The latter term meant students who were not taking the full classics course by special permission of the faculty.

Until the time the university issued lists of certified high schools in 1874, students were admitted to the university on three or four bases. Any student who presented himself on opening day could be admitted to college classes by passing satisfactory examinations in Latin, Greek, and mathematics. If he failed these tests he had to enter the preparatory school and take up to two years of classes. If he came from another college and could produce a certificate of satisfactory work done he was admitted. Occasionally a mature minister of the gospel was admitted to classes on the basis of his experience. It was not until the opening of the spring term of 1864 that the faculty authorized the president to purchase a permanent "matriculation book."

It was difficult for the earlier university board and faculty to make up their minds about the proper arrangement of terms. Possibly there was some consideration of the farming cycles in the early university, and there appeared some mention in early board and faculty minutes of this fact. Also, there was not always a full registration in semesters in which boys had to remain at home to help their families. Indiana College in 1828 began its first or winter term on December 1, 1829, and closed it the latter part of April. The second term opened on June 1 and closed the last week of September. In 1837–38 classes began on the first Monday of November and closed the last Wednesday in March. The second term began the first Monday in May and ended with commencement in the last week of September. October and April were vacation months. In 1851–52, the first year after Andrew Wylie's death, the academic year was divided into three terms. The fall session opened seven weeks after the first Wednesday in August and closed on December 24; the winter term began January 2 and closed the first Wednesday in April; the summer term began early in May and closed the first Wednesday of August.

Students were required to attend classes three hours a day, six days a week. The schedule of classes was preset for them, and only under extraordinary circumstances could a student change his schedule. To be absent from a boring class was to court sharp censure if not disaster. Until David Starr Jordan assumed the presidency the university was almost solely a morning school, with classes held at nine, ten, and eleven o'clock. After the morning's classes professors were free to pursue their own affairs. Except for Andrew Wylie and Richard Owen, there exists no real evidence that faculty members did research and writing. Some of them were ministers and worked at that task. Some were in demand to give public lectures. At the beginning of each term the faculty met and the president produced a simple handwritten class chart which showed hours that each man was to meet his classes. The schedule was not made until immediately before the meeting, but since student courses were set there were no conflicts. It was not until 1860 that a published copy of the semester schedule appeared in the catalogue.

The students' scholarly habits are almost impossible to document. Much was said about this in general terms in faculty minutes, but when did they study and under what conditions? Basically the professor assigned at the outset a portion of the classics for each semester and the student recited on a portion of the assignment at every class meeting. He did outside written work only in the years he took English composition, and then he prepared a composition every ten days.

Classroom procedures in most of the courses were rigidly set by the faculty. Students stood when called upon and recited verbatim from the text. Any deviation, snickering, argumentation, or mumbling resulted in a low grade, accumulation of demerits, and sometimes a tongue-lashing from the professor. The faculty approached the classroom with funereal seriousness, and any slight to their dignity was quickly resented. The professor himself adhered to a rule of rote, and sometimes students were critical when he allowed other students to go beyond the prescribed text. On one occasion the faculty spent four days quizzing witnesses over a dispute that arose between J. W. Jefferson, a student, and the eccentric Hermann B. Boisen over the translation of a Latin sentence in class. Boisen ordered Jefferson from the room but he refused to go. In the argument he called the professor an "old man." The faculty censured the student for his behavior and instructed him that henceforth he should cease wasting classtime by asking questions. Occasionally a professor lectured to his classes. This was especially true in philosophy, logic, history, political economy, the Constitution of the United States, and evidence of Christianity. This privilege of free range was reserved largely to the sage Andrew Wylie and his successors.

In mathematics, physics, chemistry, natural philosophy, and astronomy the professors often performed the experiments or demonstrated to classes the principles they wished to communicate. In mathematics, physics, and chemistry, students placed problem solutions on blackboards and signed their names underneath.

Faculty minutes reveal how jealous the early professors were of their prerogatives and dignity. Some of the charges they made against students reveal clearly the boring nature of their classroom procedures. Nevertheless, they worked at William Daily's stated objective of 1854 to achieve in the student "the development of intellectual and moral faculties, and correct habits of thought and study."

Every day a student was enrolled in the university he came under the tyranny of the professorial record books. He began the day by answering the roll call in chapel, he had to answer three more times that day in class, and on special occasions he was asked to give an account of himself. Professors kept a merit check on deportment, and in 1853 the Board of Trustees adopted a resolution that deportment reports should be sent to parents at the end of each term.

Grade records were kept in several forms. Apparently the earliest scale ranged from 1 to 10. Sometime after the Civil War the scale was increased from 1 to 100. Because registries were destroyed in the university fires it is impossible to determine precisely what system was used and at what given time. The catalogues are silent on this question. Examinations varied. Professors at times seemed to use oral examinations; sometimes they exchanged classes to be examined with each other; sometimes a small committee did the examining. Seniors submitted to a comprehensive examination at the end of their final semester. This continued to be true until the 1880's. The Board of Trustees was the official examining body. These final examinations were public affairs to which all the intellectuals of the community were invited, and the general results were published in the local newspaper.

On December 24, 1878, the faculty recommended that the system of awarding class honors be dropped and a new grading system adopted. Boisen, Atwater, and Clark were given the responsibility of designing a new system. A month later they suggested use of the designations "excellent," "good," and "satisfactory." If a student was down in deportment he was not to be awarded a grade of "excellent" no matter what his grades were. Four days later they recommended that by secret ballot of the faculty the best students be declared to be "graduated with honor" or "graduated with high honor." Use of these terms and the general grade designation was voted down by the faculty, and the numerical scale was continued.

Rules governing classroom examinations were changed on May 10, 1884. Examinations were to be oral in part, and questions to be worded in such a manner as to preclude ponies or English translations. Groups were not to exceed twelve or fifteen, and seats were to be arranged alternately. Each examiner was to have an assistant. There was to be no communication of any kind. The janitor stood by to pass out paper, and only university paper was permissible.

The faculty were assiduous record-keepers. In some periods the principal business of many faculty meetings was to compare roll books. By the time a student had attended four years of classes his professors knew him better than his own father and mother. Completion of work leading to a degree depended upon classroom responses, a student's behavior, and even a periodic appraisal of his moral character.

Down through the Civil War and Reconstruction years courses leading to a bachelor of arts degree were set forth in precise detail in the annual catalogues. To deviate from this schedule required considerable faculty discussion and voting. Before 1852 only minor changes were made in the stated curriculum. These changes were most often additions to the original classics requirement. The most important departures resulted in the addition of what were considered, if not so classified, scientific courses. At first students enrolling in the scientific curriculum were granted a certificate instead of a degree. In 1854 courses were instituted to anticipate an agricultural science program. The agriculture curriculum was similar to other outlines. The student farmer was required to take natural philosophy, organic and inorganic chemistry, vegetable and animal economy, growth of plants, mineralogy and geology, and analysis of soils, marls, and manures. Electives were permitted in Hebrew, Spanish, and French but these were offered for information rather than credit.

The annual catalogue issued in 1851, the year of the revision of the state constitution, divided the five areas of academic emphasis into as many departments. These included moral philosophy, natural philosophy and chemistry, languages, mathematics, and law. These divisions were used more to categorize learning than to establish disciplinary departments for academic administration. A decade earlier, in 1841, the board and faculty revised Andrew Wylie's basic philosophy that students should concentrate on a single topic at a time. After this date the general areas outlined were considered of coordinate importance, and courses in these areas were offered concurrently.

In 1851, following the enactment of the new charter for the university, a normal school curriculum appeared in the catalogue. It consisted of the theory and practice of teaching, reading, elocution, writing, linear drawing, mental and written arithmetic, bookkeeping, geography, English grammar and composition, surveying, history, vocal music, and didactics. This broad course of studies also led to the granting of a certificate rather than a degree and quickly became popular with students. The addition laid the foundation for the university's later boast that it had trained more college presidents than any other school.

After the death of Andrew Wylie and the slight revision in the legislative mandate, the demands of the Indiana student emerge somewhat more clearly in the instructional program. Perhaps this reflected the impact of changing times in the nation itself more than actual internal pressures for revision of the university's narrow instructional program. Older concepts of American education were being challenged, and American colleges were moving further away from the traditional English public school or academy approach to education.

There appeared in the catalogue of 1840, in the student classification column, three categories, "regular," "irregular," and "preparatory." Years later the "irregular" courses were formulated into a scientific curriculum, and the first roster of students in this area appeared in the catalogue in 1841. The bachelor of science degree was first granted in 1855, at which time four seniors received degrees. The 1841 university catalogue stated, "The principles of science and literature are the common basis of all high intellectual attainments. They supply that furniture, and discipline, and elevation of the mind, which are the best aids in the study of any profession." This was the first major break with the revered British grammar school tradition. William Daily wrote in the catalogue of 1855, "This title [bachelor of science] borrowed from French Colleges, has already been introduced into the Lawrence Scientific School of Harvard, to mark the graduation of a similar class of students."

It was not until 1860, however, that the science curriculum was lifted onto an even plane with that of the bachelor of arts program. Under this new classification the academic programs were listed as "regular" and scientific. By 1868 the scientific course was lengthened to four years, and the full-time students in this course were given freedom of choice between the classical and modern languages. This liberalization led further to the freedom of choice of electives instituted by David Starr Jordan in 1885.

Frankly, the academic course work in the university was often pedantic, dull, and uninspiring. Bright youthful minds sometimes cloyed on the mundane procedures, and had it not been for the fact that other activities in student life compensated for the three daily hours of imprisonment plodding through Homer, Horace, Ovid, and Cicero, there would have been an even more limited enrollment. Almost from the opening of the first classes there existed a literary society. Baynard Rush Hall encouraged his students to organize the Henodelphisterian Society. By 1830 this organization had disappeared and in its place were organized the Athenian Society and the rival Philomathean Society, which was chartered by the remaining members of the Henodelphisterian Society. The Athenian Society had nine original members, three of whom had come west in the "Pennsylvania migration." The literary societies in the first three-quarters of the nineteenth century were as necessary institutional adjuncts as sports and fraternities came to be in the twentieth century. Down to 1890 the societies had at least three major objectives. The Henodelphisterian emphasized classical interests; members even assumed Greek and Roman names. For the unsophisticated country students the literary organizations filled a social and intellectual void. Many a boy unleashed his tongue for the first time in a speech before a society. Too, the boys learned to express themselves in the written essays required of society members. These organizations were important training grounds for future Hoosier politicians, ministers, and barristers.

The university provided the two societies with club rooms equipped with a platform, a lectern, library, pictures, and society records. These organizations were chartered directly by the General Assembly. Society libraries in the earlier years perhaps offered more cultural benefits to their members than did the tightly supervised university library. It would perhaps not be too much of an exaggeration to say that many students even received more polish and self-assurance from the society meetings than from classroom exercises.

Literary society halls were regarded as secluded islands where members, within certain bounds, could cast off the parental tether of the faculty and feel free to express themselves. Since there were no intercollegiate sports or other forms of extra-university rivalry, members took an almost militant pride in their affiliations, and they guarded this independence with Jacksonian fierceness. Frequently issues arose between society members and the faculty, and, sometimes, between the societies and the Board of Trustees, as to who had ultimate control of the organizations. On one or two occasions these disputes brought up fundamental questions of freedom of speech within the university community itself.

In November, 1863, because of lingering sensitivities over the Prather stovepipe affair, a fight occurred in the Philomathean Hall in which the president of the society was hit over the head with a chair. This incident seems to have been caused immediately by violation of a rule of the society that all members would remove their shoes on entering the hall, not because they observed some Oriental custom, but because the campus was muddy and boots were nearly always smeared with dirt. The society did not wish to leave its carpet soiled. A recalcitrant member asserted his independence by keeping his boots on, and a scuffle occurred. Perhaps there had also been some pointed speaking and debating of the faculty's handling of the Prather case. At any rate Philomathean's speaker policies were dragged into conflict by the ever-meddlesome Board of Trustees. This issue was considered by the faculty and trustees as early as March, 1863. The trustees adopted resolutions ordering all literary society members to submit their speeches before delivery for inspection by the faculty. Too, the faculty was to approve all outside speakers whom the societies invited to address them on special occasions. The board's order was transmitted to the societies by Professor Daniel Kirkwood in a patronizing letter. He informed them that by refusing to comply they were being led inadvertently into error. He asked members to make an immediate response to the board's resolutions.

Both societies tabled the board's resolutions and refused to act. A year of faculty investigation and faculty-student argument followed. The faculty called society members before them one at a time and grilled them on their failure to act. The societies themselves held special and joint meetings in which the board's mandate was discussed, but these always ended by tabling the board's demand. On March 11, 1863, the Philomatheans met in defiance of the board's order. Professor James Woodburn was present as a faculty observer. Joseph G. McPheeters, a former member of the society, and later to be a member of the Board of Trustees, spoke for both societies. He declared that the organization had received the board's resolutions, had held joint sessions to discuss the issue, had resolved that they would hold no more public exhibitions and members would be expelled from membership if they submitted their speeches and essays for prior inspection. The audience was dismissed *sine die*.

Following the meeting described above, the societies contended they were beyond board and faculty control because they held charters directly from the legislature. They would go off the campus and find quarters; they would adjourn themselves indefinitely. In case the faculty and board did not back down they would organize new societies, would encourage the organization of a citizens' lyceum to which students could belong, and, if necessary, would take other extreme steps. On Friday, February 5, 1864, James F. Foster and a group of Athenian members did take such a step by breaking into the Athenian Hall. Foster and his raiders were prosecuted on charges of malicious trespass, forcible and unlawful entry, and riot. The magistrate dismissed the case, however, when both parties agreed to a different resolution of the issues.

For a year the faculty discussed the literary society rebellion. Their minutes were filled with the records of hearings, letters, and resolutions. At no place did a professor contend that the students had a valid point in resisting the board's arbitrary denial of freedom of speech and writing. The president and professors took the side of the Board of Trustees unquestioningly and undertook to browbeat students into conforming. They even went so far as to suspend six members of the Philomathean Society until they would accept the terms of the board's resolutions. The Athenians backed down finally, but the Philomatheans stuck to their guns until everybody was worn out with the issue. With something akin to vengeance the Philomatheans invited the minister William Daily to be their fall commencement speaker. The faculty grudgingly accepted their choice but petulantly raised the question of honoring the board's speaker resolution. Perhaps the eloquent and suave Daily soothed both sides into a state of intellectual coma. Anyway, the speaker issue was dropped. This was Indiana University's first really important test of the principle of academic freedom.

When Sarah Parke Morrison was admitted to the university in 1867 she sought to participate fully in university life, which involved membership in a literary society. The men, however, held the line and refused to admit Miss Morrison to their masculine retreats. During the session of 1870–71 the Hesperian Society was organized for women. This organization was conducted along similar lines to the older men's societies. The girls declaimed, debated, and socialized in the same way as their brothers. James A. Woodburn described the visitation of a male spy who reported with some degree of amazement that the girls had minds and ideas of their own. Earlier there had existed in the Female Seminary the Neotrophian Society. The women's rights movement furnished impetus, topic, and brimstone for co-ed debaters down to the adoption of the constitutional amendment granting women the right to vote and hold office.

For approximately three-quarters of a century the literary societies formed a central part of student life at Indiana University. Youthful orators from 1825 on were ready and anxious to mount the speaker's platform on any occasion. They celebrated Washington's Birthday, the Fourth of July, the admission of Indiana to the Union, God, home, and mother. Their debates and essays covered the universe.

A strong spirit of rivalry developed between the Athenians and Philomatheans, and student loyalties rested as much with the societies as with the university. Many a budding politician came from these halls of eloquence to enthrall gaping Hoosier audiences in the campaign hustings, or to enliven court trials as much with their eloquence as with legal logic. These were the years in which the American eagle flew high and cast a broad shadow over an ever-widening domain. Often a university graduate was judged more by his oratorical powers than by the quality of his learning. One can imagine the young Hoosier Demosthenes, Theopompous Jones, rendering his soaring oratory as described in an Indiana *Student* satire. "When genius bows her crested head & stoops to wear a coronet," said Theopompous, "the world's intelligence laments. The jewels of an earthly crown are dust beside the living stars that shine upon the head of greatness. The tears of millions tarnish the lustrous fame of him who sways the sceptre, but paeans of applause make music in the ears of the patriotic hero." In a peroration concluding his address, a contemporary, Longinus Locke Tumbleson, concluded, "If ever we can grasp the awful immensity of this thought in all its mighty fullness, a new light will break in upon our benighted vision, all its ills will flee away, & the world will assume its garb of glorious & unending prosperity."

The age of Theopompous and Longinus, not the ills of man, passed. The rostrums of the literary societies were left to gather dust and memories. Indiana students, however, did not desert the lectern in numbers until David Starr Jordan departed to found Stanford University. In Jordan's day the orators competed in intercollegiate oratorical contests with the same zeal they had begun to demonstrate on the baseball diamond.

Essentially the literary societies had served the purpose of filling the social lives of students, and in this respect were forerunners of the Greek-letter fraternities. In 1837–38 Charles Henry Hardin, a native of Kentucky, entered Indiana University as a sophomore and remained until 1839. In the latter year he transferred to Miami University in Ohio, where he graduated in 1841. Hardin was initiated into Beta Theta Pi Greek-letter fraternity, which was organized in Miami on August 8, 1839. At that time there were six fraternities in existence, and Beta Theta Pi was the first one organized in the West. On August 17, 1845, Gavin Riley McMillan, a young South Carolinian, initiated Thomas Blake Graham of Dubois County; this marked the beginning of fraternities at Indiana. By 1870 there were four chapters on the campus. Phi Delta Theta was established in 1849, Sigma Chi in 1858, Phi Kappa Psi in 1869, and Kappa Alpha Theta in 1870. This marked the beginning of a new era in Indiana University history, in which many students developed a way of life within an organization but somewhat apart from that of the university. Fraternities by no means destroyed a student unity or common purpose. To a degree the Greek fraternities have perpetuated some of the activities of the literary societies down to the present.

So long as there remained the Board of Trustees and the faculty on one side of the generation line, the students on the other, there were issues in which there could be no meeting of minds. Andrew Wylie and his successors may have talked of the parental responsibilities of the faculty; students had other views. In their adolescent ways they occasionally struck back. At one graduation, in an oratorical contest, when there were ten faculty members, students were entrusted with the responsibilities of decorating the chapel. When the commencement audience assembled it was horrified to see hung up about the auditorium the drawings of ten jackasses. This also was the beginning of an era when malicious students quickly discovered the high nuisance value of anonymous publications, or boguses, as they were called. The first bogus was a commencement program which was thrown into the chapel door, and which conveyed confusing and idiotic information, and made naughty remarks about the participants in the program. In 1869 wounded gentlemen of the literary societies had a bogus program printed in Bloomfield. This bit of tomfoolery was printed at the office of the Bloomfield *Democrat*, and was also thrown into the chapel. The professors believed it was the handiwork of Toland Youche, who years later became a member of the Board of Trustees. Its main objective was to throw the Philomathean Society's program into chaos. The professors spent over six weeks in 1869 trying to identify the culprit but finally had to give up in defeat.

There appeared on the campus in March, 1873, a bogus paper called *The Dagger*. There were external indications that it had come from the Hesperian Literary Society, or from students who attended its "special." The paper made an appraisal of the faculty, many students, and possibly of the Board of Trustees. No one can be sure because no copy is known to survive. The Board of Trustees offered a reward for identification of the publishers, but no one came forward to collect the money.

Sometime in 1878 *The Dagger* struck again. Written in good college journalistic style, this four page bogus declared it had its origin "in a depraved condition of your college. Three years ago," said the editor, "four professorships in the State University were filled by persons odious to the students, and highly disgraceful to the State. The high positions of these personages enabled them to practice and encourage frauds of the deepest dye." *The Dagger* said its purpose was to remove these frauds, and it proceeded to name them and to give the public a close-up student's view of the professors. The paper thought Lemuel Moss was a man and teacher of the truest sort only if some of his past indiscretions could be cleared up. Dr. Nutt had "touched the dead corpse of the University and it stood upon its feet." Kirkwood was a "man of wonderful reputation. The astronomer royal had crossed the Atlantic to see him." The students agreed with the King's astronomer. Hoss was a source of dependable advice. He no doubt could lecture if he would leave off his bombast. Thomas C. Van Nuys met with *The Dagger*'s full approval. Dear old "Bally" (Elisha Ballantine) had rendered wonderful service in his time, but the hoary locks of the old savant betrayed his lack of ability to go further. Poor old "Atty" (Amzi Atwater) in the *The Dagger*'s august opinion was "nothing but a hypocritical runt of a teacher." The editor said he rode a pony in teaching Latin, and the alumni would burn him in effigy. He proclaimed, "Seven to one for Atty! Hurrah! Atty has decided on one point. The first time that this idiot ever passed sentence on a point in Latin was on May 22, 1878, when he decided that a verb was in the singular, because its subject was pure, a singular noun. He is a more profound reasoner than I conceived him to be." He was asked by the authors of the paper to resign. The erratic Boisen impressed the paper as having the most original mind on the faculty. William Ballantine was a worthy assistant teacher of Greek. Walter R. Houghton was "a brutal tyrant," and Uncle Tommy Spicer was the best janitor a college ever had. His only fault was his peculiar faculty for catching students in mischief, but he redeemed himself by not telling. Finally Joseph McPheeters was an enterprising postmaster, but a notoriously poor picker of public lecturers. It does not take much imagination to envision the Bloomington scene when this juicy sheet appeared on the campus. Nor does it take much to understand the palpitations in the faculty meetings. This by no means was to be the last time an omniscient anonymous editor would toss from behind the curtain of darkness a printed appraisal of those who made up the faculty.

Repeating in the catalogue the phrase that Indiana University was a parental institution did not stem the tide of change. In the post-Civil War era all American society was undergoing a mild revolution. The context of life was greatly enlarged, and this was especially true for university students. The antebellum student had to develop his physical entertainment and get exercise where he could find it. The woods were still nearby and he could chop his own firewood, or he could ramble over the countryside in long exploring adventures. Occasionally students paired off in wrestling matches, or tempers flared and they pummeled one another in fist-fights. As yet, however, there were no organized sports. Earlier students may even have indulged themselves in the childish games of marbles and mumblety-peg, so famous on the frontier.

There were occasional community picnics, the Fourth of July was celebrated in a large patriotic gathering, and apparently there were fall festivities. These things emanated from the community rather than the university. There was little more a student could do in Bloomington except go to church, sneak into a saloon, and play pranks on townspeople—even painting naughty graffiti on their houses and walls. The end of the Civil War brought a new breed of students to Bloomington. Many of them had been soldiers and had become accustomed to more robust entertainment.

One of the things the military veterans brought home from the army with them was the knowledge of the new game of baseball. On April 20, 1867, students submitted a request to the faculty seeking permission to use the southwest corner of the campus as a baseball diamond. This request was granted provided no changes were made in the grounds. To insure that no abuses occurred Professor Theophilus Wylie was charged with overseeing the campus.

At first students played the game for joy of the exercise. Quickly, however, a team was organized with Edwin C. McIntyre of Bryantsville as the barehanded catcher, and Acquilla Jones, a preparatory student from Bryantsville, was pitcher. The team called itself the University Baseball Club. Although the faculty permitted use of the grounds to the team, it would not allow it to to leave Bloomington to play "match" games. On one occasion the "Nine" had issued a challenge to an out of town club and had made all the arrangements for the game, only to be refused permission to play by the faculty. The challenged team claimed the "ball," and students contended that faculty members should pay for it. After some wrangling the faculty offered a ball, but the captain refused to accept the gift.

The editor of the Indiana *Student* climbed down from his stool in May, 1867, and strolled across the campus. He saw what he thought was a crowd of boys chasing butterflies, but it turned out to be the baseball team taking exercises. He reported the players had great confidence in their ability to play. One player told the editor he had just taken the "33rd degree" and could beat anything in Indiana. So good did the University Baseball Club believe itself to be in the latter 1860's that it challenged Yale, Harvard, Greencastle, and Hindustan in Monroe County.

This first club seems to have been altogether intramural. By 1878 there were several baseball clubs, and the campus in May and June was atingle with excitement. Baseball had come to stay. In June, 1873, the University Club played Spencer in the first matched game. It was not until a decade later, 1883, that a move was started to organize an intercollegiate association. By this time baseball had become a highly popular college sport. The Indiana *Student* gave its fatherly blessing by saying that it was both pleasant to watch and heartily invigorating to play, and much less expensive than billiards.

Apparently the first intercollegiate game played by an Indiana team was on May 12, 1883, when the Asbury University nine came from Greencastle to humiliate the University Club by a score of 23 to 6. The student reporter said the local team lacked professional sophistication. He described the opponents as being "nine gentlemanly men from Asbury clad in neat white uniforms, met a hastily collected club of our boys in the campus & beat them twenty-three to six." For five innings the game was even, then catcher T. W. Wilson's hands became so bruised he had to exchange positions with the right fielder. This ended Indiana's hopes. The next year the "Bloomingtons," as they were now called, retaliated with a score of 33 to 13. By this time the university had launched an intercollegiate athletic program. Students now began to talk of need for a gymnasium, and a note in the *Student* said a Michigan team had gone east in search of competition. In Indiana, the *Student* said in October, 1882, "following baseball, has come football—but, second thought, we will leave this matter to the prep. reporter." Apparently this game was first introduced in the town among men and boys, and then a preparatory school team was organized.

College life was undergoing fundamental changes in the postwar years. More and more students became conscious of themselves as members of a general student body rather than as members of a literary society. The dawning of the athletic era tended to focus attention upon the institution itself and its pride and honor. The baseball and debate teams created a new sense of loyalty. In May, 1867, the student newspaper learned that students at Asbury University had adopted ermine as a college color. "Let us have something of the kind," the editor said. "All the colleges in the country have some badge by which to recognize their fellow-students. Prompt action should be had on this." As organized sports grew more popular Indiana University students found athletic rivals in the new state and denominational schools.

Early in the spring of 1883 word got around among the colleges in the Old Northwest that a baseball association should be formed to compile playing rules, organize playing schedules, and to encourage a sports program in collegiate institutions. The *Student* felt that Indiana University should belong to such an association because "It will have a regenerating effect upon enervated muscles, & introduce a new variety of heroes." Spring was the time when baseball was in the air, "the merry diamond is again resonant with the dialect that Americans use when they wield the willow," said the *Student*.

Time rushed on for Indiana University. Lemuel Moss had gone, and a livelier administration with a youthful outlook came to Bloomington with David Starr Jordan. The president and faculty could take a broader look at educational approaches; they grew conscious of the physical man. By 1885 the students' frame of reference when they entered the school was no longer bounded by the narrow horizons of backwoods cabin, farm, and village. The world was coming into fuller focus and looked to the universities for fresh leadership. Indiana college students had become men and women largely on their own instead of kneeling obediently at the knees of Andrew Wylie and his ministerial successors.

[IX]

The Bootstrap Decades

I N HIS ANNUAL REPORT to the Indiana legislature in 1841 Andrew Wylie observed,

> It is an appalling fact that no Literary Institution has ever yet flourished under Legislative Management. This institution, when the undersigned took charge of it, ten years ago, was a mere Grammar School, without a Library, without apparatus, and with but two professors, having a strong tide of prejudice and opposition to stem. In these circumstances, "None was so poor as to do it reverence." It was with difficulty a quorum of the Board could be got together once a year.... Yet the legislature no sooner began to be moved about it, than it sank at once. And this is now cited, all over the land as another proof that no Literary Institution can prosper, which is even liable to legislative influence.

As university faculty and friends stood about the main building watching flames devour it on July 12, 1883, there must have dwelt in their minds the troublesome question of whether they could again raise from the ashes a new university and have it flourish after this second disaster in a quarter of a century. The history of Indiana University throughout its existence had been fraught with severe financial problems. Only after the school failed to secure support from the Morrill Act did the legislature move to give direct aid to the university in 1867. Until this date the "strong tide of prejudice and opposition" had worked against it.

At this date it is hard to fathom the minds of the founders. So much of what they said appeared in the form of grandiose oratory and vision that they actually concealed their innermost thoughts and fears. No doubt a more sensible question is whether the pioneer fathers had any concept of the burden of financing a seminary of higher education. How high did they aim? Clearly they were most unrealistic about the monetary requirements for even the simplest college. Blinded by these bits of frontier optimism the founders stumbled along with high ideals and little cash. First, they believed that public land prices would be boosted by an inrush of settlers. Second, they did not take time to calculate how much two townships of public land would yield under the most propitious conditions of sale, and, finally, they apparently failed to consider all of the failures, human foibles, and even political chicanery that might occur in such sales. Maybe they were blinded by the federal land law of 1820 in their failure to understand that under local political control all sorts of self-serving pressures would be exerted on state land commissioners, trustees, and legislators. The early Hoosier settler might have stood in some awe of the federal government, but he seems not to have feared the state.

All the vacillating over land policies by the state is clearly reflected in the income of the university from 1825 to 1876. In these five decades the university had an expendable income of $396,-055.96. Expenditures were $324,948.81. These figures at best are only approximations because neither the Board of Trustees' report to the legislature in 1848 nor the auditor's and treasurer's report are clear on this point. The Board of Trustees' report to the legislature in 1848 said: "The average annual amount of interest which has been drawn from the state Treasury since 1843 up to the present is $3,688.29 which with the tuition or contingent fee of $1,200 has constituted the fund for payment of salaries." Oftentimes the auditors confused pure income with several other administrative cost figures involved in land sales and damages. The above statement of income is based upon approximate student fees and interest from the endowment funds. Income from land sales went directly into the capital endowment trust and none of this money was available to the university as operating capital. The annual professorial budget for these years averaged approximately $4,000 to $6,000. Income from collective student fees from 1825 to 1885 was in the neighborhood of $67,298 and this is doubtless a generous estimate.

There were some miscellaneous sources of income, and perhaps as much as $35,000 was collected during this period from preparatory students. These, however, do not figure in the registrar's official tally, which is used in this study as the basis for enrollment count. There were expenditures such as janitorial services, building repairs, library purchases, and the cost of scientific equipment. These costs did not amount to more than $25,000, if in fact they were that high. There were many years when the university's operating budget fell below $6,000. Professors' annual salaries after 1838 averaged approximately $1,100 each.

In 1876 the Indiana auditor said in his published report something which had appeared obvious from the outset. There were grave uncertainties about the management of the university funds. At that date the endowment totaled $116,384.13. The auditor commented,

> It has been the custom of this office, at the close of each fiscal year, to close the account of the College Fund Interest, with all other subordinate accounts of the fund, into the account of the College Fund Principal. This system has doubtless in the past deprived the University of money that legally belonged to it, as in many instances at the close of the year there would be a balance [operation funds] on hand not taken up, and by this method was merged in the permanent fund.

The problem here was that ignorant or willful auditors arbitrarily managed the university fund in the easiest way for themselves, and the Board of Trustees and university presidents were left most of the time entirely in the dark. There is evidence in the auditor's and treasurer's report that both treasurers and auditors used the university monies as a glorious slush fund to cultivate political goodwill. Records are so vague and confused, however, that possibly no complete picture of the university's financial assets can ever be isolated and accounted for with certainty. The Secretary of the Board of

Trustees was almost as careless as the auditors in stating clearly year after year the budget and financial transactions of the institution. The figures given above must be considered approximations, but they are reasonably dependable gauges of the university's income and expenditures.

The Board of Trustees for its part gave more attention at times to increasing the endowment fund to $100,000 or more so that the 6 percent income from this capital source, plus student contingent fees, would properly finance the school's instructional program. It was believed that once the endowment exceeded $100,000 the institution would be permanently in sound financial condition. This attitude clearly reflected the board's willingness to maintain the status quo. Thus only emergency planning for the future was possible, and no appreciable additions could be made to the plant, program, or faculty. This accounts for the fact that, when an expansion in the program was made, the faculty, accordion fashion, and without added cost, had to make room in their schedules for taking on additional classroom teaching. Building the endowment fund from public land sales, however, was a constant uphill struggle. It is now impossible to do more than surmise what political and personal forces were at work but beyond the trustees' power to comprehend or control. No one can say how much the vigorous political partisanship of these decades cost Indiana University in income, breadth of program, and vital growth. At times the institution was faced with bankruptcy because of the indifferent if not corrupt management of its funds. Some loans made to individuals, banks, and counties were secured by insufficient collateral. Not all borrowers were carefully checked before receiving loans, nor were they coerced to pay their debts on dates of maturity. A more disturbing fact was the readiness with which legislators granted debtors relief from delinquent obligations, and then allowed them to begin all over again on the terms of the initial sales, seldom if ever taking into consideration advances in land prices or the added assets of improvements.

There is no doubt that everybody in Indiana in 1820 believed a college or university could be maintained without calling upon taxpayers and legislators for support. Too, it was a remote chance indeed that students could be admitted to the college free of tuition payments. From the moment Indiana Seminary opened to the present it has been the thought that at some time in the foreseeable future the university would be sufficiently well endowed by the public to do away with such costs to students. Frontiersmen were strong for free education, but they never quite discovered how to absorb the cost without paying taxes to do so. Obeying the original mandate of the legislature, "as soon as possible," that students would be admitted free of charge to the university classrooms was observing the letter of the law but not the exigencies of practicality. Instead of calling the fees levied tuition, the legislators and trustees did a clever semantic sidestep and euphemistically designated them "contingent fees."

From the moment Baynard Rush Hall was employed to begin the first classes until the arrival of David Starr Jordan as president, a majority of the staff members were ministers, and public attitudes toward professors' salaries were precisely the same as those exhibited toward ministerial salaries in general. There was no hard and fast obligation to pay the preacher, and a preacher turned professor was regarded in the same penurious light. Indiana University professors for the first sixty years of the institution's history were patient, long-suffering, and self-sacrificing in the matter of salaries. They were paid no more than a subsistence wage, and sometimes it was doubtful that they actually maintained their families on their pay.

When the Congress in 1816, or technically in 1820, awarded to the Indiana Seminary the remaining portion of the Gibson Township and all the one in Monroe County, it opened a complex and sometimes devious chapter in the annals of public land management. The Congress land was accepted by the new state and was placed under the administration of state land commissioners. The first land official who had responsibility for selling school lands was John Badollet. On April 18, 1811, Albert Gallatin wrote the land registrar that the Territorial Legislature had misinterpreted the terms of the land grant. It was never Congress' intention, said Gallatin, that the legislature assume administrative authority over the public school lands, and sales, and sales made by authority of the legislature were invalid; only Congress had the power to dispose of the lands. This letter created some panic among land purchasers, and the trustees of Vincennes University wrote Congress for permission to validate sales already made. Apparently this request was honored, because purchasers remained in possession of their holdings.

On July 15, 1816, Josiah Meigs wrote John Badollet that an additional township would be granted Indiana for seminary use. He designated the new township to be number eight, north of the base line in range one, and west of the principal meridian line. Contrary to tradition President Monroe only authorized this grant *pro forma* and did not personally select the township. Behind this grant of two townships was the precedent of the Ordinance of 1785 with its school lands reservation. In making the provision for reserved sections of public lands the special committee was less interested in endowing a public school system than in creating a device by which lands could be made attractive to future purchasers.

This fact was revealed by Timothy Pickering, a major land speculator, on June 16, 1783, in a proposal to Rufus Putnam. Jefferson's original ordinance, drafted in 1784, did not contain the school reservation. Pickering saw the addition of such a provision for a reserve section of school lands as a good future sales argument in the disposal of homesteads from the large speculative grants. This land grant also appears to have been a motivating factor in the grant of certain administrative provisions for the Indiana townships. Later when the committee located the seminary this also appears to have been a motivating factor in its decision. When the committee later located the seminary on the edge of Perry Township, David Maxwell had voiced practically the same sentiments as Rufus Putnam. The location of the school, wherever it might be placed, would be a major incentive in land sales.

The committee appointed to locate the seminary in Perry Township in 1821 was composed of men who were involved in land development and speculation. It was they who were given authority to appoint a sales agent and to entrust him with the disposition of seminary lands. The location committee was instructed to report progress at the next session of the General Assembly. Perry Township was virgin territory; to date no sales had been made in it, and there appear to have been no troublesome squatters on the cession. Gibson Township, which the state appropriated to Indiana Seminary in 1820, however, presented a highly confused picture. It contained originally 23,040 acres. Of this 4,000 acres had been sold soon after 1804, and there had been other sales. Squatters had moved onto the land, and there was uncertainty as to how much land the Vincennes University Trustees had sold, or to whom the ceded tracts were deeded.

At its meeting in 1825 the legislature once again considered the administration of seminary lands. John W. Lee, the agent, was authorized to rent improved areas of the township at less than $0.625 an acre, per year, the income to be deposited in the seminary fund. At the same session the legislators granted the contractors for the new college buildings permission to go into the Monroe forest and cut such timber as they needed for joists, rafters, and columns.

Soon after 1820 it became apparent that the land agents left much to be desired in their dealings. An act was passed to permit township trustees to remove an agent at any time for cause and to name his successor. This plainly implied that matters of integrity and judgment of management were involved. The legislature in 1828 authorized the public sale of seminary lands on the first Mondays of May, August, and October, 1828. In the same session the lawmakers instructed the trustees to deposit all land monies and special gifts to the seminary with the state treasurer to become a part of the state's public loan fund. This was the beginning of a second and badly muddled chapter in the university's financial history. Citizens of Indiana could borrow up to $500 from the loan fund at an interest rate of 6 percent per annum, and the loan was allowed to run for five years. As collateral the borrower had only to give a mortgage on the land he had bought on credit provided it was judged to be worth twice the amount of the loan. This scheme opened a velvet path for speculators, schemers, and rascals. This was also the day of the "deserving common man," and his political affiliations had almost as much to do with his securing a loan as did his integrity and collateral.

Almost yearly the legislature undertook to assure honesty in the seminary land sales. In 1829 provisions were made that a list of all lands sold be sent to the clerks in Gibson and Monroe counties so a determination of damages could be made in tax suits. As the federal land officers had learned, it was difficult under the best of circumstances to sell land on any date, and the national liberalization of land laws in 1800 and 1820 eased the conditions under which the public domain could be sold. The Indiana legislature in

1829 revoked the specific sales dates and instructed the seminary land commissioners to sell any time they had purchasers. They were held, however, to the previous terms of the state law regarding price and credit. A year later the latter provisions were revised and a new scale of prices was issued by the assembly. These ranged from $2.50 per acre for lands of the first class down to $0.75 for those listed in the third class. The land agents were given freedom in making classifications.

On the first Monday in May, 1831, a public sale was held in Bloomington in which seminary lands were sold to the highest bidders. Lands that remained after this could be sold at private sales. The legislature found it necessary at this time to pass an additional law requiring sales commissioners to remit to purchasers the unauthorized commissions which they had collected from the sale of plots of less than eighty acres. From 1830 on, however, the township lands were broken up into small tracts of forty and eighty acres, and sales were made largely to yeoman farmers.

By 1833 legislators showed some concern with educational financial problems, and extended their interest on a broader scale than mere sales of reserve township lands. They hoped further to encourage education by the provision that any person who paid $1.00 into the public seminary funds could be excused from county militia duty. This act is not specific as to whether or not it applied to county seminaries alone. Further relief was granted the individual in 1834 when a law provided that debtors would be relieved of taxes on the Monroe and Gibson lands until the purchasers had paid their debts. At the same session the assembly added to the college's fiscal woes by providing that one student from each county could attend the institution free of tuition cost for a period of two years. Preferably this student should be indigent. There is no indication, however, that the legislature was concerned with either the student's educational preparation for college or his mental competence. All he had to submit to the president was a testimonial of good moral character.

A loan office was established in Indianapolis in 1838 in connection with the treasurer's office for the purpose of making individual loans from the college fund, and for sale of Gibson Township and Monroe County lands. Funds were to be loaned to citizens of Indiana, and the amount available to each borrower was limited to

$500 or one half the value of the real estate purchased. Interest was charged at a 6 percent annual rate payable in advance. Loans could be executed for five years and no longer. Inevitably there was to be politics in the administration of such a public fund and in the election of university land commissioners. There were to be two agents elected by joint ballot of both houses of the legislature for terms of three years. After February, 1840, the commissioners were paid 4 percent on money collected for rentals, leases, and land sales.

No one in the university's administration had control of the institution's funds, not even the Board of Trustees. The legislature and the state treasurer made all the basic fiscal decisions. For instance, the Board of Trustees had little idea as to what funds were available from one year to the next until they received the information from the state treasurer. There is ample evidence that this state official was inefficient in the management and reporting of university funds, and as a result no one could be certain that the report given the Board of Trustees represented the actual funds available. On one occasion when an attempt was made to determine the precise amount of the so-called endowment income the board found that the treasurer's records were kept on bits and scraps of paper which gave only the vaguest indication that they were accurate, and they gained no precise information as to the total amount of the funds. An example of this carelessness was the fact that in September, 1842, a question arose as to whether President Wylie and the faculty had been paid double their salaries in 1841–42. The auditor said there was evidence in the vouchers to prove that this had happened. The board disputed this, saying such a thing was impossible. What had happened was that the Board of Trustees drew warrants against the state treasurer, but that official neglected to issue payments. The treasurer then issued a second set of vouchers, and when the auditor received the duplicate records, he spotted an overpayment of $1,175.00, or rather the treasurer's duplication of payments. Even more disturbing was the fact the records of the loans were in a chaotic condition. Auditors undertook to correct this by publishing several pages listing debtors and the amounts of their loans in the reports of later years. This, however, in no way assured the security of the loans or alleviated other conditions which mitigated against their collection.

A new loan policy was instituted in 1841, when legislators instructed the treasurer to invest university funds in state bank stocks, but in less than twelve months the lawmakers had second thoughts on their decision and repealed the law. There is no indication how much, if any, stock was purchased. Possibly there were no readily available funds to invest at the moment because the legislature granted an extension to debtors for five years, provided they made new notes and produced additional securities for the extended loans. Realizing that the land management had been slack and careless, the Assembly in this year asked for a strict accounting of the amount of land sold, the amount unsold, amount of money received, amount of land leased or rented, and probable value of the unsold tracts. This time the Assembly asked that the report also be given to the Board of Trustees of the university. The board in turn was asked to make a precise report to the legislature of all expenses, including professor's salaries and apparatus purchases. It seems in requesting this information legislators had in mind the abolition of tuition payments if they found that the university was in sound enough financial condition to permit a reduction of income. Legislators felt the time had come when the Assembly should comply with Section 2, Article 9, of the Constitution. To add further strain to the miniscule university budget the legislature increased the number of free students from each county to two.

Occasionally a purchaser of university lands walked off and left his bargain behind, unpaid for. Others farmed the land over the five-year period and when they were unable to meet payments they sought relief from the legislature. One such case was that of William Alexander of Monroe County, who had paid neither interest nor capital. His tract was restored to him on condition that he pay the state treasurer his back interest before August 1, 1843. This in time became a common story. In case an owner lost his land because of nonpayment of taxes after 1844, he could redeem the payments, less interest payments which he had made. But even with all of this mass of legislation the land purchasers asked for more relief. In 1845 they succeeded in getting the time limit extended to six years, and there is implication that the commissioners had gone beyond the terms of the law in granting more liberal conditions to purchasers. Thus it became necessary once again for the legislature to regularize these transactions by enacting a law to cover whatever ex post facto terms were made by the agents.

Year after year there were supplicants before the legislature picking away at the existing laws and seeking enactment of legislation favorable to their economic predicaments. In time the land laws became so badly confused that it is doubtful that the courts could say with certainty what laws applied to an individual case, far less what the laws might be after the next meeting of the Assembly. For instance, in January, 1846, the legislature declared that if lands were lost by mortgage foreclosures they could be sold for the balance of the principal and interest. If the commissioner reappraised them at less than this value then they could be sold for whatever they would bring. Under this law a debtor could redeem his land and improvements within four weeks after he was listed as a delinquent at the new rate by paying the remaining part of his mortgage, at the reduced price, interest, and cost. This opened a veritable Pandora's box of foreclosures and reclamations.

A legislative act of 1848 dealt further with the admission of two free students from each county and added a second condition that students studying medicine could be admitted to a public medical school on half tuition. There is doubt as to what the legislators had in mind in this latter provision. Possibly someone, maybe DePauw University, had sought by charter to establish a medical school in Indianapolis. Sometime before 1850 Indiana University was given a plot of land in the city designated as section or lot 25, or State University Square. In January, 1850, this square was offered to Asbury University for the purpose of erecting on it medical college buildings. From this date down until the first decade of this century the University Square was more of a thorn in the school's side than an asset. As has been pointed out elsewhere, this lot figured prominently in the university's loss of the land grant funds to Purdue University. In the meantime the Board of Trustees spent a considerable amount of money in lawsuits trying to gain possession of the tract.

The background of land management in behalf of Indiana University gives some indication of the complex issues involved. When Congress conveyed to the new State of Indiana in 1816 the townships, the conveyance included only the unsold portions of Gibson and all of Perry Township. The Act of Congress preceded by the Ohio Associates rule, however, specified two "entire townships." Specifically, the *United States Statutes at Large*, April 19, 1816, reads "also, one whole township should be designated by the President for use as a seminary of learning—this township in addition to one already reserved for its use." In time the dispute over Gibson Township was to cause the university one of its most vexatious moments in its financial history. The issues which arose over this land between 1838 and 1854, technically, had no direct bearing on Indiana University, nor was it a party to the upcoming lawsuits. Yet the Vincennes University contentions later threatened the institution with almost sudden death. At no time during the future court sessions was the Board of Trustees of Indiana University represented in court. Yet this case must be considered with as much care as though the institution had been a party in the cases. In time this litigation was to have an enormous effect upon the university's administration and friends.

Specifically involved in the cases in court were the State of Indiana and Vincennes University's Board of Trustees. Were it not for the Assembly's near irresponsibility in crediting the Vincennes threat the case could now be dismissed in a sentence or two, and Indiana University's history would not be cluttered with it. This, however, was not to be.

The revival of efforts to reestablish Vincennes University as a public institution came about largely because the town of Vincennes needed land for expansion. Involved was the sale and drainage of a swampy area known as the Vincennes Commons which had been donated to the town by congressional act of 1791. Residue of the funds involved in this sale was to go to the university. For much of the two decades between 1816 and 1838 the Vincennes trustees had been largely inactive. Some of the members had died; others had moved out of Indiana. In fact at the later date there was a question as to whether the board actually existed. An appeal was made to the legislature for relief, and this was forthcoming in the act of 1838. This piece of loosely considered legislation had the effect of reviving the Vincennes University charter of 1807, and of reinstating the powers of the Board of Trustees. However, the act denied the trustees power over the Gibson Township lands.

Immediately following the enactment of the 1838 law the "new" board met in Vincennes on June 11, 1838, for purposes of reconstituting itself. Present were two shrewd lawyers, Samuel Judah and George R. Gibson. Judah supplied the legal talent and tenacity, and Gibson assumed leadership of the board. The body had no money, and its only prospect of acquiring any was to reclaim and sell the old university building and to institute a claim for recovery of the Gibson County lands, even though the act of 1838 specifically denied the board this right. The old building had been in the hands of Knox County Seminary and the Vincennes Academy, and there was a mortgage of $1,800 against it which had to be cleared before the trustees could make any disposition of the structure and the plot on which it stood. Among several institutions involved in the confusion was the Vincennes Medical School, which also had a vested interest, but this institution failed in 1839 and left no active claimants.

In 1842, after considerable negotiation with the Catholic Diocese and other persons, the Vincennes University was brought back into existence, and it needed a new building. Ignoring the specific statement in the act of 1838 that the lands of Gibson Township were beyond the legal reach of the Vincennes Board, Judah and Gibson began the process of abstracting all the laws relating to the university and the Gibson grant. By 1841 this abstract was ready, but nothing happened until 1843, when Samuel Judah was instructed to prepare a full abstract of the laws and history of Vincennes University to submit to Chancellor James Kent of New York for a preliminary judgment.

In a lengthy decision Chancellor Kent reviewed the acts and intent of Congress, the charter rights of the Vincennes board, the actions of the Indiana legislature, and the ticklish issue of adverse possession. He held the Vincennes charter to be valid and the Board of Trustees to be legally viable. The actions of the legislature had in fact renewed the charter, and the intent of Congress in 1804 and 1807 was clear. However, Chancellor Kent was vague on the issue of adverse possession of individuals or the state. He thought Vincennes University had just reason to expect the state to compensate it for its loss of lands. If, however, the Board of Trustees sought to enter suit against individual purchasers, unregistered squatters, and other claimants, then it would embark upon a long, questionable, and expensive legal fight which might be unsuccessful in the end. A change in approach was made in 1845, when the plaintiffs agreed to drop any suits they had instituted or proposed to institute against the individual landholders of Princeton and Gibson County.

The legislature agreed, on January 17, 1846, to permit a suit to be brought against the state.

Legislators said most of the land in Gibson Township had been sold to private citizens who had bought and held their titles in good faith. The impending Vincennes suits would destroy faith in the Indiana land titles and otherwise cause distress on the part of the people. "The state therefore gives *permission* for a suit to be brought against it by Vincennes University." There is indicated, but not clearly revealed, the fact that considerable maneuvering had occurred in the statehouse. The plaintiffs were as anxious as the state not to become involved in the issue of adverse possession, which Chancellor Kent had said was at best a foggy one. The law of 1846 was emphatic that the state would defend its rights in the case, and not allow the Vincennes claims to go by default.

The first suit in the Vincennes case was brought in the Marion County Circuit Court, and the plaintiffs won. The Indiana Supreme Court quickly reversed the circuit court's decision. Then the plaintiffs appealed the case to the United States Supreme Court in *Board of Trustees of Vincennes University* v. *State of Indiana*. In its December term, 1852, the Court heard Samuel Judah plead that the congressional act of 1804 was a valid grant, and the territorial legislature had been given administrative powers over the university lands.

O. H. Smith argued on behalf of the state that Vincennes University had at that late date no corporate existence. Twenty years had elapsed, hence the power of adverse possession had set in; the act of 1804 was a mere reservation, not a grant of land; the case in point did not plead public or present use; the enabling act of 1816 deposited legal title with the state; and the lands were clearly in the public domain. The Supreme Court justices were divided in their opinions. Justice McLean for the majority denied essentially that the state had any power over the lands, basing his opinion on the phrase in the 1804 grant restricting territorial powers. In short, the majority opinion upheld the viability of the board, the rechartering of the university in 1838, and held that titles to the lands had never been vested in the state, and consequently it had no powers of sale. The enabling act of 1816 did not in fact transfer the Gibson Township lands to Indiana. The Vincennes charter was further supported by the *Dartmouth College* v. *Woodward* decision of 1819.

Chief Justice Roger B. Taney and two of the justices dissented. They contended the Vincennes trustees had to show legal title to the lands; the state had used the lands in conformance with the congressional mandate, and the act of 1816 clearly gave the state possession in fee simple. The case was remanded to the Marion County Circuit Court for rehearing, and this court held to its original decision.

On February 10, 1853, the legislature acknowledged loss of the Vincennes case, and began a search for some means to secure from Congress lands to replace the loss to the state. A bill to this effect was introduced in the House of Representatives by Thomas A. Hendricks, and in the Senate by Jesse D. Bright. These bills were debated in February, 1854, and passed. The governor of Indiana was authorized to select 19,040 acres of lands from the public domain, provided they "Shall be, and forever remain, a fund for the use of Indiana University." Actually this bill passed with almost no debate in both houses, but a careless clerk misplaced the enacted bill and it was not signed by Millard Fillmore. The Indiana representatives at the next session of Congress reinstated the bill, but in the second debate members of the House argued that such an act would set a dangerous precedent. They properly raised the question of whether the State of Indiana had actually lost anything by the adverse court decision for which the federal government could be held accountable.

Actually Indiana University was able to keep the funds derived from the Gibson Township sales, and was given additional lands by congressional mandate. The Indiana Board of Trustees complained to the legislature late in 1854,

> The land recently granted by Congress to the state for the use of the Univ. ought, in the opinion of the Board, to be made productive at as early a date as practicable. As these lands were selected at a late period, when but little public land remained unsold from which selections could be made, their value cannot be placed at a high figure, in order that the most may be realized from them, the Bd. would propose they be sold on easy terms to the purchasers.

The legislature was asked to grant authorization for a general public sale before private negotiations were begun.

On April 9, 1854, the university's immediate prospects of success were gravely clouded by the great fire; immediately following this the university had to face the calamity of the adverse court decisions. The courts ordered a judgment decree of $60,000 against the state in favor of Vincennes University. This judgment in turn was ordered discharged by the treasurer and auditor, "out of a fund in the charge of the state, & which is designated in the State Treasury as the Univ. fund."

The greater part of the university fund accumulation had been derived from land sales in the Perry Township, and the Indiana Board of Trustees stoutly maintained it belonged exclusively to the university. The Vincennes Trustees were adamant in their request for reimbursement and sought a court order to compel the auditor and treasurer to pay the indemnity at once out of the university's endowment. In the meantime the Indiana University trustees entered a bill in chancery seeking a decree to enjoin payment of the judgment from its funds. They maintained rightly that the university was not party to the Vincennes case, and that it was the responsibility of the legislature to take immediate action to satisfy the claim from state funds other than those of the university. This judgment, said the trustees, should be quieted in such a way that the university would not be destroyed in the process. The board further contended that the university's endowment policies must conform with the legal injunction that they "Remain inviolate, and be faithfully and exclusively applied to the principal purpose for which the trust was created."

When the news reached Bloomington that the legislature, on February 13, 1855, had passed the bill ordering the state to assume the $60,000 judgment held by Vincennes University, students assembled in the chapel to express their joy. Theodore Read moved that a committee be appointed to arrange a victory demonstration. That same evening the students assembled and marched through the town in a torchlight parade accompanied by the raucous "Bloomington Saxe-horn band" playing a spirited tune. They went first to President Daily's residence and gave "three hearty cheers." Daily, ex-Governor Dunning, and Judge Hughes addressed the students and assembled citizens. Judge Hughes reviewed the rocky financial past of the university but said he now saw a ray of light for the future. This same sentiment was expressed by Benjamin

Wolfe and Professor Daniel Read. What the celebrants did not know was the fact that the bill had passed the House by a comfortable margin, but in the Senate the vote was tied and the outcome had to be decided by the lieutenant governor Ashbel Parsons Willard. This one vote saved the university from almost immediate destruction.

The loud shouts of joy sent up in Bloomington might have been premature. The Vincennes issue had created bitterness in the Assembly, and possibly as a result the university was denied direct support from the legislature for several years to come. It was clear from the tie in the Senate that at midcentury there still was no burning zeal for the cause of higher education in Indiana. The legislature of 1846 was bemoaned for its stupidity in allowing the state to be made a defendant in the Vincennes case. Though innocently drawn into the lawyer-created maelstrom to collect damages from the state, Indiana University no doubt was injured by the enemies made for it in the legislature, and by the cloud cast over its credit rating. It is not possible on the face of the record to determine what kinds of pressures and persuasions were used to get a vote favorable to the institution. It seems to be clearly indicated in the record that left to its normal course of action the legislators in Indianapolis would have killed the university without misgivings.

Following the legislative actions, the Board of Trustees found itself confronted with a couple of ticklish matters. McDonald and Blackford, the Indianapolis law firm, represented the university as advisory counsel in the Vincennes matter, and then lost the case before the Marion Circuit Court. They sought a fee of $1,000 each for their services. The board had based its agreement upon the grounds that the lawyers would win the case. The matter of whether to honor it dragged on in the board meetings for some time to come, and the lawyers were finally paid.

Representing the university in the feverish maneuvers in the legislature in 1855 were William Clayborne Tarkington, who on April 2, 1855 was elected university treasurer, and Samuel H. Buskirk, a Bloomington citizen. Apparently these men worked in Indianapolis for the university on their own initiative. They reported decided support for the Vincennes claim in the legislature. In the face of this situation they took it upon themselves to hire "lawyers" to lobby for the university and agreed to pay them—again without authorization—$1,236. In the trustees' meeting on July 30, 1855, the question of paying this lobbying fee was introduced, and the board refused to pay until it knew to whom the money was due and for what specific services. Tarkington and Buskirk refused to reveal these facts because they said they had assured the "lawyers" they would not disclose their names or divulge the fact they would receive pay for their services.

John I. Morrison, Chairman of the Board of Trustees, was present in the legislative halls, but Tarkington and Buskirk said they neither consulted him nor revealed their plans to him. On August 2, 1855, Tarkington and Buskirk explained their position in a letter to the Board of Trustees. They wrote,

> In reply to your interrogatory, as to whether John I. Morrison, the President of the Board of Trustees was consulted, and knew and approved of the employment of such persons, we say that for the reasons given that he was not consulted, but we are of the impression that he had some knowledge, that we were using money, but in this we may be mistaken.
>
> We very much regret that our zeal induced us to expend our own money for your use and benefit. We should have permitted the bill to fail, and blotted out of existence the state University.
>
> If we have to lose this sum of money, it will teach us wisdom in the future. We would very respectfully suggest to you, that if you have an impression, that improper influences were brought to bear upon the Legislature to procure passage of the bill, you had better return to the State Treasury the money improperly obtained.

Certainly the above letter did nothing to alleviate the board's suspicions; if anything it heightened them. Board members knew well enough what went on around the legislature, and they no doubt knew more about this case than they were willing to record in the board minutes. They refused to pay the fees, twice tabling requests to do so. If this bill was paid at a later date there is no record of the fact in the minutes of the Board of Trustees. There does appear, however, a note in the state auditor's report that Tarkington and Buskirk were paid $673.76 in 1855. The historian can only infer, as it seems board members did at the time, that this was an outright case of chicanery if not bribery.

Someone was paid some money to use his influence in behalf

of the university. It is clear, as Tarkington and Buskirk told the board, the university was saved by the narrow margin of one vote, and influence had been used to accomplish its salvation.

While the Vincennes matter was being resolved in Indianapolis the Board of Trustees was engaged in another vital struggle. The fire in the main building on the original campus left the university with sorely limited housing facilities. A new building had to be constructed and equipped as quickly as possible. The insurance money collected from the fire was little more than a start. Private subscriptions were rather small, and the university endowment was beyond the trustees' reach. There was only one way in which the school could raise money and that was by issuing bonds.

The trustees believed they could sell all of their bonds in Indianapolis and Indiana. William M. French of Jeffersonville was appointed sales agent. He failed to sell any bonds in Indianapolis and had no better luck in Louisville and Cincinnati. He reported to the board that it was impossible to borrow money in the state or in the Ohio Valley and suggested that he take the bonds East to seek buyers.

After a conference with William Daily and John I. Morrison and consulting with Judge McDonald, French went to New York. Then, without direct consultation with the Board of Trustees, he altered the date of maturity of the bonds from ten to three years but to his surprise found no permissive resolution of the board on record regarding his right to make alterations. The only change that he could legally make was to provide for semiannual interest payments. French even sent the bonds back to Bloomington to be revised, but President Daily returned them to him unaltered.

When French was unable to sell the bonds in New York he approached the Savings Bank at Norwich, Connecticut, where the president of the bank agreed to pay $0.83 for them, but when the bank's board of directors met they reneged on the agreement. French sold only eight bonds at $0.70, and left the others with John M. Lord in New York to be sold if possible. He also left some bonds with William Bradley of that city. In all the university had issued $5,600 in bonds. The failure to sell these bonds left the university in an extremely weak financial position.

The financial committee of the Board of Trustees reported on December 5, 1855,

The embarrassed condition of the finances of the University is such, the Board having this morning very properly, as we think, ordered the withdrawal of the unsold Bonds from the market, that other means for raising funds for immediate relief must be resorted to, or the whole concern wound up and closed or at least suspended for a time. Your committee in looking for some mode of relief less ruinous than the sale of bonds, whereby but little more than fifty cents on the dollar has been realized, have been very naturally led to devise some measure by which the lands donated to the State for the benefit of the University may be made available.

Some money was raised by offering the "perpetual scholarship," and some by land sales. It is difficult, however, to explain just how all the money for the construction of the new building was raised.

Before the fire in 1854 the Board of Trustees gave the legislature an estimate of the worth of the university's physical property. The ten acre campus was valued at $1,000 and the buildings at $21,800. Thus in that dark moment in December of 1855 the physical worth had been reduced to $10,300, scarcely enough, if sold, to pay half the cost of the new building.

The university barely met its budgetary needs from 1855 to 1867. In these years, with one or two exceptions, the income of the institution was under $6,000, and expenditures just slightly lower. Collective salaries paid professors were actually under $5,000. In the latter year the legislature made its first direct appropriation to the university.

There were some years in Indiana University's history which may be considered as pivotal in the institution's development; the year 1867 was one of these. In this year the first woman was admitted to the university's classrooms, a final chapter was written in the location of the land grant college at Lafayette, the students began the publication of *The Student*, the first baseball team was organized, and university enrollment increased to 140 students, only once later to fall below this number. Yet the next decade, 1867 to 1876, was static, if not actually dreary. Friends of the university thought they saw by the end of the latter year promise that it would progress.

A closer look reveals that the university on the whole had met with as much or more success than could reasonably be expected with its severely limited financial support. To talk about hiring an abler faculty, broadening the curriculum, or improving fundamentally the quality of instruction was purely academic. At the end of the school year in 1867, the state auditor reported the university's income to be $6,667.65, and the professorial budget was $4,971.40. This was the lowest level of salary expenditures since 1845.

The most casual investigation of other university budgets revealed Indiana's inferior position. As early as 1852, Wisconsin's budget was $8,480.27. In 1841–42, Dartmouth had an income of $15,763.14. Columbia had in 1845 a budget of $93,361.16. Missouri in 1849 received $11,631.50; Princeton had an income in 1863 of $70,000, and on the eve of the Civil War, Thomas Jefferson's University of Virginia received $44,351.

After its initial one-year grant to the university, in 1867, the legislature continued its support but often only grudgingly. It was not until 1875 that the public income of the university was boosted to $23,000. Unfortunately the increased capital income did not immediately affect salaries. This was a critical period in which the university's outlay for its plant placed an inescapable burden on the Board of Trustees.

Judge George Buskirk, who spoke to a political audience in Bloomington in May, 1870, painted a sad picture indeed of the university's plight. The Bloomington *Progress* on May 25 quoted him as saying,

> It is now in a more critical condition than it has ever been. That the legislature during the time Judge [James] Hughes represented us, appropriated eight thousand dollars to the Institution in a year; that at the last session of the Legislature, he Mr. Buskirk procurred an additional appropriation of seven thousand dollars a year; that these laws were temporary in their character, and liable to be repealed at any time; that I introduced a bill at the last session to remedy this trouble, but it was defeated by the Democrats breaking up a quorum to prevent passage of the 15th Amendment[;] that a law making these appropriations permanent in their character should be passed; that the success and prosperity of the University might not depend upon the whims and caprices of each succeeding Legislature.

Buskirk thought that unless the legislature made a substantial appropriation the Board of Trustees would be forced to sell the

Owen geological and anthropological cabinet, for which it had paid $20,000, to meet its obligations. He also warned his Monroe County neighbors that there was a formidable combination of interest bent on moving the university to Indianapolis, and he believed they would attempt to defeat appropriation bills for the school during the coming session. If the opposition succeeded the removal would take place shortly. He further assured his audience that the dangers he had described were real, and not just campaign bluster. At no time in its history, he said, has the university "been so much in peril."

This period endured. At its meeting on June 12, 1876, the Board of Trustees reported a crisis. The university was $5,000 in debt and had to save its slender resources most stringently. Actually the Indiana auditor reported the year's income at $31,966 and salary expenditures at $28,300. This was the highest income in the university's history, and the salary budget was at a high point. These optimistic figures, however, in no way reflected the actual financial condition of the university. At this meeting the board called the faculty members before it and persuaded them to take a $200 cut in salaries. The salary of the newly employed Lemuel Moss, however, was left intact.

Writing many years later, W. J. Davis, commenting on the Indiana legislature's treatment of the university, said, "The Indiana Solons in 1876–77, seemed to think a University should live and thrive like a tree toad on a liberal supply of fresh air and sunshine." He accused the legislators of actually wishing to destroy the university and said they would have succeeded had its friends not rallied vigorously. "After strenuous opposition," said Davis, "the legislature finally appropriated $23,000 for the support of the University for one year—almost sufficient to buy kindling wood for Michigan University today [1922]. People of that time thought it was wrong to tax the whole population of farmers, doctors, lawyers, preachers, business men, and candlestick makers in order to educate the sons of a few high brows."

Indiana University was scarcely better off in 1884 than it had been in 1838, when it was raised to university status. It was not competitive with the state universities in the Old Northwest. Legislators continued to view it as a charitable institution which came annually begging alms. It took an enormous amount of emotional energy and practical political horse trading to secure any public support at all.

No historian now can fathom the pressures and picayune human prejudices exerted against the university by the rising influence of the denominational colleges. Yearly decisions of the Assembly clearly showed that the legislators could not differentiate between schools organized to serve narrow sectarian objectives and the broader based public university which served as a liberal arts and professional institution. To the end of Lemuel Moss' administration the Indiana General Assembly had borne out eloquently Andrew Wylie's dire foreboding, "no Literary Institution *can* prosper, which is ever *liable* to legislative influence."

[X]

The "Star of Jordan"

Y 1884 the Indiana University community had become accustomed to the fact that presidents left the institution with
such suddenness that they did not take time to deliver farewell addresses. The haste with which Lemuel Moss departed
Bloomington, however, caused a serious hiatus in the school's
operation. His place was filled temporarily by the beloved Elisha
Ballantine, who was asked to serve as acting president at a salary of
$2,000 until a permanent appointment could be made.

Moss' departure did not clear the Board of Trustees of the
delicate problems connected with the cause of his leaving. Miss
Katherine Graydon asked that the case be reopened. She said she
had taken time to reconsider and she felt the board should hear
her plea that she resigned "inadvertently" and by "mistake." She
asked the trustees for an opportunity to present formally her defense
against any charges which she believed might have been made
against her. This request was tabled, and a month later, December
11, 1884, the board ruled that since no formal charges had been
lodged with it, Miss Graydon's resignation must stand accepted.

A much graver situation faced the trustees. Indiana University
had definitely reached a period in its history when changes had to

be made in its operation if it were to survive as a useful institution of American higher education. Its days as an isolated secondary liberal arts college were ended. Immediately following the departure of President Moss an Indiana *Student* of January, 1885, expressed an awareness of this condition. It gave a strong hint that atrophy had set in many years before. In the editor's opinion, "It is not necessary to have a theologian at the head of a state institution where sectarian tenets are not touched upon. Indeed, the present faculty, composed largely of men identified with religious organizations & entirely of men of religious lives, will not fail to impart proper moral instructions to the students both by precept & example." This youthful editor sensed the changes in attitudes of his age, in which Ezra Cornell, Andrew D. White, James Burrill Angell, and James McCosh were the new type of university president. This was also the age in which William Rainey Harper, William Torrey Harris, Josiah Royce, Andrew Draper of Illinois, and even Charles Kendall Adams of Wisconsin delineated educational philosophy and universities met public demands. Unfortunately too few Hoosiers gained a sense of the burgeoning of a new American educational and literary age. They still quibbled over the old jealousies and chipped away at already inadequate appropriation bills.

The Board of Trustees began an immediate search for a new president without first formulating the precise qualifications it wanted in the new man. A committee was appointed to keep watch on the quality of work done in the university and to make certain that Ballantine and his colleagues did not go astray. Later it reported that "Old Bally" was running the machine like a veteran. Never in its history had the university done such good quality work. This was a relief because the board could take its time in searching for the "right man" to be president.

According to David Starr Jordan several candidates must have been brought to Bloomington. In *The Days of a Man* he said one of the "more acceptable" candidates was asked to speak in chapel. The visitor discussed his travels in Europe, "and incidentally in Holland, remarking that he had 'visited Edam, Rotterdam, Amsterdam, and other dam places.' That bit of humor chilled the audience, and his name was not again mentioned." There is no indication as to who this jocular candidate was.

By the time the Board of Trustees met in Indianapolis in mid-December, 1884, the search committee had compiled a list of forty-seven possible candidates for the presidency. On the morning of December 17 the trustees began to read recommendations, and for the next two days they were engulfed in this task. Late on the afternoon of the eighteenth they decided to elect a president at that meeting, but members had not settled on a specific name. Among the forty-seven candidates were John M. Coulter of Wabash College, ex-Governor E. B. Fairchild of Michigan, Seaman Knapp, president of Iowa State College, and David Starr Jordan of the Indiana University faculty. On the afternoon of December 19 Jordan received all eight votes of the board in a test ballot and was declared unanimously elected. At the same time the board elected John M. Coulter to be professor of botany and geology.

The elevation of David Starr Jordan to the presidency opened a new era for the university. In nearly every phase of its existence the institution was in a state of major transition. Years later Jordan wrote of his Indiana experience,

> notwithstanding the handicaps of poverty, antiquated methods, and lack of popular appreciation, Indiana University, as I have implied, did some really excellent work, and among its professors in the '70's were four, grown old in service, who were justly held in high respect by all capable of recognizing a good man. These were Daniel Kirkwood, Theophilus A. Wylie, Elisha Ballantine, and Richard Owen.

All four of these men had served the university faithfully through several periods of utter poverty and frustration. Daniel "Daddy" Kirkwood was a genuine scholar who, perhaps more than any other man of this time at Indiana, gave status to the academic program of the university. One can only speculate on what reputation he might have made as an astronomer had he had access to a good observatory and been able to work in a more liberal atmosphere. Richard A. Proctor, called by David Starr Jordan "a distinguished English astronomer," referred to Kirkwood in an address in Bloomington as the "Kepler of America" because of his original work in astronomy. No less capable were Owen, Wylie, and Ballantine. These professors, however, were gentlemen of the "old school," a fact which is eloquently reflected in the faculty minutes.

In Jordan's eyes the dissidents who wanted to move the university to Indianapolis might have had some reason on their side. He described the town of Bloomington as a drab country village marked by the courthouse, "then a shabby building surrounded on Saturdays by the saddle horses and teams of the neighboring farmers— all Monroe County, after the fashion of the rural South, aiming to spend Saturday afternoon at the county seat." There were three brands of Presbyterians in the town, and representative congregations of the other Protestant denominations. To Jordan, however, the most interesting citizens were Henry S. Bates, shoemaker, and James Karsell, grocer. Long after he had gone to Stanford University he wrote students in Bloomington about Bates and his "shoe-shop school of philosophy." Hammering away at his customer's shoes, Bates carried on discussions with students and professors about the "problems of life and literature." Karsell was hardly so voluble, but he too was well read and had just as inquiring a mind as the professors.

It is not clear what the Board of Trustees had in mind for the university when they chose Lemuel Moss' successor. Because they compiled such an elaborate list of names and spent so much time reading recommendations, the trustees seemed to have no fixed notion of what they did want. Too, there appeared on the list the names of many individuals who fitted into the traditional pattern of Indiana University's past presidents. The trustees did not fully appreciate the philosophy or scientific ideas of Jordan. His image in Indiana was an exceedingly popular one. He was an energetic, eloquent, and intelligent member of the faculty. He made a strong appeal to students; he shared their enthusiasm for debate, the outdoors, and sports. A story, whether apocryphal or not, followed the twenty-six year old scientist to Bloomington. It is said that in 1877, while he was a professor at Butler, Jordan got into an argument as to whether a baseball pitcher could throw a curve ball. His doubts aroused the ire of the Indianapolis professional team. The Butler faculty sided with Jordan, and the "sports" with Eddie Nolan, the pitcher. The athletes set up an elaborate pitching range behind the Maryland Street Fire House; Nolan was to throw his fast curve through a series of paper flags. The ball was coated with chalk to leave a pattern of its course. When Eddie threw a perfect ellipsis the professor was confounded, and the baseball team vindicated. This was a case of physics versus brawn, or more properly ichthyologist versus physicist. Born January 19, 1851, Jordan lived on an upstate New York farm near the village of Gainesville, fifty miles south of Rochester. He was the son of Hiram and Huldah Jordan, a member of a pioneer family. There were two creeks near his parent's homestead, and in his youth Jordan said he fished in the streams and developed an early interest in the habits, species, and distribution of fishes. This interest went with him through life, and formed the base of his professional career. In school the lad orated in good nineteenth century style before school and Sunday school audiences, read adventure literature, and dreamed of traveling to strange places. This interest also remained alive through the years. He said his earliest scientific interest was in the stars, and that early he had access to Burritt's *Geography of the Heavens*, a fact which "persists curiously in the middle name I have ever since borne, and which I myself chose for two reasons. The one sprang from love of astronomy, the other had to do with my mother's great admiration for the writings of Thomas Starr King." He said, however, his overweening interest was terrestrial geography.

The farmer Jordans had an extraordinary interest in reading. Both father and mother were former school teachers. Their son David waded through Dickens, Macaulay, Bret Harte, Thackeray, the *Atlantic Monthly*, Horace Greeley's New York *Tribune*, and everything else available. He was keenly aware of the great issues of the moment, and followed the course of current American politics. Later in Castile Academy and the Gainesville Female Seminary the youth was prepared for admission to college—which both he and his father thought would be Yale University. Before he could go on to college, however, Jordan served as teacher, and strict disciplinarian, of the boisterous South Warsaw, New York, public school. In the spring of 1869, at age eighteen, he took a competitive examination for a scholarship awarded by the newly founded Cornell University, and in March of that year he went to Ithaca with seventy-five dollars in his pocket to seek a college education. By hard labor and extreme self-sacrifice he was able to work his way through college. In June, 1872, he was graduated from Cornell with a master of science degree. His thesis was in botany, on the wildflowers of Wyoming County, New York. At Cornell Jordan had many friends, none of whom had a more far-reaching influence than President Andrew D. White.

David Starr Jordan's first teaching assignment was at Galesburg, Illinois, as professor of natural sciences in Lombard College, and at the end of the year he went to Penikese Island, eighteen miles offshore from Bedford, Massachusetts, to study in Louis Agassiz' Summer School of Science. In this summer institute Jordan became a confirmed Darwinian, and formed invaluable friendships with Agassiz and his promising young scientists, who were shortly to become leaders in their fields. Agassiz offered him a position as curator of fossil vertebrates in the Harvard Museum, but instead he accepted a professorship in the Pestalozzian Appleton Collegiate Institute in Appleton, Wisconsin. It was in this part of the Northwest that Jordan revived his boyhood interest in fishes. The Collegiate Institute failed after its first year, and the young teacher returned to Penikese the following summer without a job. On this second visit to the island he learned about the newly founded Woods Hole Marine Laboratory.

In 1874 Jordan took a job as science teacher in the Indianapolis city high school, but he stayed only a year before he was job hunting again. He was turned down for a job at Princeton because James McCosh felt his explanation of his views on religion smacked too much of Agassiz liberalism, idealism, and German theism. President James B. Angell at Michigan turned him down because he was not a specialist in zoology, botany, geology, and physiology. He was elected professor of natural history at the University of Cincinnati by Henry Turner Eddy, but the trustees refused to ratify the appointment, and finally he was tempted to accept a professorship in the Imperial University of Tokyo, an offer he refused.

In the midst of his job hunting, Jordan and Charles H. Gilbert of Indianapolis went on their famous southern journey seining streams, listening to political speeches in Kentucky, visiting Civil War battlefields in Tennessee, collecting valuable biological specimens, and making some keen post-Civil War social observations. That winter, 1876–77, Jordan did extensive biological exploration and served as professor of the sciences in the North Western Christian University (Butler) in Indianapolis. The following summer he again made an extensive exploration of the South, this time accompanied by Charles Merrill of the Bobbs-Merrill Company, Barton W. Evermann, Theodore Hill of the Smithsonian Institution, and Elliott Coues.

In 1879 Jordan and a Butler instructor, a Cornell graduate Alembert W. Brayton, came to Bloomington to judge an oratorical contest. Richard Owen, the much beloved professor of the natural sciences, had just retired, and the board was seeking a replacement. Brayton asked Jordan to appear before the board in his behalf, but the trustees were so impressed with the young visitor's presentation that they selected him to the chair instead of Brayton.

As a professor in Indiana University Jordan began at once to explore the natural resources of Monroe County and southern Indiana. He already knew something of Indiana University through his friendship with Hermann B. Boisen, the eccentric Schleswig-Holsteiner who had served as professor of modern languages from 1870 to July 1, 1874. Jordan regarded Boisen as "one of the real men of the faculty, remarkably successful as a teacher and sincerely loved by his students." From Brown County to San Francisco, to Europe, Puget Sound, the Fraser River, the Indiana professor of the natural sciences went in search of fish and culture. On his return to Bloomington from these adventures he was much in demand as a speaker. Jordan was never at a loss for a subject. He described everything from the catching of a rare eel—*Anguilla rostrata*—in the Rockcastle River of Kentucky to climbing Lookout Mountain, scaling the Matterhorn, explaining the theories of Charles Darwin, and describing his exploration of the Florida Keys. No doubt he was correct in saying that he had known no one when he came to Indiana, but in a short time he knew someone in all ninety-two counties. Thus it was that in December, 1884, the Board of Trustees selected a man for president who was already well known and popular among the people of Indiana. He was not to join the line of cautious, narrow, ministerial administrators who preceded him. He would not be satisfied to take the buffetings of critics because he and the university simply marked time in Bloomington.

Before Jordan lay the challenge of making a viable university of the institution in Bloomington, and of selling the people of Indiana the idea that higher education had values which could be translated into the acceptable terms of a practical minded, agrarian society.

By 1886, Jordan had become the most widely publicized professor in Indiana educational history. The Indiana papers from 1879 to 1891 carried numerous stories of his activities. The Smithsonian Institution sent him to the West Coast to assume charge of taking a fish census in that part of the country. Nearer home his "tramps" about Bloomington, trailed by a company of nature lovers, were ever newsworthy, as was his work with Charles H. Gilbert in preparing a book on the fishes of the world. By January, 1883, he had published some 124 books and articles, some of them with Charles Gilbert. He was rapidly becoming the Constantine Rafinesque of the late nineteenth century. His name got abroad and offers of jobs came from Illinois and Mississippi universities. He was offered a two thousand dollar salary and a house at the University of Mississippi, and when he turned it down the Indiana *Student* remarked, "it is not good taste for Indianans to say anything derogatory to the state of Mississippi after this." Jordan turned Illinois down because he did not like the flat muddy lands about Urbana, although he was attracted by the fact that he believed that university to be much stronger than Indiana.

Faculty minutes reveal that Jordan was often absent from meetings because he was late returning from Europe, or off making arrangements to go to the West Coast, or seining for fishes in the South. In February, 1884, he was awarded a gold medal by Albert, Prince of Wales, at the International Fishery Congress in London. This prized medal he brought home and showed to students of the university following a morning chapel service. This caused the *Student* to boast, "We, of the Indiana University, U. S. A. feel quite large, thank you."

In April of 1884 Jordan led a party of sixteen South Hadley Seminary ladies through the Adirondacks. That fall he was busily engaged until December arranging an exhibit of fishes for the great Cotton Exhibition in New Orleans. The United States government was even looking ahead to the time when Jordan would seine the rivers and lakes and complete as nearly as possible a collection of the fishes of the United States. It was hoped especially that he could investigate the trout streams of the Great Plains and western mountains.

During part of the crowded summer of 1884, Jordan was busy with the assignment from the United States Bureau of Fisheries seining American rivers. Sometime during these months he visited Cuba, began seining at Ottumwa, Iowa, and worked southward to New Braunfels in Texas. He had just returned to Bloomington from this expedition when the Moss incident occurred. He said in *The Days of a Man* that the Board of Trustees asked him to go over its extensive list of presidential candidates and appraise each man. After doing this he urged the election of John M. Coulter of Wabash College. Jordan declared he was surprised at his unanimous election to the presidency. He also said that he did not desire the job because his ambitions "ran in the direction of Natural History and exploration." He said he actually hoped to be appointed to a permanent federal job in connection with the Fisheries Bureau. In accepting the Indiana job temporarily, Jordan sent along a letter of resignation to become effective at the end of the first year—a document which, he said, was "promptly lost by the Secretary of the Board."

Reaction to the election of David Starr Jordan to the presidency was generally favorable. The editor of the Indiana *Student* was jubilant over the selection. "A man of international reputation," said the editor, "*is* put at the head of this institution, & thus have we ever prayed." Students felt this was an answer to the petition which a hundred of them had signed. They had actually backed Richard A. Proctor, but this was because Jordan had persistently said that he would positively not accept the appointment. In the minds of the students only one thing was needed to put Indiana University on the road to becoming a thriving school: "Give us Coulter now as Professor of Natural Sciences," they said, "& Proctor by & by—as Professor of Astronomy—with *a good round sum to 'buy books'* & to back us; & we'll be fixed."

In January, 1885, the thirty-four year old Jordan took up the duties of president. In his opening lecture in the college chapel on January 11 he displayed a modest amount of reserve mixed with a decided air of cockiness. He told the audience,

It has been said reproachfully of Thoreau, that, with a genius which might have directed great enterprises, he preferred instead to lead a huckleberry party. In this matter I have always sympathized with Thoreau. It is easier to find leaders in the battles of the world than pioneers in the fields of science. Science demands singleness of purpose, & scientific men have always been loth to leave their own pursuits to accept duties & trusts from the schools of the State.

He took great pride in the fact that he was the first scientist, since the elevation of Karl Linnaeus to the presidency of the University of Uppsala, to become a college president. With certainty he assured his audience that Sunday afternoon that he knew the size and shape of the problems before him, and "There are certain things which I know I can do well, & which I can train others to do well." He then appealed to the faculty, students and townspeople to help make Indiana a university in fact as well as in title.

One thing the audience assembled in the chapel learned was that though Jordan expressed great admiration for Thoreau he had none of the New England philosopher's traits. He was a Darwinian extrovert among Hoosier fundamentalists, but his students in years to come would give back to the state well trained minds which would be of great benefit. "We have the essentials of the University," Jordan said, "though the surroundings be those of a huckleberry party."

The huckleberry party that David Starr Jordan began to lead in January, 1885, had to make its way through a tremendous tangle of economic, academic, and political brambles. The university's central problem was simply that of growing into a mature institution as measured by the current advances of American higher education. The new president realized that he had assumed leadership of a rather intimate local college which had been faithfully served by a small faculty that had grown old and set in its ways. The curriculum suited an antebellum classical college rather than a modern state university. Jordan said the enrollment was 135; a later registrar, however, said 156, and the yearly income of the university was in the neighborhood of $35,000. Beyond this were the additional problems involved in settling the institution in its new home in University Park. Because of this there was the appearance of backwoods rawness about the buildings and grounds, and an inordinate amount of disorganization and confusion.

First of all Jordan had to secure from the state more financial support, and this required the utmost loyalty from alumni legislators, the people of Bloomington, and the student body. The two new buildings were "quite insufficient." In Indianapolis the old enemies of the university were waiting with sharp fangs to devour it. One group, the sectarians, was led by John R. Gordon of Greencastle, and the others were Jordan's personal enemies. Gordon led a vigorous forensic onslaught, not only to cut the university's request for funds but even to close the institution. He declared it a waste of money "to throw it into that sink hole." Another clique wished to unite Indiana and Purdue. James H. Willard, Chairman of the Senate Finance Committee, objected to giving any support to the university so long as Jordan was president. Willard was angry because the president had in earlier years given a speech on college oratory in which he had singled out one of the senator's "greatest efforts" which was "famous like the others for rotund periods and florid adjectives." Jordan had admonished his students to forswear all attempts to rival the member from Floyd. Willard met Jordan in a capitol passageway and snarled, "You little dreamed when you laughed at me before your students that very soon I would be chairman of the Senate committee of finance and you would come before me begging for appropriations." The university asked for a $50,000 appropriation through Representative Cartwright and this amount was cut to $30,000. In February of that year the educational committee of the legislature was supposed to come to Bloomington on a special train, but only four of the nine members actually arrived. At a chapel period Jordan introduced the visitors, and one or two citizens of the town made some remarks about the university and its needs. The indifference of the absentee members, however, was an ill omen. The Bloomington *Republican Progress* said, "Committees have visited us before, but none more intelligent, more genial, gentlemanly and friendly than the one which was here last Friday."

Already the House of Representatives had passed a bill giving Purdue $40,000. In the second reading of the university's bill Representative Gordon moved to cut the appropriation to $20,000, and spoke for an hour declaring that Indiana University was in fact the "University of Bloomington." The local *Republican Progress* charged the representative with acting in bad grace as a graduate of Asbury University. "It shows on its face that his opposition results more from jealousy than from any earnest conviction of a principle involved." Gordon evidently did damage because the appropriation was set at $30,000. On March 4, 1885, Joseph G. Mc-Pheeters, Jr., and Robert W. Miers went to Indianapolis to support the $30,000 allotment when it came before the Senate. By April 8, the Senate had restored the amount to the original $50,000, and the Bloomington paper assured legislators the university needed every dime of the money. "This will put the University on a good basis, and it will start out on its new year with brighter prospects than it has ever known in all its history," said the editor. The Indiana *Student* expressed great pleasure at the increase in appropriation, "and right here & now, presents its thanks for the same." Rejoicing was premature, for Gordon was still active, and he succeeded in cutting off $7,000. Even at that the Bloomington *Republican Progress* thought it was "A very handsome sum, and one that will do a vast amount of work if properly applied."

The university could not always be certain that the treasurer would actually deliver the amount of money appropriated to it by the legislature. The sums appropriated were to be paid semiannually, but for the years 1879–80, 1880–81, and through 1883 installments were overdue. The treasurer maintained that payments should not be made until six months after appropriation and in the case of the back payments, he claimed the funds had lapsed with the results that the university had lost $10,000; the board refused to test the case in the courts.

These were the external problems which confronted the university. Internally there were two concerns which could no longer be put aside. First of these was the selection of a new faculty. The old professors had either outlived their usefulness or retired. Richard Owen was gone, Kirkwood approached dotage, Ballantine was aged, and so was Theophilus Wylie. Actually the faculty had to be reorganized almost throughout. Of the older staff there were left Amzi Atwater, James A. Woodburn, William J. (Lowe) Bryan, and Thomas Carlton Van Nuys. In an extensive report to the board in June, Jordan suggested a considerable revision of the whole instructional program. In some cases he wished to coordinate subjects into departmental relationships, and in others to get away from the older pattern of suiting the schedule to professorial convenience and residual rights. In addition to the rearrangement of professors and course classifications he also recommended that the joint office of registrar-librarian be created.

[2 1 3]

He told the board, "I submit that the President should not be required to spend any large part of his time in purely clerical work. Much of the work of registration is now done by Mr. William W. Spangler, & all should be under his direction."

Before this the president of the university had not only kept the records, collected fees, and registered students, but he had looked after many of the petty financial transactions of the school. He prepared all of his correspondence personally and in longhand.

Jordan's first faculty in 1885 consisted of Theophilus Wylie, physics, Daniel Kirkwood, mathematics, Amzi Atwater, Latin, Thomas C. Van Nuys, chemistry, Orrin B. Clark, English, John G. Newkirk, history, Samuel Garner, modern languages, Horace A. Hoffman, Greek, and John M. Coulter, botany and curator of the museum. There were the four associates, Arthur B. Woodford, political science, John C. Branner, geology, William J. Bryan, philosophy and English, and Joseph Swain, mathematics. The aggregate of salaries for this faculty was $24,800. This was far from the eager and aggressive faculty Jordan had envisioned, but in time he made other additions. He sought younger and better trained faculty members who could help steer Indiana University into the new educational age.

There is plenty of evidence that Jordan made a full-scale academic analysis of the university's program during his first six months in the presidency. By June, 1885, he submitted to the faculty a new curriculum and a revised teaching schedule. Daily recitation periods would be reduced from more extended periods to one hour. Juniors and seniors were to be permitted to elect subjects of special interest to them, and all courses of an advanced nature were to be revised in order to accommodate the central objectives of the elective system. The new curriculum leading to the bachelor of philosophy degree would include intensive work in philosophy, history, and political science. A junior and senior specialty was to be developed in English language and literature. Juniors and seniors were to take five hours consecutively and weekly to meet specialty requirements. Literary students were required to have backgrounds in Greek, Latin, and English philology.

The above was only a starter in curriculum revision. In February, 1887, the faculty announced profound revision of the university's program. Required courses consisted of daily lectures in English for a year, and the student had to take two years of one foreign language, or two languages in one year. English composition was a required course of all students one hour a week for a year, and every student had to take a one-year course in basic mathematics.

In addition to required courses every student had to choose a "specialty" to be pursued daily for four years. The head of the specialty department was required to select courses for majors. The student, however, had freedom to make a choice of any course provided he pursued the subject for two years. This erased the old curriculum even if some of its elements were retained for many years.

Once reforms were under way in Bloomington, Jordan took to the academic hustings to sell the university and desirability of specialization. In a speech at Richmond, Indiana, on the subject of "The Value of Higher Education," he told an audience of young men that "It may do many things for you if you are made of the right stuff, or it may do little or nothing, for you cannot fasten a $2,000 education to a fifty-cent boy. The fool, the dude, and the shirk come out of college pretty much as they go in. They dive deep in the Pierian springs, as the duck dives in the pond, and they come up as dry as the duck does."

Jordan explained that he and the faculty at Bloomington were deepening the Pierian spring. Efforts were being made to assemble an able faculty, and in his mind, "The ideal college professor should be the best man in the community. He should have about him nothing mean, or paltry, or cheap." His own philosophy of higher education, he said, was partly shaped by his contacts with Louis Agassiz. All professors should be eminent in some branch of the learned sciences or literature and should spurn the reading of textbooks and staid lectures. Their real teaching should flow from original works in which they had made substantial investigation.

There was little of the McCosh and Angell philosophies behind Jordan's search for teaching talent. He wanted young ambitious men, and revealed little or no concern for their religious views or broad specializations. He was scientist enough to know that a successful professor of the new type was one who gave intense study to a given area. Somehow he gathered the information that there was a bright young Johns Hopkins graduate, a student of

Herbert Baxter Adams and Richard Ely, teaching history at Bryn Mawr College, and he sought to hire him for Indiana. On February 1, 1886, Jordan wrote Woodrow Wilson that the chair of history held by Newkirk "may become vacant in June. Salary $1500–$1800. Would such a position in a flourishing State University in a faculty chiefly composed of young men of modern training offer any attractions to you?" The job was actually offered to Wilson on March 19. Woodrow Wilson might have accepted the Indiana offer had it not been for his eagerness to go to Michigan, but instead Wilson went to Connecticut Wesleyan. Too, there was doubt in his mind as to how well his wife Ellen Axson might adjust to the kind of environment which Jordan described in his letter.

As a selling point to the Hopkins graduates, Jordan informed them he had just hired Baron Hans Karl Gunther von Jagemann, who had a doctorate in language from the Baltimore school. At that time Jagemann was professor of modern languages in Earlham College.

By June, 1886, Jordan had made up his mind about what Indiana University needed. In his annual report he informed the Board of Trustees, "The state university can only win or claim patronage from the good work it does. The value of this work depends on the character of its teachers. The University must have on its faculty only men of character and men of scholarship: men whom the students respect as men, and men who are masters or are becoming masters in the type of work they are employed to do." The youthful president was quick to reassure the public that not many well trained men fell short in these respects, a sentiment which was not borne out in his innermost thinking on the matter.

While Jordan was engaged in his study of the faculty and curriculum of Indiana University, he found his faculty involved in a slight whirlwind of local resentment. The German-born professor Felix Adler of the Society for Ethical Culture lectured in Bloomington in December, 1885, perhaps in the university, on the good life. He felt that all blue laws should be scrapped. Places of amusement should be thrown open on the Sabbath and the day should be turned into a grand holiday. Headlines in the papers implied that Adler was an Indiana University professor. He was a professor, but not at Indiana. The Jordan Darwinian liberality did not propose to go so far as the free-thinking Adler thought the city should go.

At the board's annual meeting in June, 1886, the president reported a number of faculty changes. Kirkwood and Wylie "have resigned their active duties & will henceforth honor our faculty roll with the title Professor Emeritus." John G. Newkirk and Samuel Garner presented their resignations. Newkirk did not resign voluntarily, as was indicated in a letter from Richard H. Dabney to Woodrow Wilson. Whether his unhappiness involved more than friction with Jordan is not indicated. At any rate he protested the financial terms in his case, and sought pay for another year. In hiring Dabney, Jordan promised him a salary of $1,500 to $1,800, but when Dabney arrived in Bloomington he found that the amount had been reduced to $1,000; the $500 difference was to be used in paying Newkirk's salary until December.

Other faculty changes included the employment of Arthur B. Woodford as professor of political and social sciences and Joseph Swain as professor of mathematics. Allan B. Philputt was made associate professor of Latin and Greek and Percy Burnett was elected associate in Germanic literature and languages. William A. Rawles was employed to take James A. Woodburn's place while the latter was on leave. Richard G. Boone was elected to fill the new chair of pedagogy and moral philosophy. The Bloomington *Telephone* reported on January 18, 1887, that the full-time university faculty numbered eleven professors, four associates, and two tutors. "The faculty," said the paper, "is composed of young men, the average age being only thirty-two. They are chosen without regard to political or denominational relations. Among them are graduates of Harvard, Yale, Johns Hopkins, Virginia, Michigan, and Indiana universities, and some have studied at Berlin, Leipzig, Frechtberg, Heidelberg, Munich, Tubingen, Geneva, Paris, Edinburgh, and Glasgow. Ten are natives of Indiana." This was a broadly educated group and reflected the fact that Jordan was caught up in the new wave of emphasis on graduate study.

As liberally educated and widely chosen as the new Indiana faculty was, there still existed dissatisfaction with one aspect of the Jordan staff. It was all male, and the president seemed to ignore the enormous feminist pressure being exerted on institutions at the time. He told the trustees in June, 1887, that there was real agitation for the appointment of a woman to the faculty. He, too, wanted to elect a woman member, but she had to be a "woman of scholarship, tact, social experience, and maturity of mind and character." She could be of great value to the university. "A woman whose scholarship was not such as to place her on a fair equality with the men in the faculty could not succeed as the occupant of a chair in the university." Then he uttered a gross understatement that "such a woman was rare." Few or no men met the level of perfection which he outlined. He thought that there was only one woman in Indiana who could be considered and that was Miss Mary E. Nicholson of the Indianapolis Training School.

Organization of the faculty was only half of the Jordan program of reform. The key to the university's future progress was the nature of its curriculum. It is doubtful that Jordan brought much originality to the revision of the Indiana program. He came to the presidency at the moment when the introduction of an elective curriculum was the central issue in American Education. The old presidents and professors stood for the old line classical college curricula. Charles W. Eliot said, "The manners & customs of the Yale faculty are those of a porcupine on the defensive. The other colleges were astonished at first, but now they just laugh." Johns Hopkins asked Noah Porter for advice and he refused to answer the letter. In the end, and after much ill-tempered storming by Porter, Yale had to give in to the new curriculum with its system of electives. Yale lowered its quills, and the head porcupine, Noah Porter, seems to have drifted into the new age. More and more the term "real university" entered educational parlance and into the future planning for Indiana University.

Eliot went so far in his liberal views as to declare that requiring students to study Greek was an anomaly in a democratic country. It was from Andrew White of Cornell, however, that the young president of Indiana University took his cue. Cornell under White dealt with the masses of rural and small town students better than did the denominational colleges. It undertook to serve students with even such esoteric and practical training as in pharmacy. White and Eliot were in full agreement when the latter answered an address by President Arthur T. Hadley on thirteenth century European universities. Eliot declared the American university had nothing to learn from medieval universities, not even those still in existence.

Other forces felt in this period were demands for training in the new sciences and for the liberal type of graduate work then being undertaken in some universities abroad. Some of the reformers began to inject the idea that research was a basic part of the university's mission.

Before Indiana could pursue the liberal course, Jordan told the trustees, "We need in each of the several departments of learning within our scope rigorous men to represent before the students, & before the state, advanced culture & original work, in that field." He was highly critical of the fact that botany in Indiana University could be taught by assistants in mathematics or psychology, or even by the professor of chemistry. Before anybody could lead the university to growth and maturity of its program there had to be more first class men on the campus, and there had to be a revolutionary reworking of the curriculum. More books for the library, specimens for scientific displays and experiments had to be purchased, and more buildings had to be constructed.

Jordan reviewed for the trustees the conditions in the university, man by man and subject by subject. He proposed a new departmentalization of the fields of learning, and a completely new approach to the appointment of professors to fill posts. He proposed, for instance, that the program in modern languages be separated and given precedence over the classics. With the coming of Karl von Jagemann, German became a major language. In fact Jagemann had hardly arrived on the campus before there was a demand for two professors in the subject. This continued to be so even after Jagemann resigned. His successor, Gustaf Karsten, continued to cultivate good will for the subject by exciting teaching. The effects of the expansion of the modern languages was reflected in the Bloomington *Telephone* report of March 25, 1887, when the editor said since Latin was no longer compulsory only two sophomores had elected to take it.

In the social studies Jordan's university made some significant changes. In June, 1885, the Board of Trustees created the Department of History and Political Science. Again the president was influenced by "Andy" White, who had advocated that every entering freshman have a course in general history. It is difficult to discover what if anything Professor Newkirk had done with the subject, or whether he was actually a professor of history with any authority to revise plans for teaching his subject. The appointment of Richard Heath Dabney on June 8, 1886, was the actual beginning of an organized, separate program of history in the university. There had been courses of sorts going all the way back to Andrew Wylie's time. By the fall of 1887 Dabney had introduced courses somewhat in the style of Johns Hopkins and the German universities. He offered introductory courses in classical history, but he emphasized advanced work in American history and politics and gave a seminar in the field. By the fall of 1888 there were fourteen "specialists" in history in the graduating class, and Dr. Dabney's work was growing in favor. The *Student* recommended that all ministers and lawyers take it.

When Andrew White visited Bloomington in October, 1888, he reported to Jordan that the course of history offered in Indiana University was the best one in the West. R. H. Dabney was an interesting man. He was an independent Virginian and scion of a family whose name was well regarded in the South. When Dabney left Bloomington to spend the Christmas holidays in 1886 in Richmond, Virginia, the *Saturday Courier* took pains to note that he was the nephew of the much publicized Dr. Robert L. Dabney, who had fought efforts to institute public education in the South. The *Courier* was concerned that the uncle had been appointed to a federal position. The newspaper press all across the North screamed over the fact of this appointment. Richard H. Dabney took care to assure the people of Bloomington that these were monstrous lies, and that his uncle had nothing to do with Andersonville Prison, as was implied in the Indiana newspapers. A fifteen year old lad in 1865, Robert Dabney had taken no part in the war, and he had secured his federal position by an honest civil service examination.

Professor Dabney was to create a minor furore of his own when he published an article in *The Nation* exposing corruption in Indiana local and state politics in the Benjamin Harrison era. This commentary received a lot of local attention in Indiana. The Bloomington *Saturday Courier*, December 8, 1888, said, since certain people were printing insults in a Bloomington paper about this, it felt obliged to write an editorial defending Professor Dabney's right to express his views. Note: the attack on him was printed in the *Telephone*. The *Courier* said that at the meeting of the next legislature the university would ask for an appropriation of $100,000 to complete its physical plant. Since the legislature was Democratic and the people conservative it anticipated no trouble, but the *Telephone's* attack on Dabney was "doing a notable work toward securing the desired legislation." The *Telephone* finally agreed to stop its attack, but advised Woodrow Wilson's bosom friend to crawl into "the artesian well hole." The *Courier's* editor retorted, "There is a larger and deeper hole yawning for the editor of the *Telephone* where the sulphuric atmosphere is much stronger." The *Courier* said it thought one of the "cheekiest" things at all was for the "*Tellelie*" to pretend that "Its utterances would have any influence toward securing an appropriation after it abused and insulted everything Democratic about the institution."

This incident led indirectly to Richard Heath Dabney's resignation from Indiana and to his acceptance of the professorship of history at the University of Virginia, where he spent the rest of his life. Apparently Dabney's wife never came to Bloomington. In May of 1889 she became seriously ill and her husband rushed home, but she died before he could get to Richmond. Dabney never returned to Bloomington.

There was obvious friction between Dabney and Jordan. There is no doubt that Dabney wore his tender Southern pride on his coat sleeve. On November 6, 1886, he wrote Woodrow Wilson:

> I am anxious to see the war issues dropped entirely and the old parties dissolved, but the Republicans must lay down their arms first. They must cease to wave the bloody shirt & to damn the South before I will vote for a Republican for President. So long as they continue to call the southern people "traitors" & the like, so long do I wish to see the South "solid" no matter what becomes of civil service reform, the labor question, the tariff question, the silver question or what not."

Obviously the professor of history had decided views.

Dabney wrote Woodrow Wilson January 27, 1887, about his plans to be married if he could earn $1,500 a year. He felt he would make a better salary, "Even though I be obliged to be connected with a hypocrite like Jordan. . . . Jordan appears to be satisfied with my work, & has told me as much, but he *may* be plotting to put me out for some reason unknown to me." Earlier he had written Wilson, "For although Jordan is a snake-in-the-grass & a hypocrite of the rankest kind (as I am now still more convinced than before I came); it is not necessary for me to have very much to do with him; and although the average Hoosier is far from being a savoury animal, I am nevertheless of the opinion that this place is on the rise & is destined to become much more important than it is." In December of that year Dabney again wrote Wilson, "Still I have such a loathing for Jordan, who is as contemptible a rascal as I ever met, and such contempt for Hoosierdom in general that, even if you were not at Bryn Mawr, I should be strongly tempted to get there."

There was room for a clash between Jordan and Dabney. Dabney had come fresh from the German universities, where, as he told Wilson, he spent a year without taking a drink of water. He had savored to the fullest the German university life, and the raw new ground of "University Park" in Bloomington seemed a world away from Heidelberg. Dry Monroe County with its militant temperance lectures irked the more liberal scholar. Too, there arose between Jordan and Dabney a hot dispute over a cheating case. Dabney had caught the daughter of a prominent local family cribbing, and when he reported her to the administration Jordan equivocated and refused to punish her. In Dabney's mind this was confirmation that the man was an opportunist who lacked moral fibre. Dabney's anger persisted throughout his life, and he sometimes discussed his frustrating Bloomington years with his son Virginius. Changes came to Indiana University the hard way; professorial personalities sometimes clashed with that of the strong-willed and energetic young president.

By May, 1888, Dabney's tolerance of Jordan was exhausted. He told Wilson that the president had announced an elaborate program in history without consulting him. He confided that out of spite he had added a biting footnote to his article which appeared in the Indiana University *Bulletin* disclaiming any knowledge of Jordan's statement of curriculum. "The footnote," he told Wilson, "may have shown you that the article was in part intended as a defiance of Jordan, who is not only a humbug in general but has endeavored to force me also into the humbug business. The alleged 'original work' which his special students in ichthyology do is, in my opinion, largely a waste of time."

Jordan instituted a course in geography in his new program. This was not the first time such a course had been included in the curriculum, but it was the first time it had been given such solid status. The *Student* commented in October, 1885, that "the demand for topographical geologists is already large & is constantly increasing, while there is almost no supply whatever. The Indiana University is the only institution in the country today where such work can be learned as a part of the college course." A chair of geology was created in June of that year to take the place of the old geology-botany combination. After considerable correspondence Jordan persuaded John C. Branner, a practicing geologist of Pennsylvania, to come to Bloomington as director of the Geological Survey and professor of geology. Branner was an industrious man who made his presence felt in the university. The fall of his arrival he was appointed to represent the state in the famous Cotton Exposition in New Orleans. He assigned his students a rush project of making a topographical and geological survey of Bloomington Township to be included in the exhibition. He also prepared paleontological and archaeological materials to be displayed. A competition grew up over who would have the most elaborate display in the Exposition, Branner with his geology or Jordan with his fishes. Branner was almost as active in moving around as Jordan was. In 1886 he was appointed an assistant on the United States Geological Survey. The next year he was given two years' leave of absence to make a geological survey of Arkansas.

No department in the university received greater impetus than did zoology. This subject had been taught in some fashion in the university since 1838, if not earlier, under the heading of the natural sciences. With the curriculum revision of the Jordan years the older branch of the subject was taught during the first two years. In fact most of what had been the university's original program was moved back to the beginning years. In zoology the system of majors working under direction of a major professor involved more than mere laboratory exercises; emphasis was added on special research and advanced work in one field.

Jordan's intense interest in ichthyology set a pattern. Zoology became in the 1880's one of the best covered fields in the university. Both students and faculty members began publishing the results of their researches, a tradition that has continued. It may also be true, as Dr. Barton W. Evermann told the Indiana Academy of Science, that the twelve years Jordan spent at Indiana were the most productive of his life. Certainly he and his associates made the school a center of even international interest in the field. In the years 1885 to 1891, the Indiana biological scientists were Charles H. Gilbert, Barton W. Evermann, Douglas H. Campbell, J. S. Kingsley, Carl Eigenmann, and David Starr Jordan.

Because of his interest in oratory and elocution, Jordan was quick to support the newly formed department of English. In November, 1886, he announced in his annual report that he was in favor of stiffening the English requirement for every student entering the university. The next year the Bloomington *Telephone* said that more than fifty students were enrolled in the course of American literature. To help keep them interested in the subject the Board of Trustees in 1889 appropriated $25 with which to purchase portraits of Oliver Wendell Holmes, James Russell Lowell, John Greenleaf Whittier, Henry Wadsworth Longfellow, Nathaniel Hawthorne, Ralph Waldo Emerson and William Cullen Bryant. Except for the purchase of the Laocoön for von Jagemann this was probably the first direct investment that Indiana University made in the fine arts.

Curriculum changes elicited little faculty opposition, largely because new and more progressive professors were brought into every department in the midst of change and President Jordan started fresh in building his staff. He was not, however, so fortunate with the students who straddled the two periods. In the February, 1886, issue of the *Student* the editor complained that the university faculty had recently broken faith with the students already enrolled in classes. About ninety of them were in courses which led to the degree of "Bachelor of Letters." This indicated they had made a fair start in the modern languages and other courses that went with this background. When these students enrolled in the university they placed their faith in "permanence of the university—for four years at least. Now they had only two choices, "swing on the new fangled Ph. B. or join the dry boned minority of A.B.'s without a bit of Greek in their course." Said the editor,

There is little enough in a degree at the best, make it however permanent, distinct & difficult to attain; but when an A. B. is to be traded for a B. L. & a B. L. for a Ph. B., that may mean anyone of six different things with no certainty that it meant either, from the fact that elections are so free, it looks like returning to the days of our primitive corporation high school where we boys went to school till we wore out the arithmetic & quit school when corn-planting began, only to do the same thing over next winter.

Not only did the faculty change the titles of degrees, but it also changed other rules. After June, 1887, a senior thesis was required of each graduating senior until 1888, and every student until the later date was required to write at least one essay under the immediate supervision of Professor James A. Woodburn, the head of the department of composition. Professor Woodburn must have had his hands full with 273 term papers each semester.

The problem of degrees dogged the university. Various revisions were made in the list of undergraduate degrees offered from 1828 to 1885. At every commencement there were candidates for the Bachelor of Arts degree, and a few for the Master's degree. The Master's degree was awarded on the European plan. After the lapse of two or three years the Indiana graduate could apply for a Master's degree on the basis of work done independently, which led to intellectual advancement in his profession, or under the guidance of a professor. From the beginning the trustees at each commencement conferred honorary degrees on favored individuals. These were usually ministers and neighboring college presidents. David Starr Jordan carried this practice a step further and began conferring the doctor of philosophy degree as an honorary citation for scientists. At the June commencement such a degree was conferred on J. C. Branner, the new professor of geology and botany, at the same time that James A. Woodburn was awarded the Master's degree. The next year G. Brown Good, Director of the National Museum, and one other candidate were made honorary doctors of philosophy. Ten honorary Master's, one of whom was William J. (Lowe) Bryan, were awarded in the same commencement. In the graduation exercises of 1889 Carl H. Eigenmann and Oliver P. Jenkins were given doctorates for their "original research in ichthyology." Apparently they were the last recipients of the doctor of philosophy degree until the university instituted a genuine graduate program which led to this degree after substantial advanced study. The history of graduate work in Indiana University up to 1890 is obscure. Graduate courses were given from time to time, and there was a keen desire to institute a full program, but lack of faculty, money, classroom space, and laboratory equipment prevented offering enough work to constitute a school.

Jordan inherited the lingering problem of reinstating the law school, which had been discontinued in 1877. He began agitating for the revival of the school to meet student demands for training in the legal profession. By November, 1885, the new president had found time to give some serious attention to the teaching of law. He prepared a report for the Board of Trustees and the matter was turned over to a special committee consisting of Robert W. Miers, Robert D. Richardson, and Robert S. Robertson to investigate the possibility of reinstating law courses. The Bloomington *Saturday Courier* said that space for classes could be found in the old building, a tuition fee charged, and a professor hired. "We ought to have the Law School again," said the *Saturday Courier*'s editor, "and there doesn't seem to be any good reason why we should not have it." In June, 1886, the committee on the Law School reported that because of the uncertainty of the university's income, and because of the failure of the state treasurer to make available the semiannual appropriation, the organization of the Law School would have to be postponed.

It was not until two years later that the question of teaching law again came before the board. This time a legal affairs committee was appointed and given power to act. On November 12, 1888, the trustees finally approved the idea of reinstating the Law School, but again lacked funds. In his report the year before, David Starr Jordan had suggested that the Law School organization be held in abeyance, but that a professor of law be appointed to give legal courses as a part of the regular university program. These courses were to be arranged on a three-year cycle. Still in 1889 he was insisting that such a program be instituted, but this time the board responded positively. At their meeting on March 19, 1889, the trustees suggested that a law school be established and that two professors, one of whom was to be dean, be employed. Law classes were to be started in September, and work would be conducted on a two-year cycle. Further, the trustees proceeded to draft courses of study, specifying the areas of law to be taught. The degrees of Bachelor of Arts and Master of Arts were to be granted law graduates. At the June meeting of the board Judge D. D. Banta was elected Dean of the Law School at a salary of $2,500. The Indiana *Student* announced the organization of the new school, and said that W. P. Rogers of the well-known firm of Louden and Rogers would teach equity and jurisprudence, and Judge Robert W. Miers would offer pleading and practice and preside over the moot court. In September classes were begun with thirty-two enrollees.

Jordan's years at Indiana were filled with responsibilities. His main job was to reorganize and expand the whole university program. The staff was in an almost constant state of change, and course fields were divided and subdivided. The trustees in 1889 employed Jeremiah W. Jenks of Knox College to head the courses in economics, and after R. H. Dabney's resignation Earl Barnes was elected to the chair of history. After a failure to entice Martin D. Leonard away from Johns Hopkins University, Thomas McCabe of Michigan was employed as von Jagemann's successor in German. In 1891 Jordan was to add the last professorial star to his crown. He persuaded the young sociologist Edward A. Ross to come to Bloomington to develop courses in his specialty. Ross remained only one year before moving to Cornell, and later to Stanford.

Internally the administrative organization was expanded. In order to give Jordan more freedom from picayune details, Amzi Atwater was made vice president, and Henry S. Bates was appointed registrar. Actually the work of the newly created registrar's office (November 12, 1888) was done by Sophie Sheeks, who was transferred from the Library. She was paid fifteen cents an hour until 1891, when President John M. Coulter persuaded the Board of Trustees to stabilize her salary at $300 a year.

The new and ambitious professors kept a jump ahead of the bustling Jordan. In June they presented a request that a scholarly bulletin be published by the university. This project would require the appropriation of $500, and the *Bulletin* would be the official university publication. The faculty selected von Jagemann as editor and Orrin Banner Clark and Darwin P. Kingsley as associates. The Bloomington *Telephone* announced on September 23, 1887, that the new bulletin was about to appear. "It is to be conducted on the plan of the Johns Hopkins *Bulletin* and will be the only publication of the kind in the state. It will appear six times during the year in the form of a 16-page pamphlet, some larger than the *Student*. It will be the organ of the faculty." Instead of appropriating the $500 requested of it, the board contributed only a hundred dollars, and the rest of the cost had to be made up from twenty-five cent annual subscriptions.

No doubt one of the sorest problems which Jordan faced in his six-year presidency was that of getting the physical plant in order. The *Student* said in February, 1886, that "Of the three new buildings, two—the larger and best equipped—are devoted to science. The third, a poor little frame, is used for a chapel; & stored away in its attic are four or five little rooms, about 12 x 16, where the student must get his philosophy, political economy, literature, languages, & etc." The chair of philosophy was vacant, but that man of all subjects, William J. Bryan, taught "English, logic, rhetoric, and occasionally Mathematics & Languages, doing at the same time a large amount of lecturing in the interest of the University."

The campus was little more than a muddy woodland in which the dirt from the foundations of the new buildings was still bare. The roadway and walks were either muddy or dusty. The first brick walk into the campus was finished in November, 1888, and the walk in front of Owen and Wylie halls was laid in the summer of 1889. Before these buildings was the magnificent clump of Dunn's Woods. The Bloomington *Saturday Courier* said, "The forest trees in the new college campus now present a scene of true magnificence. Never was there a lovelier scene than the one presented there last Sunday October, 1885. It was a lovely Indian summer day, and the earth, the air, the clouds, the sky, and the roseate tints of the stately forest streets seemed to vie with each other in presenting a scene of gorgeousness never excelled by nature." The editor was in an ebullient mood.

Not all Bloomington householders were as intoxicated with the beauty of the Park. They grazed their cows in the woods and meadows, occasionally a drunk stumbled into the bushes to sober up, and hunters shot squirrels from the stately walnuts and beeches. Students complained they had to wade in the mud to get to the new college, and everybody charged that the city council had neglected to fulfill its promise to build a sidewalk along the street to the university. As a defense against trespassers the university enclosed its campus with a wire fence, which a Bloomington editor thought a jarring note of the glorious October festival. If the stock laws were properly enforced, said the university officials, the fence could be removed.

While stumbling through mud and dust, Jordan viewed two lingering problems through darkened glasses. The first was the eternal nagging issue of charging students a contingent fee to supplement income from the endowment fund and the state appropriation. In 1889 the public management of the endowment was no better off than it had been in 1829. Joseph Swain and Nat U. Hill were sent to Indianapolis to make a thorough inspection of the loans with the auditor. They brought home cheerless news indeed. Interest payments lagged in many cases as much as four years, and there was due a sum of fifteen or sixteen thousand dollars in back payments. Many loans had been made through obvious political influence and were secured with insufficient collateral. The auditor explained he had good intentions of clearing this matter up at some future time, but Swain and Hill believed the only way the university could ever expect to be dealt with honestly was to appoint a full-time debt inspector to make sure that loans were paid and capital funds properly invested. At that date the endowment fund had increased to $123,946.34, and interest returns in theory, at least, approximated $6,300.

Jordan's other major problem was a double-headed issue which had also plagued the university since the registration of its first students. Indiana had not made proper advancement in the field of college preparatory education and the university had been forced to operate an extensive preparatory department which had always hindered the university's promise to do more advanced work. Too, the standard of work in the university had to be lowered in order to have any students enrolled. In April, 1887, the president announced that he thought the preparatory school should be closed, and only applicants qualified to enter the freshman class admitted to the university. In June, however, he reported to the board that there was considerable demand for preparatory work by country and small-town students where no high schools existed. It was not, in his opinion, the business of the university to bridge this gap, and the preparatory school should be suspended even if it did result in a reduction of enrollment. He advised the board to discontinue the school at once, or set a term of years it would be allowed to continue, and not drag it along in a constant state of emotional uncertainty.

Tied to this problem was the one of charging a contingent fee of both university and preparatory school pupils. The board, however, voted in May, 1887, not to discontinue the collection of the fee, even though it hoped to reduce the amount. The Bloomington *Saturday Courier* in 1889 inquired why the university continued to advertise itself as not charging tuition when students were required to pay $6.00 a quarter to attend the school. It was the editor's belief that removal of the fee would result in a much larger enrollment. At its June 6, 1890, meeting the board finally abolished the preparatory school, but retained the contingent fee.

When continuation of the preparatory school was being threatened, the university faculty recommended that the friendliest relations be established with the Indiana high schools. This could be accomplished through a series of visits. A proposal was made that after 1889 professors would visit schools to give reading demonstrations in English classes in an effort to familiarize prospective university students with the British and American classics such as Tennyson's *Enoch Arden*, Charles Dickens' *Nicholas Nickleby*, Shakespeare's *Julius Caesar*, James Russell Lowell's *Vision of Sir Launfal*, Thoreau's *Walden*, and Washington Irving's *Sketch Book*. The professors suggested further that applicants for admission to the university should prepare "a neat composition in good penmanship, correct spelling, capitals, punctuation, grammar, paragraphing, and expression."

At last Jordan felt the university was making progress. The legislature of 1889 appropriated $60,000 for the construction of a library and other buildings. At the same time it had appropriated $30,000 to the general fund, which now gave the institution an annual income of approximately $40,000. The *Student* shared the president's enthusiasm. It said in June, 1889,

The year just closing has been the most successful in the history of Indiana University. More students, better faculty, and a better work are the elements of success. It was a happy day for the educa-

[2 3 0]

tional interests of Indiana, when David Starr Jordan was elected to the presidency of this institution, & began his aggressive administration. Formerly it was the policy that the student should seek out the University, but now, thru its representative men, the University had impressed itself upon the people of the state.

Earlier in the year this optimism had been clouded somewhat when the Reverend T. A. Goodwin, a misplaced rural preacher, attacked the university in the Indianapolis *News*, and later in a slender privately printed pamphlet. He contended the university was a beggar that had no place at the legislative appropriation table. In a long maudlin argument he said that the framers of the first constitution never meant it to be a public university. He said that Joseph Ristine had tried to destroy it in the Constitutional Convention in 1851, but had been able only to reduce the mandate. Again in 1867 Ristine and T. A. Hendricks had undertaken to defeat the appropriation of $8,000, but this bill had been introduced into the legislature too late to be assigned to a committee, and therefore it was passed. Higher education, in Brother Goodwin's opinion, should be entrusted to the religious bodies. Goodwin thought it might be all right to support Purdue because it was a "practical" institution, but nevertheless it, too, was entangled in the "nefarious affairs" at Bloomington because of the university's influence on the State Board of Education. He also claimed that Indiana had spent $3 million for nothing in supporting the university. He left his readers in the dark as to where all this money had come from, or what authority he had for specifying that amount. The time had come, the preacher thought, to call a halt to supporting the university even if it would involve great loss.

> And now what have we to show for these millions? A cluster of costly buildings and an assortment of mechanical appliances, and a corps of overpaid and underworked professors, whose business methods are such that tuition costs are approximately twice as much per capita there as in non-state schools, and yet the average saving to the student is less than 40 cents a week as compared with the expenses at other schools.

It mattered not that universities in Michigan and New York were better schools. Goodwin thought perhaps even they should be closed because they also exploited the people. He was uninterested in the outcome of the immediate skirmish over the annual appropriation and the state school board issue, the ultimate battle could end only one way. "The people will not be driven to build colleges by the neglect of the state to supply the want, and then not only be taxed to support a college no better than theirs." He argued that above a certain amount the church-related schools were taxed to support Indiana University. This was a heavy blast, but Jordan had met it head-on in Indianapolis, and for once Indiana University won both the skirmish and the battle.

Goodwin's plea that the legislature withdraw its support seems to have resulted in the institution being given the most solid public support it had ever received. Jordan could feel confident that the university was on solid ground from other indications. It had adopted an entirely new curriculum which was open-ended and looked to future expansion. Young professors gave a strong air of intellectualism to the new order of teaching, and the student body now showed an increase with the opening of each year. Jordan started his administration with 156 students, and in the fall quarter of 1890, there were 324. The high schools had multiplied and matured, and the old fear that some time or other the institution would fail to register enough students to justify keeping its doors open was gone.

Neatly printed invitations asked friends and alumni of the university to assemble on January 20, 1890, to celebrate the seventieth anniversary of the institution. A special feature of this celebration would be the presentation of a pageant adapted from Baynard Rush Hall's *New Purchase*. Then Dean David D. Banta and David Starr Jordan would speak. Later the Indiana *Student* reported that this was one of the most pleasant days in the university's calendar. Two distinct views of the university were presented by the speakers. Judge Banta reverently closed the door on the past by reciting the history of the heroic, but somewhat grim, past. The occasion was brightened by David Starr Jordan's prophecy that Indiana would at last become a university in fact.

[X I]

The Age of Transition

Indiana university found itself in a state of change by the middle 1880's, and its guardians were hard-pressed to explain the impulses which set its future course. To date, whatever may have been the details of its history, and the nature of the stirrings which had lifted the institution from one plane to a slightly different one, the university had held to one central ideal; it existed for the primary purpose of granting the Bachelor of Arts degree within the narrow parochial limitations of the classics. Earlier institutional contacts with the emerging world of higher education in late nineteenth century America were severely limited by provincial leadership, an aged faculty, and chronic lack of financial support. Before 1885 there had been too little opportunity for the university to organize its program in such a way as to engage in any broader public service than that of professors acting as supply ministers for local churches, and conducting a speaking campaign in the public schools of the states and before educational organizations. Education as a "practical everyday affair" in the age of limitless material expansion enjoyed almost no expression in Indiana in a period when private church-affiliated colleges wielded so much influence with the public and politicians.

The nearest Indiana University had come to contacts with the everyday society of Indiana was in its biennial attempt to gain some consideration from politically oriented state legislatures. After 1850 there was a liaison of sorts between the university and the state government which was maintained by the politicians of Monroe County and by the members of the Board of Trustees. These efforts were seldom pleasant, and by no means always constructive. They involved the institution directly in the mundane affairs of statehouse corridors and caucus rooms. In a more direct way the university was frequently dragged into conflict with taxpayers and the denominational colleges. Thus educational planning had to be conducted largely at the precinct level of partisanism, and within the selfish mores of a provincial society.

Isolated though Indiana University was, the inflow of changing American educational concepts and ideas was unavoidable. By the time David Starr Jordan assumed the presidency many American universities were caught up in an intellectual renaissance. There arose a continuing debate between the apostles of the old academy concept of the educational function and the newer approach of balancing instruction with original research. No longer did the set curriculum or highly prescribed set of courses fit the needs of a people who at all levels were in the exhilarating throes of an industrial revolution. Nowhere was this fact more noticeable than in the departmentalizing of education itself. In the social and humanistic fields fundamental change stirred defenders of two or three different points of view. Historical research now became almost as important as the teaching of textbook history. The Johns Hopkins Seminar had wide impact in this area, and the departmentalization of the subject under the management of young men imbued with modern and Germanic ideas demanded a place in the new university curriculum. English professors debated the approaches of the classicist and those of the newer cultural and philological partisans. Sociology emerged above the ruffled surface of the generality of politico-economics, and psychology was torn between Hegelian idealism and the thrust of the new sciences.

At Indiana University the bustling young President Jordan broke the parochial Hoosier shell by devoting himself noisily to research in the biological sciences. In his speeches to faculty and public he emphasized the role of the sciences, while upholding the place of the social studies and humanities. Whatever Indiana University did in the future, Jordan was convinced that it should dedicate its program to the concept that university education must move in the direction of reality and practicality. The test of the university graduate should be whether he had prepared himself to harmonize the forces of daily life.

By January, 1886, it was clear that the new regime at Indiana had broken with the institution's cloistered past. The Board of Trustees was made conscious that thenceforth the institution would become a practical social and scientific laboratory in which the student would prepare himself to serve the larger objectives of a rising technological society. This was the age in which much attention was focused on the democratization of academic society.

Up to 1885, the Indiana University faculty presented a paradox. Though the school was located in an isolated town, off the main stream of population and flow of travelers, many of its faculty members had a national and international educational background. Most of them had taught in other schools in the Midwest or East. Yet in Bloomington they conducted their activities on a purely parochial basis. Little or no comparison was made between Indiana University and its neighbors. It was not until the impulse of Cornell, Michigan, and the German universities was felt in the opening of the Jordan years that a broader perspective developed. The organization of interest-centered associations in the 1880's and 1890's brought about professional communication, which had been almost impossible before that date.

As explained in a previous chapter Indiana University took a strong line of departure in realigning its program to meet growing public demands. The young president worked both sides of the road at once. Inside the institution he undertook to adjust the academic program to reflect changes then occurring in the most progressive schools and to organize a young and better trained faculty. On the other side of the road, he sought broad public approval and support for the university. By 1887 Jordan had spoken in all ninety-two counties and had worked assertively and effectively with the legislature. In fact by 1889 he had become an expert lobbyist. He demonstrated with personal energy what he meant by leading the university into a world of reality and practicality.

At the grassroots of his school's existence, Jordan had to reckon with a local Monroe County constituency which three times had been called upon to make substantial contributions to the support of the university, and which now had a heavily vested interest in the institution.

Bloomington was still a backwoods courthouse town and its people were still Jacksonian in political outlook. The new buildings of Indiana University were said to be 3,000 feet from the courthouse and, as one carping student said, "Well on the way to Brown County." At the time Jordan assumed the presidency of the institution there was mud chin deep in the streets, and the dilatory City Council had not built a sidewalk down Kirkwood Avenue. The *Republican Progress* said in November, 1885, that grading for two or three blocks along the street was being completed. Thirty or forty members of the student body were women, and the editor felt it was beneath the dignity of the town to invite ladies to come from other parts of the state and then compel them to wade through almost impossible swamps of mud. If anybody thought this "a strong statement let them attempt to walk to the new college buildings after the next rain." The city fathers were warned that the students had been patient and uncomplaining but the time had come for action.

Theodore Dreiser, a student at the time, in 1888 viewed Bloomington and the university through the eyes of a somewhat timid lad who had been sated on the scenes of a raw Chicago. Of the university he said,

> There were, in addition, six or seven other buildings, of brick or wood scattered rather casually over a large and physically varied campus, which to me as I first saw it, and especially after my confined Chicago days, seemed very beautiful. A wide brick walk led from the principal street of the town up a hill, at the crest of which and to the sides as one approached stood these several buildings. . . . And to the east, northeast and southwest, were hills and seemingly heavy growths of trees leading interminably hence.

Dreiser found Bloomington to be a charming old town to look at; it was a respite. Life in the town seemed to go at a leisurely pace. The fall was a time when a student could dream away his days, something Dreiser tended to do.

Since its beginnings the university halls had been illuminated by sputtering and smelly lard oil or kerosene lamps. That part of the city's population which was astir after sundown depended on tallow candles and lamps. It was difficult indeed to move about after dark because of the absence of sidewalks, the muddy streets, and lack of public lighting. On July 3, 1886, the Bloomington *Saturday Courier* announced that electric lights were turned on for the first time, to the delight of everyone. The streets were lighted except for out of the way corners. There were thirty-five lights in the downtown buildings, two of which were in the cupola of the courthouse. A new era began for Bloomington and the university. In a short time the university itself entered the electric age by lighting its classrooms.

A year after David Starr Jordan assumed the presidency, and after another effort to move the university to Indianapolis failed, the Indiana *Student* told its readers that Bloomington with all its mud, flickering electric lights, and indifferent city officials was a good place for the university. It had a population of 3,500 inhabitants. There was not a registered saloon in town, and there were a good public school building and twelve churches. "We feel safe in the assertion," said the editor, "that no young man or woman can select a more healthful place, morally, mentally or physically, for the acquirement of a thorough education than that chosen by the state for her children."

In the first year of David Starr Jordan's administration, the attention of the university community was distracted from the main issues by two tragedies. At the end of the first semester the faculty and students were shocked by the accidental death of Edward A. Hall of Kentland. One of the main amusements for many students in Bloomington was hiking across the countryside and exploring the creek beds and caves. Theodore Dreiser graphically described in *Dawn* the harrowing experience of being lost with a greenhorn companion in a limestone cavern near the town. In May, 1885, the sophomore botanical students set out on an extended cross-country hike toward Brown County. Their route lay along the meanders of Salt Creek, where winter floods had dished out deep pan-bowls. Three boys who traveled out well ahead of the main party decided to cool off by taking a swim in the creek even though a neighboring farm hand had warned them that the green pools were treacherous, and especially so for nonswimmers. Edward A. Hall, unable to swim, slipped off the slick shoulder of rock and was catapulted into deep water, where he sank and drowned immediately. This accident ended the hike, and disrupted the university schedule. Hall's body was packed in ice, and David Starr Jordan and a representative of the student body accompanied it to northern Indiana for the funeral.

Hardly had Bloomington gotten over the shock of the Hall tragedy before Susan Bowen Jordan died. Mrs. Jordan was as energetic as her husband, and in the short time she had been in Bloomington had become a popular figure. Born in Berkshire County, Massachusetts, she was a graduate of Mount Holyoke (Hadley) Seminary and had planned to be a biological scientist before she met David Starr Jordan at Louis Agassiz' Penikese summer school. She had married the president just after he came to Indianapolis in 1875. At her death the town and university community went into mourning. Faculty members arranged the funeral and served as pallbearers, while Elisha Ballantine, Amzi Atwater, and T. A. Wylie conducted the burial services. Thus at a time when Jordan was working intensively on the reorganization of the university he had to bear the personal grief of two major tragedies.

There were other interruptions. In October, 1886, a freshman named Steele walked out of Bloomington leaving behind him all of his personal possessions at Mrs. McCoy's boarding house. He left no clues as to his whereabouts, and the university community worried that he had become the victim of an accident or foul play. The record is not clear as to what became of this lad; perhaps, he, like several college students in this period, got fed up with the trials of an entering freshman and went on a soul-liberating hobo trip. Edward Hall's death and Steele's disappearance gave the university adverse publicity which it had to outlive.

Jordan's Bloomington was comparable to other university towns: Ann Arbor, Oxford, Urbana, Madison, Columbia, and Iowa City. All of these were relatively new towns struggling in that muddy and uncertain era between the raw frontier and the more sophisticated educational centers. Cows still wandered in the streets of all of them, and city fathers did no more than was necessary to keep the populace out of the mud in streets and on sidewalks. President Jordan felt constrained to tell prospective professorial appointees that they would have to endure some of the inconveniences of an earthy frontier courthouse town. He tried to prepare them in advance to live in a town where their every act would be watched, reported on in the newspapers, and gossiped about around the square. Overshadowing all else was the fact that the university was growing physically and academically. The mud and inconvenience of the new campus in Dunn's Woods symbolized a phase in the institution's history. This came about because the institution was building an entirely new plant.

Students, however, were slow to make the transition from the older customs of the university to the establishment of new ones. Upperclass students gave haircuts to the freshmen and, sometimes, also to fraternity and literary society rivals. Student pranks persisted despite efforts to check them. Professor Amzi Atwater may have been as puzzled as to the point of the joke in placing a birch bark canoe mounted with a red lantern headlight on his lawn, as is the modern reader. Macabre humor was involved in mounting the "College skeleton" atop the Wylie Hall tower. It required fifty feet of new rope to get it down. Heavy stones had to be removed from the base of the cupola in order to permit Janitor Stewart to reach the bony guardian. The janitor informed bystanders that he knew who the offenders were, and his price for silence was the replacing of the stones.

Despite his scientific liberality, David Starr Jordan still retained many of the characteristics of the country school teacher of Warsaw. When a student turned off the gas in the midst of a chapel lecture he could be as stern as any of his colleagues. He was opposed to drinking, and, perhaps, dancing. He undertook to break up the various class and society "scraps." Nevertheless both Jordan and the faculty must have been amused at the escapade which occurred in May, 1885, when the seniors threatened a face-saving commotion because one member of the class had been taken snipe hunting. This lad had held the bag until 2:00 A.M. The *Student* reporter asked the rhetorical question, "Is higher education a failure?"

An Indiana student in 1885 was a far more independent individual than were his predecessors. However much the Board of Trustees and faculty might have wished to exercise strict parental authority over their charges, the age when this could be done was past. The university could not embrace the new national educational changes and freedoms which were sweeping the country without recognizing the fact that students, if given greater freedom in the selection of courses, had to be granted more freedoms in personal and group affairs on the campus. This aroused conflict at Indiana University. Older faculty members, townspeople, and members of the Board of Trustees were reluctant to grant wider latitude in student behavior and morals.

By 1887 David Starr Jordan felt himself pushed into the corner by student squabbling over use of the university chapel, interfraternity and literary society rivalries, class scraps, and other organizational problems. He ordered a halt to what he called the "two horned" affairs. There must be no further argument if students expected to use university facilities for their extracurricular meetings. Later that year the president asked the board to formulate rules to apply to drunkenness, cheating, disorderliness, impudence, and prankishness in college buildings at night.

The university had no direct control over boardinghouse situations, and once a student passed out of the university gateway he was largely on his own. He could misbehave in various ways and get away with it so long as he did not run afoul of the Bloomington constabulary or get drunk. Theodore Dreiser described in his autobiography some aspects of university life as he viewed it from the perspective of a diffident lad. If his descriptions are accurate, one segment of the student body had a much gayer time than is indicated by the more formal historical sources. Unquestionably some students departed from the straight and narrow path to enjoy such favors as the young ladies of Bloomington might bestow. Dreiser described a journey to Louisville with a couple of girls and a fellow student which sounds definitely unorthodox. This party's visit to the great Ohio River fleshpot was largely frustrated by the devastating cyclone of 1889, which had practically destroyed the city. As Dreiser implied, it was hard to sin in a place where people were grief-stricken and in ruin.

In Dresier's eyes the university social community had become sharply stratified by the rise of fraternities and sororities. A snobbism had sprung up on campus, largely erasing the early nineteenth century egalitarianism that had existed in the Jacksonian university. It was still true that rural middle class boys and girls registered each fall, but even many of these behaved more in keeping with their aspirations than with their social and economic past.

The fraternity movement gained fresh momentum in the

1880's. Kappa Sigma was organized on the campus in 1887, and Delta Tau Delta was reorganized. This brought the number of fraternities and sororities in the university to seven. The old literary society aspects of these organizations were being neglected, and the chapters more and more became social clubs. The fang and claw rivalries among the Greeks were dissipating as a matter of self-preservation. On March 9, 1888, there was held perhaps the first panhellenic banquet, which the *Student* said was the great social event of the year. In the editor's opinion, "The Greek spirit at Indiana University has changed materially in the last few years and for the better we are glad to say, until it finally reached a culmination in this pleasant occasion." The paper hoped this would become an annual affair.

Fraternity men had to find some outlet for their youthful energies besides girls and liquor. They announced in 1887 that the time had come for the university to issue a formal class annual. The *Semi-Weekly Telephone* thought this a good advertisement for the university and urged professors and students to support the undertaking. This move bore fruit, and the first issue of a formal publication appeared at commencement in June, 1888. Possibly this was only an extended issue of the *Student*, because it is now bound in the file of that periodical. Since around 1879 a fairly voluminous class commemorative volume had been issued containing photographs of university buildings, faculty, and students. In some of these volumes a lined page was included in the forefront for autographs of special friends of the owner. It was not, however, until 1894 that the *Arbutus*, so named for the tiny mayflower which is indigenous to the Bloomington area, was first published. By 1890 most of the campus rivalries had become calm enough to permit a compromise between fraternities and "barbs" (non-fraternity members), and a student named Foster was chosen to represent the two groups in university-wide councils.

David Starr Jordan was an advocate of outdoor activities and physical exertion. He had learned about baseball in Indianapolis in the "curve ball" incident, and in Bloomington he developed good rapport with students in both athletics and oratory. Athletic contests among the colleges of Indiana had come to involve a lusty kind of competition and school pride. An athletic association had been formed, possibly in 1885, and by 1886 students were looking forward to a fuller participation in sports with other colleges. Professor A. B. Woodford introduced the game of football on a formal basis in 1886. Two players were added to the first line-up of the baseball team, and on trips this combination engaged opponents in both baseball and football.

The first football players wore tight-fitting white canvas suits. Shirts were laced up the front, and some of the players cut blades from broad grain scoops and strapped them over their chests. The athletic association consented to participation in the state championship playoff in its first season in Indianapolis. The City Athletic Club offered as enticement a gold medal to the champions. The *Student* announced that the university team was practicing for its meeting with Butler in the first of the state championship games in October, an event in which Wabash College was victorious.

Indiana University athletes went on a road trip in October, 1887; at Greencastle they played DePauw in baseball, and at Franklin they played football. They tied DePauw and lost to Franklin College by two points. It was said the team had not had enough practice in football because it was playing its baseball schedule at the same time. Apparently the Indiana teams met one another several times during the season, as Indiana defeated Franklin 10 to 8 in a game in Indianapolis.

Students complained to the trustees that they gave no really serious attention to repeated requests that a gymnasium be built for all students to use. They claimed that one reason Indiana University athletes made no better showing in competition was the fact that they had no opportunity to condition themselves during the colder months of the year. Eastern institutions had been able to separate their football and baseball seasons between fall and spring months because they all had gymnasiums. Indiana had just as good material for football as Yale, but it needed a place to practice, and the university needed a fully organized athletic association. If a gymnasium was not established by the university, the students proposed to rent and equip a hall out in town for physical education.

Reviewing the athletic situation in Indiana University in October, 1888, the *Student* boasted that the baseball team had repeatedly won the collegiate championship by beating the strongest combinations of student clubs. The football team had not been so successful but it had kept up its courage. Tennis had reached a feverish pitch of popularity, and the local club had enjoyed success in intercollegiate competition. Lack of a gymnasium, however, had handicapped other forms of physical expression. Since its frontier days Indiana had cherished an athletic spirit; all it needed now was local encouragement. "The state," said the *Student*, "can give thru appropriations for a gymnasium and a continuance of the kind of interest and approval of the faculty [for the university] to become pre-eminent in athletics as we are in the sciences and philology. . . ." Whether or not Jordan had a hand in influencing his alma mater to take Indiana's champion pitcher onto its baseball team is an open question. Indiana students were proud of the fact that Fred Cornell went to Ithaca to pitch for Cornell University at $250 for the season.

If need for a gymnasium was reflected in football scores then the legislators and trustees should have been duly impressed in November, 1889, when Wabash defeated Indiana at football, 40 to 2. The Wabash team was said to have been carefully trained and played an alert game, while the boys of Bloomington did much to engender pride at home but labored under genuine handicaps. Not enough local interest in football had been manifested to recruit a second eleven to permit competitive practice, and not all members of the first team had ever played together. Evans Woollen of Indianapolis had been with the team only two days. In his last year as president of the university, Jordan was to learn how frustrating athletics could be in a university program. For some reason of internal confusion the Indiana baseball team failed to finish the season in 1890, and perhaps forfeited the state championship. The student paper said the season should be completed "as it is an honor to the University, sets no bad precedent, and sends abroad no false impression of Indiana University grammar and morality." One of the last refrains David Starr Jordan heard on his departure from Indiana in 1891 was the *Saturday Courier's* query, "What is the matter with Indiana University putting out a football team? All the other colleges are making great preparations to have a strong team. It seems as though Indiana University should have one in order to keep up with the procession."

The element of professionalism had crept into American collegiate baseball, as was indicated by pitcher Fred Cornell's departure for Ithaca. Professor Orrin Banner Clark, in March, 1891, moved that the faculty investigate to see how many members of the university baseball nine were bona fide students. He also suggested, and the faculty approved, that the team be denied use of university grounds, excuses from classes, or any other favors, if any members received pay for their services, for such professionalism would be harmful to the integrity of the university. No doubt the faculty had ample reason to suspect professionalism, as the current issue of the *Student* lamented that baseball seemed to have departed Indiana forever. A movement was already underway to establish class teams.

Maybe, after all, it was not a stern faculty rule which discouraged baseball so much as the faculty-senior game played in June, 1891. The sports reporter of the *Student* said,

> to be sure, there were only twenty-four men given their bases on balls and so many errors were made that it required a calculating machine to note them all down. Nevertheless the game was interesting. Davisson deserves special mention for catching Gilbert's erratic delivery without the aid of a step ladder. The race between Bryan and Woodburn as to which could make the most errors was decided in favor of the former. Jenks excited the admiration of the crowd by the way (like unto an ice wagon) in which he ran bases. Swain was model first baseman, and were it not that he plays with Jordan's aggregation next year, doubtless could get a position with the famous Ellettsville team. The umpires, Justice-of-the-Peace Louden and Judge Brill, did as well as could be expected of such men. In order that the game should not be continued by the light of the moon it was called at the end of the sixth inning.
> Faculty 14—Seniors 30.

The introduction of intercollegiate athletics into American colleges brought about the use of nonsensical college yells. The Indiana Seniors yelled "88 is I. U.! I. U.! Hurray, Hurrah, Hurrew, Hoopla, Dipla, 88." In January, 1890, the Indianapolis *Sun* said that a contingent of fifty or more Indiana University students had rumbled into town aboard the "Southwestern Limited." When these Indians left the train they

> gave the college cry, one of those yells so devoid of sentiment and sense and replete with noise. One of the callow criers was asked

by a reporter to spell out the gibberish. He frankly confessed he could not. Several of the students who waited here to take other trains spent their leisure time saying those giddy nothings that characterize a college boy's courtship.

By 1891 the college spirit ran strong in Indiana University. Students took pride in their yells, class loyalties, and gibberish nonsense. Perhaps nothing appealed to their sense of humor more than to confuse the English university man with their college yells. Said the *Student* for February that year, "He [the Englishman] at once sets to work to prove how even educated Americans follow the custom of the savage Indians, his war whoops being perpetuated in the college yell." It was said that Indiana University students went to a circus and scared the elephant to death with their cheering.

At the time the seniors decided to publish an annual in 1888, they also selected university colors. The question of colors had been discussed much earlier when the university baseball team first engaged in competitive play. Apparently colors had been chosen for the university, as the *Student* for December, 1887, announced "The colors of the university are crimson and black." That year those of the upcoming senior class were cream and gold. On November 13, 1903, the *Student* again discussed the subject of colors, this time saying positively that cream and crimson "are the official colors adopted fifteen years ago. It appears that seniors in 1888, confronted with the problem of selecting binding colors for their annual, mixed the class and university colors to produce the cream and crimson combination." Before that time, said the campus reporter, "There had been no official university colors so the class of '88, thirty-nine in number, met to decide what Indiana's future colors should be. The cream and crimson were chosen without a dissenting vote."

The Jordan age was also an age of the straw-hatted, foppish, loose britched adolescent man of the world who tapped on the door of opportunity with a tennis racket, and greeted fate with a "sis-boom-bah!"

The coming of the athletic age to Indiana University saw the closing of another era. Whether or not athletics lessened interest in oratory is a moot question. There seems to be more positive evidence that introduction of the elective system into the curriculum was more influential in diverting student interests away from the old pursuits of literary culture. Since the opening of the university's doors the orator had fought the air on the campus proclaiming man's virtues, bemoaning his shortcomings, and gilding the glories of the heavens. The newly organized *Student* said on May 17, 1867, that orators had implored audiences repeatedly to accept the proposition that George Washington, Patrick Henry, Daniel Webster, and Henry Clay were great men, that Christopher Columbus started a job which Benjamin Franklin and Cyrus Fields carried on by snatching fire from the heavens and tying together two great nations in instant communication by a slender strand of wire. The Greeks, the Romans, Martin Luther, the English bards, and Hoosier notables were paraded before long suffering literary society and commencement audiences. Each spring brought out of the ground a new crop of Hoosier elocutionists and poets who declaimed everything from full-scale plagiarisms of Addison and Steele to the immortal words of Oliver P. Morton. Battlefield ashes were stirred from Marathon to Gettysburg, and adulatory soldiers found standing-room only.

Patriotic holidays, commencement, and literary societies' exhibits annually brought forth enough eloquence to raise a full blown tide in Spanker's Branch. On February 22, 1875, the four-piece university band kept an impatient audience in abeyance until orators could release it emotionally. The stage of the chapel was decorated in the cherry tree motif, and behind the speakers was suspended a large hatchet on which was inscribed, "I cannot tell a lie." No doubt this was an added precaution against the musty charges that many speeches were outright plagiarisms or feeble Hoosier imitations of the originals. "Cicero said," "Emerson said," or "Henry Clay said," hacked many a piece of filched plunder into eloquent chunks of nothing.

The Indiana Oratorical Association enjoyed much higher esteem before 1890 than did the athletic organizations. Speakers competed for statewide honors, and cheering sections went along with favorite contestants to befuddle judges with their catcalls and applause. David Starr Jordan was an active participant in all of this as judge and observer. He was an able speaker himself, often holding audiences spellbound with his descriptions of the hazardous trip up the Mattherhorn, or assuring parents of the values of higher education. He nevertheless grew weary of what he called "flavor-less foolishness." The *Student* in November, 1882, published his wonderful encyclical on college oratory. Said Jordan,

> The time of the singing of birds is come, the dandelion's head grows heavy in the tall grass, the Greek accents are slanting wearily to the grove, and the ichthyosaurus becomes a burden. And now, from behind tall trees, from the lofts of old barns, from the shores of Clear Creek, from the top rail of the garden fence, the voice of the senior is heard in the land. The ghost of Patrick Henry lurks behind every corn crib, and even the very mud has in it a reminder of Henry Clay. Apostrophes to George Washington, Pericles, Cicero, the American eagle and the Goddess of Liberty float down on every summer zephyr."

In his address Jordan dissected college eloquence and concluded that the great defenders of liberty lay moldering in graves in Massachusetts, Virginia, and at the Hermitage in Tennessee, and unless some drastic changes were made college oratory would soon lie beside them. "Generally speaking," he thought, "there is little originality in a man without some degree of humor. There is not much lightning in a fog. "

There may not have been much intellectual lightning in the fog of Bloomington, but in time there arose so much bickering and ill feeling over oratorical contests and society exhibitions that the faculty, recalling the Asher affair of 1883, and the eternal noise generated by charges of plagiarism, voted in March, 1886, to recognize no one as the official representative of the university in the state oratorical contest. Students could hold as many contests as they pleased and choose as many representatives as they liked. This hasty decision resulted in bitter factionalism in which two representatives, J. W. Fesler and C. E. Sims, were chosen for the state contest. Sims was backed by the fraternities and Fesler by the student body in general. This division came about because of an attempt not to permit the nonfraternity students to participate in the contest.

No doubt David Starr Jordan and the faculty rued the day they voted to leave selection of contestants to students. The *Saturday Courier* of April 17, 1886, observed wisely that the campus conflict on this subject should have been settled at home. Two Indiana representatives and their respective backers presented themselves at the English Opera House in Indianapolis to participate in the state oratorical contest. When Indiana University was called to the stage, both contestants came forward and began their orations amidst cat-calls, hisses, and moans. The din became so offensive that the opera house manager had them removed from the stage, and the judges disqualified the university from further participating in that contest. A week later the faculty refused to excuse class absences of contestants who wished to participate in the interstate contests at Lawrence, Kansas. Too late to halt contests, however, this body voted in November that year to forbid students to use the name of the university in public contests unless it approved such use. The faculty also assumed future management of the University Oratorical Association, and there would be no more of what Jordan called "abject lessons in public."

This move by the faculty did not immediately solve the infighting over the contests. Actually this type of intercollegiate contest was losing broad state interest and the Indianapolis debacle did nothing to improve its cause. All the Indiana college presidents agreed in April, 1887, that it would be wise to disband the Oratorical Association, but the students and public were not quite ready to accept this solution. Indiana students themselves made renewed efforts to restore oratory to its high place of interest, and to some extent they succeeded. In 1891 Frank Fetter won the interstate contest at Lawrence, Kansas. This was a day of rejoicing. The *Student* sent up the lusty cheer:

> Here's to Old I.U.,
> Drink her down, drink her down!
> Hurrah for Old I.U.! Hurrah! Hurrah! Hurrah!
> Fetter! Fetter! Fetter! first Place!

The paper ran numerous comments from over the country about the young Hoosier's victory, giving him credit for having left well behind the objects of Jordan's criticism of college orators not to descend into literary mud puddles.

If oratory waned after 1887, so did the literary societies. In October, 1890, there were the Philomathean, Athenian, Eureka, Hesperian, Independent, Century, and Union societies. As the internal strife increased in the old societies, and as students' interests turned to other social and intellectual channels, the literary clubs found it more difficult to carry on with the traditional enthusiasm. The *Student* reported they had done little in the literary line, "but now that our bark is launched we hope to spread our sails and glide smoothly on." Such, however, was not the will of Poseidon. Total membership in the societies had dropped to fewer than one hundred, and the secretaries' books indicated that not half of these attended meetings regularly. The *Student*'s editor thought something drastic had to be done. To allow the literary societies to go by default would deny the university admission to all sorts of literary contests. The implication was clear; the days of the literary societies were numbered.

While the new age was being born, the university made a departure in the field of music. Music had always played a slight role in the institution. President Wylie in his famous confrontation with the old carpenter in the Presbyterian Church was accompanied by a makeshift band of four or five pieces. Later a harpsichord or piano was used in chapel song services. By 1885, the musical contingent of the school had maintained its numbers only, and maybe it had made certain instrumental advances. Miss Clara Orchard played the organ, Oaks and Howard Tourner played cornet and flute, and Miss Esse Fee was pianist. Opening of an entertainment in March, 1885, was delayed for forty-five minutes because the gas burners of the lighting system could not be lit and the musicians could not read their scores. As the *Republican Progress* said, the gas pipes were "out of shape," and Uncle Tommy Spicer had to bring out his dirty old oil lamps. In the meantime the rowdies in the crowd threatened to tear up the auditorium. These lads had a gleeful time by cheering loudly the arrival of every couple. Not even Miss Fee and her band could calm the commotion. The editor was of the opinion that the university's authorities should clamp a tighter control on such audiences, but first they should get them out of the dark.

The era of Jordan's presidency at Indiana University was a highly vocal one for all American society and universities. As mentioned earlier, the public lecturer was loose in the land, and Bloomington came more and more to be a point of interest to him. Both town and university attracted these speakers and performers.

In May, 1885, Hoosiers had an opportunity to hear their favorite poet James Whitcomb Riley speak in Mendelssohn Hall, and after the lecture he went home with the Phi Psi boys, who cheered both his literary and gustatory accomplishments. Aside from Professor Felix Adler, who upset the equilibrium of the sabbatarians, the Redpath Concert Company served the College Lecture Association with John Bascomb, George W. Cable, Henry Ward Beecher, and Lieutenant Schwatka in 1885–86. Tickets to these lectures went fairly fast, and their financial success was assured. Riley was back in May, 1886, with Bill Nye to offer "the richest treat of the season," and to justify the great expenditure of energy on the part of Professor D. K. Goss, chairman of the lecture series.

Not all of the lecturers were as successful as Riley and Cable. The editor of the *Saturday Courier* thought an occasional circus would be more entertaining. Better than a circus was the appearance of the highly publicized Henry Ward Beecher. On April 3, 1886, a large crowd gathered at the depot to welcome Mrs. Theodore Tilton's lover to town. From Beecher's voluminous publicity the crowd no doubt expected to see a towering giant step off the cars. The *Student* editor said, "To one who had never seen Mr. Beecher he was, physically, a surprise. He is of very low stature, but with a well-rounded aldermanic person that speaks of a quiet, happy contentment both with himself and the world at large." Older people standing about the train remarked that Beecher reminded them very much of Lemuel Moss; the two had something in common. Beecher lectured in the old College Chapel that night on "Government by the Common People," and approximately 700 waded through a "blinding snow storm and slush and mud to hear him."

In this era of reforms, speakers discussed tariff and civil service and all the ills of the day. In October, 1886, Senator William Dudley Foulke lectured on civil service reform, and the *Saturday Courier* said the university staff was mortified by his talk because he turned it into a vituperative tirade against the Republicans. The editor thought it would be some time before another political stump speaker would be invited to the chapel. On Foulke's heels, however, came Congressman Horr of Michigan, who spoke two hours without using notes on labor and capital. The *Courier* was certain that everybody went away feeling "that it had been good for them to be there."

The next year Henry George came to lecture on his single tax program. On February 13 he spoke on "Land & Labor." The *Student* reported that few persons present at the lecture agreed with him *in toto*, but many were impressed with his sincerity and desire to better the conditions of the laboring man and thereby the quality of American society. George displeased the Republicans, thought the *Saturday Courier*, because he voiced strong anti-tariff views. Jordan, however, was fascinated by George's ideas and engaged him in an extensive conversation as to how private property might be brought into control, and how corporate business might be brought into the system without creating a totalitarian state. It was Jordan's thought that individuals would suffer the most. Henry George was extremely vague in answers to the president's questions.

The eccentric Bronson Alcott did not have a proper audience in crusading for his esoteric form of society. He drew little positive response from the university audience. As David Starr Jordan said in later years, Alcott did not even stimulate the "Bates School of Philosophy" to any serious comment. It wasn't what Alcott said that piqued the Bloomington citizens so much as his eccentric manners. His hostess had prepared a good Southern feast of roast turkey, scalloped oysters, chicken pie, boiled ham, and served jellies, pickles, preserves, layer cakes, ice cream, and everything else imaginable only to have her hospitality curtly refused by the visitor. He explained that "he ate next to nothing and little of that."

One of the most timely lecturers was Senator Blanche K. Bruce of Mississippi, who had gained national fame as the Reconstruction Negro senator from that state. He was candid in his discussion of the race problem in America, and especially in the South. The campus paper said,

He is quite hopeful as to the future of his people and considers the present course of Americanization in the light of *sinqua non* [sic]; that the status of the race is one of degree and not of kind; that the carrying of a rabbit foot and the hanging of a horseshoe bespeak no wide distinction; and lastly that the freedmen are no longer a "benighted people halted in hesitating wonder on the twilight threshold of civilization and enlightment," but rapidly advancing to claim the merit of integrity and intelligence.

All of the popular figures of the day seemed to have visited Indiana University. Among these was George R. Kennan, who enlarged upon his popular article on Russia which had appeared in the *Century Magazine*. Max O'Rell lectured on "John Bull and His Isle and America." The *Student* became excited when its editor learned that Edward Bellamy was to visit the school. In time, however, the popular lecture series of the Jordan years was topped off by the appearance in the college chapel on March 29, 1890, of the robust young Chairman of the Civil Service Commission, Theodore Roosevelt. The school paper thought the "stolid bureaucrat's" speech was "masterful, instructing and instructive." On this trip David Starr Jordan accompanied the young politician as far as Indianapolis. They missed connections at Limedale and had to spend the night in the lonely station waiting for the next train. During this wait the thirty year old Roosevelt disclosed to the university's president his political ambitions. Jordan felt these ran pretty high for so young a man. He, however, made this appraisal many years later and from an altogether different perspective. No doubt Roosevelt went away feeling that the young university president's ambitions also ran high.

A university audience was introduced to another of the world's problems on February 11, 1891, when Stergius Stepnick, an exiled nihilist, discussed, in his broken English, Russia's great needs, and designated the areas in which the United States could be of real assistance. Broken English or not, the *Courier* reported that Stepnick caught and held the interest of the audience.

Less exciting speakers who appeared in chapel in a virtually unending procession were temperance lecturers, who seemed many times to have invited themselves. They carried on a noisy unilateral debate with demon rum. Egged on by local members of the Woman's Christian Temperance Union and other dry organizations, they gave the impression that there lurked on the periphery of Bloomington a scheming ravenous horde of saloonkeepers who were ready to pounce upon Indiana University with the fork of destruction. In March, 1885, the new president Jordan and the aged patriarch Elisha Ballantine led a stout band of seven enemies of rum onto the chapel stage, and in an extended session they did the "old cuss" in with a thunderous oratorical pounding.

The following year the W.C.T.U. held its state convention in

Bloomington and in the chapel, three of its top sergeants, Frances Willard, Josephine Nichols, and Mrs. "Governor" Wallace exposed the evils of drink to students who by that time were moaning that the only thing they could find to drink in the perennial droughts was a jug of distilled water, and this enjoyed public sanction only because of emergency conditions.

David Starr Jordan early in his administration undertook to solve the nagging problem of compulsory Sunday afternoon chapel. The ultraconservative Board of Trustees was scarcely conversant with changes that were occurring in the rising state universities. They wished to hold students in line with the vanished part of the ministerial presidents by requiring compulsory chapel attendance every day and Sunday too. Jordan was more liberal than his board, and was able to work out a compromise by offering a series of popular informational lectures, some tepid entertainment, and a series of nonreligious lectures himself. In these he slyly gave the rock-ribbed chapel patrons a popular insight into evolution and Darwinism, and made them ask for more.

A large audience came out on a November Sunday afternoon in 1886 to enjoy the autumn color of Dunn's Woods and to hear General Lew Wallace of Crawfordsville lecture on the Turks and Turkey. Father Zahn of Notre Dame discussed the Catholic Church and the new science on a Sunday afternoon. Young William J. (Lowe) Bryan captivated a Sunday afternoon audience with a finished lecture, and thus helped along a career of public speaking. So pleased was the *Courier*'s editor with this local son's speech that he predicted a brilliant future for him. Another local luminary, Governor Albert G. Porter, pleased his neighbors with an apolitical lecture on William E. Gladstone. Again the ebullient *Courier* editor was quick to bestow the editorial laurel wreath, "Never before were the citizens of Bloomington permitted such literary treats in the way of free lectures, and the credit for the enterprise is due to Dr. Jordan."

Not all the chapel cultural programs were speeches. There was an interest in music as well. Frederick N. Innes, the Englishman, described as the "world's greatest Trombone soloist," was a popular musician acclaimed by newspapers across the country. He came to Bloomington fresh from triumphs in the Cincinnati and Louisville expositions. The Chicago Madrigal Club gave a performance. The local Mendelssohn Society gave a competent recital which pleased the audience and saved money for the lecture association. The Belgian violinst Monsieur Musin and the Spanish pianist Carlos Sobrino, a Mr. Hatch and Miss Fannie Kessler caused the *Student* editor to comment in November, 1887, "He who has not been moved by concord of sweet sounds at the entertainment given by the Musin Concert Company certainly has no music in his soul."

In Jordan's last year as president the Lecture Association brought the newly organized Boston Symphony Orchestral Club to Bloomington. This orchestra had several accomplished artists, including the Swedish prima donna Mademoiselle Augusta Ohrston. Other musical organizations appeared at the university in time, adding to the townspeople's growing enthusiasm.

By 1890, however, interest in forensic culture began to lag in Indiana University. Not even Jordan could stir new interest in this means of intellectual communication. No doubt students, like the Bloomington editor earlier, felt the time had come for some mental unwinding, and a focusing on lighter cultural fare such as the circus and football. The *Courier*, on May 17 of that year, lamented that students were not attending the lectures. "It is not very encouraging to the faculty," said the editor, "or gratifying to the lecturer to address empty benches."

In every area of his life David Starr Jordan, like his beloved "Andy" White of Cornell, took himself with the utmost seriousness. He thoroughly entwined his private life about that of the university. On November 3, 1886, he reported to the Board of Trustees in the most businesslike manner that he was going East to marry Mary A. Jordan, head of the Department of English of Smith College; the wedding would take place on June 23, 1887. In a vein of academic objectivity he told the trustees that he believed, "This most earnest and successful teacher will be felt for good by all connected with the University." His statement left the impression that he was guided by the philosophy, "If you can't hire them, marry them." To amplify Miss Jordan's intellectual pedigree the *Courier* announced that the bride-to-be had been offered the presidency of a female college, but it was believed she preferred matrimony and climbing the Alps on a wedding tour.

Both the President and the local records are silent as to what happened to this matter-of-fact Jordan romance. So quick to make the announcement of his approaching marriage a part of the official university record, Jordan failed to explain what transpired, nor did he even hint at this blighted romance in his autobiography, *The Days of a Man*. Students had anticipated the arrival of Mary Jordan. The *Student* announced under a heading of "Wedding Bells" that it was pleased with the news. "The woman who is to become one of us as the wife of our President has the right ideas for a woman's life and mission. She has fought and won for herself recognition among the educators of the East, and doubtless she will exercise the same influence, when she becomes first lady on the faculty." It was said that the students and citizens alike congratulated Jordan on his wise action.

In October, 1887, the Indiana *Student* announced that David Starr Jordan had married Jesse L. H. Knight of Worcester, Massachusetts, on August 10. Jordan had spent the first part of the summer in the Harvard Museum of Comparative Zoology helping assemble Agassiz' collection of Brazilian fishes. Marriage seems to have been only an incidental event of the summer, for in a remarkably short time Jordan and his bride were in Virginia with a party seining creeks and rivers. Jesse sat on the creek banks of the swift clear rivers "while we men drew the necessary nets; incidentally we both enjoyed the summer 'scented' piney woods."

Professor James A. Woodburn saw the honeymooning couple in Richmond on August 27, and brought to Bloomington the news that the new wife was an exceedingly pleasant lady, a small and dark brunette, quite sociable, and he believed she would fit in well in Bloomington society. Though she was a graduate of Cornell University, neither Woodburn nor Jordan mentioned her prospects as a professor of English. Jordan had met her in Ithaca when he attended a meeting of the Cornell Board of Trustees. He described her as petite, brunette, with a trace of her ancestral Huguenot olive coloring. It may have been that Jordan was fickle, and had broken off his engagement to Mary Jordan. Possibly he was captivated by Jesse L. Knight when he first saw her in Ithaca.

When the Jordans arrived in Bloomington late in the afternoon of September 4, the local people scarcely gave the couple time to unlock the door at their Morton Street residence before they began to call. The bride was able to read in the September 6 issue of the *Telephone* that the callers went away and passed many pleasant compliments on her. Still the unsentimental scientist-president informed the public in later years that, true to James Stephens' observation, "to marry a university woman is to have ever after a critic on the hearth." He doubtless needed such a critic.

Returning to his desk in the fall, Jordan found it full of nagging administrative responsibilities. The new campus demanded expanded services. The enrollment had reached 273 and the staff had grown to twenty or more members. The water supply was ever a problem, but it grew more so as the student body increased in size. Provision had to be made to supply water to the new heating system. Janitorial needs now exceeded Uncle Tommy Spicer's capabilities, and Jesse Stuart was hired to assist the old man. The fact that the new janitor had rented the Tobe East house was reported by the *Courier* as a news item of almost equal social importance to Jordan's marriage. Jordan informed the Board of Trustees that with an increase in demands the time had come to name a purchasing agent. Students for several years had clamored for a university bathhouse, and the everlasting problem of sanitary provisions demanded immediate attention. The board responded to the latter call by instructing a special committee to see to the construction of such a building near Wylie Hall. Later in 1891 this committee reported that it had given careful attention to its charge and had had constructed a Roman type forum with ten stone pillars at a cost of $177.26.

Jordan took pride in reporting to the board at its annual meeting in 1888 that there were twenty-eight staff members, the president's salary was $4,000, and professorial salaries ranged from $1,300 to $1,800. Income from the endowment and direct legislative appropriation permitted the adoption of a budget of $43,375. Indiana University, though still not competitive in this area with its neighbors in Michigan, Ohio, Illinois, and Wisconsin, was making genuine progress. The president was an eloquent salesman of the idea that the state university had become a central part of the American system of higher education. Along with meeting his classes, going on fishing expeditions, and attending to his increasing administrative duties, Jordan found time to speak and write on the subject of state university education throughout the Middle West. He also carried on voluminous correspondence with American, British, and European scientists. In all this rush, the president took time to have his office carpeted, and as the Bloomington *Telephone* said, to add "necessaries of other kinds." This bustling president apparently did not follow up Lemuel Moss' gesture to the technological age by using the typewriter; his correspondence relating to university matters was written in longhand.

Although 321 students did not place an unbearable burden upon either president or professors in giving personal attention to their charges, there had grown up in the Jordan years a feeling that the gulf was widening between the two segments of the university community. Disgruntled students gave expression to this feeling at times. For example, on the morning of September 17, 1890, many of the people of Bloomington awakened to find on their door steps a crude and vulgar underground "bogus." There had been several boguses before, but this one was unusually adolescent in character and fecal in language. Both professors and townsmen were horrified by the onslaught against faculty members and students and were alarmed that it had found its way into print and into their homes. In many cases children read the bogus before their parents discovered that it existed.

The distribution of the bogus stirred the community into a furore. The local newspapers fired the cauldron of local wrath by publishing running stories of new developments. The *Saturday Courier* self-righteously wrung its editorial hands. Later, with some glee, this paper announced that the boys had been caught and dismissed, and it hoped the law would take its course, but it failed to specify what course. The *Courier* said it was Professor Rufus L. Green of the Mathematics Department who had uncovered the identity of the offenders. In the heat of the moment students and citizens collected $150 to be awarded to the person who revealed the authors of the bogus, but there is no information as to whether Professor Green received the purse.

In dealing with this offensive tirade against the faculty and human decorum nearly everyone lost his poise. In an undated memorandum Jordan said the paper had the flavor of the Beta Theta Pi point of view, but he seems not to have known whether the Betas originated the sheet or whether it was intended to injure them. One thing he learned quickly was that the brothers of Beta would not divulge the secrets of their order. The citizens of Bloomington and the trustees became emotional about the language and charges of the bogus. Letters arrived in the president's office condemning the paper in the strongest possible terms—its authors were called "dastards," "fiends," "vipers," and "corruptionists." J. N. Wallingford wrote Jordan demanding quick action, and Jordan, without knowing who the culprits were, replied defensively, "The boys were carried away with the excitement of a midnight adventure." The trustees, however, were not so easily mollified. In their minds this act, if unpunished, would lead to the university's destruction. In May they hired the Pinkerton Detective Agency to handle the case for them. One investigator, known as J.H.S., appears to have just stepped out of the newest Nick Carter thriller. He officially branded the paper a "vile publication," suggested calling the grand jury into emergency session, and asked the Indiana attorney general to throw out a legal dragnet so that none of the "gang of infamous devils" would escape. "This course," he said, "at all events will have a healthy influence with this crowd of vipers, and will tend to prevent a repetition of this." J.H.S. asked the grand jury to issue subpoenas wholesale to catch everybody.

The Pinkerton dramatics seem to have been taken bodily out of one of the old railroad dime thrillers. The story of the origin of the bogus began to unfold quickly, but not because of the Pinkerton man. It turned out that seven boys, members of the Beta Theta Pi fraternity, were disgruntled about some of the things which have always irritated college boys and they had struck back in a childish manner. Clarence H. Beard of Spiceland did most of the writing, and Nicholas A. Robertson with the help of two or three other brothers read copy. When the manuscript was ready it was sent off to Spiceland to be set in type and printed by Clarence H. Beard's seventeen year old brother Charles Austin Beard, editor of a little country weekly. The printed papers were sent to Bloomington by express and delivered to the authors. Once they held in hand printed copies of their handiwork, some of them lost their nerve and suggested that the paper be burned. Nicholas Robertson locked the papers in his trunk, but while he was at his boarding club Clarence Beard and John S. Shannon opened the trunk and rescued the paper, and that night W. H. Bloss, Frank Post, Beard, and Hal Read distributed them in the town.

Nicholas A. Robertson was the son of Trustee Robert Stoddart Robertson, and it was his confession which quickly reduced this fiendish band of "vipers" to a frightened bunch of naive college boys. Young Robertson was charged with being a ringleader, which was to cause friction among board members. The elder Robertson, though mightily embarrassed, defended his son, and demanded a full-scale investigation in which witnesses would be sworn and compelled to testify. This, however, never happened. Once the officious Pinkerton man was removed from the case and trustees and faculty took a calmer view of the incident, the seven boys were expelled. The boys' parents were hurt by the incident but the case was closed. The most pitiful situation was that of the Beard family. Clarence and Charles Beard's mother was in extremely delicate health, and her husband wrote President Jordan that he feared she would die if she learned about the furore over her sons. This is a tremendously touching letter from a grieving father. All the parents were surely troubled by this incident. One or two of them had made strong pronouncements against the culprits before they knew who they were. Nearly all of them told Jordan how they had sacrificed to send their sons to the university.

In June, 1892, the faculty relented in the bogus case. Degrees were granted to five of the expelled lads, and the Board of Trustees voted to reinstate all seven of them into good standing with the university. J. W. Youche, who had in his own day been charged with publishing a bogus, served as a one-man committee and reported that the bogus was "the result of thoughtlessness and spontaneous evil impulse rather than portraying evidence of a depraved nature. Your committee believes that notwithstanding what occurred these young men will be useful citizens and worthy members of society." In fact they became excellent citizens, and one of them, Walter Howe, had a long and highly respected career as a Texas judge. The others did equally well in their professions. One became a pioneer registered pharmacist in Chicago. At this date one cannot help but speculate on what influence this incident had in steering Charles Austin Beard to DePauw instead of Indiana University.

David Starr Jordan did not reveal himself as entirely judicious in his handling of this incident. His letters to some of the boys were sharp and grilling, and at times he seemed to credit the "viper" and "fiend" labels. Perhaps Uncle Tommy Spicer could have handled this with more sobriety and human understanding than did the president and trustees. With the passage of a couple of years everybody concerned seems to have regained his equilibrium and to have felt a sense of guilt that so trifling a thing had reached such great proportions. In future years Judge Walter Howe must have recalled this needless commotion when he had a prisoner before him for sentencing. College capers such as this one were adolescent reactions to college restraints and boyish frustrations.

An era of Indiana University human relationships came to an end on June 9, 1890, when the Board of Trustees received a communication couched in the polite language of the old professorial school. The seventy-eight year old British-born janitor, Thomas Spicer, asked to be relieved of his responsibilities. Uncle Tommy said he was unable to further discharge his duties. "I most respectfully tender to you my resignation," and he expressed the hope that the university would "still grow in all directions." Many an alumnus of the university would have quivered if Uncle Tommy had written his memoirs and told all he knew about the foibles of student life at Indiana.

Uncle Tommy's resignation was soon followed by that of David Starr Jordan. In the past seven years Jordan had ridden the Midwest circuit preaching the virtues of the state university. Early in March, 1891, he was in Urbana, Illinois, speaking on the function of the state university at the dedication of a new science building. In the midst of the speech he was handed a telegram from President Andrew D. White of Cornell, instructing him to "Decline no offer from California till you hear from me."

Waiting for him back in Bloomington were Senator and Mrs. Leland Stanford, who had arrived at the Monon station aboard a Union Pacific private train. They were returning from a visit in the East, where they had conferred with Charles Eliot, Andrew D. White, and others. The Stanfords had shocked Eliot out of his Yankee reserve by asking him in essence how much it would cost to buy a university. They had offered the presidency of their fledgling university to White. He refused it, but recommended Jordan to them. Thus on March 21, 1891, the Stanfords were in Bloomington in search of a president for Leland Stanford Junior University. At that time Senator Stanford presented the physical embodiment of the popular concept of the robber baron. He stood five feet eight inches tall and weighed 298 pounds, his white hair covered his collar in proper senatorial style. He was an impressive figure of a rich man.

Word spread fast in Bloomington that the "Governor" of California was waiting over at the hotel for President Jordan to return to offer him the presidency of the new western university. News got around even faster when Mrs. Stanford and Bertha Brenner attended church services and listened to a young student preacher propound the might of a wrathful God. Mrs. Stanford put a five-dollar gold piece in the collection plate, and was startled when the minister met her at the church door and offered to return the coin because he believed it had been dropped in the plate by accident. This bespoke something of the care with which Bloomington church-goers watched their money. The young minister received a mild lecture from Jane Lathrop Stanford, who said her God was more gentle than the one he had described.

It took Leland Stanford a remarkably short time to convert the seven-year apostle of state university education into a private university president. The difference was partly reflected by a four thousand versus ten thousand dollar salary. Jordan lost no time accepting the Stanford offer to organize the new university. There is a hint in the Jordan-Stanford literature that the Senator offered his new president a bonus for each good Indiana professor he could persuade to follow him to California.

The Bloomington *Saturday Courier* reported on April 4, 1891, "From the talk about town and the newspaper reports, it seems that Dr. Jordan is not only going to Stanford University, but he is going to take the whole of Indiana University's faculty with him." This gossip was stimulated further by the arrival from Cornell during that week of Orrin Elliott to serve as secretary to Jordan, and to aid him in the hiring of a faculty. News leaked out that Joseph Swain and Douglas Campbell were resigning. Jordan formally submitted his resignation to the Board on April 8. He told the trustees that he could better be spared then than at any other time in the past six years. He assured them that the university's prospects were brighter than ever before, and that the people of Indiana were alert to the importance of their state schools. He asked for immediate leave of absence and a $400 reduction in salary to permit him to devote his time to hiring a faculty for Stanford. He also requested that he be allowed to purchase $1,000 worth of fish he had collected, but the board ruled that he could only have duplicate specimens.

At its June meeting the trustees discovered how injurious Jordan's departure was to be to the school. They received the resignations of Douglas H. Campbell, Joseph Swain, Earl Barnes, Joseph P. Naylor, John C. Branner, John Matzke, E. B. Cubberly, and Charles Gilbert. This made staggering inroads into the Indiana faculty of twenty-nine members. Jordan thus led away many of the ablest members of the staff. He had tried to entice Bryan away and had his eyes on other men whom he approached in later years with offers. In all, twelve Indiana men went to Stanford, eight of whom were heads of departments. This necessitated an immediate restaffing of the university faculty at an unreasonably late date in the year to find good men.

David Starr Jordan had given the best of his younger years to Indiana University. It would hardly be historically correct to say that he served the institution with thorough unselfishness. His correspondence, however barren of material about the university, reflects his ambitions as a scientist who climbed toward preeminence in his field of ichthyology. Every time he had an opportunity, he was away from the campus collecting specimens or traveling abroad. His interests were catholic, and he developed a wide circle of associations. Looking back, it seems almost miraculous that a university bound down for so much of its history by an extremely conservative parochial approach to education should hire at the strategic moment one of the leading apostles of what Jordan called "scientific and volitional education."

Indiana University did not truly become a university under the administration of Jordan. He only prepared the way for the broadening of the future institutional base. When he left Bloomington there were still only two colleges, liberal arts and law. By old standards the budget had been greatly increased, but it was still too low to enable the school to meet its challenges. There were fewer enemies attacking the school than at any time in the past, but still enemies existed. Gradually the number of counties represented in the student enrollment increased, but some still were unrepresented, and the senators and representatives from these districts had to be converted to support the university. David Starr Jordan had visited all the counties, and his face and name had become familiar. The news-papers gave the president an immense amount of publicity. Wher-ever he went to speak he was given prominent notice and his comments on evolution, public education, oratory, and the adven-tures of travel were listened to and appreciated.

Jordan's greatest influence, however, lay in bringing Indiana into the main stream of the new education of late nineteenth century America. He had the good judgment to realize that this could only be accomplished by hiring the best young faculty members avail-able. In his seven years as president his choices were on the whole exciting ones. In the sciences he had hired Gilbert, Branner, Camp-bell, and Naylor. In the languages he had brought to Bloomington von Jagermann and Karsten, in history Dabney, Newkirk, Von Holst, and Barnes, and in English Clark. Three of these were graduates of the university and figured prominently in the institu-tion's future. These were William J. (Lowe) Bryan, James A. Woodburn, and Carl Eigenmann.

Internally Jordan had brought about a reorganization which helped to place various administrative responsibilities in the hands of competent assistants. The registrar's office was created along with that of purchasing and business, and the academic department heads were given a fundamental role in the educational develop-ment of the university. Like Moses of old, the ubiquitous and ego-tistical, but imaginative, young scientist had brought Indiana to within sight of promise, but he left it to others to scale the mountain to university status and academic maturity.

Reporters from the *Student* interviewed David Starr Jordan many years after he had left Indiana, and he told them, "I once reminded the Board of Trustees that they need name no building for me. I asked only that the brook coming through the campus should be called the River Jordan." This was done, but they did still better: for the meadow across the brook they named Jordan. This was the year that the new University campus was being loca-ted along Spanker's Branch, which dissected Dunn's Meadow and Woods. This tiny spring branch trickled through the new campus and the city to feed Clear Creek. Shrewdly Jordan eyed the future. Buildings could burn or be torn down, but Spanker's Branch, in this pre-bulldozer age, promised to flow on forever, and so long as it gurgled its way through the heart of the campus, and boys and girls surrendered to the ides of spring in Jordan's Meadow, he would not be forgotten in Indiana University. Thus like the eternal flow of the River Jordan, the man's personal influence and impact on the history of the university has remained fresh and virile.

[XII]

The Age of Science

D AVID STARR JORDAN may have accepted the presidency of
Stanford University and hustled away from Bloomington
at the earliest possible moment; but he was reluctant to
relinquish his personal hold on Indiana University. He wished to
assure the continuance in Bloomington of the strong science and
elective programs he had instituted, and to see the state university
justify its position at the head of the state school system. In 1884
he had strongly recommended John Merle Coulter, professor of
botany in Wabash College, to head the list of forty-seven candidates
to succeed Lemuel Moss. When the board again appealed to him
for advice in 1891 he made such a strong recommendation that
Coulter was chosen without opposition, and apparently without
much discussion in the trustees' meeting of April 8, 1891.

In June the new president was on hand to accept the responsibilities of his office and made plans to permit a minimum of disruption
in closing out the Jordan administration. Coulter came to Indiana
with only two strong background qualifications: he was a dedicated teacher-scientist, and he had a wide reputation for agreeability.
The forty year old executive was born of missionary parents in
Ningpo, China, November 20, 1851. Actually the family lived in

[2 6 5]

Chicago, which ostensibly was Coulter's first home. He was educated in Hanover College, taking a baccalaureate, a master's, and doctor of philosophy *pro merita*. He had demonstrated that he was an excellent teacher in the fields of botany and the general sciences. Contemporary evidence indicates that he was held in high esteem by his students, and, as indicated earlier, his popularity had become known to Indiana students. There is no doubt that Coulter's interests lay more with the teaching and research phases of education than with administration.

Coulter was a handsome man with an appearance of lingering youth. Like Jordan he was a good speaker, and for a research scientist was unusually gregarious. He had a keen sense of the importance of strong public relations in a state that still had a good number of counties unrepresented in the university's student body. Coulter knew something of the nature of Indiana politics and realized that legislators could be as fickle where higher education was concerned as were the winter mistrals of the Ohio.

It can hardly be said that the scholarly Coulter brought any innovative educational ideas to Bloomington. He gave no indication that he was fully cognizant of the kind of expansion and change that was then going on in American colleges and universities. He was satisfied to accept his predecessor's program and to carry forward Jordan's ambitions in the area of scientific interests. Coulter believed that the major-elective system was a sound one, and stoutly opposed any suggestion of a revival of the old classical academic college of narrowly prescribed curriculum and highly restricted baccalaureate degrees.

The new president and his wife were in Bloomington for the commencement week. Judge and Mrs. Robert Walter Miers gave a reception for the couple, and they were introduced to the university and its commencement visitors. Jordan had become so emotional in his farewell address that he had two-thirds of his audience in tears and sobbing with him. Instantly he changed his tone and predicted a brilliant future for Indiana University and its new leadership. There is no way of telling what emotions stirred in John M. Coulter's breast. He doubtless wondered if he could fill Jordan's place in leadership and affections of the people, but in a more practical vein he must have wondered how he would fill with competent professors the many major vacancies created by the Jordan resignations. Too, he must have contemplated the progress which the school would have to make in the new age of the modern state university.

The *Student* for that June did nothing to reassure the new president that his job would be easy. "Never, perhaps, in the history of Indiana University has there been so great a change in the faculty," said the campus editor, "and so complete a revolution in the management of the institution as is to take place this year." The paper then recited for the third or fourth time the list of professors who were leaving for Stanford or other appointments. There was some solid comfort in the fact that left behind were William J. (Lowe) Bryan, Carl H. Eigenmann, David M. Mottier, Gustaf Karsten, Horace A. Hoffman, David D. Banta, and James A. Woodburn. Coulter's first session, 1891–92, opened with a faculty of twenty three full-time members and four or five instructional assistants. In fact his faculty in 1891 was to be basically that of the university for the next twenty years. This faculty for the most part was made up of men who were thoroughly acquainted with Indiana University because many of them had graduated from the institution.

By 1891 the new physical plant of the university was taking form. George W. Bunting of Indianapolis had designed four of the new buildings, Wylie, Owen, Mitchell, and Maxwell halls. These buildings gave little or no indication that they were designed by the same architect, and varied radically in attractiveness. The original Maxwell Hall, designed to temporarily accommodate Latin, Greek, philosophy, oratory and rhetoric, also contained a general assembly room, which resembled a large period Indiana family dwelling. The Indiana General Assembly had made a $60,000 appropriation in 1889 to finance the construction of a library building. This structure was finished in January, 1891, and was already occupied by the 14,000-volume library and the Law School. Classrooms for English, history, political science, and pedagogics were also available in this turreted structure. The university retained possession of the old main building on the original campus. Thus Coulter had the use of five buildings, four of which still form the heart of the older part of the present campus. These buildings were not adequate to accommodate the enrollment of 326 students. An urgent demand existed for two gymnasiums, one for women and the other for men. Early in 1890 an appropriation was made for a gymnasium, and provisions were made in Wylie Hall for a women's exercise room where the Sargeant and Swedish systems of physical education could be taught. On January 20, 1892, the 40 by 60 foot frame gymnasium for men was dedicated. The catalogue for that year said the building was unpretentious, but that it was built after approved gymnasium plans and was well adapted to the purpose for which it was to be used. For many years this structure also served as a general assembly hall.

When the new library building was completed in January, 1891, it was given the name of Maxwell Hall, and the frame building which had borne this name was changed to Mitchell Hall to honor J. L. Mitchell, a graduate in the class of 1858, and a trustee from 1883 to 1894.

As the university community developed more of the academic services necessary to efficient functioning of the institution new demands for space arose. One of these services which matured during the Coulter years was the cooperative book store. Located as it was in a small town, the university clientele had no access to a satisfactory book outlet. Students and professors felt local dealers who did carry books charged too high prices for them. In the age of the burgeoning cooperatives in many fields across the country, Indiana faculty and students felt the time had come to organize a university book and supplies store which could sell merchandise at lower prices. On April 1, 1890, a Cooperative Association was formed for the main purposes of selling books, stationery, and student supplies. Shares were sold in the undertaking, and stockholders received both cheaper prices and a dividend from the net business transacted during the year. This venture was a success. The first year the cooperative grossed $1,500, and by 1894 it did an annual business in excess of $10,000, with a saving of 25 percent to student purchasers. The *Student* advised newcomers to purchase shares in the cooperative and save several dollars during the year. This organization was to thrive until 1904, when its stock was redeemed by a university-owned bookstore.

The financial condition of the university in 1891 was not as sound as a new president faced with reworking a faculty organization might have desired, but compared with the past it was not wholly poor. Jordan left behind a total budget of $65,459.92. This permitted Coulter to pay faculty salaries which ranged from

$1,200 to $2,000. His own salary was $4,000, and that of Judge Banta, Dean of the Law School, $2,500. Coulter's actual professorial payroll was $38,100. One substantial change had already occurred in the administrative organization under Jordan; Amzi Atwater was made vice president of the university in 1888 at a supplementary salary of $100 per annum, but this office was abolished on April 9, 1891, at the time Coulter accepted the presidency. Instead of supporting a vice president the Board of Trustees made an appropriation of $300 with which the new president could employ office help of his choosing.

With the organization of the university set for the next session, Coulter apparently did not move to Bloomington until late in the summer. The record does not indicate that he made an unusual effort to recruit new faculty or to make extraordinary plans for the next session. It might have been wasted effort for the president to remain in his office between sessions. Jordan never did so, nor did most of his predecessors. The school had a miniscule administrative staff, and professors and students were either away from Bloomington or otherwise employed. Janitors cared for the buildings and grounds, and the local trustees looked after many of the housekeeping details. There were no dormitories, dining halls, or services to be readied for a new term. This was a time when President Coulter could do some field work in the natural sciences and move his household from Crawfordsville. It may also be that he spent part of the summer preparing speeches to be delivered around the state the next year.

In September the university community reassembled. That fall 326 students were enrolled, an increase of two over the preceding session. A considerable amount of shifting and rearranging of instructors and classes took place, but even so the year was begun with remarkably little confusion. On the third Sunday afternoon in September, Coulter gave his first public lecture, on the subject of "Christian Patience." A large audience assembled in the Old College Hall, but there seems to exist no contemporary comment on its quality. It seems clear it contained no intellectual stroll with Thoreau as had Jordan's inaugural address in 1885.

Public speaking was to form a pattern which prevailed through the rest of Coulter's administration. He agreed to give six lectures in a public normal course in Bedford in late September and early

October. He hardly had time to go by Bloomington before rushing on to Indianapolis to give the opening address before the local literary club. This was possibly an initiatory address upon the president's being admitted to membership in this prestigious organization.

During the first Christmas holidays, the president had time enough away from the classrooms and the lecture circuit to refurbish his office. He bought a Munson typewriter, painted the walls, and ripped out Jordan's worn carpet and put down a new one. The Bloomington *Saturday Courier* told its readers that Dr. Coulter's office "Now looks something like what the state ought to provide," the implication here being that the university offices were shabby in appearance.

Times were changing in other ways. There was no genuine anxiety about enrollment. It seemed obvious that each year would see more students come to Bloomington, and in time all ninety-two counties would be represented. Coulter was soon predicting the arrival of 600 students. The high schools were greatly improved. In 1891 there were 108 commissioned high schools in Indiana, and each year more schools were being added to the list. On June 6, 1890, the Board of Trustees had voted to discontinue the university preparatory school and depend altogether on the public high schools to supply prepared students. The university admitted students on one of two qualifications, graduation from a satisfactory high school, or examination in four or five major high school subjects.

The university had made a real effort for several years to cultivate the favor of the high schools and to foster the impression that it was head of the public school system. One of the things the board did was to appropriate $100 with which to purchase enough copies of the *Student* to send one to each of the commissioned high schools. Something published in that paper in 1890 must have disturbed the trustees because action was taken at the June meeting providing that local members of the board, and the president, could withhold any issue of the *Student* which they felt was unsuitable for high school students to read. A good part of this burden of censorship fell to John Coulter.

As Indiana grew in wealth and there was a substantial increase in urbanization, many of its prospective university students were better provided for economically. Strict controls were relaxed, and there was greater freedom for the student on campus. Although this does not imply that the people in Indiana had surrendered to liberalism, the inflow of the manners of the "gay nineties" was noticeable. Fraternities and sororities gained a much stronger foothold in the center of the campus social and political stages, and much of the simplistic old social democracy of the rural commonwealth was pushed into the background.

Students over the years grew weary of having to attend the Sunday afternoon chapel services, and David Starr Jordan had tried unsuccessfully to communicate this to the Board of Trustees. Daily chapel services were fairly well attended, in fact on many occasions there was not room enough in the building for all of the students who wished to hear a speaker. In October, 1892, the Sunday service was discontinued. Campus religious expressions had begun to take other forms. Carl Eigenmann and a student named Fitch reorganized the Young Men's Christian Association in January, 1885, but in May the *Student* said, "It is the general sentiment that the Y.M.C.A. fared badly under the supervision of Fitch and Eigenmann. Public sentiment will out on these matters." By 1891, however, both the Y.M.C.A. and the Y.W.C.A. had at least taken over part of the religious role of the chapel.

In other areas of academic life special clubs such as the Scientific Association, The Civil Service Reform Club, the Mathematical and Physical, Shakespearean, Progressive, Psychology and Philosophy, Sociological, and Pedagogical clubs had been organized. In fact the two years of Coulter's presidency saw a tremendous expansion of campus organizations. These tended to diffuse student interest more than in the Jordan days. On top of the special interest area there were the Democratic and Republican clubs.

The town of Bloomington did not always keep pace with university progress. It was subjected, however, to some of the fermentation which stirred the campus. On June 29, 1891, the *Telephone* reported the city still had only twenty-five electric outlets and a demand for five more. It was doubtful that the existing generator could withstand the burden of additional bulbs. Not until after Coulter's years, in 1894, did the post office achieve second class status by having more than $10,000 annual receipts. That same year W.T. Hicks bought the telephone franchise and prepared to construct lines. The *Student* reported as late as October 17, 1893, that ox teams were not unknown sights on the streets of the town.

The most serious problem of all was housing and boarding the increasing numbers of students. For almost the first three quarters of a century the university still had built no housing or dining facilities, except for the early Boarding House on the old campus. Students were thrown upon the housing resources of the town for rooms, and upon the various student-run boarding clubs for meals. On August 12, 1892, Professor Rufus L. Green told the *Telephone*,

> the greatest need of Bloomington is new houses of first class. I am aware that there have been a large number of good houses erected for rent, but they are all rented, and the demand now is for large houses. Within the past two weeks the University has been compelled to reply to eleven families from a distance and tell them that there were no houses that could be rented at any price, and as a result a number of students will be lost. Persons . . . can build houses from $1000 to $1500, and they can rent them at good figures.

Coulter himself looked for a house in Bloomington and finally had to give up and rent rooms until he could have one built.

The university had no control over the local boardinghouses, and there arose problems of cost, sanitation, health, safety from fire, and discipline. The latter problem caused concern because parents were reluctant to allow their children, especially girls, to be exposed to such conditions. These problems were not unique to the Coulter administration, of course, they only grew more complex and demanding of solution with the expanding university enrollment.

Coulter's own professional interest in botany showed some progress, and he supported an expansion of facilities for the teaching of the sciences. Forty-four tables were installed in Professor Robert E. Lyon's chemistry laboratory, and still there was not enough table space to accommodate the fifty-one students crowded into the undersized room. The Bloomington *Telephone* thought this spoke well for Lyons and Van Nuys since their work in chemistry was not a required subject. The following August the Department of Chemistry received from Germany thirty-six boxes of chemicals and apparatus valued at a thousand dollars. This alone marked a significant advance from the early 1870's, when Theophilus A. Wylie had taught chemistry in the basement of the old building with little more than a hundred dollars' worth of materials and equipment, and the Board of Trustees refused to pay his bill for distilled water.

While facilities for the teaching of chemistry were undergoing improvements in 1892, the Department of Botany received from New Zealand 1,230 specimens collected by the Englishman T. Kirk. At the same time the John Ball collection of more than 2,000 European specimens had arrived in Bloomington. In February that year, the Herbarium received a set of mounted plants of New England, Lower Canada, and Pacific Slope specimens. This latter collection was said to contain approximately 10,000 different items. The *Telephone*, on February 12, 1892, boasted that with the addition of these new materials Indiana University had the largest collection in its Herbarium of any university west of the Allegheny Mountains. The specimen collection was greatly strengthened by the addition of fifteen volumes of botanical literature purchased in Germany. These new additions were written in Latin, German, French, and English. Since the Botany Department was preparing to publish a study on cacti, one or two of the new volumes were of immediate service. This cacti study received further aid from the National Herbarium in Washington, which supplied a gift of forty cacti specimens gathered on a Death Valley expedition. Coulter was able to continue work begun by Douglas H. Campbell in 1887 when the department was organized. Campbell abolished the old natural science courses which merely rehashed Gray's lectures, and introduced discussions and illustrations of planograms and advanced cryptograms, vegetable histology and vegetable physiology. During his two years as president, Coulter was able to maintain a continuity between Campbell and David M. Mottier in botany.

In geology advances were made possible by the purchase of specialized equipment in the form of microscopes which permitted students to do advanced work in petrology, thus maintaining some of the momentum given the subject by J. C. Branner. Foundations were laid in three or four of the sciences for deeper study when additional financial support was forthcoming. The university was still in desperate need of money with which to buy apparatus and materials, and to employ more professors in special areas. By 1893 it was clear that Indiana University's liberal arts students were becoming more and more interested in training for scientific careers.

In order to maintain a high level of university work in all fields, President Coulter carried on a continuous campaign to encourage improvement of the Indiana high schools. During the fall of 1891 he and his staff prepared the *Indiana Bulletin*, number 3, which was mailed to all principals. This publication was intended to be a guide for the upgrading of high school courses to enable Indiana University to raise its standards of admission. Even more important than raising standards was the fundamental issue of aligning the high school curriculum with that of the modern scientific and social science courses being offered in the university.

One of the most satisfactory mediums for making the work of the university known, and at the same time bringing about a marked improvement in high school work in Indiana, was the operation of the Indiana University Summer School. This adjunct to the regular academic program was organized and operated first in the summer of 1890. David Starr Jordan thought that this service was necessary, even though the faculty pay was exceedingly poor. It brought teachers into Bloomington and helped to enlarge their concept of university education. The summer school of 1891 was such a marked success that Coulter recommended in his annual report that it be placed on the same basis as the summer schools in other state universities. The professors should be paid the meager fees, "which will be very poor compensation for services rendered," but this would bring good return to the state. Subjects should be restricted to those which suited only school teachers.

That the summer school and its special pedagogical courses offered during the regular sessions paid dividends was demonstrated in a report in May, 1892, of a survey made in ninety-three high schools. There were twenty-three university graduates on the faculties, and it was boasted, "There is a greater demand for Indiana University talents this year than ever before."

The university began offering extension work in March, 1891, when a faculty committee reported that there seemed to be a demand in Indianapolis for two or three courses a year. The committee expressed the belief that there would be sufficient patronage to pay expenses and believed the question should be taken up with the Board of Trustees for its approval. David Starr Jordan told the trustees through a public address that a movement had originated in Oxford University known as university extension. He saw this as a means by which American universities could increase "their reputation with the public at large." Jordan said that during the winter of 1891–92 Professor J. W. Jenks had given lectures in Indianapolis on Friday evenings and Saturday mornings under the auspices of the University Extension Society of the College Alumnae of Indiana. After a fashion the botanical lectures which Coulter gave in Bedford and at other so-called normal institutes were a form of extension work. So were the numerous "normal" sessions taught by the university's professors in various parts of the state. In 1912, when Dean W. A. Rawles made a detailed report on extension work in a move to bring about the organization of an extension division of the university, he gave only a brief background history of this work. In 1892 John R. Commons had taught classes in Rochester, Indiana, and Chicago. James A. Woodburn reported as chairman of the extension committee that three-fifths of a term credit be allowed for twelve lectures, and no credit be given for less time spent in class.

Between an enormously demanding list of public speeches and attendance at educational conferences, John M. Coulter found little time to listen to students requests and complaints. Nevertheless he had to deal with these. In 1891 an interest in courses in military science and tactics was revived. The *Student* reported in December of that year, "Some of the boys are becoming very much interested in military tactics. They fought in the armory for practice more than 'once a week with more to be heard from.' " In May the paper reported an agitation to add a military instructor. The university, it was said, was entitled to a "detailed officer." As the decade wore on and the rumblings of war with Spain increased this became a more vital issue to the university. The earlier military science program had been dropped because of lack of student interest in the subject.

On the complaint side, students felt that it would be to their advantage to rearrange class schedules so that the class week would begin on Tuesday and include Saturdays, thus leaving Monday a free day. The faculty refused to grant this change on the grounds that professors already had their programs arranged for the year and to make a change in midsession would be too disruptive. A promise was made that the proposition would be considered again the next year. Some students complained that the university calendar allowed too little time for the Christmas holidays, and in 1893 the faculty refused to end classes early because of the opening of the Chicago Columbian Exposition.

Although emphasis on oratory in the university was being reduced, the state oratorical contest continued to create excitement. The Indiana University contestant won in 1891, and in 1892 C. M. Hubbard was selected to represent the school. His subject, "The Higher Selfishness," had impressed the local judges. Hubbard was a Phi Gamma Delta member, and had defeated two strong opponents to win the right to go to Indianapolis on March 11. The Monon Railroad offered special excursion rates of $1.80 round trip to the capital if as many as fifty of Hubbard's backers went along. The next year Walter Wood of Seymour, went to Indianapolis, where he won second place. He was accompanied by a host of students and the Glee Club. He spoke on the subject "Realized Possibilities," but was defeated by H. H. Hadley of DePauw University. During the contest R. W. Payne of Franklin College fainted in the midst of his speech and had to be carried off stage into a sideroom to be revived. The Indiana Glee Club relieved the tedium of the moment by singing several numbers.

Some social stratification was taking place in Indiana, and the state and the nation were enjoying more prosperous times. New crops of high school graduates arrived in Bloomington with less wonderment in their souls than had past generations of rural students. Older customs were being dropped and new ones adopted. Chapel services gave way to special religious organizations, and the literary societies surrendered to the clubs and fraternities. In November, 1892, the Bloomington *Telephone* announced that the Philomathean Society had died a natural death and "the obsequies will be held this week." This was indeed the cutting of a last major tie to the university's past.

There was one area in university-student affairs in which Coulter had little direct influence. David Starr Jordan left him the legacy of a badly organized and demoralized athletic program. Apparently Stanford University offered financial inducements to athletes, and the Indiana *Student* in December, 1891, lamented that Jordan had taken away a number of students. The reporter said, "Although it [Stanford] promises gigantic proportions, some queer developments have evolved as to the manner in which it secured certain students. Near the close of the spring term in 1891 it was learned that several of our juniors were intending to graduate the following year at Leland Stanford Junior University. Others of the sophomore and senior classes were also intending to go." It was said that nearly all these students were offered financial inducements to go to the California school. This was quite a contrast to President Coulter's behavior. He had advised Wabash students not to follow him to Bloomington. In all, thirty-seven Indiana students went to Palo Alto. It is not clear how many of these students were athletes, but one thing is certain: Indiana's athletic fortunes were at low ebb.

At a meeting of the Athletic Association in January, 1892, "the deep despondency of its members was obvious." The university, it was said, was simply not supporting athletics, and money and popular enthusiasm were lacking. There was urgent need for a new gymnasium, and a proposition to tax each student $2.00 to support the teams was discussed, but tabled. A month later the *Student* was thrown into high dudgeon by a charge in the latest issue of the *Rose Technic* that Indiana University hired most of the players on its teams. The *Student* said the *Technic* looked down the list to see who was strongest and charged that team with being professional. There was one discrepancy: the Rose Polytechnic paper failed to mention the fact that the Terre Haute professionals were used by the Technics without the formality of matriculating.

The university used every sort of scheme to improve its athletic situation. A concert was given on February 5, 1892, to raise money to pay the Athletic Association's debt, an effort which yielded only twenty dollars. An attempt was being made to raise more money without a direct solicitation from students. It would not be possible, said the *Telephone*, to have future competition until the debts were paid. There were signs of hope, however, in another quarter; fifty students had registered for gymnastics, and the class was "not a month old."

In November of that year, during a heavy snowfall, Indiana played Purdue in Lafayette. The *Student* reported, "A defeat, of course, with a score of 68 to 0. The team had a pleasant time, for there was a friendly feeling existing between the teams. The friendly jokes which were exchanged during the game are a novelty in football games." They must have been short and pithy jokes with all that running and scoring. The baseball fortunes of the previous season did something to make the joking at Purdue more bearable. In the previous June the Indiana manager was challenged by the DePauw manager to a sporting proposition that their respective teams would deposit $200 apiece, and the winner would take the purse and the gate, but the Methodist brethren rejected their own challenge in that it was not sporting—it was out-and-out gambling—and refused to play. The DePauw students expressed sorrow that the note was sent in the first place.

Indiana was without a football coach, and the Athletic Association decided this problem had to be solved first. At a mass meeting in April, 1893, President Coulter and Professors George E. Fellows and Carl E. Woods spoke in favor of more support for the Indiana teams. One hundred dollars was collected by popular subscription and further exploration was made of the idea of hiring a coach. In May plans were under way to construct a high board fence around the playing field so that from that date on spectators would have to pay to see games. Heretofore anyone could view contests without paying admission at a gate. Coulter did have one pleasant memory of athletics from Indiana; in June, 1893, the faculty defeated the seniors in baseball, 17 to 0.

Perhaps the faculty was cheered on by the singing of the new Indiana song. J. T. Giles was said to have spent the school year 1892–93 composing the song, to the tune of the Cornell *Alma Mater*. The introduction of the school song and a sharp revision of athletic policies in the spring of 1893 in reality marked the beginning of a new era in the university's history. Its student activities became more highly integrated with the functioning of the university itself, and the bases of school sentimentalities were rapidly being relocated. Thus the Coulter years were highly transitional ones. It is a marvel that he kept in such close communication with the internal changes in the institution when so much was expected of him in the areas of public service.

Though the literary societies vanished one by one, Hoosiers still relished public speaking. At times John Coulter must have felt that he had stepped onto an oratorical treadmill. During his years as president one news story after another reported his speaking engagements. He was in Evansville to address an extension group. He began a series of lectures on botany in New Albany; at the Bloomingdale Academy he again spoke on botany. From Bloomingdale he went to Olivet, Michigan, where he spoke on Charles Darwin and then rushed south to Florida to lecture for ten days on botany on the southern Chautauqua circuit.

He seems to have kept up with his work back in Bloomington. At the end of his second term in March, 1892, the *Telephone* reported, "The affairs of the institution were never in a better shape, and . . . satisfaction among the students is general. During the two terms of Dr. Coulter's first year, now closing, there has not been the least disturbance, and the institution has never enjoyed a more prosperous period, either in point of numbers or in the class of work accomplished."

Hardly had the ink dried on the *Telephone* story before a rumor was afloat in Bloomington that President Charles Eliot of Harvard had offered Coulter the position of director of the Harvard Herbarium. Coulter admitted to the Indianapolis *News* reporter that President Eliot had often talked with him about the botany department at Harvard. The income of the Herbarium directorship, however, was too small to attract the Indiana president. It was the belief of the newspaper that the salary would be increased, as President Eliot had been in Indianapolis the past week. In the meantime Coulter kept up his grueling public lecture routine, and in between times he worked at his university administrative duties.

In June, 1892, Coulter gave the Board of Trustees a clear concept of the needs of Indiana University in his annual report. First was the necessity for constructing additional buildings. He proposed a large general purpose hall without laboratory facilities to serve the literary departments, and he believed such a building could be constructed at a cost of from $75,000 to $100,000. The second building should be devoted to sciences. It could be as small as Owen Hall so long as proper equipment were installed for the teaching of laboratory courses. This building, Coulter believed, would cost $125,000.

In addition to building needs, the President said serious attention had to be given to strengthening the faculty. Edward A. Ross had just resigned the chair of economics and social sciences, and Coulter proposed that the Board appoint John R. Commons of

Oberlin College to the chair of social studies. There were other needs such as an extension of the university's electric system. Twenty-eight lights had been installed in the chapel at a recurring service cost of $7.00 a month, but lights were needed elsewhere on the campus. There was still the water problem, and finally, the campus itself needed constant attention.

Every president of the university had had to concern himself with the water supply. Jesse W. Starr, a contractor, announced on July 26, 1892, that construction had begun on the new Blooming-ton waterworks, and if no trouble developed the city would have one of the best water systems in the West. As a hedge against another failure of the public supply, the old well in front of Wylie Hall had been deepened five feet in order to supply drinking water. On November 28, 1893, the *Student* said, "The franchise of the water works has been revoked by the city council, & the students' dreams of bubbling fountains on the campus & hot & cold baths in the gymnasium have been rudely shattered." At that time water works had not been placed in the university buildings.

At the June meeting of the trustees Isaac Jenkinson and his colleagues added their approval to that of the *Telephone*. Jenkinson reported, "We find the institution in excellent shape. Under the care of Dr. Coulter there had not been a jar nor a friction during the entire year. In addition to this, he has carefully guarded the financial interest of the institution, and everything is run upon business methods with which Dr. Coulter is connected."

Coulter must have been one of the most royally invited guests of the Columbian Exposition. One mail brought him three elaborate requests to be present at the opening of the great international display. One of these had come to him as editor of the *Botanical Gazette*, of Wisconsin, which he edited for much of his professional life. In October, 1892, Coulter brought even greater honor to the institution when he was appointed one of three of the American representatives of the standing committee of international botanists at a meeting in Genoa, Italy. In December he had to take time out from his speaking engagements and the university to work with D. H. Campbell in making arrangements for the World Botanical Congress which was to be held the next year in Madison, Wisconsin.

John Coulter had an altogether different personality from

David Starr Jordan, but he possessed all of Jordan's industry and much of his imagination. Wherever he went he inspired trust, and was able to catch people's attention. In two years he had a remarkable impact on Indiana, almost more beyond the boundaries of the campus than within the university itself. He was elected president of the Indiana College Association in December, 1892. At about this time James A. Woodburn was elected president of the state's historians and Horace A. Hoffman became vice president of the philological society. Later that month Coulter was made president of the state Y.M.C.A. Hardly had the newspapers stopped congratulating him upon his new appointments when a highly disturbing rumor began to circulate.

A leak in information indicated that the Indiana president had been offered the presidency of Lake Forest University in Illinois. The rumor was more or less confirmed by a Chicago paper which said definitely that a Lake Forest trustee had confirmed that the job had been offered to Coulter, and he was of the opinion that Coulter would accept. The Illinois salary was to be from seven to eight thousand dollars, a four thousand dollar advance over the Indiana salary.

At the same time the Lake Forest rumor was hot, word came that Coulter had been elected president of the University Department of the Bay View Assembly in Michigan. This was called the Chautauqua of the Middle West. The pay in this summer job was liberal, and Coulter's family could take a summer vacation in a pleasant place, said the Bloomington *Telephone*.

Coulter had still another offer: the University of Chicago offered him the headship of its Department of Botany at a salary of $7,000. He told the *Telephone* reporter that the Chicago position was more attractive than the presidency of Lake Forest. On March 3, 1893, Coulter was unanimously elected by the Board of Trustees of Lake Forest and that afternoon he confirmed to a local reporter that he had received the offer but had not finally decided to accept it. Three days later a copy of the Lake Forest College student paper arrived in Bloomington. It said that Coulter would be the college's next president and ran a picture and biographical sketch of him. By March 17 the Board of Trustees of Indiana University publicized the fact that it would meet in ten days to begin the search for a new president, and to make plans for an additional building. The Chicago *News Record* publicized the fact that on March 9 Coulter had formally accepted the Illinois presidency. That paper commented that Coulter's management of Indiana University had been highly successful, and as an internationally known descriptive botanist and professor he was an adornment to any faculty. He was a good organizer, and had attractive personal qualities. Nearer home the Wabash student paper regretted the fact that Coulter had accepted another college presidency: "We cannot but feel that a college presidency is not just the place for Dr. Coulter. He is preeminently a botanist & his time should not be taken up with other duties. One of the great universities should put him at the head of their Botanical Dept. & give him all the assistance and facilities he wants. In doing so they would be conferring a benefit on the country at large." This is what eventually happened. Coulter went to the University of Chicago as head of the Department of Botany in February, 1896.

Under Coulter's presidency the university maintained the momentum it had gained under Jordan. It would not be too extreme to say that Coulter advanced the institution pretty well beyond the reach of the reactionary forces which still wanted to return it to its pre-Jordan academy college status. An attractive and willing lecturer, Coulter in his two-year presidency did almost as much to gain public good will, to bring the university before the Indiana public, as Jordan had done in seven. It is doubtful that Jordan enjoyed any more scholarly distinction than did his successor, as demonstrated by the offices he held in scholarly organizations. Coulter, however, was neither pioneer nor innovator. He was an efficient administrator and an excellent scholar, but he really started no new programs nor attempted to expand the university fields of service. He never seems to have considered even in his own mind organizing some new divisions within the university, although the universities of Michigan and Wisconsin had done so.

Coulter's biggest contribution was to bring to maturity those projects which had been started in the last years of Jordan's administration. Among these were the introduction of extension work, the development of the university cooperative, expansion and improvement of the new campus, opening the new Library in Maxwell Hall, creation of the psychology laboratory under William Lowe Bryan's direction, building the men's gymnasium, and advancement in the summer school. Possibly the most important original thing Coulter accomplished was the reorganization of the faculty. He, like Jordan, succeeded in employing some highly promising outsiders, such as John R. Commons in economics. By the time he left the Indiana presidency he had organized a faculty which would be a vital part of Indiana University history until the 1930's.

Coulter accommodated his successor, Joseph Swain, by doing a bit of faculty "housecleaning." On March 27, 1893, the Board of Trustees notified Amzi Atwater, former vice president, James Kirkwood Beck, George William Saunderson, and Orrin Branner Clark that the departments of Latin, English, rhetoric, and oratory would be reorganized, and that their resignations would be acceptable at the end of the academic year. The official record does not explain the reasons for this major dismissal of faculty members. Amzi Atwater had a reputation among his students and colleagues of being a poor teacher. The other three men, however, had been solid professors in the faculty. They were thus summarily dismissed without any question from other faculty members as to the causes or any public notice. The entry in the minutes of the Board of Trustees reveals no more than the bare request for their resignations.

Student enrollment advanced to 392 in the latter part of Coulter's administration, an increase of approximately sixty students over the two-year period. There was an air of genuine optimism about the future. Like Jordan, Coulter brought Indiana no closer to being a university than it had been in 1891, except that the school had successfully diversified its science and social studies programs. The creation of the necessary divisions to give the school true university status had to await the coming of a later president and a new country.

[XIII]

Educational Crossroads
of the Nineties

W HEN JOHN M. COULTER ANNOUNCED in March, 1893, that he was resigning the university presidency, the Board of Trustees turned to him and to Jordan to suggest a successor. Jordan said in *The Days of a Man*, "Upon my further recommendation, again at the board's request, Coulter was succeeded by Joseph Swain, already for two years professor of Mathematics at Stanford." The two men agreed on Swain as their successor in Bloomington. The Jordan program would proceed under the direction of a staunch convert. The board quickly chose Joseph Swain, and again without much, if any, extended discussion or searching for additional candidates. The new president was thirty-six years of age, a Quaker from Pendleton, Indiana, and a man who had a solid asset in Indiana friendships. He was a graduate of the university in the class of 1883, and held the Master of Science degree, awarded in 1885.

For four years, 1886 to 1891, Joseph Swain was professor of mathematics at Indiana University. In the latter year he resigned his professorship to join the Jordan hegira to Palo Alto. The Indiana *Student* for May, 1891, said, "The mathematical students are especially regretting that Professor Swain will leave them next year. He is not only excellent in the classroom, but every student considers him a personal friend." Swain was a large and heavyset man with a kindly face. He lacked the fire of Jordan, and the ready speaking ability of Coulter, but he inspired trust in his integrity through what almost seemed a fierce honesty.

The Bloomington *Telephone* on March 24, 1893, reported gossip that Benjamin Harrison would be chosen to head the university.

> It may be only talk, but a number of friends of the institution are insisting that it would be a good thing. The idea is not that he should stay here all the time, but that a part of his time only is to be devoted to the work, and a vice president will look after details. It is argued that as it is a state institution, it would be a matter of pride with General Harrison to assist in its up-bringing.

The editor said everybody who had talked about the matter was highly in favor of the arrangement. In Indianapolis the General would not talk so the local papers interviewed his son-in-law Mr. McKee, "who was not slow in expressing his opinion and said, 'I have not talked with Mr. Harrison, but you may quote me as saying that he will not take the presidency of any State University. He is going to Leland Stanford as you know.' In this connection it is interesting to add a fact not generally known, James A. Garfield was offered the Presidency of Indiana University and had it in his mind to accept, but finally declined." What the editor could not possibly foresee was the fact that Benjamin Harrison spoke in Bloomington in 1896 and never mentioned the university. There appears to have been some friction between the man and the institution, but the Harrison rumor was to persist.

By April 18, 1893, the Swains had rented a new home which Amzi Atwater was having constructed on Kirkwood Avenue, and for which, the student paper announced, they would pay $30 a month. The editor said the people of Bloomington and the university community were happy that the professor was coming home. "He is in perfect harmony with the spirit of the institution," said the *Student*, "& will carry out the policy of Dr. Coulter, whom we hold in such high esteem, & who so ably took up the work begun by Dr. Jordan." This paper said that Swain preferred administrative work to classroom teaching.

When President and Mrs. Swain arrived in Bloomington on June 8, 1893, they were met at the train by a hospitable crowd, and later a large number of students surrounded Professor Robert J. Aley's home, where they were staying, and the Glee Club serenaded them. Swain already knew something of the task awaiting him. The first obligation was that of reading proof for the new catalogue. This gave him an opportunity to review intimately the university's program, and to discover what changes had occurred since 1891. When this chore was finished, he, like Coulter, went off to the Columbian Exposition, where he gave several lectures in some of the special institutes, one of which was the National Educational Congress.

Joseph Swain was a person Hoosiers could understand. He had a friendly open nature and never flaunted his learning before them. In some ways he could have been called a stolid man in his public dealings. On occasion, in dealing with state officials, his integrity and determination showed to excellent advantage, and his Quaker firmness stood him in good stead when political inroads threatened the validity of the university. He did not enjoy a national scholarly reputation comparable to that of Jordan or Coulter, but this did not reflect on his competence in his academic field.

Like Coulter, Swain was faced with the task of hiring faculty members. The Board of Trustees had created some of the vacancies. In addition to the boards dismissal of Orrin B. Clark, Amzi Atwater, and George William Saunderson, vacancies were created when E. W. Huffcut resigned to go to the Northwestern University Law School and when Benjamin Snow resigned to accept an appointment in the University of Wisconsin at a considerable advance in salary.

Swain not only had to fill key vacancies on the staff, but he promoted several younger instructors to professorships. There is little room for doubt that the ablest scientist left at Indiana was young and eager Carl H. Eigenmann. This round-faced German lad, born in Flehingen, Germany in 1863, had spent his boyhood near Rockport on the Ohio in southern Indiana. His parents had brought him as a small child to this country when they came from Germany. They forgot to declare him as an alien, a fact which was to have some comic reverberations later on. In 1883 Eigenmann entered the university as a classics major, but falling under

Jordan's seductive spell, he shifted to the scientific curriculum in his sophomore year. About this time he ran afoul of acting President Theophilus A. Wylie. He and six other sophomores balked when the aged professor directed them to take front seats in the chapel so he could keep a closer eye on them. This resulted in the boys being suspended from the university for a brief period. All through his life Eigenmann was to show this stubborn streak in his nature.

In 1893 Eigenmann was well on the road to professional success. He had inherited Jordan's enthusiasm for ichthyology and was already restoring much of the original collection of fishes destroyed in the fire of 1883. Following his graduation in 1886, he was given an apointment as an assistant in science courses while he pursued his graduate studies. In 1891 Eigenmann was named a successor to Charles Gilbert, at $1,200 on a year's trial, and in November the next year he was elevated to a full professorship on a professor's pay and tenure. From that date on the professor of zoology became almost as active as his idol Jordan. He seined Indiana caves for blind fish, exploited the waters and creeks of the whole Ohio Valley, and became equally avid as a hunter for research funds. In time the names Eigenmann and Indiana University became almost synonymous.

A second alumnus on the faculty in whom Swain placed trust was Robert J. Aley, who, like Eigenmann, received a bachelor of arts degree in 1888, his master's degree in 1890, and the doctorate from the University of Pennsylvania in 1897. In 1893 he was elected secretary of the faculty, but in 1894 Swain and Jordan worked out an exchange arrangement by which Aley would go to Stanford for a year, and Professor John A. Miller would come to Indiana. Aley had told Swain he wished to live on the West Coast for a short period, but before the president would consent to the exchange he extracted a firm promise from Aley that he would return to Bloomington, which he did in June, 1895. In a sense Aley was a replacement for Swain in both universities. A year later he was given another leave to complete work for his doctorate.

Swain's administration began in September, 1893, with forty-two faculty members. Some of the strongest of these were John R. Commons, William Lowe Bryan, Carl Eigenmann, Arthur L. Foley, Ernest Hiram Lindley, James A. Woodburn, William A.

Merrill, and David Rothrock. This was the largest faculty in the university's history. Many of the members, however, were young and fairly inexperienced. Of the forty-two about fifteen were of the instructor rank. Swain's budget was $65,336.71, $30,000 of which was derived by direct appropriation from the legislature, $17,700 from endowment interest, and $6,773.50 from the contingent and library funds. The remainder of the above sum came from miscellaneous accounts.

Coulter's plea to the legislature earlier in 1893 was for an annual appropriation of $40,000 to be paid in quarterly installments. In addition the building fund was reduced far below what the president had requested. The university received $50,000 with which to erect an assembly and recreational building, and this modest amount was to be paid in two annual installments. This fell far short of the requests for two substantial buildings. Swain, however, was somewhat encouraged that in the future there would be more money. Later the legislature agreed to the levying of one sixth of one mill on every property tax dollar levied in 1895, the fund thus collected to be distributed among Indiana University, Purdue, and the Indiana State Normal School. An amendment to the act required each school to file a complete financial statement with the state auditor before it could collect its share of the fund. Later provisions were made for the governor of Indiana to name a committee of legislators to investigate the financial condition of the state institutions. This committee was then to fix the amount of appropriation for each institution for 1894–95.

The $50,000 appropriation mentioned above hardly dented the university's need for housing. Earlier Benjamin W. Snow had been forced to equip a small laboratory in the basement of Wylie Hall, and Vernon F. Marsters organized a museum-laboratory for paleontology in the basement of Owen. Swain no doubt agreed with the *Telephone* that, "The existing buildings are simply too crowded." In 1894 a bacteriology laboratory was located alongside Marster's classroom in Wylie Hall.

In February, 1893, the Board of Trustees and university administration were faced with a serious dilemma. They had money enough to make plans for a new building, but not enough to construct it. This was to be a fairly large structure with classrooms for Greek, Romance languages, home economics, German, and the

Extension Division. Swain also suggested, as had Coulter before him, that the new building should contain library space, an assembly room, and space for the sciences. This was the genesis of what was to become Kirkwood Hall. Parker and Jeckel of Anderson were the architects, and bids were called for on May 1, 1894. The board had already decided to name the structure for Daniel Kirkwood, a revered professor of past years.

Kirkwood Hall specifications were more generous than those for any other building. It was to be 130 feet long by 76 feet wide. The basement was to be eleven feet deep, the first story sixteen feet high, the second fourteen, and there was to be a large attic; the structure was to be topped off by a tower reaching 100 feet high. On May 8, 1894, the contract for construction of Kirkwood Hall was awarded to E. E. Thompson, also of Anderson, for $39,742. Work was to be started in June and was to be completed by January 1, 1895. The trustees were able to secure the services of Father Boqueman, a Catholic priest who had an interest in architecture, to oversee the construction of the building. In October, 1894, the fifteen foot long slab of stone bearing the legend "Kirkwood Hall" was hoisted into position. This three foot wide block bore in two-foot letters Daniel Kirkwood's surname in what the *Telephone* called, "plain English." The contractor kept his agreement and by the first of the next year the new building was ready for occupancy by the departments of physics, philosophy, Greek, Latin, French, German, and the Law School. Another addition to the university buildings was the gymnasium bathroom accommodating eight persons at a time. The *Telephone* was certain, "The boys are delighted with the prospect of obtaining this much needed equipments." Up to this time taking a bath was a considerable undertaking for many students because of a lack of facilities.

On Founders' Day, January 15, 1895, Governor Claude Matthews and committees from both houses of the legislature were on hand to dedicate the new building. Isaac Jenkinson, President of the Board of Trustees delivered the principal address. He reviewed three quarters of a century of the university's history and concluded by saying there had never been "as a whole an abler, a more earnest and a more industrious faculty in the university than the present. We have had strong men taken from us but we have found other strong men to take their places. And as long as wealthier institutions are able to outbid us there will constantly be gaps in our faculty to fill." He then made a plea for more adequate salaries, saying that Indiana youth had as much right to receive able teaching as those of other states.

The *Student* drank an editorial toast to "Indiana University at Bloomington forever." Then it reported

> yesterday, will be long remembered as a red-letter day in the history of this honored Univ. city. Enjoying her hospitality were the Governor, the Secretary of State, more than 40 members of the legislature, two congressmen, three ex-congressmen, the Mayor of Indianapolis, the President of Michigan Univ, and more than 100 persons whose reputations are not confined to state lines. Everybody had on their best bib and tucker, and Streets and residences were scenes of beauty with their wealth of cream and crimson—the colors of Indiana University.

The only person missing was Daniel Kirkwood. There were companies of militiamen, visitors' and students, in all sorts of vehicles, and train-loads of visitors, 3,000 in all. The dedicatory services were held in the old chapel, where the university quartet opened exercises by singing *Lead Kindly Light.*

The modern age was forcing other physical considerations on the university. On November 12, 1895, the Bloomington *Telephone* announced that the Board of Trustees had about decided to install an electric light plant. That May work was begun on the fire cistern located in front of the Library, or Maxwell Hall. The institution had increased its physical liability by the addition of Kirkwood and fire protection was a prime necessity. Water had to be found nearby because the whole country about Bloomington faced disaster during droughts. In the university the new rage for bathing did nothing to alleviate the problem. The *Student* predicted on October 8, 1895, "It will not be long till an increase of the student body will demand individual locks & baths to say nothing of more space & apparatus."

As much space as Kirkwood Hall furnished, there were other needs. There was the question of furnishing an adequate women's gymnasium. The existing quarters were poorly ventilated, difficult of access, and could not be properly supplied with water. Swain knew that he and the board would get nowhere if they went to the legislature with a request for a men's and women's gymnasium. He was convinced that gymnastics were an important part of modern education, but it would take a long educational campaign to convince state officials of this fact. In order to get a new building the purposes had to be mixed, and he suggested asking for a building which could be used for a general assembly hall in which all sorts of university gatherings, including commencement crowds, could be assembled. It was estimated that such a building could be constructed of wood for around $12,000. Some trustees felt that to request a cheap wooden building of the legislature might result in forming the notion that all future buildings should be so constructed. There were others who wanted to wait a year before approaching the lawmakers for fear they would charge the university with never being satisfied. Swain was opposed to this idea of waiting and expressed the hope the Trustees would do nothing inexpedient. In August the board finally consented to the construction of a gymnasium-assembly hall at a cost of $10,300, and a contract was let to the Thompson builders from Anderson. It was to be 65 by 125 feet and have a seating capacity of 1,200-1,600 persons. This structure, the Assembly Hall, was completed by March 20, 1897, when President Swain reported to the Board of Trustees that it had been paid for and was in use.

President Coulter really never solved his personal housing problem in Bloomington and there were ample indications that Swain was having no more success. At the November 7, 1896, meeting a proposal was made to the trustees that President Swain be instructed to arrange for private builders to construct a president's home at a cost not to exceed $15,000, and to bear an annual rent of $900 to $1,000 a year.

To solve the student housing problem, which had grown steadily worse, the university officials suggested that two dormitories be built near the campus, one for men and the other for women. These buildings would be constructed with private capital and operated by their owners, and be ready for occupancy in the fall of 1897. The university reserved the right to supervise them. The plans for the buildings were drawn by Scott, Edelsord, and Fortin of New York.

In June, 1897, Swain and the board began a long discussion of erecting a heating plant. They had the advice of Professor Goss of Purdue, who explained in detail the kind of system needed, and took up the matter of location. This caused some serious debate because it was thought at first that the plant would obstruct the Dunn graveyard on the outer edge of the campus. Assurances were given that this would not be so. The next year the Bloomington Coal and Gas Company ran pipes into the campus to supply the university with gas for its lighting and laboratory needs. Sometime in the past the school had installed a "gasoline plant" to supply these services, but it was said that the commercial gas would not be any more expensive, and perhaps would cost no more than $300 a year.

By 1899 Indiana University had approximately half again as many students as it had in 1895. This increase in size of the student body placed every sort of strain imaginable upon the staff and physical plant of the university, and upon the town. No doubt legislators looked upon President Swain and the trustees as mendicants who plodded to Indianapolis every two years to wheedle out of the legislature the largest sum possible for buildings and salaries. The lawmakers had little or no real concept of what was occurring generally in American higher education. Little of the intellectual throb of the new university age had reached them, and even if it did they most likely misunderstood it. They were poorly equipped by educational background or first-hand experience to understand the urgency of President Swain's statements in his annual report to the trustees and legislators that the need for space in the university had become in fact an emergency which controlled the very quality of the educational program of the institution. Books stored in the basement of the new Maxwell Hall under the Registrar's office and the Board Room were going to pieces because of dampness. There was no place to hold some English classes, and other classes were crowded into inadequate rooms.

The prospect for building funds in 1898–99 were dim. Under the recently enacted $700 mortgage exemption law there was danger that all the state's colleges would be unable to do more than realize their meager salary budgets from public appropriations. At Indiana University, President Swain had in mind saving enough money to finance the building of a new wing on Maxwell Hall. He knew that what the university needed most, however, was another large classroom building.

Rooms in the older buildings were shabby. Swain told the trustees on June 8, 1899, that they needed refurbishing and re-furnishing. The refurbishing could be done with paper, paint and tint. He felt, however, that a committee of the board should visit the buildings and see for themselves the unattractive conditions of the rooms. In the November meeting of the Board of Trustees the president reported that the university had on hand cash resources of $37,000, $12,000 of which was needed for operating expenses, and the remaining $25,000 could be used to purchase books for the library and equipment for the science laboratories. The wisest thing in his opinion was to make a start on a new building and hope the legislature would be generous enough to complete the job with an additional capital appropriation. If the board believed that the full cost of the building could be procured in Indianapolis then the accumulated funds should be used for the purposes for which they had been saved. In addition there was urgent need for several new professorships. Specifically, Swain recommended pro-fessors of music, and physiology, and a dean of women.

At the time the above report was made, Professor John A. Mil-ler submitted a request to be allowed to purchase an astronomical telescope with a twelve inch optical glass. This instrument and its proper use necessitated the location of an observatory site and the construction of a suitable building. The board granted the request and then spent considerable time in the future discussing the proper location of the observatory. Miller believed a building could be con-structed for as little as $800. He thought it unwise, however, to keep so valuable an instrument as the new telescope in a flimsy frame building. He suggested that the observatory, whether of wood or stone construction, be named in honor of Daniel Kirkwood. After considerable discussion in trustee meetings, the observatory was built at the southeast corner of the campus, near Maxwell Hall, and named for the university's first astronomy professor. The permanent building was designed by John Nichols, and was built by the Henry Taylor lumber company of Lafayette at a cost of $6,225. Eakin and McKinley of Bloomington constructed the dome at an additional cost of $250. This contract was awarded by the Board of Trustees on June 16, 1900. In June, 1901, Joseph Swain assured the trustees that the Observatory had already justified its cost because it "has quickened immensely the interest in the students of Astronomy. . . . There is no doubt that we have value received in this observatory."

While president and trustees confronted the severe shortage of building space on February 7, 1900, the upper story of Wylie Hall caught fire, and before the Bloomington Fire Department could extinguish the blaze the ornamental tower and the entire upper story were ablaze. The damages were estimated at $19,404.40. It was necessary to remove at once the charred debris, strengthen the overhead joist, and install a temporary roof over the damaged structure to permit the continuation of classes. In rebuilding the hall, the upper story was replaced by a box-like extension in which the tower was left off. The central objective was to create the maximum amount of space possible for classrooms.

Following the Wylie Hall fire the board felt it would have better luck before the legislature by requesting that a state appropriation be made outright to finance the construction of a new building to house the sciences. In January, 1901, legislators discussed this request. Louis H. Gibson had prepared plans, and had proposed an unusually tall three-story structure to be constructed of oolitic limestone. This new building was to be built on the southern angle of the campus row between Kirkwood Hall and Third Street, and near the head of Bohannon's Hollow or ravine. The board resolved to go ahead with this building and ordered that the cost be held under $100,000. Apparently they made this determination whether or not the legislature granted the money. In his annual report, Swain asked the board to select an architect, locate the building site, and give the structure a name. In the meantime he secured a copy of the plans of the new library at the University of Illinois, and the plans of the physics building at the University of Chicago. It was decided at the outset that the new hall would be named Science Hall, and in later years it was named for Professor Ernest Hiram Lindley, professor of psychology and pedagogy from 1893 to 1917, and later president of the universities of Idaho and Kansas.

In his annual report on March 27, 1901, Professor Swain submitted a plan for distributing space among departments: Owen Hall would house zoology and botany; Wylie, law, political science, geology, and chemistry; Kirkwood, fine arts, languages, English, and history; and the new science building, physics, psychology, philosophy, pedagogy, mathematics, and the administrative offices.

By November 1, 1901, a contract for $115,000 had been awarded, and the sum of $4,906 was held in reserve for heating and plumbing fixtures. Dedication was set for Founder's Day, 1903. Aside from constructing new buildings, Swain was challenged with the problem of bringing the wooded campus into harmony with its usage. The woods were wildly beautiful, but left entirely in a state of nature they became shaggy and brush entangled. In March, 1899, W. R. Ogg, father of Frederick A. Ogg, the famous Wisconsin political scientist, was employed at a salary of thirty dollars a month to be university gardener. He was nominated by his trustee brother Robert A. Ogg who told the board, "I do not like to suggest my brother, but he knows all about doing what we are doing here." Before this date the professor of botany and his colleagues had supervised a limited beautification program of planting shrubs and removing dead trees and limbs. On May 19, 1896, a touch of sentiment was added to the new campus when the sundial, which had so long been a landmark on the old campus, was removed to a grassy mound at the southeast corner of Maxwell Hall. Along with the sundial came the old folk story of Cyrus Nutt striking a light on a dark night to see what time it was.

The appointment of W. R. Ogg was indeed the wedding of a man to the land. It was he who turned the picturesque natural tract of the rough ground of Dunn's Woods or University Park into an appealing garden. He served the university over a period of twenty-two years. Later Ogg reported to the Board of Trustees a strange phenomenon: at a certain period of the year the campus red squirrels gnawed the bark off the stately beeches, causing their top branches to die and give a shaggy appearance to the trees. Master gardener though he was, Ogg could never bring the squirrels under control.

Joseph Swain may be regarded as the builder of much of the older angle of university halls, and as the developer of the campus as a park. He was forced to these accomplishments because of the rapid increase in student enrollment (392 to 790) and the expansion and maturing of the academic program. By no means had Jordan and Coulter, active as they were, solved the university's curriculum problems. Jordan's electives blueprint, and its execution by Coulter, was but a pointing of direction for the new university to follow. In 1892, following the discontinuance of the preparatory school, the Bloomington *Telephone* reported,

> The large number of students who have entered Indiana University this year who with work to make-up in Latin, Mathematics, and English is so large that some action on the matter is expected from the Board. As the University has no preparatory department, it does not agree to prepare students for entrance, but leaves that to the high schools. All the conditioned students make that much extra work for the faculty, and it has been quite a problem to arrange this work.

The editor proposed that poorly prepared students be asked to pay sufficient fees to hire graduate tutors, as was being done at the universities of Michigan and Wisconsin.

A misunderstanding arose between the university and the commissioned high schools in 1893 over the meaning of the special certified requirements in English. Because of this the university agreed to grant credit for two terms of study, but thereafter the rule of reduced credit for lack of preparation would be strictly observed. In late 1892, said President Swain in his annual report of 1902, only 20 percent of the applicants for admission to the university passed the entrance examination in English. In 1902, the proportion had risen to 70 percent. The state normal school had some influence over the improvement of teaching. Too, the percentage of Indiana University graduates who entered the teaching field went up from 14 percent in 1871 to 1880 to 61 percent in 1895 to 1900.

The *Telephone* said in January, 1894, "Indiana University, long famed for its continued interest in the welfare of its graduates, announced the establishment of a small 'Teacher Agency' under the direction of the Registrar, Mr. Bates. The idea was to prepare a list of all the students who wanted to be teachers, and to serve them as well as organized teacher's agencies serve their patrons." This was an important milestone in the shaping of the Indiana University tradition at the turn of the century of being a producer of teachers. While the trend of the number of graduates going into the teaching profession skyrocketed, the trend in the number of lawyers went into reverse. Between 1830 and 1870, 40 percent of the university's graduates became lawyers, while in the years 1896–

1900 only 11 percent entered the legal profession. In subsequent years fear that the public would come to regard Indiana University as a second state normal college became a problem of vital concern to the institution.

Another problem which the Swain administration faced at the outset was to prevent students under the system of elective courses from overloading themselves with work. The faculty ruled in September, 1893, that except in special cases, students would be permitted to carry no more than three courses a term. This rule, however, was subjected to constant change because of the variations in class offerings. For instance, Carl Eigenmann offered a popular two-hour course in heredity to accommodate John R. Commons' students in sociology. Two seminars were offered, one in English and the other in Physics, and George E. Fellows broadened his course in European history in such a way as to make mandatory a reconsideration of units of credit. All of this reflected student demands that the faculty help the students broaden their horizons. By 1895, 105 different courses were being offered, and there were 120 different class meetings daily. One of Swain's major ventures outside of the Jordan-Coulter curriculum was the introduction of the fine arts and drawing into the course of study. Alfred M. Brooks of the Boston School of Technology was employed in 1896 to offer these courses. The curriculum was broadened in other areas. Alexis V. Babine, the new librarian, offered the first course in Russian, and Ulysses G. Weatherly suggested that courses in commercial subjects be offered. Just before this latter suggestion John R. Commons had taught courses in sociology which seem in fact to have dealt largely with labor relations in the rising impersonal American industrial system. Commons no doubt was too liberal and raised too many questions to suit many Hoosiers.

President Swain informed the trustees that commercial courses were being offered at Ohio, Illinois, Wisconsin, Minnesota, and Michigan. He thought this a good way to bring Indiana's businessmen into closer touch with their university. He believed this would do for Indiana University in the field of business what agriculture did for Purdue and the farmers. Already there was a stirring in the university and the state which really demanded that both break out of the shell of the past and the restrictive old line liberal arts college.

To do this required a tremendous change in many areas. Special interest groups in the state had to be enlisted to support the institution. In November, 1899, the president reported the appointment of a press committee composed of Isaac Jenkinson, Charles T. Henry, and Joseph Swain. Its duties were ostensibly to answer newspaper articles and publications which sought to hurt the institution. This action was provoked by a furore stirred up by the Indianapolis newspapers. In a pamphlet, said to have been published by the church-related colleges of the state and by the contentious Thomas A. Goodwin, D.D., and Will Craig, vicious and dangerous charges were levelled at the university. These attacks basically were made against all three state schools. Joseph Swain felt the best strategy was to assume an unaggressive approach until the gauntlet was down, and then to answer every charge in detail.

Thomas A. Goodwin of Indianapolis and Will Craig of Noblesville gave the press committee plenty of charges to be answered. Goodwin was more plausible and persevering in his campaign. He argued from the false premise that Indiana University was a private corporation chartered as such by the first constitution and by legislative act. Hence, he contended, it was unconstitutional for the General Assembly to appropriate money to support public higher education. The university's friends felt it would not take much of this kind of opposition to be injurious. Swain answered the Goodwin attack and successfully prevented the people and the legislators from taking the irate preacher seriously. Perhaps the Board of Trustees Press Committee had other positive effects. In answer to the paranoiac fulminations the university was able to call attention to itself in a most inoffensive yet informative way. Joseph Swain and the trustees sensed at the turn of the century that the university had to broaden its academic base to survive competition from other institutions. It had to prepare to serve the needs of a rapidly changing society in Indiana, and it had to keep abreast of university education in the Old Northwest, where it had pioneered for so long.

Most of the pressure for a greatly enlarged program came from the new breed of students entering the institution. The improvements in commissioned high schools was inevitably reflected in the quality and motivation of the university's student body. It would not be too farfetched to say that the Swain years were the most important ones in a transitional sense in the history of the university down to 1903. The Indiana *Student* noted almost monthly progress of this revolution. In March, 1893, it asked,

> What is more ridiculous in modern college life than a fight be-
> tween Freshmen & Sophomores over the burning of Horace? But
> few of either class know what Horace is. As a text in our Univer-
> sity it is less known than "Henry George." Horace is now only an
> excuse for a "scrap." No one knows what the contest is about, nor
> does any one care. Soon it will follow other traditional college cus-
> toms to a shelf prepared for it.

In April that year the paper discussed another dying custom. "Some of the old abuses in the east end of the library building have ceased," said the editor, "yet a few gentlemen eat 'terbacker' & fail to swallow the 'broth.' " Anyway the Dukes of Durham sup-plied the college sports with a more sophisticated use of tobacco with their cigarettes.

Along with the age of the cigarette came the various musical organizations, the straw sailor hat, and the mandolin. The Glee Club which serenaded the Swains upon their arrival in Blooming-ton in June, 1893, had been recently organized. In October of that year a new club was assembled under the direction of M. B. Griffith. At the same time twelve of the "straw hatted and striped blazer boys" organized a mandolin and guitar club. This was the era when the seniors rent the air with the outcry:

> Rip War, Blood and Gore . . . '94
> Indiana Evermore, That's us.
> Every cuss, make a fuss . . . for '94

The crusaders found new causes to inveigh against. John R. Commons and Edward A. Ross had tried to raise criticisms of the American social and economic system. The temperance leaders were still able to shake a bony finger in the face of demon rum. The new fad of cigarette smoking lifted eyebrows, even those of the old tobacco worms. The *Student*, which since 1867 had bemoaned and ridiculed tobacco chewers, on October 8, 1895, turned on the smokers. "We are democratic enough not to wish to interfere in the slightest degree with the private rights of anyone," said the editor. "Among these rights belongs the use of tobacco & the modern compound known as cigarettes. We believe it is not undemocratic to say that the use of the cigar and cigarette in public is not a private privilege. . . . The practice is offensive to many not only from a moral view but also from the physical aspect." This came near connecting smoking with the evil of drinking.

The Indiana University student of the 1890's was quite capable of expressing himself militantly if necessary. In all the tugging and hauling over moving the university to Indianapolis or leaving it in Bloomington, there were irritations which kept people in a state of some anxiety if not anger. The "removal" partisans wore badges which offended townspeople and many of their fellow students. On hand on January 25, 1895, to greet the visitors to the university were the Mechanics Band and Company H of the Indiana National Guard. Ostensibly the soldiers were present to form a guard for Governor Claude Matthews and the members of the General Assembly. There was no apparent reason for such a heavy military guard even for honor's sake. When the distinguished guests filed into the chapel entry way the National Guardsmen separated and allowed them to pass between the two lines of soldiers. When the "removal" lads came along the militia captain ordered his men to snatch off their offending badges. This resulted in a general fight in which badges were ripped off, men and women students were knocked down, and the overwrought soldiers even drew bayonets on some. A public furore over this incident followed. The *Student* reported on March 12, 1895,

> Much indignation was aroused among the student body last Friday by an article in the columns of one of our local contemporaries concerning the student-militia company controversy. An effort is being made by some students and citizens to have members of company "H" indicted by the grand jury for their mistreatment of students on Dedication Day. The action of the Company was a flagrant violation of civil as well as military law, & justice would demand that the members be prosecuted, but our esteemed local contemporary openly counsels the grand jury to take no hand in the matter.

The local newspaper thought that enough had been said about the matter. It felt that since the university was just then seeking an

appropriation from the legislature all past differences and bickerings should cease. Everybody should join in building up the university for the general welfare of the community. The *Student*
was of the opinion that there was more at stake than mere university
support and local community peace of mind. People had been
knocked down and harassed for expressing an opinion.

Joseph Swain was the first president of Indiana University
who had to deal with an open student revolt. This incident of student unrest and rebelliousness came about because Washington's
birthday in 1896 occurred on Saturday, which caused students to
feel that they were being cheated out of a holiday, because they
had no classes on that day anyway. Since Lincoln's birthday oc-
cured on Wednesday a segment of the student body sought to have
that date declared a holiday, but the faculty refused this request.
The students then chose to "bolt" classes. A small group gathered
at the entrance to Kirkwood Hall on February 12 and sent up the
college yells. In a short time a crowd had gathered and soon it
became an audacious mob which was emboldened to charge into
the building shouting and misbehaving. Students rushed the classrooms and dragged non-bolting students out of the classes. They
raided the English end of Maxwell Hall, but they were driven out
when President Swain appeared. They made a second raid on the
Kirkwood classrooms and again Swain drove the noisy mob away.
The screaming students then rushed downtown, gathered the assistance of a drum corps and returned waving an Indiana banner,
and filled the chapel. A cold rainstorm, however, helped mightily
to chill the students' ardor for a cause that had no substance from
the outset.

On February 14, 1896, a faculty committee composed of William Lowe Bryan, Horace A. Hoffman, and Robert J. Aley sent
out letters addressed to the bolting students in which they asked
for reports in writing to the students affairs committee as to why
the rebels had not been present in class on the twelfth. They asked
these students to state their connections if any with the Lincoln's
birthday commotion. The recalcitrants were also requested to have
their replies in the hands of the registar by the seventeenth. The
tone of this communication seemed to imply punitive action would
be taken, but the "bolters" pretended to regard the letters as valen-
tines and fifty of the communications were posted in the window

of Axtell's store downtown. On Saturday afternoon the absentees and their friends held a meeting in the Opera House to discuss their predicament. It was said "the meeting was cool and determined." The attitude of the students seemed to be one of personal respect toward the faculty, but of determination to refuse to comply with the requested submission of reasons for the bolt to the faculty committee. Resolutions were drafted saying that the assembly felt no punishment should be administered to the rebels. The *Student* said the following Monday that the situation demanded that some one back down or there would be a second explosion. The editor stated the position of his paper, that the students should be allowed to stay away from classes if they wished but with no right to interfere with those who wished to attend classes.

When the faculty received the "Saturday resolutions," notices were again prepared and posted about the campus saying that punishment was not implied in the original letter, but students must reply to it or be dealt with on an individual basis. All but thirty students replied, and the hold-outs met in Mitchell Hall and soon found themselves deadlocked in a stormy debate. President Swain called a meeting at his residence of the Advisory Board of Students early in March to discuss the dispute. Swain said the faculty's attitude was one of noninterference so long as students could govern themselves, but if they failed to do this the faculty would have to take a decisive hand. On March 3, 1896, the *Student* said,

> We have seen the strange spectacle of a body of students dragging their fellows from classrooms; students receiving notices from the faculty and pasting the same on a shop window fronting the public square; students in mass meeting assembled resolving to ignore these notices from the faculty; faculty notices on bulletin boards threatening students who refused to recognize notices received; & students in second mass meeting wrangling over their action in the previous meeting & adjourning without coming to an agreement.

This all wound up in a Shakespearean farce of much ado about nothing. It was the first outright student rebellion, and it clearly marked the end of what remained of the tradition of *in loco parentis*. Both faculty and students learned something from this adolescent quarrel.

On top of the quarreling over Washington's and Lincoln's birthdays, the Associated Press erroneously attributed to Indiana University a reported scrap between the freshmen and sophomores at the University of Illinois in which the freshmen had surprised the sophomores in bed in the early morning hours, and had tied them hand and foot and hauled them out to the country and bound them to trees. A fight was said to have ensued, in which a boy's skull was fractured and others were badly beaten. The Hoosier editor observed, "Indiana University has no need for unearned notoriety; and we suggest that if the Associated Press correspondent wished the world to know that the freshmen and sophomores indulge in such luxuries as class scraps, he would do well to underscore the word *Illinois*."

The Associated Press reporter only confused specific details in the above story. Despite rising opposition the class scraps continued in Indiana University. Annually the burning of Horace, Caesar, and mathematics textbooks brought out swarms of "braves" who sought to create as much pandemonium as possible. Each year in the 1890's students seemed to decide to discontinue this barbarous custom. In 1895 they resolved to allow February 22 to pass peaceably, but the juniors and seniors broke over and had a scrap. In 1896 letters threatening torture to both freshmen and sophomores were afloat on the campus. This resulted in a free-for-all on North College Avenue in which both sides took captives. Boarding houses were raided and students were handcuffed and taken off to secret hiding places. A day and a half of searching for "prisoners" ensued, with sporadic fighting among the classes.

The *Student* on February 25, 1896, described the scenes of warring about the campus,

Early Saturday morning large squads of Freshies and Sophs were seen here and there searching for some of their imprisoned classmates. Occasionally some of these would collide when a regular scrap would occur. About the middle of the forenoon everything became quiet. Promptly at 12:00 a phalanx of Sophs broke into the Southwest corner of the campus with the blazing Horace in their midst. The Freshies expected them from the woods in the rear and for this reason were not prepared to receive them. So Horace was burned. The hostile parties stood, eyed each other and dispersed.

Again, in 1899 the "muttering storm" in January was heard in the distance. Upperclassmen were urging freshmen and sophomores into a fight. It took a little more urging than in the past, and the campus editor felt the time had come once more to usher in spring without breaking heads and noses.

At present, the barbarous custom of appealing to brute force would again test the relative strength of the lower college classes. Why? To maintain a time-worn custom which like the cap and gown should be relegated to the past, that of burning Horace. How many of the Sophomores can without an interlinear translate the first page of Horace? How many of the class knows the origin or can give a single reason for maintaining the custom for which they so bravely fight?

The Board of Trustees on February 10, 1900, expressed strong agreement with the notion that the "scraps" if they ever had any relevancy, were now outmoded. They commended Joseph Swain for his efforts to suppress the class fights, and the painting of class numbers on buildings. This official mandate, however, was not immediately honored. President Swain reported that the Committee on Student Affairs had tried for several years to end the fighting, and during the winter, 1901–02, ten students had been punished for violating university rules. Students proposed a "color rush" in which the freshmen colors would be placed in a tree for one hour after an athletic contest in the men's gymnasium. If the sophomores could remove the colors during the hour they were victorious, if not, the freshmen won. It was said the new policy was better, but still there was roughness. This new scheme let off some animal energy. "They [underclassmen] need some outlet as much as a steam engine needs a safety valve," said the *Student* editor.

The Swain administration saw changes in other areas of university life. The Bloomington *Telephone* announced on May 1, 1896, that Mr. Simone in the corner store was that morning taking orders for senior caps and gowns. There were over a hundred graduates and they would present a striking appearance. The paper said, "On the day of graduation all the seniors wear a black gown that falls loosely from the neck over the shoulders down to the feet, and a black mortar-board cap." This was a new departure for Indiana University, even though the cap and gown had been worn by graduates in Eastern colleges for many years. So proud were the seniors in '96 that most of the class appeared at the Swains' reception in graduation garb.

The faculty and students were uncertain as to whether the grading system was satisfactory. In May, 1894, after extensive discussion, the faculty decided to abolish the older system and adopted an early version of "pass-fail." A month before this action the *Student* said,

> In our judgment the faculty of Indiana University lost an opportunity to increase the educational efficiency of the institution when they failed at their last meeting to vote on a proposition to abolish all distinctions between all students whose work is deemed worthy of the University's credits. Comparisons and distinctions between persons associated together are always odious and most odious in the classics atmosphere of a great university.

The editor was certain that students favored the system of "fail, conditioned, passed, and turned down." He neglected, however, to distinguish between "failed" and "turned down." At their May meeting the faculty acceded to student wishes, "to their great delight." The *Student* thought "the action of the faculty is a recognition of the constantly increasing democratic tendencies that prevail throughout the whole country." It was believed that Joseph Swain was eminently fair in initiating this system, and students congratulated him for his action.

Grading at Indiana University had a mixed history. Up to 1851 students seemed to have been graded in professorial conferences which appeared to have considered deportment as well as class work in determining a student's standing. Between 1851 and 1862 the faculty used a numerical system based on a 1 to 10 scale. Later the scale was based on a 0 to 3 basis, and in 1894–95 the faculty adopted, as described above, the three stages "failed, conditioned, and passes." This system prevailed until 1908, when the present

"A, B, C," scale was adopted. This action was in keeping with grading history in American universities generally.

The movement to revise the grading system was intimately tied in with a rising sense of academic democracy. In 1868 Ezra Cornell had proclaimed his university to be a place where anyone could study without having to be subjected to a form of grade snobbery. The University of Wisconsin experienced a period of doubt that grades were wise, and some of its leaders contended that a degree obtained with a "C" was as valid as one representing superb marks. Michigan banned Phi Beta Kappa on the grounds that it created a grade-conscious aristocracy. Michigan and Stanford experimented for a while with the idea of no differential grades, in fact no grades at all. Sweeping the country in the two decades 1890 to 1910 was the feeling that public institutions should dedicate themselves to the highest possible degree of academic service. This was in keeping with Charles Kendall Adams' thought that the University of Wisconsin was a people's university, and should remain a place where folk wisdom could be exercised. In Indiana there can be little doubt that the university was looked upon as a people's institution that had sought since 1865 to reach as large an element of the state's population as possible.

By 1899 Joseph Swain and his administration had more fundamental issues to deal with than mere grades. In his annual report to the Board of Trustees, the president took a searching look at the university's academic program. The number of students pursuing work leading to the Bachelor of Arts degree was relatively large as compared with those of neighboring institutions. Indiana had an enrollment in 1899 of 1,050, approximately 950 of these were registered in liberal arts courses. Michigan, for instance, had only 1,200 registrants in its liberal arts programs. In 1899 Indiana had more liberal arts students than either Illinois or Wisconsin. Joseph Swain realized fully that his institution was headed for serious difficulty unless some drastic changes could be made in the university's organization. The challenge was clear: Indiana needed to organize at least a half dozen divisions serving the new demands of the modern American student. Until this was done, Swain felt, as did several of his predecessors, the term "university" was purely an ornamental one.

It was difficult if not absolutely impossible at the turn of the century to increase the field of educational service in Indiana University because of a lack of building space, or an adequate and specialized faculty, or money to organize what inevitably would be an expanding program. In highly realistic terms Joseph Swain told the trustees that the university in this era would do well just to keep its doors open and remain functional in a severely limited way with its current financial support. Unless new departments and fresh inducements could be added enrollment would drop off. Expanded programs in other universities surrounding Indiana would attract away from the state some of its brightest and most ambitious students.

On April 9, 1895, the *Student* noted that the presidents of Illinois, Indiana, Ohio, Michigan, Wisconsin, Minnesota, Missouri, Iowa, Kansas, and Nebraska had met in Evanston, Illinois, and formed the North Central Association of Colleges and Secondary Schools. Plans were made for an annual meeting of this body, and accreditation standards were being formulated. This was an important step for Indiana University because it brought the institution into a more pronounced position of comparison with its neighboring universities than ever before in its history. This gave everybody, president, faculty, and trustees, a clearer perspective of what was happening in higher education, and especially in the state universities.

Indiana was founded primarily as a liberal arts college, despite the breadth of scholarly approach specified in the constitutional clause. There was, however, from the beginning, a strong implication that technical and professional schools would be developed. Only law was added in the first eighty years, although valiant attempts were made to institute courses in engineering, agriculture, and teacher training. Since the Civil War Indiana's economic interests were centered in the land and in the practical matters of organizing banks, building railroads, roads, and manufacturing establishments. It still remained a monumental challenge to the president and the trustees to sell agrarian legislators the idea of a broadly based university. This became even more difficult after the creation of Purdue.

As early as 1894 Swain reported to the Board of Trustees that he had been examining the catalogues of forty colleges and universities, and he found that 385 Indiana students were enrolled outside the state. He explained this drain in concrete terms of dollars and cents, saying that $150,000 was spent annually by these expatriate Hoosiers, and he estimated the loss amounted to as much as a half million dollars. "Give us the money to make a great institution of learning," he pleaded, "and Indiana will not only have the greater part of one half million [dollars] in the state, but she will bring the sons and daughters of other states to spend a half million more." President James B. Angell said that many talented students came to Michigan from Indiana and settled there when they had finished their education. This was the loss which counted, and the state, in the president's opinion, foolishly allowed many of its best youth to go elsewhere.

In December, 1894, Joseph Swain, addressing the Indiana State Teachers' Association, said the state universities had become potent factors in the development of the states. This fact was early recognized in the constitutional provisions of the new states of the Northwest. Now that the pioneering era was past the universities had clearly defined missions in the new "science, literature and learning." He asked the question, "Is Indiana taking her natural place in this national movement? Is Indiana looking to her own interest by seeing that her sons and daughters have as good opportunity for culture and liberal learning in her own border as they can receive in other states?" Under Swain's guidance the university attempted to meet this broad challenge.

[XIV]

On the Threshold
of the Future

T HE CHALLENGES OF CHANGE had confronted Joseph Swain
at Indiana University since that day, June 8, 1893, when
he returned to the campus from Stanford University. Every
aspect of university life and activity was caught up in demands
either for expansion or for serious revision. Although he was no
militant apostle of revolution, nor even of mild change, the forces
of the times denied the new president the privilege of maintaining
the status quo. He still faced the unsatisfied demands made upon
David Starr Jordan and John Merle Coulter of adjusting the people
of Indiana to the fermenting age in American higher education,
and at the same time of converting a liberal arts college into a
university.

The latter task Swain had to accomplish with one hand bound
behind his back by a stringent financial cord.

One of Swain's first statements to the Board of Trustees and
legislators concerned keeping a good faculty. He told them if David
Starr Jordan was worth $10,000 a year in California he was worth
every cent of it in Indiana. John Coulter was worth as much to
Hoosiers as he was to their neighbors in Illinois. Jeremiah Jenks
was paid $4,250 by Cornell University and he could have been

just as influential in Bloomington. Richard G. Boone and John Casper Branner were most worthy of their hire at Michigan and Stanford, and they drew twice the salaries paid them by Indiana University. The remedy for all of this lay in larger legislative appropriations, and their expenditure by the trustees as an academic investment, not as a penny-pinching financial bargain. There was no reason why Indiana should do less for its university than was done by Illinois, Michigan, Wisconsin, and Minnesota.

The University of Michigan received an annual income of $375,000, and a property tax increase of one-sixth mill yielded $188,000. This enabled the university to add an extensive heating plant. Its physical plant otherwise was worth $1.25 million, and it had just finished an $85,000 law building and a $133,000 gymnasium. Illinois had just dedicated a $160,000 physics and English building. Even poorer Missouri had appropriated $1.5 million to its university since 1891.

Legislative support in Indiana was still minimal, and demand for buildings, as discussed previously, far exceeded any possible promise of satisfaction. The new president had to prevent the institution from slipping backward in its academic program; nor could he allow legislators to settle for second best in the construction of flimsy wooden secondary buildings. It was clear that the new breed of Indiana students was unwilling to lose a generation of study or be cheated out of the advantages of a sound college education. Students came to Bloomington in ever increasing numbers, no matter how pressed the physical facilities were to accommodate them.

Aside from the housing crisis, university officials were faced with the constant problems of water supply and the health of the students. In the summer of 1892, as described earlier, Jesse W. Starr, the contractor for the local water company, said that he had begun work on a Bloomington reservoir, and that within three months Bloomington would have one of the best water systems in the West. Swain had hardly been in office a year before the city council and the students' dreams of bubbling fountains and hot and cold baths in the gymnasium were shattered. Mr. Starr had failed to deliver on his boast. The university renewed one or two of its wells, but in the fall of 1896 Joseph Swain posted a notice cautioning students against drinking well water unless it were thoroughly boiled. "A strict observance of this caution," he said, "will save many from an attack of typhoid or malarial fever."

In his report to the Board of Trustees on November 1, 1897, Swain said that the drinking water supply had been exhausted during the dry season. He warned that some provision had to be made to prevent a recurrence of this condition. The university had to create a water reserve for its drinking and boiler purposes in case the city's supply was exhausted. He expressed the opinion that snow water was better for drinking than any to be found about Bloomington. The most immediate remedy the university could apply to its water situation was to fit up the large cistern near Maxwell Hall to contain drinking water, and connect the two north cisterns by pipes to the boiler house. The Maxwell cistern could be equipped with a filter to protect the purity of the water.

Year after year the university was beset by the ancient problem of its water supply. In November, 1898, Swain again warned the Board of Trustees that something had to be done to relieve the institution of this worry. The local agent of the water company wanted to charge the university $520 a year for its water supply. Swain told the trustees this was too high. He believed that, scarce though water was, $1.00 a day was ample charge. If the water company refused to accept this payment then the university should think seriously about building its own waterworks. This solved nothing. The next summer was a dry one and Bloomington was again without water, no matter what the price. The campus went dry, and the university carried insufficient insurance on its buildings, which most surely would burn down completely if they caught fire. News of the drought had kept some students from entering the university that fall. Thus this problem took on almost the same proportions as need of money and the demands for an expanded academic program.

Because of the recurring water shortage there was a constant threat to health. On November 14, 1893, the *Student* said,

The shocking prevalence of typhoid & malarial fever in this city this fall is not without a cause, & is not without a cause the city could easily remove. The University has already suffered & will probably continue to suffer from the shameful, if not criminal, negligence of the City Board of Health, (if such an organization there be). It is high time the town take some action. Students have gone home, sick, to the four quarters of the state & the sanitary condition of Bloomington is rapidly becoming known. . . . On Sun. the 15th inst., the day of the fire, when the hose burst in front of the Presbyterian Church & the water flowed down the west side of Walnut Street, there arose from the little stream a combination of stenches that would have the Chicago River smell sweet in comparison.

The editor pointed to other places where there were rotting vegetables, calling these places disease centers. If the city authorities refused to clean up the streets and piles of rotting vegetables and cisterns, then the editor said, "if there is to be no remedy, no relief, then let us arise as one man, student, faculty, trustees, & demand the instant removal of the University to a healthier city." The editor of the paper believed that the large number of cases of typhoid fever among the students could not just be a "happen so, unless it 'happened so' at other places in the same proportion."

By 1895 the health situation had become so precarious that students proposed the idea of organizing a student's guild of mutual benefit by which members would care for one another in sickness. It was thought a house might be rented and equipped for a hospital, and a trained nurse placed in charge. The house could be fitted with bathrooms for general as well as hospital use. A solicitation of funds would be made, not as donations, but as a business investment in a necessary facility. The *Student* announced on October 22 a set of rules and conditions under which such a hospital would be organized and operated. Two rules seemed rather strange. No person suffering from a contagious disease would be accepted to membership, and no person on the eve of sickness would be admitted. The pending condition of the supplicant patient would be determined by a medical examination. The committee thought the cost of equipping such a house would run to approximately $100. This effort, however, failed in the beginning because students did not respond to the canvass for members. The next year a student committee met with Joseph Swain and William Lowe Bryan in an attempt to create a workable plan to effect a permanent organization to care for sick students. This may have impressed the two administrators more then than at another time because most of the faculty was in bed with "la grippe."

Not only did typhoid, malaria, la grippe, and dysentery threaten the welfare of the student body; annual outbreaks of smallpox were frightening. It was said that the attendance of the spring term in 1899 was reduced because of a threat of smallpox. Enrollment dropped from 765 to 717. Six students, four men and two women, contracted the disease. Their houses were fumigated, and the university furnished a nurse, and cooperated with the city in a quarantine which cost the institution $700. Virus or vaccine was secured and nearly the whole student body was vaccinated. Fortunately the epidemic did not spread.

Swain told the Board of Trustees after this experience that the university should build a small pesthouse off on a corner of Jordan Field to care for smallpox victims. "This year," he reported, "I believe considering all the circumstances the University should take care of cases of smallpox. If a small and inexpensive house were built in the northeast corner of Jordan Field it would serve the purpose." But in 1901 it was reported that the house had not been built. In 1902 a sum of $1,500 was set aside to provide a building for smallpox victims, but it was necessary to confer with city commissioners on the subject. There were strong objections to the location of such a house in the city, but finally it was agreed to have the architect Nichols prepare plans for a six room cottage, which would cost approximately $900. A man named Pryor who had survived a smallpox infection was approached to be caretaker and nurse. By the fall of 1902, President William Lowe Bryan reported that smallpox was increasing and with such virulence that it would be necessary to provide additional funds to minister to the sick. As this fall wore on and public health became very much an issue, the campus editor took the administration and faculty to task for not seeing to improvements in local sanitary conditions. In areas of student life the faculty had a responsibility to see that students did not injure their health by overexertion or foolish habits. One of the things that should be corrected was limiting the university dances to certain hours so that students could get home and to bed on time.

Almost as much of a problem for Joseph Swain was to strike a happy religious balance in the institution. He managed to bring about a reasonable compromise between the pro- and anti-chapel groups by holding chapel every Tuesday at ten o'clock, and having a public lecture given by a faculty member or a prominent citizen every Thursday. The Thursday lecture did not necessarily have to be on a religious subject. Another compromise was to add a course in Bible study to the curriculum, taught by William Lowe Bryan. Swain told the board in November, 1898, "This work together with the teaching of the Bible classes in students' rooms led by students is one of the most useful and interesting movements in Bible study I have ever known." Two years later he reported that the idea of Bible study had been growing on him. He was not thinking in ecclesiastical or denominational terms, but in the sense of history and ethics. The present generation was lacking in knowledge of the Bible and this was a chance to catch it up. However, the course would be worse than useless if not taught by the right man, one of large heart and mind, and one in whom students and faculty had confidence. In Swain's opinion S. R. Lyon, president of Monmouth College, was just such a man. Already he had talked over his ideas with both President Lyon and David Starr Jordan, and Jordan assured him that if Indiana did not hire Lyon, Stanford would. By the end of his administration Swain had consented to turning over chapel services to the various campus organizations, which varied in their religious emphases. The *Student* thought this was a good idea which would bring new students into touch with the university, and renew the interests of older students.

Since 1867 the Indiana *Student* had played a significant role in Indiana University history. It not only was the monthly chronicler of events, but its editorials no doubt had significant bearing on university policies. Student editors seemed to exhibit genuine courage. While they spoke of the faculty in most respectful tones, seldom taking a caustic poke at an irritating professor or speaking harshly of presidential decisions, they left little doubt about how the students were thinking. Newspapering was a popular profession in a politically minded rural state. In the fall semester of 1895, courses in journalism were added to the curriculum. These consisted of two years of English, economics, and history. Not only was there a new course, but a new subdepartment was added which aimed to prepare students for newspaper work in much the same fashion as men prepared for the practice of medicine. This department was actually an adjunct of English. The Indiana newspapers were said by the *Student* to react favorably to the idea of the newsman's trade being taught in the university, especially since assurances were given that Indiana would avoid mistakes made by other departments of journalism in other universities.

Almost immediately students agitated to convert the *Student* into a daily. The editor in May, 1896, thought that if a daily were published

> it should be issued by the class in journalism with the instructor as permanent editor and general manager. Our idea is to conduct the paper in the same manner as a laboratory. Let it be a laboratory in journalism with the entire responsibility upon the department to which it belongs. Then we would have a course in journalism free from the taint of [the] "impractical" and using the same methods in vogue in all modern [press] rooms.

He was not in favor of a nonstudent paper because the student body would then have no way to express its opinions. Swain reported in the fall of 1898 that the *Student* had become a daily on September 26, and he requested the board to purchase $150 worth of issues to be distributed to the high schools of the state. This paper had begun as a monthly publication and then was published semiweekly. The editor disagreed with President Swain on the distribution of copies to the high schools. He believed the paper was no longer suited for this purpose, and in time the board agreed with him by refusing to distribute certain issues.

The tenor of university life during the Swain years underwent rapid change. The president noted with genuine pride in March, 1898, that the Glee Club had greater success than in other years. It had gone out of town during the Christmas holidays, to the northern part of the state, and had filled several engagements during the summer. The following June, however, brought a severe blow to his pride. He informed the board that on the spring tour in the southern part of the state three members had got drunk in Kingsland between Hartford City and Huntington. One of the lads never returned to the university, and the other two were expelled. Swain went to Hartford City and made an investigation which resulted in further checking on student habits back in Bloomington. As a result "a number of students were pledged to abstain from the use of intoxicating drinks under any condition."

When Joseph Swain became President of Indiana University in 1893, there were 193 women students registered in classes, and as more and more emphasis was being placed on high school teaching this number promised to grow rapidly. While it was true that the university had admitted women students in 1867, its faculty had never quite decided what role they should play in the institution. Both president and faculty seemed to feel that if women maintained a genteel Victorian decorum problems of coeducation would not arise. In earlier years Sarah Parke Morrison had been assigned —in addition to her English instructorship—to seeing that the girls behaved in the ladies' room, and that some semblance of control was exercised over their nocturnal activities; otherwise the girls were on their own. Since earlier girl students had boarded in private homes or lived with their parents there had been little need for university supervision. As the number increased, however, this problem demanded solution. Elsewhere across the country the position of dean of women had come to be a significant one in university administrative organization.

By 1899 Indiana had 318 women registered, or 30 percent of its student body. No comparable recognition of this fact had been made in the appointment of staff members. Only Katherine Graydon, Sarah Parke Morrison, and Sophia Sheeks had been employed in the past. Later Louise Maxwell was given a position in the Library. At the same time presidential and professorial wives were almost invisible in the academic community, except for Mrs. Wylie and Mrs. Swain. Jordan's two wives were noted, even in the official records of the institution, but they seem not to have played significant roles in the university life. Women appeared in generous numbers at all university and public affairs, but they appeared as almost faceless individuals so far as the university was officially concerned.

A serious handicap to women students was that both institution and town were poorly prepared to house men students, and much more so to offer suitable living quarters to any considerable number of girls. There is plenty of evidence that at this time there prevailed a sort of open-housing scheme, and this continued to be so in a limited way down to the 1920's.

In 1894 there was some evidence that the crusade for women's rights had made an impression on Indiana University. The *Student* described this situation: "The girls of Indiana University are far from belonging to the short-haired woman's rights type but they evidently take an interest in politics. They were all there [in Mitchell Hall] and we may add, as a logical though unnecessary deduction that their gentlemen friends were with them." The occasion was one in which Miss Helene Slack read a paper on the United States Supreme Court's recent decision on Ben Tillman's South Carolina Liquor Law, or "the palmetto blown in a bottle." There followed a debate on the Populist platform of 1892 and the McKinley Tariff. There is no evidence that co-eds joined the debate, but they rendered loud applause.

A doubting Thomas showed that the most pronounced weakness in an otherwise well informed girl was a startling ignorance of contemporary history and politics. He felt Indiana University co-eds rarely read newspapers and hardly ever spoke of current issues. It would be a good idea to organize a newspaper class to meet once a week, and ask the girls to give synopses of the most striking events of the past fortnight. If this were done people could say, "The girls are beginning to talk sense."

Joseph Swain had more pressing problems than seeing that his co-ed charges read the newspapers. He told the trustees in his annual report on November 1, 1896, that it was becoming increasingly difficult for girls to find places to live. He expressed the belief that private homes were the best places for college girls to board; these kept Indiana's daughters near the hearthside, but the number of co-eds in 1896 was overrunning Bloomington's private facilities. Besides, Bloomington landladies showed a decided preference for male boarders.

Swain told the board that he had asked an architect to prepare tentative plans for a club house to accommodate twenty-five to thirty girls. The building was to contain a reading room, bed and bathrooms, and dining facilities. He estimated the cost at $9,000 but this amount would have to be supplied from private capital. A matron would be placed in charge of the house, and he hoped board and room could be held down to $5.00 a week. This was the inception of Forest Place, which later became Alpha Hall, constructed and managed by Colonel John H. Louden.

The woman student at Indiana University found herself in an anomalous situation. Most of the girls came from strict homes.

They arrived in the university bound down by admonitions, taboos, and inhibitions. Under the title, "Girl Life at Indiana University," the *Student* in November, 1897, said the co-eds never made an outcry about their rights, "they simply take whatever they want." The men, to their everlasting honor, said the editor, never opposed them. The co-ed had to learn early to be self-reliant. Chaperones were said to be absent. "People who come to visit us have expressed surprise at her absence, and though we have told them, proudly and freezingly, that we are quite able to take care of ourselves, in our hearts we have been just a little doubtful," said the "girl life" author. The girls said they believed a chaperone might actually allow them more freedom than they were willing to accept on their own. The sororities took the places of mothers, sisters, and chaperones, but not all Indiana University girls belonged to a sorority.

Not only did the university need to consider housing under its own administration, and other physical accommodations for women, but the time had come by 1898 to consider the employment of a dean of women who would look after feminine welfare generally. "It is generally believed by those who had made a study of this matter," Swain told the trustees, "that there should be in the university a woman of superior training and refinement who shall have special care of college girls." He believed the way things were organized at Indiana such a woman should be a physician, provided the trustees could be induced to provide the necessary salary to attract such a person. "No woman should be placed in such a position," he said, "unless she has proper training, special fitness and a gift in leading college girls without seeming to do so." In other words Joseph Swain sought an angel with an M.D. degree.

Behind Swain's move to appoint a dean of women was the urging of his wife and the Women's League which she had organized with hopes of enlivening social life for women students. The board responded favorably to the suggestion and authorized the university administration to employ Dr. Rebecca Rogers of Indianapolis to give ten lectures in health and hygiene to the co-eds, provided she would come for $100 or $125 and expenses. Mrs. Swain and other faculty wives attended Dr. Rogers' lectures and said they felt that the lectures were well worth the cost.

In June, 1900, Joseph Swain reported that he and Mrs. Swain

had visited Michigan, Vassar, Western Reserve, Chicago, Smith, Mount Holyoke, Barnard, Pennsylvania, and Bryn Mawr to investigate the matter of a dean of women. He also had letters from Presidents Edward A. Birge, James B. Angell, and Andrew S. Draper on their experiences in the employment of deans of women. Draper said a dean was to look after women students, not control their conduct. She should attend social functions and act as counselor. All three agreed that the successful dean would use her influence naturally, and they told the Indiana president that desirable deans of women were difficult to find. Swain knew this better than did his respondents.

The Board of Trustees in its November meeting, 1899, told Swain to search for a dean, and to begin the building of a women's dormitory if private investors could be induced to support such an undertaking. These recommendations came as a direct response to the president's annual report.

Life for women students at the turn of the century was described in the record as being fairly dull. Entertainment attractive to young women was severely limited. At some period around 1897 the girls began playing basketball, and once a year they played a spring exhibition game for women spectators only. In 1899 the first public game was played, and after 1901 the competition was between the freshmen "whites" and the senior "reds." The teams were coached by a Mr. Liard.

On March 29, 1901, Mrs. Joseph Swain appeared before the Board of Trustees to discuss the construction of a women's building. Both the president and his wife had been active in opening the campaign for this building. They attended alumni meetings in Evansville, Louisville, and Vincennes where they had discussed the idea. They told the trustees that the movement for the women's building furnished a means for uniting the alumni. It was suggested that a secretary ought to be appointed to help Mrs. Swain with her correspondence with former graduates. The 1901 *Arbutus* announced that the proposed building would contain a women's gymnasium with modern equipment, an auditorium, parlors, committee and resting rooms. Campaign centers had been organized wherever there were concentrations of alumni, and already the president's wife had $6,500 in subscription.

In their arduous search for a dean the Swains felt that Emma

M. Perkins, professor of Latin in Western Reserve University would be highly acceptable. She was forty years of age, a graduate of Vassar, and had taught twelve years in the Cleveland university. Professor Perkins had a national reputation as a fluent speaker and was a leading member of the National Association of Collegiate Alumnae. The big drawback for Indiana was whether or not she would come to Bloomington for $2,300. The trustees approved Miss Perkins' appointment, but in November the minutes reveal that the Swains were still combing the country for the "right woman." By this time the university had raised the ante to $2,500. Susan Peabody was approached, but bearing a proud family name, and wedded to the East, she refused to come "West." The job was then offered to a candidate closer to home and a native daughter, Mary Cox of Huntington, Indiana. There followed offers to Ada Wing of Brown University and Ann McKeag of Wilson College in Pennsylvania, and still no dean. Finally on November 1, 1901, the president reported a triumph of sorts. He had been successful in employing Mary Bidwell Breed, a Quaker from Pittsburgh and a graduate of Bryn Mawr. She also had a Ph.D. degree from Heidelberg, and two years' teaching experience in the Pennsylvania College for Women. She brought more than a doctor's degree to the feminine contingent of Indiana University. Her sense of decorum was Eastern, and she was strict enough to enforce her code of gentlewomanly behavior. Her first act was to end the era of "open housing," by decreeing that men and women could live only in separate houses, a ruling that placed further strain on an already highly aggravated situation in Bloomington. For six years Dr. Breed was to rule much of the collegiate social scene in Bloomington. She broke the traditions of informality in the university and the community by reordering relationships between the sexes.

While President Swain, his wife, and the Board of Trustees struggled with the many social problems created by the new era of rapidly rising enrollments, another phase of university activities came of age. At the outset of his administration in 1893, the Bloomington *Telephone* observed on October 6 that it was cheerful news to hear that the new president showed promise of taking charge of "athletic sports connected with the University, and that the faculty committee will act as censor. Heretofore athletics have mainly been a 'skin game' financially, physically and every other way, as numerous business men with long uncollectable bills will testify to their sorrow. All of which has been greatly to the discredit of the University." He might have added that a bit of not too subtle professionalism had brought college athletics in America under a cloud of suspicion. Swain returned to Bloomington with the memory still fresh of the days when as a student he had at least demonstrated an interest in sports, and he was a stellar player on the faculty baseball team which engaged the seniors each spring.

In athletics generally, and in Indiana particularly, proper coaching, game rules, and dependable business management of the teams were lacking. C. E. Syrett was given the task of teaching physical education and organizing a football team. The season of 1893 was to open on October 14 with the Purdue game. Before that date arrived, Charles Compton was nursing a broken hand, "a new man is disfigured by a broken nose," and Dick Miller had a wounded eye. These three injuries, plus lapses of rules and the freewheeling activities of team members made tighter faculty control of athletics mandatory. On October 6, 1893, a student mass meeting agreed to give the faculty athletic committee the power to veto any actions by the members of the teams or the coach which seemed to violate the university's code of behavior.

The football team of 1893 was the first to have a Negro player. Preston Eagleson, the son of a prominent member of the black community in Bloomington, was a halfback. Tall and rangy, he apparently was a valuable player. At Crawfordsville, in a game with Wabash College, Eagleson became the victim of unnecessarily rough treatment which bore a strong racial overtone, and which stirred the Hoosier press. Football in 1893 was at best a rugged and rough game, but the Wabash incident seems to have gone well beyond the usual tactics. Reflecting the roughness of the game was the campaign carried on in the fall of 1893 in which funds were being solicited for the benefit of James A. Call and Ora Herkless, who were injured. Herkless had a broken bone in his foot, an injury which was said to cause such a serious bone disintegration that there was a threat of amputation. There were other injuries which raised serious questions as to whether football was a game that college boys should play.

Safe or not, there developed considerable zeal for the game at Indiana University. Almost as great a problem as the players' safety were the difficulties of keeping the game free of professionalism, student politics, and indebtedness, and of retaining a coach. Following football seasons in the earlier years the athletic committee or association found itself in debt. There was no gate, no advance sale of tickets, and no way to conceal the game from nonpaying visitors. Income came almost entirely from subscriptions. Anyone who has sat on a modern university athletic committee can readily recognize the contrast between collegiate athletic financing in 1896 and the 1970's. In the former year the Indiana University Athletic Association received $1,491.02 from student, faculty, and citizen subscriptions, and from payments for traveling expenses and board. The committee that year spent $1,693.77, leaving an indebtedness of $202.75. To pay the deficit plus $74.75 owed when student subscribers failed to pay, the faculty signed a promissory note.

Then, as now, there was a scramble for promising players. In March, 1894, the *Student* reported that Purdue had made a financial offer to Kenneth Brewer, captain of the Indiana University team, to play football with the Lafayette school that fall. Neither college, however, enjoyed the presence of this superior athlete. The Bloomington *Telephone* announced on September 24 that Brewer had written the Athletic Association that he would play that season on the University of Michigan team.

Fans of the various Indiana colleges were ardent and vocal if not rowdy in expressing their partisanship. On October 23, 1894, the *Student* said that in a game with DePauw University, "Bloomington and Indiana University have a gang of rooters that are loyal to their eleven to a degree that they are obnoxious when on a ball ground. This Bloomington crowd should take a few pointers on decency before they leave home again, and perhaps the State University would do well in establishing a chair to teach that essential branch of an education." In Indianapolis an Indiana partisan charged the DePauw players with mistreating those from Bloomington. The *Student* editor felt it was the roughneck fan and not college boys who caused the trouble. Fans were uncontrolled either by seating arrangements or by policing. Sometimes it was almost impossible to keep them off the playing field.

A classic example of spectator interference occurred at Purdue in 1901. The game with Indiana was hotly contested, and the score became 6 to 6 when Zora Clevenger ran for a touchdown and then kicked a goal. Purdue came back to score and tie the game. Within three minutes of the end of the game Purdue fumbled and Alva J. Rucker of Indiana picked up the ball and ran 95 yards for a touchdown. The Purdue coach and players claimed that their tackler was blocked by a spectator. After a hassle on the field the Purdue captain took his team out of the game and refused to return. The referees gave the game to Indiana with a score 11 to 6. This resulted in a considerable emotional outpouring by the press. It was said that one of the game officials had reported the illegal block to the referee but he chose to ignore the information.

The older sport of baseball still retained considerable popularity. In March, 1894, the *Student* announced that the first baseball game to be played on the new field in the Dunn addition would be an exhibition contest with the University of Illinois on April 18. Robert Berryhill, the new baseball "coacher" had arrived in Bloomington to train the Indiana team for one month and was to receive $100 for his expert services. By April 10, however, he informed the Athletic Association that he would not fulfill his contract. In his place manager Auxtell procured the services of a Mr. McIntyre of Lebanon, Indiana.

The Athletic Association had high hopes that the baseball team at least could help clear up its financial deficits by playing a team in Louisville on Decoration Day. A special train was chartered, and a swarm of fans went down to the Falls of the Ohio to root for their team, but when the game was over and the gate receipts were counted it was discovered that the proceeds would barely pay expenses. There still remained a season deficit of $700, and the final game with Purdue offered no prospect of relief.

Getting out of debt was again a major challenge in 1896. On January 25 of that year the Athletic Association elected Fred King manager of the baseball team, subject to faculty approval. The faculty had made approval of activities a condition of its assuming financial responsibilities for athletics. The faculty intended to choose one of its own members to manage baseball, and the faculty attitude was generally known. However, Fred King, a student, was elected over Professor Charles H. Beeson by a single vote; students thereby expressed the strong belief that they should have a hand in guiding athletic policies. A new election was demanded by the faculty despite student attitudes, and a considerable amount of controversy followed.

It was not until March that the election of a baseball manager was again considered. The *Student* said, "This is the third time within the term. The first time they elected a man [Fred King], the committee got its gillotin [sic] and gave him a shave after the manner of the French Revolution." In the latter election too, a student, E. C. Crampton, was successful but he resigned; perhaps he had suffered decapitation on the faculty chopping block. Then "A large crowd assembled at the chapel Wednesday afternoon and were called to order by the president of the Association. Professors Aley, Newsom, and Stephenson occupied a front seat as representatives of the faculty." A. E. Williams, a student, was elected by a majority of two votes. Professor Aley then affirmed Williams' election, and told the students that the faculty did not want "to kill athletics."

Such a course would be absurd to say the least. A look into the past showed too much dirty work in athletics, and the faculty was anxious to restore integrity to the teams and their management. The athletic teams, thought Aley, were made up of mature men who could be trusted to make some decisions. In the past they had been controlled by managers who misplaced funds or appropriated them to private use. For these reasons the professors had taken a stand for clean athletics. Williams, like his predecessors, proved fickle and resigned in May, and Dr. Harold Whetstone Johnstone, professor of Latin, was elected manager in his place. Johnstone was to act as chairman of the Athletic Association for many years.

Indiana University was criticized by some of its neighbor colleges in February, 1896, because it failed to organize an all-Indiana schedule. The Athletic Association said it preferred to see the university teams play some games at least with out-of-state competition. This was the beginning of an athletic relationship in what was to become the "Big Nine" Athletic Conference.

The faculty athletic committee took unusual interest in developing a good competitive program in the university, but it demanded the right to set the local rules, and to veto policies which might be injurious to the institution's image. The committee assumed responsibility for bringing in W. D. Osgood as coach in 1894. He was said to be the best halfback in the country, a star athlete generally, within limits a good student, and a gentleman. Osgood was a graduate of the University of Pennsylvania. In these early years of athletic competition the president also took an active part in making athletic decisions. Joseph Swain expressed himself as being unwilling to encourage football at Indiana University unless the game could be freed of rowdyism and specific and safe rules be formulated. It is doubtful that the community shared the president's views. Enthusiasm was growing over the new sport, and demands arose for more emphasis on the development of a winning team.

Athletics offered a serious threat of physical damage or even death to students. In June, 1896, the university community was shocked by the fatal injury of John King Sheridan, a junior and history major from Lebanon. Sheridan was a member of the varsity baseball team and was reputed to be a good player. He was acting as umpire in an interfraternity game when he was struck in the temple by a wildly pitched ball, and two days later he died. This accident not only saddened students and faculty, but it raised questions about the safety of the prevailing rules in both football and baseball. Too, there may have been doubts as to the wisdom of holding annual intramural games and especially the one between faculty and seniors.

Football rose greatly in popularity during the Swain years. It presented all kinds of problems, many of which were publicized in the public press. At best the game was rowdy, and it took only a slight incident to touch off a serious fight. In the season of 1894, Winston Menzies from the "hills" of Posey County injured his wrist, and this no doubt paved the way for a 38 to 6 defeat at the hands of Butler in November. Later Earlham offered the crippled Indiana team $65 in expense money to play a Thanksgiving game in Richmond. No wonder the university's athletic committee found itself in a chronic state of indebtedness.

Though football enjoyed rising popularity with both spectators and players, it remained rough and to some extent unruly. At the end of the wild playing season in 1894, the presidents of Indiana colleges met in Indianapolis to adopt resolutions governing intercollegiate athletics. Football was withdrawn from the list of recognized sports by the Indiana Intercollegiate Association. The Indiana *Student* said, "In most colleges, and especially in Indiana

University, there has been very little genuine football spirit; the interest has been prompted by a desire to defeat some other college, and the game has not been played for its own sake or for the good of the players, the only reason for its existence." The paper believed that Indiana could never have much football pride as long as the team competed with clubs that seemed certain at the outset to defeat it. The presidential resolutions did not prevent the local team from playing with any competitor it chose on conditions mutually agreed upon. For several years Purdue had sought its equal in other states, and Notre Dame and Earlham, two strong teams, did not join the state athletic association. The public press seems to have approved the president's action, and no doubt a good majority of Hoosiers also favored it.

The troubles that beset football in Indiana in the 1890's arose from lack of refinement of game rules, relationships between players and spectators, and professionalism. The college presidents in their Indianapolis conference undertook to outline a brief set of rules and ethics. These, however, had only to do with the overall conduct of intercollegiate athletics, and not specific game rules. The ethical decisions were that only bona fide students could play on a college team; no student who had played for money would be acceptable. Each college would establish a faculty committee on athletics which would be held responsible for the enforcement of rules and covenants.

A year later the Indiana State Athletic Association found itself in a stormy session when it undertook to dismiss Butler University. This move failed as did DePauw's attempt to withdraw from the association. A month later the Indiana University Faculty Athletic Committee, for academic reasons, ruled six out of seventeen prospective baseball players eligible, three ineligible, and eight to be held in abeyance for further investigation. Because of this decision the team lost the services of some of its best and most seriously needed players. This was not the first time that the professors had rendered decisions adversely affecting the fortunes of university teams. Earlier, in April, 1895, "The faculty committee," reported the *Student*, "struck a severe blow at professional baseball . . . when it 'plucked' from the team a number of men who have poor records for scholarship—never done before."

The athletes were allowed to take an active part in the more immediate team affairs. The faculty committee in March, 1896, amended the Athletic Constitution to permit the players on the various teams to select their own captains, and to adopt their own uniform sweaters. There had been players' uniforms of sorts before, but this new rule no doubt applied more to dress sweaters. The football players chose a red sweater with a "white scalloped I," the baseball players chose a plain white "I," and the tennis team a white sweater with a "red I. U. monogram." Another concession granted this year was the provision of a dressing room for teams in the basement of the old chapel. This room was to be equipped with several baths.

In September, 1896, athletics entered a new era at Indiana when M. G. Gonterman, formerly of the Athletics Department of Harvard University, was employed as football coach. Gonterman surveyed the athletic prospects of the university and in November asked that a cinder track be constructed, but the university lacked land space for this enlarged facility. It was not until the fall of 1897 that the purchase of additional Dunn lands permitted expansion of the athletic playing fields. President Swain told the trustees on November 1, 1897, that the way had been opened for construction of a new playing field for football, and that it was necessary to begin grading for the running track and tennis courts.

Athletic spirits experienced a lift in May, 1896. The Oolite Club of Bloomington gave a "big demonstration" and reception for the baseball team. The *Student* said, "everyone in the town is getting struck on our baseball team." In November the university officials went so far as to dismiss college chapel to permit a big celebration because Indiana University had defeated DePauw in football. This enthusiasm, however, was chilled by Governor-elect James A. Mount, who declared himself emphatically opposed to college football in Indiana. There was some indication that a bill would be brought before the General Assembly at its next session to abolish the sport. Many prominent citizens expressed a like opinion. The governor also had the backing of the Farmer's Institute of Hamilton County, who petitioned for prohibitory legislation. On December 15, 1896, the *Student* said,

> The situation in athletic circles remains in a status quo. There is
> a very strong sentiment prevailing against the disposition of a

majority of the Athletic Association, and the "college politics" argument is meeting with much opposition. Political combinations are by no means confined to one faction. . . . However, it is sincerely to be hoped, for the welfare of athletics, that an amicable adjustment of the differences may be secured.

Athletic activities became more diversified at Indiana in the latter part of Joseph Swain's administration. Basketball seems to have been played at first as an exercise in gymnastics, and both men and women played the game, but separately. On January 23, 1899, the *Student* reported, "The 1st of a series of basketball games were [sic] played between third & fourth hour classes of the men's gymnasium last Saturday afternoon. The game was witnessed by a large crowd of students and faculty." The paper said this was a lively game, but it resulted in a startlingly low score of eight to six.

It was not until 1899 that basketball became an organized sport in Indiana University. The *Arbutus* of 1902 said basketball was only in its second year. Interest was low because the game was new. In the same year golf was introduced to the campus, and the *Arbutus* bragged, "To I. U. belongs the honor of having organized the first college golf club in the state. Known as the Dunn Meadows Golf Club, taking its name from the north of the campus." An attempt was made as early as 1897 to build a golf course and to organize a club, but the actual organization was delayed until 1899. In 1900 the course had nine holes and seventy-five members, with Professor James A. Woodburn of the department of history as president.

With the purchase of additional Dunn land it was possible for Indiana to organize a track team and to train on a suitable track. In 1895 the *Student* reported that the university was not represented in the State Field Day exercises. All the school's interest was centered in baseball and lawn tennis. Five years later the *Arbutus* editor said that three years ago no one dreamed the university would have a track team. By 1901 members of the Hare and Hound Club of distance runners were streaking over Monroe County; the hares scattered paper bits as "scents" for the hounds to follow.

When Joseph Swain resigned the presidency of Indiana University he left behind a much happier athletic legacy than had

Jordan or Coulter. The football team in 1899 defeated seven teams, including Purdue, and lost only to Notre Dame and Northwestern. Swain left a good athletics committee tradition in which a code of relationships between the athletic teams and the university and other colleges was established. The relations between colleges of the Northwest were fairly well established through the "Big Nine" Conference, and college athletics as an adjunct to university education was more clearly defined.

In 1901 Swain told the trustees that the football team had won the state championship; the baseball team, composed mostly of new players, had made a good showing, and so had the track team. It was with a note of pride that he reported these accomplishments. In his last year the football team defeated Wabash, DePauw, and Vincennes, but lost to Purdue 39 to 0.

Oratory continued to flourish despite some fundamental changes in interest during the last decade of the century. "Our debaters," Swain told the trustees in 1901, "were successful with the University of Illinois, and our colored orator took the state contest." Sylvan W. Kahn had won the Indiana State Oratorical Contest in January, 1894. He spoke, perhaps from experience, on "The Problems of Children." There were 150 students, President Swain, and several professors on hand in Indianapolis to give their representative moral support. A somewhat stormy dispute marked the oratorical contest that year. On March 19, at the annual meeting of the University Oratorical Association, the president, E. C. Toner, had expected only a small group at the business session; instead a big crowd assembled. When the secretary and his minute book could not be found, the members proceeded to elect new officers and left what the Bloomington *Telephone* called "a knotty question as to which side the right belongs." The judges of the association refused to decide in either side's favor, and it became necessary to hold a new election. This hassle continued until April, when a new election was held. The source of the dispute was largely the rivalry between fraternity and nonfraternity students; the fraternity ticket lost the election.

Oratory and debating lost ground to the more physical forms of expression on the athletic fields. On February 27, 1894, the Bloomington *Telephone* lamented, "Until this year it has been the custom of the literary societies of the University to celebrate Washington's birthday with appropriate exercises, each of the societies selecting one orator to give a short address on any subject he might select. The exercises used to rank second in interest during the college year and were always largely attended." Both George Washington and oratory were fading fast as central interests for modern Indiana University students. Writing in the *Student*, November 6, 1894, "T. E. S." felt the faculty "as a body treated literary work lightly." Reforms had to be made, and some energetic individual had to throw his influence into the struggle for survival. President Swain and John R. Commons had occasionally attended speeches, but the occasions were rare indeed when faculty members generally attended meetings of the authors' society. In four years of this particular group, "not a member of the faculty from the Department of English Rhetoric, Oratory, and Literature included so far as I can remember, has ever been in the hall." The author doubted that the faculty was really interested in the original literary work of students. General statements were made encouraging oratory and independent literary efforts, "but it is half-hearted encouragement. Its influence is like that of a pastor who preaches an eloquent sermon each Sunday morning on Christian duty, morality, and godliness, but who never goes inside the houses of his congregation." Students had become equally indifferent. Social events in the university, thought T. E. S., tended to ignore literature and literary efforts. No one reads poems and essays any more. If the faculty did not show an increased interest in oratory, then the author felt the day of that form of literary expression was ended.

In June, 1895, Indiana University was invited to send a delegation of college orators to the Bay View, Michigan, Chautauqua Assembly to participate in an intercollegiate oratorical contest. The invitation came too late to hold trial speeches so the faculty had to appoint orators to participate in the contest. The signs of *rigor mortis* were even clearer on February 11, 1896, when a student editorial declared "Oratory in Indiana University is dead. 'Died of neglect,' is the verdict. For several years she struggled against the hard fate, but at last she submitted quietly to the inevitable. Will she be missed? Yes, but her vacant chair at the State Contest will be mourned over by other colleges. Among students here she will not be missed. They care nothing for her." No one entered the contests that year, and Indiana University went unrepresented in the annual gathering of golden tongues in English's Opera House.

Joseph Swain suggested to the Board of Trustees on March 27, 1900, that Indiana University withdraw from the State Oratorical Association. Both he and Professor J. M. Clapp contended that the contests were bad for Indiana University from an educational standpoint. Swain said, "nearly all if not all state universities have finally withdrawn from state contests in oratorical associations on the ground that the ideas inculcated there are harmful, and the university is misrepresented."

If students showed an indifference toward oratory and debating, they seemed to be equally complacent about politics. Joseph Swain reported to the Board of Trustees, "The campaign this year [1898] has not been nearly so disturbing to students as usual. In fact, there has been almost no disturbances from this cause." Two years later he reported, "The work of the term thus far has been very satisfactory. The campaign has not seriously interfered with the college work." McKinley's assassination went practically unnoticed, except for news of it in the public press. Swain did not comment on it in his annual report. Perhaps this did not represent so much a trend in student thought and action as it did the absence of men on the faculty like John R. Commons, Edward A. Ross, and Ernest L. Bogart. These men had inspired contemplation of the contemporary American scene in their students.

In the more formal areas of university expression, the entertainment and lecture series during the decade of the 1890's lacked much of the zest and spice of earlier years. Either Americans had settled down to a fairly dull era of public lecturing or the old headliners were passing from the public boards. Perhaps it was both. There were still crusaders and issues but there were few Georges, Willards, Beechers, Clemenses, Alcotts, Cables, or Tiltons left. Instead there were more of the A. A. Willits type speaking on "Sunshine: or the Secrets of a Happy Life." Joseph Cook spoke on November 28, 1893, on the subject "Does Death End All?" James Whitcomb Riley, ever a favorite, appeared in Bloomington on many occasions. The lecture committee has left the impression that it wished to stir the fires of hell and to raise the stench of brimstone with Sam Jones. He was a contrast to the "Practical

Common Sense" of ex-Governor Will Cumback. John Temple Graves, the suave Southern orator from smoky Birmingham, Alabama, delivered a lecture in May, 1894, which the *Student* proclaimed "a model of good style and splendid composition such as is seldom seen or heard in these days of 'falling theories and crashing creeds.' Mr. Graves is undoubtedly one of the best orators that has ever appeared on the Old College Platform." Again in October, 1895, Graves was back in Bloomington to pluck the golden eagle's wing. He lost nothing in a second appearance, and may even have gained in fame. The *Student* editor almost shouted, "John Temple Graves is an orator, if there ever was one. The fact he is a Southerner will add interest to his eloquence. It is quite possible that he may speak of things concerning which we have deep prejudice, but we should not forget that he comes as an orator."

A lot less eloquent, but an equally fiery lecturer was the thirty-three year old Thomas Dixon, Jr., who spoke his sentiments on American problems, especially those of the South in Reconstruction. If the contents of his Bloomington speech were comparable to those of *The Leopard's Spots* and *The Clansmen* the audience got a full preview of the sectional wrath and social fulmination contained in the epic movie, *The Birth of a Nation*. It was somewhat disappointing that the lecture committee was unable to raise the necessary fee to bring to the university General John B. Gordon of Appomattox fame. His description of the last days of the Confederacy would have wet the eyes even of Oliver P. Morton's bronze statue; he would have caused the Grand Army of the Republic to praise John Hunt Morgan.

Jane Addams' lecture smelled less of age and sachet, and she was less eloquent than matter of fact. Nevertheless she gave her Indiana University audience a close-up view of the straining social seams in the flatulent years of Harrison and Cleveland. In the field of music such artists as Gunsaulus, Kate Field, and the Thomas Orchestra Company appeared in Bloomington. The latter company frightened the Hoosiers by demanding a fee of $900 for a single appearance. On January 19, 1898, the Beggar Prince Opera Company performed the *Mikado* in the Bloomington Opera House.

Perhaps the financial conditions shared responsibility with the spirit of the times for the mediocre quality of lectures and concerts at Indiana University. There was indication that town and university patronage was more indifferent to such forms of entertainment than it had been in the past. Inside the university itself the tenor of student life underwent marked changes. Some claimed that the introduction of the elective system into the university's educational program diverted student interests into areas of academic and professional organizations that not only cut across traditional class and university lines of allegiance, but opened many new and wider vistas of interest. The *Student* editor on June 3, 1896, explained, "Class spirit in Indiana University has become almost a thing of the past. The causes of this death are not far to seek. In the first place classroom work is sufficiently heavy to require all the time and energy of the student to say nothing of other demands. But besides this there are fraternities, leagues, clubs, societies, and associations, all more or less closely organized, and every one drawing heavily on the students. There is also another active influence which militates greatly against class spirit in the institution. I speak of the elective system. The specialists in each department naturally form a separate class. And, because the sources of their various interests are mutual, their dept. spirit is genuine."

To this lamentation the editor might well have added attractions such as rising interest in college music and art. Between 1895 and 1896 the university organized a band. There was a long history of band activity, but most of this was the story of cooperation between town and university musicians. For instance there was Seward's Band, which appeared at many university functions. Then there was the Mechanic's Band (which may have been in fact the Seward's Band). On January 28, 1896, the *Student* boasted that Indiana University "has a band that is a band. Many of the players are professional & all who have had an opportunity to hear them have nothing but praise for them." Members seemed to have borne the expenses of buying instruments and uniforms, anyway the girls said the band members in their white uniforms were "perfect ducks."

No doubt the *Student* was in error on April 19, 1917,when it said the university had had no band in 1898. It did have one and this organization was to figure prominently in the university's involvement in the Spanish-American War.

It is difficult to say how much this international struggle affected the university community. The local and state papers were filled with stories of the war, and there is little doubt that the *Arbutus* was correct in saying:

> Bloomington is all commotion,
> And this time 'tis no mere notion,
> For a great report of battle surges through the little town;
> Chaperons no more we ponder,
> Bowling parties are no wonder,
> Such light questions, we consider, merit nothing but a frown.

Athletes and other popular students volunteered. Among them was John Foster, the football quarterback, Edgar A. Binford, and D. O. McGovney who later became a dean in the University of Missouri. The *Arbutus* for 1898 announced that already thirteen Indiana University students were at the battlefront in Cuba. The Band of Evansville refused to volunteer its services so a band was organized in Bloomington of townsmen and university students. This organization became a part of the One Hundred and Fifty-ninth Indiana United States Volunteers. From Bloomington the musicians went to Indianapolis to be quartered at the Fairgrounds, and then were shipped away to Bull Run Battlefield in Virginia to await transshipment to Puerto Rico. Orders were countermanded, however, and the Hoosiers got away from home only as far as the mountains of Virginia and central Pennsylvania. This gallant throng had to come home and admit to their girls that they had failed them in their sentiments, "We are confident that by then they'll annihilate Poor Spain!"

The Spanish-American War was little more serious for Indiana University than playing a major football game against DePauw University. Long before the rumblings were heard which led to war in the Caribbean, demands arose for the institution to expand its teaching facilities. In the fall of 1894 Carl H. Eigenmann suggested that a biological substation be established at some suitable natural site in Indiana. He volunteered to survey several places and to assume personal responsibility for materials and instruments used in locating a desirable site where a natural laboratory could be established. Swain recommended this idea to the Board of Trustees, and the Bloomington *Telephone* said on November 23, 1894, that Indiana would have a biological substation on one of the northern lakes, possibly Lake Maxinbuckee. The station would be placed in operation in the summer of 1895.

The *Telephone* had second-guessed Eigenmann as to the location. The station was to be established on Lake Wawasee, at Vawter Park, on the south shore. That summer twenty students assembled to work under Eigenmann, William J. Moenkhaus, Fred M. Chamberlain, and a visiting instructor named Taylor from Monmouth College. The second summer Eigenmann advertised that a number of specialists, including David Starr Jordan, Professor Kellicott of Ohio University, Stephen A. Forbes, Professor Keffoid of the University of Illinois, Dr. Hay of the Field Columbian Museum, Norman Wyld, Dr. J. Loeb of Chicago, and others would visit the camp that session. This was Eigenmann expansionism at its best. The northern Indiana station turned out to be a successful teaching venture which outlived the founder himself. In 1899 the biological substation was removed to Winona Lake, where two buildings were erected on the lake front by the Winona Assembly and Summer School and presented to the university. These buildings were twenty-five by forty-five feet in size, and were two stories high. There were laboratories to accommodate 100 students, and in time the course of study was extended to cover numerous subjects in the biological field. As a matter of fact the curriculum almost seemed broad enough to support work for the doctor's degree.

Joseph Swain did not lack either the imagination or the will to establish Indiana University in a position abreast of neighboring northwestern institutions. In 1897 he informed the trustees that he had visited three of the better Midwestern universities, and he felt that on the positive side Indiana had done the most per dollar spent, but he emphasized that the university could not hope to long survive competitively at the current rate. Indiana, he thought, got the most return from its faculty for the salaries it paid, but these too had to be revised upward. He then listed the university's primary needs. Swain wished to see constructed an assembly hall for $50,000, a gymnasium for $40,000, a $50,000 science building, and a social science and humanities building which would cost no less than $60,000. The appropriation for day-to-day operations had increased from $40,000 to $60,000 from 1893 to 1903.

Throughout the history of the institution the Board of Trustees had been industrious and dedicated. Individual members gave service far beyond the call of duty, and the chairmen almost seemed to have been second presidents. As dedicated as these men were, however, they were more frugal than governors and legislators.

It may have been true that the trustees themselves were unable to comprehend clearly what Joseph Swain meant by saying that Indiana University should have a half million dollars in endowment in 1894. Times were different for state universities, he told the trustees. American educational leaders yearly gained clearer insights into their social and scientific roles. These state institutions had in fact come to realize the original concept that would make them heads of public school systems. A national demand had arisen for more and broader education to serve a practical and growing materialistic nation. In the light of these facts the seemingly large sum spent on universities in 1883 had become pittances by 1894, as compared with demands being made on them. The accumulated total spent on Indiana since 1883 was less than the annual expenditure of Cornell University, only one third the budget of Harvard, and little more than the annual incomes of California, Michigan, and Wisconsin in 1894. To answer contentions that Indiana could not afford more money, Swain cited the fact that even by low assessment evaluation the state had a total property value of $1,302,310, 250, and a one-fifth mill levy would yield over $200,000 per annum. In the last gubernatorial election 600,000 votes had been cast, and this would mean 33⅓ cents per vote. Hoosiers in 1894 paid less than twelve cents per voter to support higher education.

While clearly stating university needs, President Swain also commented on the faculty. In November, 1896, he said everybody wanted to strengthen the teaching staff by promoting the strongest men. He recognized the fact that entirely too many Indiana University graduates had been kept on the staff, and many of them had no previous teaching experience. He was personally vulnerable on this point, but his experience in the newly organized Stanford University gave him a somewhat broader perspective. In his hiring of new professors he sought graduates of various institutions to give a richer variety to Indiana University's program, and he refused to employ undergraduates as instructors.

In 1897 a member of the Board of Trustees raised the ancient question of how much time professors gave the university. Occasionally in the past this issue had been raised by other trustees.

This was a lingering question in a state where support of the university was limited. On March 27, 1900, Trustee Robert Alexander Ogg moved that a special committee be appointed to study the whole curriculum and the amount of work done by professors, and to report at the board's June meeting. This motion was carried, and Ogg, Robert L. Hamilton, and Nat U. Hill were appointed to make such an analysis.

In June of that year Swain told the trustees that he objected to an arbitrary rule governing professorial hours. Under the elective system it was impossible to have uniform teaching assignments, even if it were desirable. It was, in his opinion, much better to have good esprit de corps, proper ideals of professional obligations, and loyalty to the university. Professor James B. Angell said this issue of teaching loads had been raised at Michigan but was quickly silenced. The number of hours professors taught at Indiana University was an educational question first, and only second a public policy issue. It was true the trustees had to have a public policy they could defend, but they had to shape it in the context of sound educational policies. Indiana had to remain on a middle ground because it could not encourage professors financially as did the wealthier schools, nor could it afford to exhaust its teaching force as did the private normal schools and weaker colleges. Joseph Swain cited the teaching load of well known professors from several major universities, all of which were well under the fifteen hour loads of many Indiana professors.

Besides their regular teaching loads Indiana professors were supposed to visit as many of the Indiana counties as possible during the summer months. In 1896 at least one representative of the university on these good will visitations had reached sixty-eight of the ninety-two counties. Three years later Swain hoped the professors would visit all of the counties.

Earlier David Starr Jordan boasted that he had spoken in all the counties except Clay, Newton, and Steuben during his last four years in Bloomington. By 1898 the faculty had increased to fifty-three members, and the county visitations were somewhat less onerous than in the past. But even though railway mileage had been extended almost to its peak, it was still difficult indeed to reach some of the county seats.

The president accepted more than his share of speaking engagements. In 1894 he informed the Board of Trustees that he had accepted too many invitations. In the past year he had spoken in thirty-six towns representing thirty counties. He had addressed young people on the values of a college education, spoke to teachers' institutes and before local lecture associations. He reported in 1895 that he had filled an equal number of engagements without cost to the university. The next year Swain said he had traveled about Indiana for three years visiting two thirds of the counties, and in addition had spoken to several national associations including speeches in Denver, Chicago, and Jacksonville with less than $50 cost to the public.

By the late 1890's Swain was anxious not only to increase the size of the faculty and to retain reasonable class loads, but he wished to add scholastic strength to the staff. He reported in the annual meeting of the board in November, 1899, that there were two ways to improve a staff; first by evolution and elimination, and second by extension. In the past half decade the first system had worked fairly well, and he believed it capable of helping to make changes in the future. The university, however, needed to give very close consideration to an extension of its staff. First, the president wished to retain Ernest L. Bogart in economics. This young professor showed promise of being both a good teacher and a productive scholar. There was urgent need for six major additions. These included a dean of women and chairs of Biblical literature, psychology, music, and fine arts.

Looking back over almost a decade as president of Indiana University, Swain believed a lack of money was the institution's central problem. He undertook to save money from the general appropriation in 1898 to construct a wing on Maxwell Hall. In 1899, however, the legislature reduced the tax income of the state by granting property holders a $700 mortgaged property exemption. So seriously did this reduction hurt the university's income that the president was unable to recommend to the board the purchase of a modest amount of equipment requested by professors. Moreover the university lost professors. In November, 1900, Swain reported the resignation of John B. Faught, an assistant professor of mathematics. He had accepted a similar position in the Northern Michigan Normal School. With a touch of sarcasm the president informed the trustees, "It is a good thing for the University to provide other institutions with good men, and it is a good promotion for Dr. Faught."

So hard-pressed was the university for funds in 1902 that the president could make no recommendations for salary increases. At the March meeting of the board Swain commented on the predicament of the university. It was impossible, he said, to maintain a growing institution without increased resources. Dealing with the subject of enrollment is indeed to lose oneself in a jungle of conflicting statistics. Nevertheless, in his annual reports President Swain said these were proper enrollment figures. In 1890 there were 321 students, in 1895, 771, in 1900, 1,016, and in 1902, 1,321. The enrollment passed the thousand mark in June, 1902, in the latter part of Swain's administration. The gain for this last year was 191 students, a number greater than the entire enrollment the first year of Jordan's presidency. All but 100 of the 1,321 students enrolled in 1902 were from Indiana. If a line were drawn across the state east and west at Indianapolis, 580 students came from south of the line and 581 from the north. Since 1898 every county had been represented in the university's enrollment.

The above growth figures caused President Swain to outline on March 24, 1902, a formula for maintaining the institution at a level of growth comparable to that of other state universities. Salaries had to be raised, professors had to be given sabbatical pay, younger faculty deserved promotions and better pay, increasing enrollment increased costs in every phase of university operation, and additional instructional staff had to be added.

Capital had to be raised from some source, and soon, to finance construction of new buildings. A heat and light plant had to be installed. This was an impressive blueprint for the future, but financial promise was discouraging. At their meeting on November 15, 1901, the trustees revealed that the university budget was $179,370.88 as compared with $555, 623 for Michigan, $483,118 for Illinois, $400,874 for Wisconsin, and $475,254 for California. Only Ohio State was in a comparable bracket with Indiana, its budget was $268,006.

During the years he was at Indiana, President Swain was tempted by offers of other jobs. In 1895 he was offered the chancellorship of the University of Nebraska at a salary of $5,000, but after conferring with the Indiana board he chose to stay in Bloomington. The same year he was invited to accept the presidency of the University of Washington. This time he told the trustees they would have to give serious consideration to a graduated faculty salary scale based on the worth of men, and that his own salary should be increased to $5,000. Again in 1899, he informed the board that David Starr Jordan had offered him the vice presidency of Stanford University with indications that he would in time be made Jordan's successor. This time, however, he chose on his own to remain in Indiana "while we were in the midst of the legislative fight."

When news of Swain's invitation to go elsewhere was being passed around by rumor and gossip, the question of Benjamin Harrison's election to the presidency of Indiana University was revived. The *Student*, on December 3, 1895, reported, "The following bit of information is going the rounds of the College papers: The Indiana State University presidency has been offered to Ex-President Harrison! We suppose this is notice to the politicans at large that the politician is not without honor even in his own country." The editor thought the rumor had originated in misapprehension as to which presidential vacancy was involved. "It's at the White House, not at I. U." On April 21, 1896, the college papers were again handing around an exchange that Harrison had been offered the university presidency, and again the *Student* responded, "No, no, my friend, Mr. Harrison has received no such honor. He may have other presidential aspirations but wait & see."

In March, 1902, Swain revealed that he had been offered the presidency of the University of Kansas at the same salary he received at Indiana, but he would be supplied a president's house, and the state was committed to adequately supporting the university. He said he felt it would be easier to build up the University of Kansas than Indiana, but again he refused the offer. Nevertheless he informed the board that Indiana was quite a different institution from what it had been in 1893. Duties had grown heavier. His speaking engagements took so much time and energy that he had little of either to devote to the study of problems. He had received in all less than $150 in official expenses. This no doubt caused him some anxiety, especially since living costs were rising.

In late spring, 1902, the trustees of Swarthmore College approached Joseph Swain, a fellow Quaker, with an offer of the presidency of that institution. He countered with a proposal that they raise an endowment of $600,000, give the president power to appoint all teachers, agree that no salary was to be increased or decreased without his consent, and that no professor would be retained over the protest of the president. He no doubt made these conditions because they reflected his view of the presidency at Indiana, and, too, he may have doubted the Swarthmore Board would be able to meet his terms. They did, and on June 17, 1902, he resigned the presidency of Indiana University.

The loss of Joseph Swain was a serious blow to Indiana University. He brought both leadership and genuine perspective to his administration. Possibly over the years the notion that he was somewhat stodgy and unimaginative may have prevailed; this was not so. In his address read before the Indiana State Educational Association in 1894 he set forth a clear perception of the place of the state university in the American educational system. At the same time he issued the most direct social and cultural challenge yet made to the people of Indiana. "An examination of the rise and present condition of the state universities of the United States must convince even the casual observer that the rapid development of our state universities is the stern logic of events," he said. "These institutions have taken a firm hold on our national life." Swain had no patience with the hackneyed argument that Indiana was incapable of doing more for education. He asked,

> Has Indiana not passed that period of her development when it is necessary to give her whole strength to pioneering efforts? What is Indiana's present condition? What has she done for her Normal School? her Agricultural College, her state University? When I think of all that is possible in this state with its agricultural resources that are not excelled, with the most perfect fuel that has ever been discovered on the earth, with her mines and manufactures, with her two thousand millions of dollars worth of property, and above all with the intelligence and energy of her people, —when these things are pictured to my mind [sic], I see that the educational facilities of Indiana, while they now compare favorably with those of other states, are yet in their infancy.

In 1937 and 1938, William O. Lynch, Professor of History and editor of the *Indiana Magazine of History*, published in that magazine a revealing and detailed financial account of his student years, 1901–1903. In a thoughtful appraisal he wrote,

> The impression of Indiana University which I carried away in 1903, and it has grown on me since, was that it was an institution manned by an earnest, able, hardworking faculty. I was sure that money was only one of the things needed to make a strong University, but it was obvious that the state, though awakening to its obligations, was not permitting the building up of a great library nor creating other facilities for extensive research.

Professor Lynch felt that legislators and professional men of Indiana boasted of their support of education, but they "remained blind to the absolute necessity of promoting advanced study."

This was a point that Joseph Swain had struggled so gallantly for a decade to establish. In the summer of 1902 he left behind in Bloomington a major unfinished task. Repeatedly he had attempted to tell the Board of Trustees, legislators, and the people that they had a strong traditional college which was sensitive to the swift changes which were occurring all across the land, but he warned Indiana University still had to take the broad steps necessary to justify its title in fact.

It must have been with a certain sense of sadness mixed with satisfaction that Swain reviewed his accomplishments at Indiana University at the end of a decade of arduous labor. On the negative side he had faced severely depressed economic conditions throughout most of his years in Bloomington. In 1902 there were still vacancies on the faculty which could not be filled because of financial stringency. Even leaves of absence without pay had to be extended to tide the institution over weak budgetary situations. In a more positive vein, Swain had made considerable headway with the building of a faculty, but he was bothered by the loss of John R. Commons, Edward A. Ross, Frank A. Fetter, and Ernest L. Bogart. These men not only showed brilliant promise at Indiana, but they proved this by going on to distinguished careers in other universities.

Behind him Swain left the skeleton of the Indiana faculty which was to serve the university for the next three decades. This list included William Lowe Bryan, Horace A. Hoffman, James

A. Woodburn, Carl H. Eigenmann, Gustaf Karsten, Robert Judson Aley, Robert Edward Lyons, Arthur Lee Foley, David M. Mottier, Schuyler Colfax Davisson, Samuel Bannister Harding, Amos Shartle Hershey, Charles Jacob Sembower, Guido Hermann Stempel, William A. Rawles, William J. Moenkhaus, and others.

After Swain had gone to Swarthmore the *Daily Student* observed that before 1903 there were no Hoosiers at the Pennsylvania school. In 1907 it said, "But now all this is changed and today besides the President, Swarthmore has an Indiana Dean of Women, an Indiana Registrar, three Indiana members of the faculty, two Indiana post-graduate students, besides a dozen more from the state at large."

Unlike Jordan, Swain had taken away neither major professors nor football players, nor did he keep a watch on the faculty in the future with the intention of hiring members away from Indiana University. Instead he had left behind the legacy of having recommended William Lowe Bryan to the Board of Trustees as his successor. On June 10, 1902, he told the Board of Trustees,

> When one comes to consider all the possibilities in the case I am clearly of the opinion that the thing to do is to ask Dr. William L. Bryan, now Vice President, to accept the presidency of the University. I think no Vice President should be selected at this time. I believe Dr. Bryan is the one man who in the present situation can command an unqualified support of all factors that go to make up the influence of the University and carry the work forward as it is going today.

Swain left William Lowe Bryan the best legacy that any president of Indiana University had ever left a successor. He had brought the institution to the very threshold of the future. The three, Jordan, Coulter, and Swain, nurtured in Indiana three essential tenets of public higher education. The state had an ever-growing responsibility to support a state university that would push back the horizons of human knowledge, and the individual student should be allowed the greatest possible freedom in the choice of the content and nature of his education. No matter what flaws existed in the system, or what unfortunate mistakes callow youth might make in the choices, this, too, was a part of life. Man in society was faced constantly with the responsibility of making choices, and the quality of these choices depended largely upon the sum total of knowledge, background, and experience in which they were made. Finally these three men had established in the Hoosier mind the significance of science in a burgeoning and affluent American society where man and natural resources were so intimately associated; and science to them meant everything from flashing test tubes of chemicals before wide-eyed freshman classes in introductory chemistry, to seining for blind fish in the aquatic caves of Indiana, gathering amoebae and paramecia from Lake Wawasee, and identifying the fauna of the state, to a questioning of old folk-religious hypotheses in the light of the new Darwinism. All of this implied a mix of the teaching responsibility with that of creative research. The names that stood out in the university's history after 1885 were the names that gave the faculty a reputation beyond the bounds of Indiana itself.

Most important of all, these three presidents had proved Andrew Wylie largely wrong in his assumption of 1840 that no successful literary institution could be maintained with legislative support. All of them had struggled manfully with the legislature, had carried their messages directly to the people, and had spent a tremendous amount of time trying to educate their Board of Trustees; in June, 1902, Joseph Swain could say that a part of the battle had been won. The real victory still lay well out ahead, but a dent had been made, and it would grow deeper with the passing years.

In several of his speeches over the years David Starr Jordan had expressed himself clearly on the subjects of teaching and research. In his inaugural address at Stanford he said,

A professor to whom original investigation is unknown should have no place in a university. Men of commonplace or second-hand scholarship are of necessity men of low ideals, however carefully that fact may be disguised. A man of high ideals must be an investigator. He must know and think for himself, and only such as do this can really be great as teachers. The highest function of the real university is that of instruction by investigation, and a man who cannot and does not investigate cannot train investigators.

This ideal was fairly well implanted in Indiana University. Because of this it remained for presidents and trustees who were under pressure at all times to secure the laboratories and equipment to organize the new divisions and staffs necessary to realize the ideals that had been expressed by the founders of the backwoods seminary.

Joseph Swain defined much of the position which the modern University should assume. He, however, was unable to lead the institution onto the higher ground of university status. Though many changes had been made under the three presidents who had served since 1885, Indiana University still remained a pastoral liberal arts college awaiting the moment in the future when an administration could devise a plan to create a true university within the ever-broadening framework of the system of public higher education in Indiana.

The miracle of Indiana University in the nineteenth century is that it managed to maintain representative faculty members who exhibited loyalty to the institution under the most trying of circumstances, and many in their professional lives were both worthy teachers and good research scholars. There were moments when it took all the courage and daring a president and his faculty could muster to keep classes going in the university. Had the doors ever closed, or the trustees and faculty wavered in the pursuit of the larger dreams, the institution could not have resumed operation in keeping with its ancient mandate to be the seat of superior higher education.

Bibliography

BOOKS

Barnhart, John D., *Valley of Democracy: The Frontier versus the Plantation in the Ohio Valley, 1775–1818*, Bloomington: Indiana University Press, 1953.

———, and Donald F. Carmony, *Indiana from Frontier to Industrial Commonwealth*, vol. I, New York, 1954.

Beck, Frank O., *Some Aspects of Race at Indiana University, My Alma Mater*, Bloomington, 1959.

Best, John Hardin, and Robert T. Sidwell, eds., *The American Legacy of Learning, Readings in the History of Education*, Philadelphia: J. B. Lippincott, 1967.

Bishop, Morris, *A History of Cornell*, Ithaca: Cornell University Press, 1962.

Bollman, Lewis, *The State University of Indiana, the Causes of Its Want of Prosperity Considered*, Indianapolis: W. B. Burford, 1882.

Bruce, Philip Alexander, *History of the University of Virginia, 1819–1919*, 4 vols., New York: The Macmillan Company, 1920–21.

Bryan, William Lowe, *Farewells*, Bloomington: Indiana University, 1938.

———, *The President's Column*, Bloomington: Indiana University, 1934.

———, and Charlotte Lowe Bryan, *Last Words*, Bloomington: Indiana University Foundation, 1951.

Buley, R. Carlyle, *The Old Northwest, Pioneer Period 1815–1840*, 2 vols., Indianapolis: Indiana Historical Society, 1950.

Burns, Edward McNall, *David Starr Jordan: Prophet of Freedom*, Stanford: Stanford University Press, 1953.

Carmony, Donald F., ed., *Indiana: A Self-Appraisal*, Bloomington: Indiana University Press, 1966.

Cheyney, Edward Potts, *History of the University of Pennsylvania 1740–1940*, Philadelphia: University of Pennsylvania Press, 1940.

Coleman, Helen Turnbull W., *Banners in the Wilderness: Early Years of Washington and Jefferson College*, Pittsburgh, 1956.

Curti, Merle, and Vernon Carstensen, *The University of Wisconsin 1848–1925*, 2 vols., Madison: University of Wisconsin Press, 1949.

Dreiser, Theodore, *Dawn*, New York: Horace Liveright, 1931.

East, C. Earl, *Relive It with C. Earl East*, Bloomington, Ind., 1963.

Elliott, Edward C., ed., *The Rise of a University, the University in Action*, vol. II, New York: Columbia University Press, 1937.

Esarey, Logan, *A History of Indiana from Its Exploration to 1850*, Indianapolis: W. K. Stewart, 1915.

Fischer, Karl, *The First Hundred Years of Beta Theta Pi at Indiana University 1845–1945*, Menasha, Wis.: Banta, 1947.

Gray, James, *The University of Minnesota 1851–1951*, Minneapolis: University of Minnesota Press, 1951.

Hall, Baynard Rush (Robert Carlton, pseud.), *The New Purchase or Seven and a Half Years in the Far West*, Princeton: Princeton University Press, 1916.

Hall, Forest M. "Pop," *Historic Treasures—True Tales of Deeds with Interesting Data in the Life of Bloomington, Indiana University, and Monroe County*, Bloomington: Indiana University, 1922.

Harding, Samuel Bannister, ed., *Indiana University 1820–1904. Historical Sketch of the Course of Instruction*, Bloomington: Indiana University, 1904.

Havighurst, Walter, *The Miami Years 1809–1959*, New York: Putnam, 1958.

Hepburn, William Murray, and Louis Martin Sears, *Purdue University, Fifty Years of Progress*, Indianapolis: The Hollenbeck Press, 1925.

Hoover, Thomas Nathanael, *The History of Ohio University*, Athens, 1954.

Hoshour, Samuel K., *Autobiography*, St. Louis: John Burns Publishing Co., 1884.

Houston, Florence W., et al., *Maxwell History and Genealogy*, Indianapolis: C. E. Pauley and Co., 1916.

Jordan, David Starr, *The Days of a Man, Being Memories of a Naturalist, Teacher, and Minor Prophet of Democracy*, 2 vols., New York: World Book Company, 1922.

———, *The Philosophy of Despair*, San Francisco: Paul Elder, 1902.

———, *The Voice of the Scholar with Other Addresses on the Problems of Higher Education*, San Francisco: Paul Elder, 1903.

Kettleborough, Charles, *Indiana Historical Collections*, Vol. 1, *Constitution Making in Indiana*, Indianapolis: Indiana Historical Commission, 1916.

Langdon, William Chauncy, *The Centennial Pageant of Indiana University 1820–1920*, Bloomington: Indiana University, 1920.

Lindley, Harlow, ed., *Indiana as Seen by Early Travelers*, Indianapolis: Indiana Historical Commission, 1916.

Link, Arthur S., ed., *The Papers of Woodrow Wilson*, Vol. 5, *1885–1888*, Princeton: Princeton University Press, 1968.

Lynch, William O., *A History of Indiana State Teachers College [Indiana Normal] 1870–1929*, Terre Haute, 1946.

Matthews, Brander, et al., *A History of Columbia University 1754–1904*, New York: Columbia University Press, 1904.

McKay, Martha Nicholson, *Literary Clubs of Indianapolis*, Indianapolis, 1894.

Morison, Samuel Eliot, *Three Centuries of Harvard, 1636–1936*, Cambridge: Harvard University Press, 1936.

Myers, Burton Dorr, *History of Indiana University, 1902–1937, the Bryan Administration*, Bloomington: Indiana University, 1952.

————, *Trustees and Officers of Indiana University, 1820–1950*, Bloomington: Indiana University, 1951.

Nutt, Cyrus, *Indiana State Agricultural College*, Bloomington, 1865.

Patton, John S., *Jefferson, Cabell and the University of Virginia*, New York: Neale Publishing Co., 1906.

Peckham, Howard, *The Making of the University of Michigan, 1817–1967*, Ann Arbor: University of Michigan Press, 1967.

Philbrick, Francis S., ed., *The Laws of Indiana Territory, 1801–1809*, Vol. XXI, Collections of the Illinois State Historical Library, Law Series, Springfield: Illinois State Library, 1930.

Price, Richard Rees, *The Financial Support of State Universities*, Cambridge: Harvard University Press, 1924.

————, *The Financial Support of the University of Michigan: Its Origin and Development*, Cambridge: Harvard University Press, 1923.

Richardson, Leon Burr, *History of Dartmouth College*, 2 vols., Hanover: Dartmouth College, 1932.

Rinsch, Emil, *The History of the Normal College of the American Gymnastic Union of Indiana University, 1866–1966*, Bloomington: Indiana University, 1966.

Rogers, Andrew Denny, III, *John Merle Coulter, Missionary in Science*, Princeton: Princeton University Press, 1944.

Rudolph, Frederick, *The American College and University*, New York, 1962.

Russell, William F., ed., *The Rise of a University: The Later Days of Old Columbia College*, vol. I, New York: Columbia University Press, 1937.

Schmidt, George P., *The Liberal Arts College: A Chapter in American Cultural History*, New Brunswick: Rutgers University Press, 1957.

Shaw, Wilfred B., ed., *The University of Michigan: An Encyclopedic Survey*, 4 vols., Ann Arbor: University of Michigan Press, 1942–58.

Smith, Joseph, *History of Jefferson College, Including an Account of Early Log Cabin Schools and the Canonsburg Academy*, Pittsburgh: J. T. Shryock, 1857.

Smith, Oliver Hampton, *Early Indiana Trials and Sketches, Reminiscences by Hon. O. H. Smith*, Cincinnati: Moore, Wilstach, Keys, Co., 1858.

Solberg, Winton U., *The University of Illinois 1867–1894, An Intellectual and Cultural History*, Urbana: University of Illinois Press, 1968.

Stephens, Frank F., *A History of the University of Missouri*, Columbia: University of Missouri Press, 1962.

Ten Brook, Andrew, *American State Universities, Their Origin and Progress*, Cincinnati: Robert Clarke and Co., 1875.

Tewksbury, Donald G. *The Founding of American Colleges and Universities before the Civil War, with Particular Reference to the Religious*

Influences Bearing upon the College Movement, Hamden, Conn.: Archon Books, 1965.

Treat, Payson J., *The National Land System 1785–1820*, New York: E. B. Treat and Co., 1910.

Veysey, Laurence R., *The Emergence of the American University*, Chicago: University of Chicago Press, 1965.

Wertenbaker, Thomas Jefferson, *Princeton 1746–1896*, Princeton: Princeton University Press, 1946.

White, Andrew Dickson, *Autobiography of Andrew Dickson White*, 2 vols., New York: The Century Company, 1907.

Wise, Barton Haxall, *The Life of Henry A. Wise of Virginia*, New York, Macmillan, 1899.

Woodburn, James Albert, *History of Indiana University 1820–1902*, Bloomington: Indiana University, 1940.

Wright, George G., *Reminiscences*, Richmond, Ind.: *Daily Palladium* Book, 1889.

Wylie, Theophilus Adam, ed., *Indiana University, Its History from 1820, when Founded, to 1890*. Indianapolis: Wm. B. Burford, 1890.

Yearbook of the Society of Indiana Pioneers, Indianapolis: Indiana Library, 1959, 1969.

ARTICLES: FROM THE *Indiana Magazine of History*
(From 1905–1912, *Indiana Quarterly Magazine of History*)

"An Early Educational Report," Vol. IV, December, 1908, pp. 153-169.

Atwater, Amzi, "Indiana University Forty Years Ago," Vol. I, Sept., 1905, pp. 140-149.

Barnhart, John D., "The Southern Influence in the Formation of Indiana," Vol. XXXIII, September, 1937, pp. 261-276.

———, "Sources of Indiana's First Constitution," Vol. XXXIX, March, 1943, pp. 55-94.

Benton, Allen R., "Early Educational Conditions and Founding of a Denominational College," Vol. IV, March, 1908, pp. 13-17.

Burnett, Howard R., "Early History of Vincennes University," Vol. XXIX, June, 1933, pp. 114-121.

Coffin, Annie Morrison, "John Irwin Morrison and the Washington County Seminary," Vol. XXII, June, 1926, pp. 183-193.

Coleman, Christopher B., "Some Religious Developments in Indiana," Vol. V, June, 1909, pp. 57-71.

Estabrook, Arthur H., "The Family History of Robert Owen," Vol. XIX, March, 1923, pp. 63-100.

Leonard, Adam A., "Personal Politics in Indiana, 1816–1840," Vol. XIX, March, 1923, pp. 1-15.

Lynch, William O., "A Student at Indiana University," Vol. XXXIII, December, 1937, pp. 490-499.

——, "Cash Account of a University Student," Vol. XXV, December, 1929, pp. 312-325.

Maxwell, Louise, "Sketch of Dr. David H. Maxwell," Vol. VIII, September, 1912, pp. 101-108.

Myers, Burton D., "A Study of Faculty Appointments at Indiana University," Vol. XL, June, 1944, pp. 129-155.

Nutt, Cyrus, "A Letter of 1863 from a Western University President," Vol. XXV, December, 1929, pp. 306-311.

Reid, Nina Kathleen, "James Noble," Vol. IX, March, 1913, pp. 1-13.

——, "Sketches of Early Indiana Senators—William Hendricks, 1825–1837," Vol. IX, September, 1913, pp. 167-186.

——, "Sketches of Early Indiana Senators—Waller Taylor, 1816–1825," Vol. IX, September, 1913, pp. 92-95.

——, "Sketches of Early Indiana Senators—John Tipton," Vol. IX, December, 1913, pp. 247-268.

Riker, Dorothy, "Jonathan Jennings," Vol. XXVIII, December, 1932, pp. 223-239.

Stampp, Kenneth M., "The Impact of the Civil War Upon Hoosier Society," Vol. XXXVIII, March, 1942, pp. 1-16.

Wilson, George R., "The First Public Land Surveys in Indiana: Freeman's Lines," Vol. XII, March, 1916, pp. 1-33.

Woodburn, James A., "Constitution Making in Early Indiana: An Historical Survey," Vol. X, September, 1914, pp. 237-255.

——, "James Woodburn: Hoosier Schoolmaster," Vol. XXXII, September, 1936, pp. 231-247.

——, "Research in State History in State Universities, Vol. XI, March, 1915, pp. 59-63.

ARTICLES: FROM OTHER SOURCES

Blatchley, W. S., "A Century of Geology in Indiana," *Proceedings of the Indiana Academy of Science*, Vol. XXXII, 1916, pp. 89-177.

Boisen, Anton T., "Divided Protestantism in a Midwest County, A Study in the Natural History of Organized Religion," *The Journal of Religion*, Vol. XX, Oct., 1940, pp. 359-381.

Campaigne, Ernest E., "The Development of the Science Departments at Indiana University," *Proceedings of the Indiana Academy of Science*, Vol. LXXVII, 1968, pp. 340-345.

Coburn, John, "Sketch of the Old Supreme Court," *Biographical Sketches and Review of the Bench and Bar of Indiana*, edited by Charles W. Taylor, Indianapolis: Bench and Bar Publishing Co., 1895.

Jesse, R. H., "Higher Education in the United States," *The Student*, Jan., Feb., 1898.

"Sketch of the Life of David Dale Owen, M.D., " *The American Geologist*, Vol. 4, Aug., 1889, pp. 65-72.

Thornton, W. W., "Constitutional Convention of 1816," *Report of the*

Sixteenth Annual Meeting of the State Bar Association of Indiana, Indianapolis: Indiana Bar Association, 1912.

Woodburn, James Albert, "Sketches from the University's History: Daniel Read, Professor of Ancient Languages, 1843–56," *Indiana University Alumni Quarterly*, Vol. III, April, 1916, pp. 127-148.

——, "Since the Beginning: A Retrospect," *Indiana University Alumni Quarterly*, Vol. XI, July, 1924, pp. 297-320.

Wylie, Theophilus A., "Andrew Wylie, D.D., First President of Indiana University," *Indiana School Journal*, Vol. XIII, May, 1868.

CORRESPONDENCE, AFFIDAVITS, AND COURT ENQUIRY:
THE BOGUS AFFAIR. (All materials from the Indiana University Archives)

Beard, W. H., to David Starr Jordan, September 19, 1890.

Howe, Walter D., A Statement, September 3, 1891.

Jordan, David Starr, to Nicholas A. Robertson, May 31, 1890.

——, A Memorandum on the Bogus Affair, December, 1890.

Pinkerton, William A., to David Starr Jordan, March 5, 1890.

Proceedings of the Court of Enquiry, June 6, 1890.

Reed, W. J., to David Starr Jordan, May 3, 1890.

Robertson, N. A., Affidavit, February 11, 1890, June 11, 1890.

Robertson, R. S., to Board of Trustees, January 6, 1890.

——, to David Starr Jordan, May 31, 1890.

Shumaker, J. H., to L. V. Buskirk, May 2, 1890.

Wallingford, J. N., to David Starr Jordan, January 11, 1890, June 9, 1890.

DIARIES, PERSONAL CORRESPONDENCE,
PAPERS, AND MANUSCRIPT RECORDS

Bryan, William Lowe, Correspondence, 1885–1903, Indiana University Archives, Bloomington.

Daily, William, Personal Correspondence, Indiana University Archives, Bloomington. Collection of correspondence concerned with the publication of the 1891 "Bogus," including a manuscript note of William Lowe Bryan, Indiana University Archives, Bloomington.

Eigenmann, Carl H., Personal Correspondence, 1890–1924, Indiana University Archives, Bloomington.

English, W. H., Collection of Biographical Sketches of Indiana Legislators, Constitutional Convention Delegates, and Judges. Indiana Historical Society Collection, Indianapolis.

Jordan, David Starr, Correspondence, 1884–1892, Stanford University Archives, Palo Alto, California. Microfilm copies in Indiana University Library.

McDonald, David, Family Record, 1854–1868, Indiana University Archives, Bloomington.

Swain, Joseph, Letterpress Volumes, 1891–1902, Indiana University Archives, Bloomington.

Wells, Herman B, "The Early History of Indiana University as Reflected in the Administration of Andrew Wylie, 1829–1851," November 7, 1960.
Wylie, Theophilus A., Personal Diary, 1830–1892. Indiana University Archives, Bloomington.

INDIANA UNIVERSITY MATERIALS AND PUBLICATIONS

The Arbutus, class yearbook, Bloomington, 1894–1903.
Indiana Alumni Magazine, 1938–.
Indiana Photographic Album, 1878, 1879, 1881.
Indiania University Alumni Quarterly, 1914–1938.
Indiana University Bulletin, Bloomington, 1903–.
Indiana University *Comet*, Bloomington, 1890.
Indiana University Faculty, Personnel Record, 1824–.
Megaphone, Bloomington, 1900.

LAWS, JOURNALS, OFFICIAL RECORDS,
COURT DECISIONS, AND CONSTITUTIONS

Annals of the Congress of the United States, 1803–1804, 1816, Washington, D.C., 1852.
Annual Report of the Auditor of the State of Indiana, Corydon and Indianapolis, 1817–1903.
Annual Report of the Treasurer of the State of Indiana, Corydon and Indianapolis, 1817–1903.
Carter, Clarence, ed., *Territorial Papers of the United States* (Indiana Territory), Vol. VIII, Washington, D.C., 1939.
Compilation of the Statutes of Indiana, 1820, 1828, Corydon, 1820, 1828.
Constitutions of the United States: According to the Latest Amendments . . . , Lexington, Ky. : Thomas T. Skillman, 1813.
Constitutions of the United States of America; with the Latest Amendments, New York: Duykinck, 1820.
In the *Documents of the House of Representatives at the Twenty-Third Session of the General Assembly . . .* , "Mr. Kinney's Report from the Committee on Education in Relation to the Indiana College, January 9, 1839," Document 18, Indianapolis, 1839.
Esarey, Logan, ed., *Messages and Papers of Jonathan Jennings, Ratliff Boon, William Hendricks*, Vol. III, 1816–1825, Indianapolis: Indiana Historical Commission, 1924.
Journal of the House of Representatives of the State of Indiana, Corydon and Indianapolis, 1817–1903.
Journal of the Senate of the State of Indiana, Corydon and Indianapolis, 1817–1844, then *Journal of the Indiana State Senate*, 1845–1903.
Kola, Arthur, ed., *A Compilation of Statutes Pertaining to Indiana University*, Bloomington, 1967.
Laws of the State of Indiana (local, general, and revised), Corydon and Indianapolis, 1817–1903.

Revised Statutes adopted and enacted by the General Assembly at Their Twenty-second Session, Indianapolis, 1838.

Riker, Dorothy, *Unedited Letters of Jonathan Jennings*, Vol. 10, No. 4, Indianapolis: Indiana Historical Society, 1932.

———, and Gayle Thornbrough, eds., *Messages and Papers Relating to the Administration of Noah Noble, Governor of Indiana, 1831–1837*, Indiana Historical Collections, Vol. XXXVIII, Indianapolis: Indiana Historical Bureau, 1958.

———, *Messages and Papers Relating to the Administration of James Brown Ray, Governor of Indiana, 1825–1831*, Indiana Historical Collections, Vol. XXXIV, Indianapolis: Indiana Historical Bureau, 1954.

Robertson, Nellie, and Dorothy Riker, eds., *The John Tipton Papers*, 3 vols., Indianapolis: Indiana Historical Bureau, 1942.

Special Departmental Reports (President of Indiana University), Indianapolis, 1830–1875.

State of Indiana v. Vincennes University, Brief of Oliver H. Smith for the State of Indiana, Indianapolis: Chapman and Spann, 1847.

The Statutes at Large and Treaties of the United States of America, Vols. IX–X, Boston, 1851–1855.

United States Census, 1810, 1820, 1830, Washington, D.C.

MINUTES, REPORTS, PROGRAMS, CATALOGUES
(of Indiana University except where noted)

Athenian Literary Society, Journal, October 1, 1852–November 23, 1855; January, 1856–October 6, 1865.

Board of Trustees, Secretary's Financial Accounts, October 8, 1838–August 11, 1876.

Board of Trustees of Indiana University, Minutes, 1838–1859, 1883–1903.

Catalogue of the Library of Indiana State University, Bloomington: M. L. Deal, 1842.

Hesperian Record or Journal, October 28, 1870–November 8, 1878.

Indiana College Association, Minutes, Constitution, and By-Laws, December 27, 1877–December 28, 1896.

Indiana University Almuni Association, Minutes, Annual Meeting, 1877–1903.

Indiana University *Catalogue*, 1829–1903.

Indiana University Commencement Programs, 1872–1889.

Indiana University Faculty, Minutes, 1835–1903.

President's Reports to the Board of Trustees and the Indiana Legislature, 1838–1902.

Swarthmore College Bulletin, Inaugural Issue, October 11, 1969, Vol. LXVII, No. 5, Swarthmore, Pa.

NEWSPAPERS

Bedford *Independent*, 1865.
Bedford *White River Standard*, 1854–1855.
Bloomington *Daily Herald Telephone*, 1968, 1969, 1970.
Bloomington *Globe*, 1836.
Bloomington *Indiana Tribune*, 1847, 1848, 1849.
Bloomington *Indiana Tribune and Monroe County Farmer*, 1849–50.
Bloomington *Post*, 1838–1841.
Bloomington *Presage*, 1858.
Bloomington *Progress*, 1867–1882.
Bloomington *Religious Times*, 1854.
Bloomington *Republican*, 1859, 1860, 1865.
Bloomington *Republican Progress*, 1883, 1885.
Bloomington *Saturday Courier*, 1860–1891.
Bloomington *Saturday Review*, 1885, 1889.
Bloomington *Semi-Weekly Telephone*, 1887.
Bloomington *Star*, 1899.
Bloomington *Telephone*, 1886–1899.
Chicago *Tribune*, 1884.
Corydon *Indiana Gazette*, 1819–1825.
The Dagger (Bloomington), 1876, 1878.
Indiana *Student*, 1867–1874, 1876–1898, Indiana *Daily Student*, 1898–
    1969.
Indianapolis *Daily Indiana State Journal*, 1852.
Indianapolis *Daily Journal*, 1861–1900.
Indianapolis *Indiana State Sentinel*, 1865.
Indianapolis *Indiana Statesman*, 1851.
Indianapolis *News*, 1889–1899.
Indianapolis *Times*, 1944.
Indianapolis *Weekly Indiana State Journal*, 1852.
New York Times, 1875.
Niles Weekly Register, 1816.
Putnam *Republican Banner*, 1852–1859.
Richmond *Palladium*, 1836.
Richmond *Public Ledger*, 1824–1825.
Salem *Western Annotator*, 1829–1830.
Terre Haute *Wabash Courier*, 1851.
Terre Haute *Wabash Express*, 1851.
Vincennes *Gazette*, 1851.
Vincennes *Western Sun*, 1816.
Weekly Vincennes Western Sun, 1859.

PAMPHLETS, SPEECHES, AND BULLETINS

Addresses Delivered at Indiana University and Miscellaneous Pamphlets, 1831–1845.

Albjerg, Victor, "Richard Owen," Archives of Purdue No. 2, March, 1946.

Ballantine, Elisha, "Old Age, Two Discourses upon this Theme; Delivered the First in the Chapel of Indiana University, the Second in the Presbyterian Church, Bloomington, Indiana," Bloomington: S. C. Dodds and Company, 1879.

Coulter, John Merle, "Practical Education," Indianapolis: Carlon and Hollenbeck, 1891.

Daily, William, "Funeral Discourse for President Andrew Wylie," Indianapolis, 1852.

———, "The Powerful Pen and Eloquent Tongue," Bloomington: Philomathean Society, 1859.

Hall, Baynard Rush, "Righteousness the Safeguard and Glory of a Nation," Indianapolis: Smith and Bolten, 1826.

Jenkinson, Isaac, "Dedication of Kirkwood Hall Indiana University," Bloomington, January 25, 1895.

Jordan, David Starr, "The Duty of the Scholar Towards the Community, Being the Baccalaureate Address of President David Starr Jordan of Indiana University," June 6, 1886, Richmond, Indiana: 1886.

Parvin, Theophilus, "Address on the Life and Character of Andrew Wylie, D.D. Late President of the State University of Indiana," Indianapolis: Cameron and M'Neely, 1858.

Read, David, "A Momento to the Students of the Indiana University: An Address Delivered Before the Philomathean Society at the Annual Commencement, 1856," Bloomington, 1856.

"Semi-Centennial Anniversary of the United Presbyterian Congregation of Bloomington, Indiana," Blanchard, Iowa: Rufus Johnson, 1883.

Shake, Curtis, "A History of Vincennes University," Vincennes: Vincennes University, 1928.

Wylie, Andrew, "Address to the Citizens of Monroe County and to the Members of County Lyceum," Bloomington, July 4, 1840.

———, "An Address Delivered Before the Philomathean Society of the Wabash College, July 10, 1838," Bloomington: Franklin Office, 1838.

———, "An Address Delivered at Bloomington, October 29, 1829," Indianapolis: Douglass and McGuire, 1829.

———, "Baccalaureate Addressed to the Senior Class, at the Late Commencement," Bloomington: C. Davisson, 1846.

———, "Baccalaureate Addressed to the Senior Class on Day of Commencement, 1843," Bloomington: M. L. Deal, 1843.

———, "Baccalaureate Addressed to Senior Class at the Late Commencement, 1841," Bloomington: Deal and Bollman, 1841.

———, "Baccalaureate, Addressed to the Senior Class, at the Late Commencement, 1847," Indianapolis: C. Davisson, 1847.

———, "College Government," *Transactions* of the Eighth Annual Meeting of the Western Literary Institute and College of Professional Teachers, Cincinnati, October, 1839.

———, "A Discourse Delivered before the Indiana Historical Society," Indianapolis: A. F. Morrison, 1831.

———, "An Eulogy on Lafayette, May 1835," Cincinnati: Taylor and Tracy, 1835.

———, "The Individual: A Baccalaureate, Delivered to the Class of Seniors, at the Commencement of the Indiana University, August 31, 1851," Indianapolis: John D. Defrees, 1851.

———, "Sermon on the Sin of Duelling," Pittsburgh: D. & M. Maclean, 1828.

———, "The Uses of History," *Publications*, Indiana Historical Society Publications, Vol. I, Indianapolis, 1897.

UNPUBLISHED THESES, DISSERTATIONS, AND PAPERS

Atwater, Amzi, Reminiscences of Indiana University, 1865, paper, Indiana University Archives.

Burnett, Howard R., A History of Vincennes University, Master's thesis, Indiana University, 1936.

Cahill, David, *A History of Student Affairs at Indiana University*, Bloomington, 1967.

Cope, Garrett, History of the Origin and Development of Theatre Arts at Indiana University, Master's thesis, Indiana University, 1951.

Gering, William M., David Starr Jordan: Spokesman for Higher Education in Indiana, doctoral dissertation, Indiana University, July, 1963.

———, William Daily: Ambitious or Aspersed? paper, Indiana University Archives.

Gilbertson, Eric, Early Settlement and Government in Monroe County, Indiana, paper, Indiana University, 1968.

Lowell, Mildred Hawksworth, Indiana University Libraries, 1829–1942, doctoral dissertation, University of Chicago, 1957.

Martindale, Mrs. Clarence, Sarah Parke Morrison, paper in possession of Mrs. Kate Mueller, Bloomington, Indiana.

Morrison, Sarah Parke, Reminiscences of her Days as the First Female Student to Enter Indiana University, June 8, 1911, Indiana University Archives.

Rothenberger, Katharine, An Historical Study of the Position of Dean of Women at Indiana University, Master's thesis, Indiana University, 1942.

Index

A NOTE ON THE TYPE

The text of this book was set on the Linotype in a type face called MONTICELLO, issued by The Mergenthaler Linotype Company in 1950. It is based on a cutting called "Ronaldson Roman No. 1", a late eighteenth-century production of the Binny & Ronaldson foundry of Philadelphia. Monticello belongs to the family of transitional faces which includes Bell Roman, Baskerville, Bulmer and Fournier. The Transitionals fall between the hearty "Old Style" taste represented by Caslon's letters, and the graver-styled nineteenth-century "Moderns."

The book was printed and bound by The Haddon Craftsmen, Inc., Scranton, Pa. and the paper is Warren's Olde Style Laid.

Design by Guy Fleming.